Order and Artifice in
Hume's Political Philosophy

FREDERICK G. WHELAN

Order and Artifice in
Hume's Political Philosophy

PRINCETON UNIVERSITY PRESS
PRINCETON, NEW JERSEY

Copyright © 1985 by Princeton University Press
Published by Princeton University Press,
41 William Street, Princeton, New Jersey 08540
In the United Kingdom:
Princeton University Press, Guildford, Surrey

ALL RIGHTS RESERVED
Library of Congress Cataloging in Publication Data
will be found on the last printed page of this book
ISBN 0-691-06617-5

This book has been composed in Linotron Sabon

Clothbound editions of Princeton University Press books
are printed on acid-free paper, and binding materials
are chosen for strength and durability

Printed in the United States of America
by Princeton University Press
Princeton, New Jersey

for Peggy

CONTENTS

BIBLIOGRAPHIC NOTE   ix

ACKNOWLEDGMENTS   xi

CHAPTER I.   Introduction   3

CHAPTER II.   Philosophical Foundations   32
1. Some Premises of Hume's Philosophy   32
2. Knowledge, Belief, and Fictions of the Imagination   40
3. The Skeptical Crisis and Its Outcome   60
4. Aspects of Hume's Naturalism   67

CHAPTER III.   Hume's Science of Human Nature   82
1. The Study of Human Nature   82
2. Principles of the Imagination   96
3. The Social Context of the Understanding   117
4. Passion, Volition, and Reasonableness   136
5. Hume's Analysis of Particular Passions   147
6. The Social Dimension   160

CHAPTER IV.   The Political Theory of Artifice   189
1. The Setting of Hume's Political Philosophy   189
2. Principles of Hume's Moral Philosophy   196
3. Natural and Artificial Virtue   218
4. Artificial Virtue and Human Nature   250

CHAPTER V.   Skepticism and Politics   294
1. The Scientific Enterprise in Perspective   294
2. Naturalism, Conservatism, and Philosophic Detachment   304

3. Artifice, Order, and Political Moderation   329

4. "A Government of Laws" and An Approach to Change   348

INDEX   375

THERE is at present no standard edition of Hume's writings; a new edition forthcoming from Princeton University Press is intended to fill this need. References in this book to Hume's major works are to the following editions:

Dialogues Concerning Natural Religion. Edited by Norman Kemp Smith. Indianapolis: Bobbs-Merrill, 1947. Cited as *Dialogues*.

Enquiries Concerning Human Understanding and Concerning the Principles of Morals. Edited by L. A. Selby-Bigge. Third edition by P. H. Nidditch. Oxford: Clarendon Press, 1975. Cited as *Enquiries* (I) and *Enquiries* (II), respectively.

The History of England from the Invasion of Julius Caesar to the Abdication of James the Second, 1688. 6 vols. Boston: Phillips, Sampson, 1849. Cited as *History of England*.

The Philosophical Works. Edited by Thomas Hill Green and Thomas Hodge Grose. 4 vols. London: Longmans, Green, 1882; reprinted 1964. Cited as *Works*. (Volumes 3 and 4 of this edition, which contain Hume's essays, correspond to the two volume edition of Hume, *Essays Moral, Political, and Literary*, edited by Green and Grose [London: Longmans, Green, 1898].)

A Treatise of Human Nature. Edited by L. A. Selby-Bigge. Second edition by P. H. Nidditch. Oxford: Clarendon Press, 1978. Cited as *Treatise* or in the text as (T. —).

ACKNOWLEDGMENTS

THIS book had its origin in a doctoral dissertation submitted to the Department of Government at Harvard University in 1976. My greatest debt of gratitude is to my principal teacher and dissertation adviser, Professor Judith N. Shklar, whose good advice and assistance have continued over the years. I also learned a great deal about political theory from Professors Samuel H. Beer, Harvey C. Mansfield, Jr., and Michael Walzer, some small parts of which are reflected in this book. My work at Harvard was supported by a Graduate Prize Fellowship, teaching fellowships, and a resident tutorship in South House, which provided a pleasant environment for research and writing.

In the years since I joined the Political Science Department at the University of Pittsburgh I have received new insights into political theory from my senior colleague, Professor John W. Chapman, who has been a constant source of encouragement as I brought my "Hume book" to completion. I also appreciate the helpful attitude shown by my department chairmen, Professors Robert S. Walters and Morris S. Ogul, during this period. I would like to thank Professor Annette C. Baier of the University of Pittsburgh Philosophy Department, who read and commented on the manuscript and invited me to participate in her Hume seminar.

I presented an early version of the main argument of this book at a conference on the Scottish Enlightenment at the Society for the Humanities, Cornell University, in October 1976. I was invited by the editors of *Nomos* (the Yearbook of the American Society for Political and Legal Philosophy), J. Roland Pennock and John W. Chapman, to develop my thoughts on Hume's theory of property; the results of this effort, which go beyond the scope of this book, are contained in my article, "Property as Artifice: Hume and Blackstone," in *Property: Nomos* XXII, ed. Pennock and Chapman (New York: New York University Press, 1980).

Work on this book was supported during the summer of 1978 by a Faculty Research Grant from the Faculty of Arts and Sciences, University of Pittsburgh. The typing of the manuscript was assisted financially by a grant from the University of Pittsburgh and was ably executed by Kendall Stanley and Melanie Katilius. I am indebted to Patricia Davis and Cathie Brettschneider for editorial assistance.

Sanford G. Thatcher, Assistant Director of Princeton University Press, supported this project during a rather lengthy review process and endeavored to keep up my spirits, for which I am grateful. I would also like to express my thanks to three of the Press's readers, Professors Isaac Kramnick, David Fate Norton, and (for a portion of the work) Barry Stroud, for their helpful comments, their encouragement of improvements, and, finally, their favorable judgments on the manuscript.

It is gratifying to observe the growth in scholarly attention to Hume's political theory; this development is an aspect of the general upsurge of interest in Hume's philosophy over the past decade. This book was written before the two most noteworthy recent contributions, Jonathan Harrison's *Hume's Theory of Justice* (Oxford: Clarendon Press, 1981) and David Miller's *Philosophy and Ideology in Hume's Political Thought* (Oxford: Clarendon Press, 1981), came into my hands. I have added references to these works in connection with a few points of particular interest, but the interpretation of Hume that I offer here was conceived independently of them.

This book is dedicated to my wife, Peggy, for her indispensable support and encouragement over the years.

Order and Artifice in
Hume's Political Philosophy

Introduction

THE main elements of Hume's political philosophy constitute an integral part of his philosophical system as a whole, of which the first and principal presentation is his *Treatise of Human Nature*; much of the interest and cogency of his doctrines regarding society and government arises from the links between them and his other philosophical positions. This is accordingly a study of Hume's political thought that attempts to set its main themes in the larger context of his philosophy of mind, human nature, and ethics.

Hume's philosophy is usually regarded as skeptical, as indeed he himself characterizes it. It begins with epistemological investigations, the conclusions of which frequently highlight the limitations of the human rational faculty, and the skepticism that is developed here provides a foundation for the whole. The relation between Hume's epistemological doctrines and his political philosophy is therefore a central theme of this study. Neither religious faith nor moral values, and not even scientific reasoning (based as it is on inductive inference), appears to Hume to be susceptible of a purely rational justification, although Hume never doubts the value or utility of at least the latter two. These are all rather matters of more or less deeply seated belief, or in some cases artifices or conventions that we adopt and maintain because we find them to be, on the whole, useful. The status that both science and morality receive in Hume's system, however, seems to be less secure than many (perhaps especially in Hume's day) have supposed, and such skepticism may appear to undercut political and moral commitments and theoretical convictions of all kinds.

The negative or critical aspects of Hume's skepticism, however, although conspicuous and important, are far from being the whole of his philosophical achievement. His larger explorations of "human nature," and subsequently of history as the cumulative manifestation of human nature, are undertaken in order to discover and exhibit the foundations (such as they may be) of our cognitive and moral life. And although this enterprise is interrupted by skeptical doubts and the digressions they occasion, nevertheless it reveals in the end the operation of faculties and processes (such as feeling and custom) that compensate, in a manner that Hume finds to be largely satisfactory for human purposes, for the weakness of reason. I am especially concerned with the manner in which Hume's skeptical analyses both of the mind and (in a more restricted sense) of morals give way to positive doctrines that I believe may best be grasped under the general headings of *order* and *artifice*: the order that we create or impose on our cognitive and moral worlds through habitual adherence to the rules that are constitutive of mental and social artifices. Although the character of the distinctively political philosophy that Hume develops in this framework is my main concern, this is a question that requires a rather broad consideration of his philosophy as a whole.

Hume's political views are usually studied in the two dozen essays that he devotes to explicitly political subjects. Therefore it may seem an unusual feature of this study of his political philosophy that it concentrates on the *Treatise*, referring to the essays and the *History* mainly for concrete illustrations of points made there, and moreover that it draws substantially on all three books of the former work; some preliminary comments on the standing of Hume's multifarious writings may therefore be in order. In his lifetime Hume achieved fame and fortune principally as the author of the widely read *History of England*, the most famous sections of which established his reputation as a "Tory," and as an essayist on diverse topics, many of them political. His first work, however, the *Treatise*, was largely ignored, not receiving a second edition until the nineteenth century. Discouraged by this failure, and attributing it more to the manner than to the matter, Hume recast much of its substance as the more polished *Enquiries* on human understanding and morals, and he repudiated the *Treatise* as a juvenile and flawed work.[1]

This judgment has not been accepted by posterity, however, and today the *Treatise* is the work on which Hume's reputation as a philosopher (currently very high) chiefly depends. This revised assessment corresponds to the modern view of Hume as predominantly a philosopher rather than a historian, and in particular as the most acute epistemologist and logician in the empiricist tradition—the poser of the problems that Kant set out to solve in his own way and the inspirer of logical positivism. Hume the philosopher has also retained a prominent place in the history of British ethical thought—and as a precursor of modern ethical analysis—as a contributor both to utilitarianism and to the tenacious "moral sense" or psychological current in moral

---

[1] Hume, *Works*, vol. 3, pp. 37-38; the repudiation is of the *Treatise*'s "expression" more than of its "reasoning." Cf. also Hume, "My Own Life," *Works*, vol. 3, pp. 2-3. In this study I draw on the two *Enquiries*, like the essays and *History*, primarily to corroborate and enlarge upon the arguments of the *Treatise*; certain differences in doctrine are present, however, and will be discussed below.

philosophy. Meanwhile his several skeptical writings on religion have retained their reputation as masterpieces of logical argument, and certain of the political essays continue to be recognized as important contributions to British constitutional thought of the eighteenth century.

Hume's writings on diverse subjects have thus found places in the canons of different fields of study, but in this process important links among his various efforts have tended to be neglected. Although Hume's turn to the writing of history, for example, is sometimes deplored by modern specialists as a desertion of philosophy, there was no such disjuncture in Hume's own view of his project (in which I concur): the study of history provided an opportunity to confirm the account of human nature put forward in the *Treatise*; to record in a concrete fashion the development of a government, of which the origins are analyzed abstractly in the *Treatise*; and to observe in practice the dangers of the "fanaticism" that can result from an excessive estimate of the powers of reason or from other nonskeptical claims of insight and assurance. Departmentalization of interest in Hume has been detrimental to the interpretation of all aspects of his work, since all its parts can be fully understood only in relation to the whole and in light of certain parallels in his treatment of different issues. This point, I believe, applies with special force to his political philosophy. The explicitly political essays are relatively short and deal ostensibly with issues mainly of historical interest, such as the British constitution and parties as these had developed by around the middle of the eighteenth century. Meanwhile the nearest thing Hume wrote to a systematic work of political theory is contained within the comprehensive ethical theory of Book III of the *Treatise*, not easily accessible or fully intelligible except on the basis of the preceding, lengthy accounts of the "understanding" and the "passions." Hume's place in ethics is acknowledged by modern moral philosophers, but students of political thought have not sufficiently taken notice of the centrality of political topics in his general ethical theory: justice and allegiance are, after all, the moral qualities to which he devotes the bulk of his attention. Nor have political theorists inquired deeply enough into the relations between Hume's treatment of morals and politics and the other parts of his philosophy, especially his skeptical philosophy of mind and his views on human nature taken as a whole, as these emerge in diverse writings.[2]

[2] Comprehensive treatments of Hume's philosophy (mainly by philosophers) likewise usually fail to consider his political theory, apart from his theory of justice in relation

My aim in this study is to achieve an integrated view of Hume's philosophy of human nature and its political manifestations, calling attention to the ways in which his political philosophy follows from and is firmly grounded in his general conception of the mind, with its normal features and capacities. Hume's political philosophy as such, which I shall examine in detail in chapters IV and V, consists principally in an elaborate analysis of social "artifices" or systems of obligatory rules prescribing conduct for individuals in society. The political, for Hume, is largely equivalent to the realm of artificial institutions in this sense, embracing the judgments and choices that we make in this realm, and is not clearly distinct from what may be called the social, the public, or (in many cases) the legal. This approach no doubt has weaknesses and blind spots as well as particular strengths, which include an account of the tensions that inescapably exist between artifices and the more immediate expressions of human nature, and of the relation between rules and order. In these large themes, with their philosophical setting, resides the main interest of Hume's political theory.

Justice and allegiance (or obedience to government) are Hume's main examples of artifices or artificial virtues, and they are the ones that will be of central concern in this book. Hume studies such artifices from several points of view. In many passages, especially in the *Treatise*, he explores the relation between the establishment of rules, regarded abstractly, and the creation of social order; and, invoking what would today be recognized as a model of rational choice, he outlines the manner in which these artifices would be adopted as conventions by individuals who reflect on their interests and on the advantages of orderly social life. Elsewhere Hume treats the systems of property and government that are the concrete expressions of justice and allegiance

---

to his ethics, or they do so only briefly. See, for example, John Laird, *Hume's Philosophy of Human Nature* (Anchor Books, n.p., 1967 [1932]); Nicholas Capaldi, *David Hume: The Newtonian Philosopher* (Boston: Twayne Publishers, 1975); Terence Penelhum, *Hume* (New York: St. Martin's Press, 1975); Barry Stroud, *Hume* (London: Routledge and Kegan Paul, 1977); and A. J. Ayer, *Hume* (New York: Hill and Wang, 1980). André-Louis Leroy, *David Hume* (Paris: Presses Universitaires de France, 1953), gives comparatively more attention to political theory, and his account has the merit of emphasizing Hume's doctrines of artifice and convention. John B. Stewart's useful book, *The Moral and Political Philosophy of David Hume* (New York: Columbia University Press, 1963), was long the only thorough study of Hume focusing on his political philosophy; my objections to Stewart's interpretation will emerge below. James Moore presents a lucid survey of Hume's political views, drawing from his essays, in "Hume's Political Science and the Classical Republican Tradition," *Canadian Journal of Political Science* 10 (1977): 809-39.

as historical institutions and practices; he of course recognizes, in these passages, that as historical phenomena they have origins and courses of development that are more complex and diverse than his abstract account of them might suggest, and he draws prudential conclusions from this fact for political practice. Finally, and most centrally, Hume considers justice and allegiance as expressions of a particular type of moral virtue, constitutive of norms of right action, within the context of a developed ethical doctrine that offers justificatory grounds for these institutions.

A full view of Hume's political theory of artifice must attend to all these different perspectives. Above all, it should be recognized that a normative dimension is adjoined to and indeed closely bound up with the scientific analysis and historical investigations of artifices throughout Hume's philosophy, however much his own philosophical principles provide the basis for logical distinctions among evaluative, descriptive, and analytic statements. Although Hume's philosophy establishes epistemological and logical foundations for a positivist empirical science, and although Hume himself recommends and often practices such a science with respect to social phenomena, he at the same time makes clear the limited sphere—that comprising "matters of fact"—in which this kind of a science is competent. As a philosopher—and as a political philosopher—in a broader sense, however, Hume does not eschew inquiry into morals or values. Not only does he study and analyze opinions regarding virtues and vices, and their historical expressions, but he also advances his own ethical principles and recommendations. It becomes clear, in particular, that Hume seeks to defend and justify the appropriateness (and the priority) of the values intrinsic to artificial virtue, just as more generally throughout his largely descriptive study of human nature he is concerned to distinguish those features of it that are salutary and trustworthy—those to which a "reasonable" person would choose to adhere—from those that must properly be subjected to the discipline of rules that promote the good of orderly cognitive and social life. A defense of justice and government—beyond a formal analysis and historical treatment of them—in the context of a defense of a public realm of rules generally is thus the principal theme in Hume's political philosophy.

This move from description and analysis to normative doctrines in Hume's political philosophy replicates the basic structure of important arguments in other parts of his philosophy. Hume's espousal (in cases of conflict) of artificial virtues over natural virtues and natural feeling in Book III of the *Treatise*, which forms the foundation of his normative political theory, follows as a parallel both to his advocacy of "philosophical" standards and rules of inductive reasoning (based on the assumption of the uniformity of nature) over various kinds of imaginative vagaries and nonscientific belief in Book I, and to his similar advocacy of the "calm" over the irregular "violent" passions, and of the pursuit of "true interest" as opposed to more ephemeral objects of desire, in Book II. All these positions represent Hume's considered preferences or judgments regarding sound practice; they are expressed in the face of his skepticism, which establishes that none of them is necessitated or justifiable by the faculty of reason, restricted as it is.

In his political essays this normative enterprise is continued in the more specific form of advocacy of a legal and constitutional regime, an embodiment of the kind of artifice that Hume treats more generally in his philosophical works. Here Hume indeed often appears—as he is frequently classified—as a constitutionalist liberal, his defense of limited government linked to the interest of individuals in personal security and in forms of personal liberty that are consistent with a larger social order. Prescriptions such as this, however, are typically combined with a cautious, conservative attitude toward political action and change, an attitude that is itself grounded in his view of the limitations of reason and thus of the defects of rationalism in morals and politics. These particular elements of Hume's political theory, although they are interesting on their own account, are far more compelling through their being grounded in a larger, systematic philosophy of human nature, and especially in the elaborate doctrines of epistemology and psychology that occupy the first two books of the *Treatise*. The full cogency of the doctrine of artifice, and the significance of Hume's practical teachings, that is, cannot be grasped apart from a view of the philosophical principles and account of human nature that form the larger context of the treatment of moral and political issues in Hume's work as a whole.

From time to time I point out some of the limitations and difficulties that attend Hume's methods, but I am more concerned to argue that there is, on the whole, a high degree of coherence and cogency throughout his philosophy, from the initial critique of reason (which I consider in chapter II) to the ensuing account of the compensatory operations of such innate mental dispositions as custom, feeling, and association (discussed in chapter III) and to the moral and political philosophy that follows. In particular, I accept the force of the epistemological criticisms that constitute Hume's distinctive type of skepticism and the cogency of the naturalistic method by which he at least provisionally overcomes his extreme skeptical doubts sufficiently to proceed with the more positive aspects of his philosophy: these topics provide the essential foundation on which the subsequent moral and political arguments are developed. It is not my purpose to challenge Hume's premises and methods in any fundamental way (although of course this can be done) but rather to draw attention to the connections and the noteworthy degree of continuity that are present among the different parts of his work. Whatever their vulnerabilities, Hume's various doctrines have earned a solid reputation as positions to be reckoned with, each in its own right; their plausibility and force are greatly enhanced through their being united in a largely consistent and thus formidable whole.

This is especially the case with Hume's political theory, which he conceived and presents as an integral part of the whole and which needs to be interpreted as such. The *Treatise*'s account of justice, for example, when read out of context may appear to contemporary readers as a somewhat thin piece of formal theorizing, although it is the sort of account that has been quite important in recent analytic social philosophy and therefore may be congenial in its approach to many social theorists today. In the context of Hume's larger philosophy of mind and human nature, however, his account of justice acquires much greater solidity; its premises reveal themselves to be far from arbitrary, and its plausibility is enhanced, when it is supplemented by themes developed elsewhere in the work. The concept of a moral artifice such as justice, as Hume presents it, and its operation as a social practice must be seen in relation to his previous account of the nature and sources of moral judgment, his substantive view of human nature and motivation, his account of the place of habit or custom in mental and social life, and ultimately his mitigated skepticism. The constitutionalism and the endorsement of moderation that make up his practical political teaching, although defended with brief forcefulness in his essays, likewise acquire greater stature in light of this philosophical background. An adequate interpretation and a fair assessment of Hume's political philosophy must thus consider its grounding in his work, with its continuities, as a whole.

Hume is a pivotal figure in modern thought, much of modern Anglo-American philosophy flowing from him—taking up its problems as he set them—in much the same way that other important streams of philosophy flow from Kant and Hegel. I refrain from entering into the profound issues that would be raised by a confrontation of Hume and these other intellectual traditions, and I make no attempt to assess their comparative merits and difficulties. The extent and depth of the influence of Humean philosophy in the English-speaking world, and the putative implications of this philosophy for our politics, provide in themselves reasons for undertaking a study such as this, in addition to whatever value there may be in the exegesis of texts as important as Hume's doubtlessly are. It is a worthwhile exercise for anyone familiar with (or perhaps conditioned by) the methods of current American political science and political practice to consider the philosophical assumptions on which these methods, in large degree, ultimately rest. Hume contributed decisively, in particular, to the development of two of the most fundamental (if underlying and therefore often tacit) sets of premises that govern our approach to political matters.

The first of these is the dominant positivism and empiricism of modern social science in its theoretical aspect. Although undoubtedly great refinements have been made in such areas as quantitative methods, modeling, theorem-testing, and the like, it is nevertheless the case that many social scientists today employ methods that presuppose a basically Humean epistemological position, and indeed methods that he recommends as appropriate in light of this position. Second, I refer to the utilitarianism that not only still commands the attention of philosophers but that also, more broadly speaking, provides the most commonly accepted ethic or practical attitude of social scientists and of the politicians and administrators who draw on the findings of social science in order to solve the problems of public life. Utilitarianism has received various formulations in its development over the last two centuries, some of them quite precise and quite foreign to anything Hume actually says, as is pointed out in chapter IV. Hume is correctly seen, however, as a proponent of a version of the general utilitarian method of ethical justification, especially with respect to social institutions (or, in his terms, artifices), that is at least implicitly present in most of our political deliberations. Positivism and utilitarianism as terms and as precisely formulated doctrines are not found in Hume's writings, and he must be carefully interpreted as a precursor and not necessarily as a proponent of these positions as they might be expressed in the twentieth century. Still, it is Hume's philosophical principles with which any modern advocate or critic of these methods ought to be conversant if approaches and convictions that are commonly taken for granted are to be seen in perspective.

In Hume's work, moreover, both these methods—the one theoretical, the other practical—are presented in close relation to each other and to the empiricist (or "perceptualist") foundations of his philosophy. They are developed in complementary fashion, by self-conscious steps, as viable alternatives to a previous skepticism that momentarily threatens to inhibit further inquiries or the adoption of any positive doctrines whatever. They are thus advanced as provisional guides to right reasoning and moral conduct while a lingering, moderate form of skepticism persists, preserving an awareness both of the limitations inherent in the chosen methods and of their final tentativeness.

The location of an influential scientific method and of a familiar and plausible type of ethical sensibility within a single philosophical system is of some interest in itself. Their parallel derivation from a common original skepticism, moreover, contains lessons regarding what Hume advocates as the proper philosophical (or scientific) state of mind, one that he often characterizes as "diffidence." Finally, over and above these questions of method, we find that Hume himself adopts a distinctive political attitude, which he advances in writings intended to be popular and of practical consequence. Hume's direct political teaching, as already suggested, includes constitutionalism of a fairly conservative sort (in a sense to be discussed in chapter v)—an application of his general defense of rules, form, and artifice in moral life—along with a deliberately cautious or moderate approach to proposals for programmatic change. A prescriptive political theory such as this seems somewhat removed from the assurance and the intellectually confident reformism that have been characteristic attitudes of much modern social science, and yet the skeptical caution and tentativeness of Hume's practical teachings are put forward as consistent and reasonable conclusions from his preceding doctrines. Hume is a political philosopher in the traditional sense, offering doctrines concerning the nature of a desirable political regime, a reasonable approach to political practice, and the proper relation of the philosopher to the world of public affairs, custom, and received beliefs. These doctrines follow, in Hume's case, from the basic principles of his philosophy of human nature as a whole; anyone for whom these principles are at all plausible must be interested in the political conclusions and recommendations to which their author is led.

The emphasis of this study is on the positive aspects and doctrines, both theoretical and practical, of Hume's political philosophy. These doctrines, however, rest on a skeptical foundation of which we shall continually be reminded and of which a preliminary sketch may be offered here.[3] Although Hume was not alone in giving serious attention

[3] The nature and extent of Hume's skepticism is a matter of continuing scholarly controversy. Recent views range from that of Stove, who argues that Hume is on the skeptical side of any question in which there is disagreement over the conclusiveness of arguments, to that of Capaldi, who sees Hume as a "common sense" philosopher whose skepticism is therefore largely a "pretense." Stove, however, considers only

to skeptical problems of epistemology, his self-characterization as a skeptic was unusual enough to be provocative in his own time.[4] More representative thinkers of the Enlightenment, although they were prepared to welcome the contributions of skeptical reasoning against what they regarded as dogma and superstition and as a basis for intellectual tolerance, dismissed with impatience the challenges this skepticism presented when it seemed to interfere with the project of expanding and applying human knowledge.[5]

Under the influence of Cartesian rationalism and popularized Newtonian science, the Enlightenment philosophers for the most part were motivated by a conviction of the possibility of comprehensive and certain knowledge of the world, physical and moral, based on intellectual penetration into the nature and relations of observable things. The ambitious design of Hume's *Treatise* itself (his first work) manifests something of this enthusiasm.[6] The skeptical doubts that arise in the first part of that work, however, are never entirely dispelled, and Hume's later writings (frequently taking the more tentative form of essays) are nearly always marked by expressions of intellectual caution and disclaimers concerning the restricted scope of our possible comprehension of things—attitudes that are an important residue of the earlier epistemological skepticism and that mark all his subsequent work. Hume's mature characterization of Newton, for example, em-

---

questions relating to empiricism and induction; Hume's skepticism is surely less pronounced in his moral philosophy and in his practical philosophy generally (where he indeed is usually close to common sense), as I suggest below, despite his skeptical denial of a *rational* basis for values. D. C. Stove, "The Nature of Hume's Skepticism," in *McGill Hume Studies*, ed. David Fate Norton, Nicholas Capaldi, and Wade L. Robison (San Diego: Austin Hill Press, 1979), p. 209; and Capaldi, *David Hume*, pp. 30, 200-203.

[4] Hume's explicit defenses of skepticism are found in the *Treatise* i.iv.7; *Enquiries* (i), pp. 40-41 and sec. 12; and "The Sceptic," *Works*, vol. 3, pp. 213-31, which concentrates on the sentimental theory of morals. For the historical context see Richard H. Popkin, "Scepticism in the Enlightenment," in *Studies on Voltaire and the Eighteenth Century*, ed. Theodore Besterman (Geneva: Librairie Droz, 1963), vol. 26, pp. 1321-45.

[5] See especially Diderot's articles on "Pyrrhonienne ou sceptique philosophie" and "Eclectisme," in the *Encyclopédie ou Dictionnaire Raisonné des Sciences, des Arts, et des Métiers* (Paris: n.p., 1751-1772), vol. 13, pp. 608-14, and vol. 5, pp. 270-93. A few earlier writers, including Bayle and Shaftesbury (both of whom influenced Hume), called attention to the benefits of skepticism.

[6] "In pretending therefore to explain the principles of human nature, we in effect propose a compleat system of the sciences, built on a foundation almost entirely new, and the only one upon which they can stand with any security" (T. xx). Hume's original plan for the *Treatise* included five books—on the understanding, the passions, morals, politics, and criticism (T. xii); the last two parts of this systematic project were largely carried out in the form of essays.

phasizes the inaccessibility of knowledge of the essential nature of causal connections in terms appropriate to Hume's own final convictions: "While Newton seemed to draw off the veil from some of the mysteries of nature, he showed at the same time the imperfections of the mechanical philosophy; and thereby restored her ultimate secrets to that obscurity, in which they ever did and ever will remain."[7] The reduced scope that Hume's philosophy permits to the rational faculty is not at all inconsistent with a carefully conducted, empirical scientific enterprise, grounded in close attention to experience, with respect to both nature and society. It does, however, diminish the usual Enlightenment confidence in our potential ability to understand thoroughly and thence to remake the social world along lines more conducive to secular happiness, and it denies the rational basis or necessity of the values that might guide this enterprise. For both these reasons, I argue, Hume is brought in the end to a distinctive, conservative approach to the practical matters of moral and political life.

Hume's explicit skepticism is one of the themes that is carried over from the *Treatise* to the first *Enquiry*, where it appears in the more sedate and "mitigated" form in which he never ceases to recommend it. The development of Hume's thought in the first book of the *Treatise* is considered in the following chapter; we may take our preliminary bearings, however, from the discussion of "The Sceptical or Academical Philosophy" with which Hume concludes the later work.

Hume begins this essay by alluding to a supposed connection between skepticism and religious infidelity—a topic that he quickly dismisses but one that we should consider, since this was one of the most common implications of the term skepticism to most people in Hume's day. The Enlightenment was characterized by a critical spirit that frequently assumed an iconoclastic attitude toward traditional bodies of belief and received opinions and institutions of many kinds; and some of its more prominent thinkers, especially in France, rejected the miracles and revelation on which Christianity is founded as being both unverifiable and, moreover, unnecessary for morals and the happiness of society. Hume contributed notoriously (though in a comparatively subdued fashion) to this current of thought, questioning the logical tenability and the evidence for certain kinds of arguments advanced in support of religion and sharing in the widespread contemporary anticlericalism.

[7] Hume, *History of England*, chap. 71, vol. 6, p. 374. On the Enlightenment's interpretation of Newton see Peter Gay, *The Enlightenment: An Interpretation*, vol. 2: *The Science of Freedom* (New York: Knopf, 1969), pp. 128ff. For the influence of the Newtonian method on Hume, see John Passmore, *Hume's Intentions*, 3d ed. (London: Duckworth, 1980), chap. 3.

Philosophical skepticism in the special sense in which Hume develops and recommends it, however, does not entail or connote the absence of religious faith. Skepticism refers to doubts and critical arguments respecting the potentialities of human reason rather than of divine revelation; and thus a genuine skeptic—while doubting certain positive arguments for religion—might with perfect consistency be a person of faith, sincerely sharing (as many modern skeptics have) the view expressed by one of Hume's own interlocutors that skepticism is the "first and most essential step" toward being a believing Christian.[8] Hume is generally regarded as never having himself taken the next step in this direction, but there is nothing in his philosophy that would preclude it. His critical writings on religion, on the other hand, reflect not his skepticism as such but rather the scientific commitments that he undertakes following the resolution of his more extreme skeptical doubts. Certain prominent arguments for Christianity, whether deriving from alleged miracles or from the observation of nature, are in Hume's view claims about matters of fact (including the reliability of historical testimony),[9] and as such they must be scrutinized according to the same rigorous scientific standards as any such claims. In the same way, Hume's frequent attacks on religious "superstition" and "fanaticism" should be seen as particular cases of his consistent opposition to excessive claims of intellectual insight and assurance, of the sort that his philosophy rules out in general. Such claims, he holds, are not only untenable in theory, but they are likely also to be dangerous in practice; and Hume's distaste for certain social and institutional manifestations of religious assurance (including the radical political programs that had been, within recent memory, allied to dissenting religious movements) is an aspect of the practical moderation that his philosophy likewise generally recommends. Thus Hume's skepticism pertains to religion only insofar as religion embodies the kind of presumptuous or fallacious intellectual claims, and their dangerous practical consequences, for which the skeptic can find no reasonable grounds.[10]

[8] Hume, *Dialogues*, p. 228. Orthodox Catholic thinkers were in fact inclined, to a greater degree than were the *philosophes*, to take skeptical arguments seriously; see R. R. Palmer, *Catholics and Unbelievers in Eighteenth Century France* (Princeton: Princeton University Press, 1939), p. 132. The union of skepticism and fideism is examined in Richard H. Popkin, *The History of Scepticism from Erasmus to Descartes* (New York: Harper and Row, 1964).

[9] Hume, *Enquiries*·(I), p. 165.

[10] Gay takes skepticism in its popular sense as lack of religious faith; hence he sees the Enlightenment as a whole as skeptical, or pagan, and Hume, the "complete modern pagan," is assimilated to the *philosophes*. This approach neglects the philosophical

The philosophical skepticism that Hume develops is the sort, he says, that arises "consequent" to inquiry into the foundations of human understanding; it is founded in doubts regarding the possibility of rationally validated knowledge, or the discovery of the "unfitness" of our "mental faculties" to attain certainty on speculative subjects, that is encountered in the course of epistemological analysis.[11] Such doubts are evidently irrefutable by reason; when insisted on in their extreme form, they constitute what Hume labels Pyrrhonism, borrowing the name of the ancient school of thoroughgoing skepticism that recommended total suspension of judgment on all intellectual questions. Pyrrhonism, however, appears to be "excessive." It cannot withstand the "blind and powerful instinct of nature" by which we normally repose confidence in our senses and accordingly believe, for example, in the reality of the external world; its "great subverter" is "action, and employment, and the occupations of common life," where people act on the basis of genuine convictions, both metaphysical and moral, the most basic of which the abstruse skepticism of the schools can never really dissolve (even in the skeptic).[12]

As a more plausible alternative, therefore, Hume warmly defends a "more *mitigated* skepticism or *academical* philosophy," alluding to another ancient school of skepticism that was marked by its efforts to develop, in contrast to Pyrrhonism, standards of probable reasoning even while acknowledging the limits and fallibility of our perceptual and intellectual faculties.[13] This mitigated skepticism, Hume says, is in part the "result" of the more extreme Pyrrhonist doubts: its cautious efforts to define standards for probable reasoning and reasonable belief, and its continuing opposition to dogmatic claims, follow from the preceding recognition of the tenuous status of all human reasoning.

---

meaning of Hume's skepticism and its consequences, and it glosses over important differences in temperament and doctrine between him and the others. *The Enlightenment*, vol. 1: *The Rise of Modern Paganism* (1966).

[11] Hume, *Enquiries* (I), p. 150.

[12] Ibid., pp. 151, 158-59. Pyrrho of Elis (c. 360-275 B.C.), the founder of skepticism, is reputed to have been a moralist who taught doubt and detachment as means to peace of mind. The logical doctrines of the school he founded were compiled by Sextus Empiricus (c. A.D. 200), whose writings were well known during the Enlightenment and are cited by Hume, *Enquiries* (II), pp. 180, 207.

[13] Hume, *Enquiries* (I), p. 161. Academic skepticism was developed during the Hellenistic period in the school that had been founded by Plato. Cicero, who studied in what is known as the "New Academy," presents its doctrines in *De Natura Deorum* and *Academica*. See Richard H. Popkin, "David Hume: His Pyrrhonism and His Critique of Pyrrhonism," in *Hume: A Collection of Critical Essays*, ed. V. C. Chappell (Garden City: Doubleday, 1966), and Terence Penelhum, "Hume's Skepticism and the *Dialogues*," in *McGill Hume Studies*, ed. Norton et al., pp. 255-61.

Hume never repudiates or denies the validity (by purely rationalistic criteria) of the extreme doubts; these constitute only a moment in his philosophy as a whole, however, which in the *Treatise* as well as in the *Enquiry* moves beyond epistemological puzzles to positive, practical doctrines with respect to both sound reasoning and moral value. Hume's dismissal of Pyrrhonism in the *Enquiry* manifests a clear rhetorical intention: Hume joins in the commonplace disparagement of a label associated with what common sense regards as absurd excesses of skepticism in order to defend all the more effectively under a different name a viable and moderate form of skepticism that he regards as both "durable and useful."[14]

Hume's philosophical skepticism expresses itself vis-à-vis all three types of possible knowledge that he enumerates at the end of the first *Enquiry*. His arguments regarding "abstract" or demonstrative reasoning, of the sort contained most notably in mathematics, are not of concern in this study; although Hume says that this is a "more perfect species of knowledge" than the others, he does suggest some difficulties with claims of certain knowledge even in this area.[15]

Of greater concern are claims of knowledge respecting "matters of fact and existence"—factual knowledge of the world, both physical and moral, or knowledge concerning natural and human objects, of the sort that makes up the empirical sciences. Skepticism expresses itself here in Hume's failure to find a rational ground or validation either for our belief in stable and continuing objects existing independently of our perceptions or for our belief in necessary and regular causation, on which depends all inferential reasoning from present observations to past, future, or general cases. These doubts call into question our ability to apprehend anything beyond the flux of our immediate perceptions[16] or to make the accurate causal judgments

---

[14] Hume, *Enquiries* (I), p. 161. Cicero's adherence to Academic skepticism guaranteed the respectability of this philosophical tradition. For the contemporary assessment of the two schools, see Diderot's article, "Scepticisme et sceptiques," *Encyclopédie*, vol. 14, p. 757. James Noxon, *Hume's Philosophical Development* (Oxford: Clarendon Press, 1973), p. 12, notes that Hume is not so explicit about calling himself a skeptic in the *Enquiries*; but Noxon disregards possible rhetorical motives that may be present in this, a popular and thus a carefully written book.

[15] Hume, *Enquiries* (I), pp. 163, 155-57; *Treatise*, pp. 71, 180-81.

[16] It is axiomatic for Hume that we apprehend only our perceptions, and that these appear to us as distinct and separable existences, without any perceptible or necessary connections among them. He does not dwell on the metaphysical conceptions that might be implied by these doctrines, but compare the following: "Nothing in the world is perpetual; Every thing, however seemingly firm, is in continual flux and change; The world itself gives symptoms of frailty and dissolution." "Of the Immortality of the Soul," *Works*, vol. 4, p. 404.

that permit us to engage in rational conduct with respect to the objects and other persons in our environment.

In the face of such doubts Hume, like the ancient skeptics to whom he alludes, seeks what the ancients called a "rule of life," or a set of provisional guidelines for the conduct of the mind and of life, even in the absence of rationally defensible or demonstrable standards.[17] Hume's psychological reflections readily reveal, as already suggested, that people by a kind of natural instinct *believe* what the skeptical philosophers cannot prove; common sense, grounded in certain nonrational features of human nature, appears to compensate for the failure of reason at the critical junctures. Feeling or sentiment, along with the strong propensity of human nature to contract regular habits, is the principal element that emerges from these psychological investigations: belief itself—including the fundamental beliefs in the reality of external objects and in the conclusion of a causal inference—is nothing but a special feeling, or vivacity of conception, accompanying the idea; inferential reasoning is based on a habitual or customary disposition of the imagination, apparently innate or natural, to make transitions from similar causes to similar effects when it has had sufficient past experience of regular conjunctions of objects.

One can, as Hume indeed recommends, choose to yield to these dispositions, setting aside skeptical doubts; one can, moreover, elaborate and adhere to a precise scientific logic, which will be nothing but the "reflections of common life, methodized and corrected."[18] Science itself, however, though an expression of human nature, lacks a purely rational foundation, and awareness of its status should properly induce caution in its pursuit. The notions of objectivity and causality on which science is based are "fictions" of the imagination, albeit compelling ones and ones that are more useful than other fictions; thus science as a whole for Hume is a kind of mental artifice. Like the conventions of the moral world, its function is to control or discipline the irregular impulses of feeling and the imagination, and to legitimate and encourage particular sorts of reasoning and judgments, with the end of advancing basic human interests. But it is itself grounded in mere psychological propensities, including ones, such as the desire

---

[17] The Pyrrhonists resolved to live passively in accordance with appearances and the rules of their society; the Academics adopted a criterion of probability. See Sextus Empiricus, *Outlines of Pyrrhonism*, trans. R. G. Bury (Cambridge: Harvard University Press, 1967) I.23, III.235, pp. 17, 483; and Cicero, *De Natura Deorum* I.12, and *Academica* II.104, trans. H. Rackham (Cambridge: Harvard University Press, 1972), pp. 15, 601.

[18] Hume, *Enquiries* (I), p. 162.

for order and regularity, that Hume regards as normally stronger than other impulses. We adopt this artifice, and determine to conduct our reasoning in accordance with its logical standards, because we find that it suits our purposes to do so: it brings order to our cognitive life and permits the sort of control over our environment that we find conducive to our well-being.[19] On this basis Hume himself pursues science—the scientific study of human nature and morals in the *Treatise*, of political institutions in his essays, and of historical processes (to the limited degree that this proves possible) in his *History*; and a careful scientific analysis of the operation of artificial virtue and social institutions in moral life underlies Hume's normative doctrines and prescriptions in this area.

Mitigated skepticism is thus perfectly compatible with Hume's obvious scientific commitments, and the continuing alliance of Humean philosophy and scientific progress belies the air of paradox that some of Hume's contemporaneous critics saw in this. The skeptic continues to reason about matters of fact, however, with caution and with an awareness of the limitations of the methods used. Scientific cognition consists in the apprehension of observable sequences and regularities in the appearances of objects, when these can be discerned; science concedes its own irremediable fallibility, systematically abstaining from claims of insight into causal or other relations among objects and eschewing speculations (except as hypotheses)—let alone invocation of special causal agencies, or miracles, and predictions based on these—in the absence of observed regularities. Science proceeds on the assumption, unprovable but necessary to reasoning at all, that the future will resemble the past or that the course of nature, including human nature and its social manifestations, will continue uniformly the same (T. 89, 134). On this assumption, which it is natural for us to make, experience can serve as a guide to reasonable expectations and reasonable conduct; and indeed in Hume's view there is no other possible guide for this purpose. Efforts to transcend experience, in thought or in action, however, although they may please the imagination and although they no doubt appeal to other capacities of our nature than those that underlie the scientific enterprise, cannot make claims either on our reason, as Hume delimits this faculty, or on the prudence of a wise or philosophical person.

Hume's philosophical skepticism manifests itself finally—although

---

[19] Passmore, *Hume's Intentions*, p. 55. The establishment of such a foundation for science, especially his proposed moral science, is said to be Hume's "methodological intention."

less explicitly and uncontentiously—in the third area in which claims of knowledge are sometimes advanced, namely, the area that embraces judgments of value including, most important for our purposes, ethical and related political judgments. In the *Treatise* Hume argues in detail that reason provides no distinctions of virtue and vice—that cognition of what *is* cannot yield judgments of *ought*—and he criticizes rationalistic ethical theories of several sorts. This is scarcely an issue in the first *Enquiry*, however, where Hume simply asserts that such matters fall outside the bounds of possible knowledge: "Morals and criticism are not so properly objects of the understanding as of taste and sentiment. Beauty, whether moral or natural, is felt, more properly than perceived."[20] Hume dismisses so cursorily the idea that we can *know* the good or the beautiful because he assumes that his readers are familiar with the moral and aesthetic theories that emphasized taste and sentiment or that made reference to a special "moral sense," which had been propounded by philosophers such as Shaftesbury and Hutcheson as well as himself and which had become widely influential. He does point out that much of what is sometimes taken to be ethical knowledge falls into one of the other two categories. For example, Locke's well-known instance of a demonstrable moral truth—"that where there is no property there can be no injustice"—is, insofar as it is a truth, simply a matter of the definition of its terms and not a new conclusion of reason.[21] Other moral reasonings pertain to matters of fact and are accordingly the product of observation and experience: inquiries into the psychological sources of moral judgments and what people hold to be good rather than what *is* good fall into this category. Much of Hume's own moral theory consists of doctrines—analytical, psychological, and historical—pertaining to these sorts of questions. Judgments of value themselves, however, are (or involve) in the final analysis expressions of feeling, according to Hume. They are therefore not susceptible of ultimate justification (or refutation) by reason, however much they may follow and be influenced by reflections concerning matters of fact and however strong or indubitable may be the sentiments and convictions on which they are based.

A denial that rational—and thus unchanging and objective—standards of value are accessible to the human mind has frequently figured prominently in skeptical philosophies. The ancient skeptics, both Pyrrhonists and Academics, were as much concerned with ethics as with

[20] Hume, *Enquiries* (I), p. 165. Arguments that moral judgments arise from sentiment are relegated to Appendix 1 of *Enquiries* (II), pp. 285-94.

[21] Hume, *Enquiries* (I), p. 163. See John Locke, *An Essay Concerning Human Understanding*, ed. Peter H. Nidditch (Oxford: Clarendon Press, 1975) IV.iii.18.

logic; with respect to the former they were in a sense the successors to the sophists, who had argued that human values and moral rules were mere matters of "convention" (*nomos*)—hence diverse and impermanent—rather than given by "nature" (*physis*). Likewise modern skeptics, such as Montaigne (who called himself a Pyrrhonist), were struck by the extent of apparent moral diversity and the evidently determinative role of custom rather than reason in fixing people's moral beliefs. The fact of diversity has thus often served as evidence for the arguments of moral skeptics; ethical relativism, or acquiescence in this diversity of historical and cultural experience, has often been their conclusion. The ancient skeptics' rule of life in moral and political affairs generally dictated acceptance of local custom as the most prudent course, in default of contrary standards given by reason, one that would conduce to the wise person's goal of peace of mind and tranquillity. Montaigne too, especially in his later essays, found contentment in custom and in the traditional religious faith, as well as in introspective detachment from the doctrinal and associated political tumults of the larger world.

Although Hume's epistemological position might appear to provide a basis for conclusions similar to these, his developed moral philosophy exhibits important differences from as well as similarities to the doctrines of his skeptical predecessors. He fails to discover logically necessary or self-evident principles of right (of the sort contained in some natural law theories),[22] and he is unable to find perceptible qualities of things or relations that determine their virtuous or vicious character. In this sense nature indeed provides no standards. We nevertheless make evaluative judgments, just as we draw causal inferences, and the lack of rational grounding does not normally—even in the case of the skeptic—prevent our making them with conviction; genuine and total suspension of belief in morals, just as with respect to causation, is impossible in life. Faced with this state of affairs, Hume, in a manner common to many skeptics, turns his attention from epistemology to the psychology of belief, and he finds that moral judgments arise from the distinctive *feelings* of approval or disapproval that normal people experience upon considering certain objects or circumstances. Moral like causal judgments, that is, depend on some deeply rooted and nonrational propensity of our nature, and indeed it is this origin that

---

[22] Not all natural law theories, however, were rationalistic. Duncan Forbes discusses an "empirical" tradition of natural jurisprudence in which moral duties are related to the observed needs and circumstances of society, to which Hume's doctrines have affinities; *Hume's Philosophical Politics* (Cambridge: Cambridge University Press, 1975), chap. 1.

gives the most basic of them their usual strength, rendering them immune, in practice, to the unanswerable doubts that philosophers may propose. Hume likewise grants the importance of the role of custom—in the sense both of individual mental habits and of social tradition—in the realm of ethics that the earlier skeptics emphasized; but here too his doctrine is more complex: some moral qualities—the "natural virtues"—he finds to be the largely invariable and direct expressions of natural impulses, whereas others—the "artificial virtues"—depend in large degree on social conventions and tradition. All moral judgments, however, involve feelings, whether immediate or habituated, and all morality is thus properly seen as an expression of human nature, with its constant features. When viewed from this perspective moral standards *are* given by nature—human nature—for Hume, even though they are not given by reason. Human nature here as in the basic questions of epistemology exhibits features such as feeling and habit that compensate in ordinary life for the defects of reason.

Hume's ethical theory does not begin, furthermore, from an awareness of diversity in moral values among different societies. The question of moral diversity or uniformity is an empirical one, one in which Hume is indeed very much interested and one that is open for scientific study. The investigations of the *Treatise*, many of which rely on introspective evidence, proceed on the assumption of the constancy of human nature in important respects, from which consistency in moral sentiments and judgments might be expected to follow; Hume's subsequent historical studies, which he undertook in part in order to collect further evidence bearing on the doctrines of the *Treatise*, by and large confirm its findings with respect to both human nature and morals. The natural virtues, such as gratitude or care of children, are as invariable as the spontaneous natural feelings to which they correspond. The artificial virtues, such as justice and allegiance to government, which prescribe conduct according to the rules of social artifices or conventions and which are frequently the products of diverse patterns of historical development, do vary considerably in their content; but even here Hume finds substantial similarity underlying apparent diversity, since the utilitarian quality of the artificial virtues and their function in sustaining orderly social life under certain widely obtaining conditions are everywhere similar. The subjective element in Hume's ethical theory is therefore not inconsistent with his observation that moral beliefs display in practice a large degree of uniformity and stability, moral agents and societies all sharing important characteristics in relevant respects. The step is short, moreover, from this observation to Hume's normative ethical doctrines, in which he offers only comparatively small refinements on what he takes to be the usual conclusions of the ordinary moral sentiments.

Moral skepticism therefore may seem an inappropriate characterization of Hume's philosophy, insofar as this phrase connotes an insistence on moral diversity or an unnerving sense of the absence of any stable standards of value.[23] Hume never doubts the reality of moral distinctions and moral motives, and he puts forward his denial of a rational foundation for morals with equanimity: the moral sentiments for Hume are as trustworthy a faculty as is the equally nonrational disposition to believe strongly that the future will resemble the past, and they operate with comparable regularity. In both cases, he concludes, the normal inclinations of human nature are appropriate for our purposes and happiness.

In the case of morals, just as in the field of scientific logic, however, Hume's philosophy retains a critical distance from the given features of its subject matter. Just as in the first book of the *Treatise* Hume specifies certain "philosophical" principles or rules for right reasoning, which he refines from among the various potentialities of the imagination, so also in his ethical theory he emphasizes the manner in which, in social life, many of our immediate feelings must be brought under the discipline of the rules constituting social artifices. He goes some distance, furthermore, toward defining a philosophical criterion of utility by which these artifices may be evaluated, just as he offers a philosophical or scientific conception of cause to serve as a critical standard for the common sense inferences of which it is a refinement. Hume thus proposes a normative ethical doctrine just as he proposes a normative canon of inductive logic, the former being derived ultimately from his own reflective moral sense just as the latter rests on his considered judgment of the most prudent and useful form of intellectual commitment. Neither position claims rational grounding;

---

[23] David Fate Norton, *David Hume—Common-Sense Moralist, Sceptical Metaphysician* (Princeton: Princeton University Press, 1982), chap. 6, provides a survey of different types of skepticism. Norton denies that Hume is a moral skeptic, since (as he correctly points out) Hume's theory upholds the reality and even the objectivity of moral standards, in opposition to contemporaneous theories of self-love and extreme conventionalism; see esp. pp. 12n., 109. By other criteria of moral skepticism that Norton, however, accepts (p. 245)—the view that moral judgments lack a rational basis, or arise from "taste," or depend on convention—Hume *is* a skeptic in morals, even though he neither calls himself one nor challenges the main forms of received morality. A weakness of Norton's book is its lack of attention to Hume's artificial virtues, where feeling and "common sense" must be mediated by convention and may be subjected to reasoned criticism or even radical challenge.

both depend, rather, on an appeal to human nature, with its normal needs and capacities.

In moral life as in science, however, important lessons of caution and moderation follow from the ultimately skeptical basis of Hume's philosophy, even when this skepticism is mitigated through his acceptance of human nature. Values are properly related to human nature, needs, and circumstances, not all of which perhaps are entirely constant. The artificial virtues, in particular, exhibit variability and change with respect to their exact form if not to their fundamental purpose, a fact that opens the way to an ongoing process of philosophical criticism and political choice in this realm of moral life. Experience is our only guide in these matters; doctrinaire programs, arising as they usually do from a presumptuous rationalism, are rejected, especially when they involve a repudiation of or a will to transcend human nature and the experience of the past. The common desire for order and continuity in moral life, such that reasonable expectations about the future may be entertained and our ends pursued with some hope of success, is in Hume's view as fundamental a manifestation of human nature as is the belief in the uniformity and regularity of physical nature. The latter belief arises from a certain powerful custom of the imagination, which may be expressed as rules of logic; and moral order is created by the artifices and rules of social life, which are likewise sustained by custom—which is thus the "great guide of human life" for Hume as for other figures in the skeptical tradition that his philosophy continues.[24]

Hume thus affirms a form of "mitigated" skepticism at the conclusion of his first *Enquiry*, his mature and more succinct presentation of his philosophy of the understanding, just as in the *Treatise* he praises "moderate scepticism" (T. 224) and concludes the first book with a determination to proceed with his philosophy "upon sceptical principles" (T. 270). In both works a more pure or extreme form of skepticism, although it is not refuted, is found to be untenable and to dissolve in the face of the fundamental dispositions of the mind: "nature breaks the force of all sceptical arguments," which might otherwise have "subverted all conviction" (T. 187). It is only by a considered (and not wholly uncritical) acquiescence in a certain *natural* tendency or instinct of belief and judgment that the philosopher can proceed with his investigations, and the same *nature* to which he appeals at this stage furnishes him with guidance at other points in his philosophy as well. Hume's skepticism is thus supplemented by a positive phi-

[24] Hume, *Enquiries* (I), p. 44.

losophy of naturalism—the discovery of at least provisional standards of both right reasoning and moral value in the normal features of human nature. This resort to nature on Hume's part provokes a question concerning the relation of the naturalistic element in his philosophy to the important theme of artifice and the related ideas of convention and custom that pervade it, ideas that I also emphasize in this study.

Nature and artifice (or convention) appear frequently in the history of Western philosophy as antithetical concepts, sometimes connoting two different, even antagonistic, sorts of norms for the guidance of human life. Moral and political philosophy began with the ancient distinction of *physis* and *nomos*, which was alluded to above in connection with the potentially skeptical implications contained in it. A similar distinction forms the basis for important arguments in modern political philosophy as well; it is invoked most conspicuously in Hume's day by Rousseau, who contrasts "nature, which does everything for the best," with the artificial inequities of modern society, but who also argues that legitimate authority must be founded on conventions rather than on nature.[25] There is a tension, too, at certain points in Hume's philosophy between the spontaneous impulses of our nature and the requirements of orderly cognitive and social life, which are satisfied through our adherence to rules and conventions: right reasoning depends on the suppression of perfectly natural "flights of the imagination" (T. 267) in favor of scientific logic; artificial virtue similarly involves a curbing of certain natural passions and motives, and the interests of society even require that the natural virtues (genuine virtues though they are) be subordinated to artificial rules in cases of conflict. At this level, then, Hume too is a proponent of artifice in contrast to nature as a standard for conduct; this is a normative position that follows upon his analysis of the conditions of social order and the long-term benefits that are to be expected from both science and the artificial virtues. Hume's political philosophy, as I argue in detail below, emphasizes the necessity of the artificial institutions of justice and government, institutions that are problematic because they frequently conflict with the immediate impulses of human nature even while serving certain of our most basic needs and ends.

In a larger sense, however, Hume's positive philosophy as a whole may be regarded as naturalistic—even his mode of defending the ar-

[25] Jean-Jacques Rousseau, *Emile, or On Education*, trans. Allan Bloom (New York: Basic Books, 1979), p. 80 and passim; and *On the Social Contract*, ed. Roger D. Masters, trans. Judith R. Masters (New York: St. Martin's Press, 1978) I.4, p. 49.

tificial institutions of social life. The rules of causal inference to which the Humean philosopher chooses to adhere correspond to one of the most fundamental propensities of the imagination—the natural belief in the uniformity of nature—even if steady adherence to these rules involves conscious repudiation of other tendencies of the mind that occasionally interfere with them. Similarly the artificial virtues, which are justified through a process of calm reflection on our needs and long-term interests, would be impossible to realize if there were not given features of human nature that could be harnessed, through social training and education, in their support: these include the capacity for reflection itself and the related capacity to suppress violent in favor of calm passions, as well as the natural dispositions to sympathy, rule-following, and customary modes of judging and behaving. The artificial virtues, which exhibit a fundamental similarity in all societies, are, Hume says, a universal product of a naturally "inventive species" (T. 484), the members of which are capable of contriving when necessary the instruments of self-restraint and social discipline that serve their larger interests. Our capacity to establish and observe social conventions is thus a remedy that nature itself provides for "what is irregular and incommodious in the affections" (T. 489); and habit, which upholds them, is "nothing but one of the principles of nature, and derives all its force from that origin" (T. 179). Although artificial virtue can conflict with human nature in the form of a variety of spontaneous feelings and motives, Hume at the same time is willing to ascribe to his rules of justice the traditional label "laws of nature"— not in one of the traditional senses, that connoting rational self-evidence, but in the sense of their universal correspondence to the requirements of human life.[26]

Nature for Hume is not, in the first instance, a source of normative principles but rather the totality of objects and their relations that are accessible to our perceptual faculties; it is the subject matter of science pursued according to the empiricist criteria that Hume recommends. Within this realm Hume himself is mainly interested in human nature—the operations of the mind, the behavior of individuals and groups, and the functioning of social institutions—as its manifestations may be recorded by an observer who brings to this material the same assumptions of stable objects and regular causation that the natural scientist brings to physical phenomena. With respect to cognitive life,

[26] Hume's conception of happiness, or of the human interests that are advanced by the artificial virtues, is entirely secular, and in this sense also naturalistic as opposed to supernatural or spiritual. On the various meanings of "nature," see *Treatise*, pp. 473-75.

the study of human nature reveals to the scientist the psychological processes and the logical presuppositions on the basis of which the scientific enterprise is possible and through the acceptance of which the scientist is enabled to continue. With respect to moral life, the study of human nature reveals a sociable dimension of experience that forms the context for political philosophy. An economic analysis brings out the necessitous circumstances of human beings with respect to material goods, for which justice and government are in the first instance remedies, whereas people's receptivity to testimony, the communication of feelings through sympathy, and the moral sentiments suggest our normal dependence on social relations for the greater part of our cognitive and affective life. In both cases the normal features of human nature offer guides that the skeptical philosopher may select as appropriate standards or "rules of life." An appeal from the philosopher's own reflective preferences to what he takes to be the fundamental interests and feelings of all people mediates the gradual and naturalistic transition that Hume decidedly makes from is to ought.

In the moral and political parts of Hume's philosophy, this transition is accompanied by a clear endorsement of the sociable potentialities of human nature, a theme on which I place some emphasis. The basic premises of Hume's philosophy appear in many respects to be individualistic, and a methodological individualism does form the starting point for its various sections. His perceptualism—the opening claim that only discrete impressions and ideas are accessible to our minds— has seemed to some to entail that each individual percipient inhabits an inescapably private world. This is an implication that, I argue, Hume struggles to avoid as he introduces and discusses numerous modes of undoubted communication and other bonds among people, which are none the less strong for the philosopher's speculative capacity to resolve them into private mental states. Humean science (and Hume's own scientific method) takes for granted the capacity of individual observers to detach themselves from the objects (or perceptions) they study, even when these are their own feelings, or from cultural phenomena in which they have genuine interests. Likewise, Hume's political philosophy frequently invokes a methodological individualism that links it both to classical economic theory and to more recent rational-choice theory in moral and political philosophy; this is especially true of the *Treatise*'s abstract account of the artificial virtues as conventions to whose establishment the private interests of reflective individuals would lead them to agree.

In Hume, however, as indeed in kindred bodies of theory, the assumptions underlying this kind of analysis are clearly formal premises, selective abstractions from the actual motives characteristic of human behavior, and the resulting doctrines constitute models of which actual systems of justice and government are only approximations. The status of these parts of Hume's political philosophy (which are sometimes discussed out of context) stands out clearly in light of his work as a whole, since he both provides a descriptive account of human nature that is far more rich and complex than is suggested in the more formal analyses, and he at least sketches the historical dimension in which social artifices actually exist and evolve. The inability of accounts based on rational individual self-interest to explain the sense of duty on which, as Hume recognizes, justice as a practice depends is remedied by appeal to a variety of other mental processes and motives that have a place in his larger theory of human nature; and the timelessly abstract quality of some parts of his political theory (sometimes alleged to be a feature of Enlightenment social thought generally) must be set against the historical arguments that are more prominent in post-*Treatise* writings but for which the central role of custom throughout his philosophy provides the foundation. Thus, for example, Hume's well-known treatment of justice as a convention of mutual self-interest must be balanced against his even more famous rejection elsewhere of a contractual origin for actual authoritative institutions and against his fuller portrayal of human nature in the *Treatise* as a whole; it should be interpreted as the deliberate abstraction, intended to illuminate certain aspects of artificial as opposed to natural virtue, that it is.

In Hume's larger moral philosophy the sociable potentialities of human nature, which make possible an actual and stable, as opposed to a hypothetical, moral life, modify to a significant degree the egoistic component that is no doubt present in his psychology; they reveal his methodological individualism to be, like his extreme skepticism, only a phase—useful but incomplete—in his fully developed doctrine. Just as Hume's skepticism gives way to a positive philosophy of belief and morals, so his individualism—which is grounded like the skepticism in his perceptualist premises—gives way to a rich account of social and political life, grounded in his substantive doctrine of human nature. Therefore, since human nature is sociable in certain centrally important respects and expresses itself naturally and universally in certain modes of social and moral intercourse as well as in the artifices necessary to social life, there is no deep antithesis between nature and artifice in Hume's philosophy. Stable artifices are desirable because they satisfy important natural needs, and they are possible in practice only because certain attributes of human nature support them; and thus even this part of Hume's normative philosophy is founded on naturalism.

Although Hume resolves the impasse created by the Pyrrhonist tendencies of his skepticism in a naturalistic manner, his philosophy nevertheless displays throughout the critical spirit and the diffidence in intellectual and practical matters that are the lasting legacy of his skeptical arguments. The limitations of reason in the design of our moral life and the provisional status of the values he adopts—always subject to reconfirmation in light of our feelings and experience—are conclusions from this skepticism, as is the attitude of caution and moderation that Hume continually recommends in matters of practice. Hume's political philosophy accordingly reflects the influence of this continuing though mitigated skepticism as well as the influence of the substantive doctrines of human nature and ethics and the conclusions of his scientific study of society that he pursues within the confines established by his epistemology.

In this study I concentrate on Hume's theory of artificial virtue as the central theme of his political philosophy, considering in detail both his general analysis of the place of artifice in social life and the features of a legal and constitutional regime that Hume defends as the most satisfactory structure of political authority. His doctrine of artificial virtue moves almost imperceptibly from description and analysis to advocacy, and it is thus a positive doctrine in two senses. As a normative doctrine it is derived, as Hume makes clear, from naturalistic preferences for social order and for the satisfaction of other needs and desires to which the artificial virtues generally stand in an instrumental relation. These preferences represent positive commitments that, like the commitment to science itself, offset the philosopher's radical capacity for doubt.

Hume's theory of artifice retains important skeptical features, however, that distinguish it from other more self-assured utilitarian social philosophies that in some respects draw on his modes of analysis. For Hume as for other skeptics (and their earliest predecessors, the sophists), the focus on the concept of artifice with respect to morals and social institutions follows from a failure to discern normative standards or patterns in such matters either in any transcendent or supernatural source or in nature as something distinct from human nature and our collective historical experience. Artifices and the obligations we have under them may be sufficiently justified by reference to our needs, desires, and circumstances; but these are matters that may be controversial, and in some respects they are subject to change. Although Hume believes as a matter of fact that the most important artificial virtues are fundamentally similar in most societies, the very concept of artifice, as he uses it, retains the connotations of impermanence and at least potential variability in specific content normally associated with conventions and custom. Artifices may therefore reasonably be criticized with reference either to the ends they serve or to their effectiveness in promoting their ends; indeed the philosopher, equipped with scientific standards of right reasoning and a more comprehensive outlook on such matters, may join in this enterprise. Hume himself, while preserving his detachment from the inevitable partisanship of active politics, seeks to promulgate not only the proper—that is, moderately skeptical—approach to reasoning about political affairs but specific conclusions of his own political science as well. The rejection of rationalism, however, precludes definitive or doctrinaire positions of all sorts and induces circumspection. As human nature is Hume's general guide, so historical experience—the cumulative manifestation of human nature—is the appropriate guide with respect to artificial moral life. Criticism and deliberate change in this realm are, for the skeptic, more properly a matter of continual adjustments and adaptation, as our circumstances and possibly our conceptions of happiness change, rather than a matter of achieving conformity to an ideal pattern.

These reflections bring us to a final theme of this study: the relation between Hume's skepticism and the conservative practical bearing of his political philosophy, a feature that also differentiates it in an important respect from later versions of utilitarianism and other modern social theories based on methodological individualism. Here, too, the ancient Pyrrhonists and Academics to whom Hume alludes offer a parallel, though an inexact one, to his own conclusions: their typical rule of life in practical affairs called for acquiescence in custom and adaptation to the given moral and political environment, coupled of course with the continuing ability to doubt and the withholding of full assent, which render the skeptic always a potential if characteristically unassertive critic of received opinion and practice. The Pyrrhonists in particular seem to have manifested a profound (if unprincipled) conservatism in social life, finding their goal of ataraxy or personal detachment to be advanced most effectively through passive observance of established moral and other conventions, even while they regarded all as doubtful.[27]

---

[27] Cf. Sextus Empiricus, *Outlines of Pyrrhonism* I.17, p. 13. Cicero's Academic interlocutor similarly is portrayed as a defender and practitioner of the ancestral Roman religion even while he grants the inadequacies of theoretical proofs of its doctrines; *De Natura Deorum* I.61-62, III.5-6, pp. 61, 289-91.

Hume's resort to history for guidance in moral and political questions and his appreciation of the paramount role of habit or custom in sustaining artificial moral rules, both of which follow from his view of the imperfections of reason and are conducive to a conservative approach to practice, bear some resemblance to these positions. Here too, however, his views may be contrasted with the more extreme position of the Pyrrhonists. Just as science, with its promise of social benefits, and not ataraxy is the objective of his philosophy, so with respect to moral beliefs and institutions Hume advances his affirmative doctrine, grounded in extensive analysis and historical investigation, in the conviction of the salutary effects it might have if generally accepted. This doctrine, however, drawing as it does on a general analysis of the artificial virtues and on the criterion of utility that underlies them, is a rather formal one; and Hume's own exploration of the necessarily habitual foundation of artificial virtue as well as his skeptical denial of ultimate rational justification for any particular institutions lead him to recommend caution and diffidence—and a presumption of utility in established practices—as the most reasonable attitudes to bring to the active affairs of political life. Although artifices by their nature are not fixed but are subject to alteration, and although they are properly the objects of potential criticism and improvement, they are rarely the products of deliberate and successful design. As they are assessed in light of their consequences over time, or by the test of future experience, so past experience (rather than abstract theory) is for the prudent person the most appropriate guide to this dimension of moral life. Thus moderation and gradualism emerge as the practical recommendations of Hume's skepticism and empiricism.

More broadly, however, the very concept of artifice, as Hume develops it, may be said to have fundamentally conservative connotations. The function of moral artifices, which prescribe judgments and conduct according to general rules, is to bring order to social life and especially to the comparatively impersonal relations of a large society. Private impulses are subordinated to public structures, to the end of rendering our moral and social environment approximately as regular and predictable as we all normally (and scientists systematically) believe the processes of the natural world to be. That past experience and established practice are the most reasonable guides to the political enterprise of contriving and modifying artificial institutions is related to the fact that the establishment of continuity from past to future, to the extent that this is possible in the moral world, is the fundamental purpose of these institutions—a purpose that is sanctioned by Hume's substantive conception of utility or happiness, grounded as this is in his understanding of human nature. Even the kind of political regime that Hume most favors, which with its legality and constitutionalism has definite affinities to liberal ideals, is grounded, as is all artificial virtue, in human nature's basic disposition to order and in the force of custom, the psychological source of order. The imperfections and fragility of such order as we may contrive in moral and political life, arising as these do from contrary propensities in human nature and from circumstances that change in ways that are beyond our control, render Hume's teaching of skeptical diffidence and circumspection all the more compelling. The possibility of improvement, to which his science is at the same time directed and which the study of history in large part confirms, is appropriately contemplated from this broader perspective.

From the vantage point of the history of political thought, Hume has close affinities to the "long tradition of skeptical and conservative empiricism in English social thought" that is sometimes associated with the pervasive influence of common law and the comparatively high degree of continuity in traditional institutions and modes of thought in England.[28] Hume himself was a Scot and not a lawyer, and the acuity of his distinctive analyses of English institutions arose perhaps both from his broader perspective as an outsider and from the origins of his political thought in a comprehensive philosophical system rather than in particular practical commitments. Hume's political theory thus exemplifies the manner in which philosophy may sometimes corroborate tradition, for example in defending the rule of law as realized in concrete and customary procedures as well as in promoting a prudential approach to political action. It is ultimately Hume's skeptical analysis of the mind's capacities and his ensuing investigation of what he comes to regard as the compensatory nonrational features of human nature that eventually lead him to a conservative defense of the necessity of artifice in morals, of moderation in politics, and of the appropriateness of custom as the guide of life.

[28] J.G.A. Pocock, "Burke and the Ancient Constitution: A Problem in the History of Ideas," in his *Politics, Language, and Time: Essays in Political Thought and History* (New York: Atheneum, 1973), p. 215. F. A. Hayek, whose works will be cited below, insists on Hume's place within this tradition. See also Anthony Quinton, *The Politics of Imperfection* (London: Faber and Faber, 1978), pp. 47-51.

CHAPTER II

Philosophical Foundations

1. SOME PREMISES OF HUME'S PHILOSOPHY

All Hume's writings are informed and united by "moderate skepticism," which he defends as the appropriate attitude of any reasonable person. It is at the conclusion of his two works on the "understanding," however, that his most famous and explicit philosophical skepticism is manifested. Hume's theory of knowledge is the starting point for this study because the analysis and the skeptical conclusions contained in it provide the foundation of his science of human nature, and because the distinctive naturalism that he develops as a counterweight to his skeptical doubts leads in a consistent fashion to his moral and political theory. In this chapter I outline certain of Hume's central epistemological positions, noting specific features and problems that contain implications for his political philosophy. I then examine the characteristic crisis of skepticism as Hume experienced and describes it, and I follow Hume, finally, to the naturalism in which the first part of his philosophy culminates and that provides the basis for his subsequent moral inquiries.

Hume's work on what today would be called the philosophy of mind or of knowledge is found in Book I of his *Treatise*, entitled "Of the Understanding," and in his *Enquiry Concerning Human Understanding*, a briefer and more popular rendition of the former work. Hume's views in these works were formed to an extent under the influence of Locke, and comparisons between the two can help in illuminating certain significant aspects of Hume's philosophical positions as well as some of the differences between their political philosophies. This is true even though the traditional view that Hume simply carried Locke's empiricist program more rigorously forward to its logical—that is to say, skeptical—conclusions has been substantially modified by recent investigations into the origins and intentions of Hume's philosophy.[1] Indeed, such a comparison reinforces the view

---

[1] The old view, associated with Reid and Green, that Hume simply carried Locke's empiricism through to purely skeptical conclusions has been (rightly) challenged by scholars who emphasize the place of ethics in Hume's work as a whole and his indebtedness to the moral sense philosophers. The older interpretation retains some va-

of the centrality of Hume's moral concerns that informs much of the recent work. It is important from the outset not to forget that whereas Locke's *Essay* addresses itself merely to "Human Understanding," Hume's *Treatise* is an investigation into "Human Nature" as a whole, of which the understanding constitutes only a part; Hume's first *Enquiry* likewise followed closely upon a series of essays on moral and political topics and was succeeded by a second *Enquiry* on morals. Thus from the beginning Hume seems to have conceived of human nature, together with its manifestations in moral and political life, as a whole. His investigation of the understanding, moreover, not only serves as a prelude to further inquiries but also reveals that the understanding cannot be regarded as standing entirely on its own. Fundamental operations of the human mind are found to be inexplicable without reference to mental faculties whose efficacy, transcending the limits of the understanding strictly speaking, extends into emotional and moral life; and inferential reasoning of a sort that cannot be logically justified is found to be adequate to the test of practical life.

These differences apart, however, Hume like Locke believes that a proper view of the operations and capacities of the human mind is a necessary preliminary to further speculation about human affairs, and that this investigation can be undertaken in advance, and to a certain degree independently, of other matters. Both identify the object of this part of their researches as the "understanding," a term that embraces elements of what would today be distinguished as epistemology and psychology. For both Locke and Hume the inquiry into the grounds of our knowledge merges almost imperceptibly with the study of the ways in which we acquire the opinions we hold. This tendency, which is common with the British empiricists, leads frequently to an environmentalism that in Hume's case, I argue, has important consequences for his moral and political philosophy later. The psychologizing tendency in Hume's philosophy, furthermore, is in a general way related to his naturalistic solution to skepticism: Hume seeks to learn how the mind works, never really doubting that it *does* so, in a manner that is adequate to our needs.[2]

Both Locke and Hume develop their philosophical positions as critical exercises directed toward what they take to be the unduly elevated

---

lidity, however, with respect to certain *parts* of Hume's philosophy, especially Book 1 of the *Treatise*; see Terence Penelhum, *Hume* (New York: St. Martin's Press, 1975), p. 17.

[2] Cf. R. W. Connon, "Hume's Naturalism," in *McGill Hume Studies*, ed. David Fate Norton, Nicholas Capaldi, and Wade L. Robison (San Diego: Austin Hill Press, 1979), p. 127.

rationalist claims of latter-day scholasticism and Cartesianism. Both characterize their goal as one of delineating the proper limits of human knowledge, by which they envision rather substantial reductions in the range of objects supposed to be susceptible of penetration by our cognitive faculties and a drastic curtailment of the field in which we may be said to have certain or logically necessary knowledge. Within the framework of this goal, however, one can discern from the outset an important difference in orientation between the two.

In the first sentence of the Introduction to his work Locke speaks of the "Dominion" over all other creatures that is the product of human understanding, and it is clear throughout the work that Locke regards ever-increasing power and "Advantage" as the appropriate end as well as the actual offshoot of knowledge. Although he warns that the "busy Mind of Man" ought to be "more cautious in its meddling with things exceeding its Comprehension," Locke goes on to emphasize that we "have Reason to be well satisfied" with our abilities, which are "very capable" of whatever "may be of use to us."[3] The promise of "dominion" (in its various senses), then, provides Locke with a practical motive for seeking to delineate the proper and effective ways of utilizing the mind; he entertains no debilitating doubts about the efficacy of attainable knowledge.

Hume suggests in the Introduction to his *Treatise* that his ambitions are, at least initially, theoretical. In that work he makes much of his youthful design to put the "science of human nature" on a new footing, and in the opening essay of the *Enquiry* he speaks more diffidently of his hope merely of achieving some clarification in the study of "mental geography";[4] but in neither place does he give any promise of power or dominion as an incentive to the enterprise. Humean sophistication in epistemology may in the long run have contributed to a sharpening of scientific technique, but this consequence is not Hume's own preoccupation; on the contrary, in the moral or social realm, where his main interests lie, he clearly doubts our capacity to modify our environment at will and to do so consistently with a reasoned grasp of the consequences of our actions. Thus Hume's works lack, for example, any such chapter as Locke's "Of the Improvement of Our Knowledge," with its Baconian themes of scientific utility as the goal, and the continuous progress of the useful arts as the criterion, of the improvement of philosophy. Hume refers to Bacon in the context of

[3] John Locke, *An Essay Concerning Human Understanding*, ed. Peter H. Nidditch (Oxford: Clarendon Press, 1975) I.i.1-5.
[4] Hume, *Enquiries* (I), p. 13.

a survey of the progress of philosophy in England, but the point he makes is the degree to which speculation has moved beyond its earlier Baconian impulse. He comments that the period of time from Thales to Socrates is about the same as that from Bacon to "some late philosophers in *England*" whose work Hume regards himself as continuing (T. xx-xxi). If Bacon holds a position analogous to that of the ancient physicist, who was credited with useful scientific discoveries, Hume evidently wishes to compare his role with that of Socrates, who made human nature and virtue rather than physics his main concern and whose starting point was the recognition of ignorance.[5] Likewise, when in his *Enquiry* Hume does refer to the "advantages" to be drawn from his philosophy, it is (modest) contributions to morality and politics that he seems to have principally in mind.[6] We shall see that the theoretical inquiry into the understanding with which the *Treatise* begins is not without practical implications: it serves as the foundation of the moral and political doctrines that follow—doctrines whose distinctive characteristics are closely related to the skeptical arguments and qualifiedly skeptical conclusions of the preceding work. Dominion, as a fact and as a boundless possibility, on the other hand, is the ground of Locke's renunciation of the skeptical tendencies latent in his approach to human understanding. The absence of this theme in Hume, along with his skepticism and the greater prominence of moral topics integrated in his major philosophical work, all differentiate him from his most renowned predecessor.

Despite these differences, however, Hume's philosophy displays many similarities to that of Locke in its starting point and methods, similarities that lay it open to some of the same criticisms, despite Hume's greater rigor in his application of the empirical mode of analysis and his willingness to confront problems that Locke bypassed. One such criticism pertains to the method of introspection that Hume shares not only with Locke but also with Descartes and other major philosophers prior to the historicization of philosophical speculation and the more recent redirection of philosophical attention to the public

[5] This point may also be seen in a passage where Hume argues that honors should be awarded to statesmen and educators rather than to inventors, as Bacon had recommended. Hume, "Of Parties in General," *Works*, vol. 3, p. 127. From the perspective of Hume's philosophy as a whole, with its emphasis on morals, the great attention that some commentators have paid to Newton's influence on Hume seems unwarranted. Cf. James Noxon, *Hume's Philosophical Development* (Oxford: Clarendon Press, 1973), pp. 75-78. Of the five writers mentioned by Hume (T. xxi), it is Hutcheson whose influence scholars have recently tended to emphasize.

[6] Hume, *Enquiries* (I), p. 10.

nature of the meanings of concepts and language. This method seems to carry with it the implicit assumption that the nature of experience in general can be grasped through the analysis of that of the reflective individual, and that the potentialities of human knowledge can be inferred from philosophers' surveys of the structure and contents of their own minds.[7] Although the divergences between Cartesian rationalism and Humean skepticism indicate that this assumption does not predetermine philosophers' conclusions, it is nevertheless true that they may, by viewing the individual consciousness in undue isolation from its environment, fail to provide an adequate account of the sources and the meaning of its contents. This method, furthermore, by making the individual (or the individual mind) the fundamental unit of analysis, may inhibit the social theorist's or historian's capacity to identify and assess collective and historical phenomena.[8] These are criticisms that no doubt have some validity, although as we shall see, Hume's discoveries respecting the mental faculties of the individual lead him to a particularly strong acknowledgment of the social sources of beliefs, feelings, and values; and his study of human nature leads him to recognize the importance of the history and development of political institutions. The possible relation, however, between epistemological and political individualism—so often alleged to characterize the philosophy of Hume's era—must be an object of our attention.[9]

Hume's method of introspection is clearly exhibited in the many first-person passages in which he reflects on his own feelings or conducts private mental experiments on his own imagination. He proceeds in this fashion despite his recognition in the Introduction that the "experimental method" that he endorses poses special difficulties in the moral sciences—that is, in the study of human nature: "By placing myself in the same case with that which I consider, 'tis evident this reflection and premeditation would so disturb the operation of my natural principles, as must render it impossible to form any just conclusion from the phaenomenon" (T. xxiii).[10] In the first book of the

---

[7] For some older criticisms along these lines, but from diverse points of view, see Leslie Stephen, *History of English Thought in the Eighteenth Century* (New York: Harcourt, Brace, and World, 1962), vol. 1, pp. 25, 47; Thomas H. Huxley, *Hume* (New York: Appleton, 1897), pp. 65, 72-75; and A. E. Taylor, "David Hume and the Miraculous," in his *Philosophical Studies* (London: Macmillan, 1934), pp. 355-58.

[8] G. H. Sabine, "Hume's Contribution to the Historical Method," *Philosophical Review* 15 (1906): 31.

[9] Cf. Amy Gutmann, *Liberal Equality* (Cambridge: Cambridge University Press, 1980), p. 116: "The very standard of introspection may presuppose a liberal understanding of the self as partially concealed from society. . . ."

[10] This admission of difficulty in accurate reasoning in psychological investigations

Treatise, however, it proves impossible for Hume to apply the alternative he recommends—that of controlled experiments or, more plausibly for the kinds of questions he seeks to answer, a method of objective and systematic observation of human life. Therefore much of Hume's science of human nature—especially that concerning such mental subjects as thought patterns, the passions, and the faculty of judgment—consists largely of reports on what he finds within himself. A fundamental uniformity of human nature in the relevant respects is generally assumed, and it is not clear how Hume could deal with claims to the contrary. Hume at least acknowledges the limitations of this method, as in the following passage concerning personal identity, in which he characteristically appeals from his own introspective conclusions to those of his readers: "If any one upon serious and unprejudic'd reflexion, thinks he has a different notion of *himself*, I must confess I can reason no longer with him. All I can allow him is, that he may be in the right as well as I, and that we are essentially different in this particular" (T. 252). Hume of course doubts strongly that people are "essentially different" from one another in important respects, but he cannot prove that this is the case, and his philosophy proceeds on this tentative (and never repudiated) presupposition.

Although the assumption of a basic uniformity of human nature, along with the methodological individualism to which it is related, may have the effect of inhibiting a full and wholly satisfactory account of mental and moral life, it by no means entirely determines the result. The usual criticism of this method is that such an isolated view of the mind may lead to the neglect or the underrating of the social or culturally variable factors that enter into the formation of individual characters and consciousness; but in practice it may be observed that an individualist starting point does not necessarily culminate in a doctrine of mentally or morally self-sufficient individualism, nor does it lead to the social and political conclusions that may appear to follow from this. The introspective method as practiced by empiricists, and by Hume to a much larger degree than by Locke, reveals quite readily that the great bulk of what any individual believes has its source in the testimony of others and in social tradition and emulation, a state of affairs that commonly arouses in the investigator a strong sense of the importance of education, cultural patterns, group prejudices, and the like in the formation of the individual. The precise ways and the

---

should be compared with Hume's more general warnings about the ways in which sentiments may obstruct reasoning, and conversely about how the very effort of thought may interfere with the sentiments that are necessary to belief and may thus fail to arouse conviction in its conclusions (T. 185-86).

degree of success with which Hume transcends the limitations of his initial assumptions and method are questions that will be addressed below.

Another preliminary assumption of Hume's philosophy, one that is presented as though it were self-evident in the brief opening section of the *Treatise*, is that all the contents of human awareness are reducible to the basic data that he calls "perceptions," which Hume divides into vivid and immediately present "impressions" and the "ideas" that are the "faint images" of impressions present to us in thinking or in memory. It is plausible to suggest that a perceptualist theory of knowledge such as this carries with it momentous implications for epistemology and psychology. Since each individual's perceptions— that is, mental experience—are entirely private, the possibility of communication or of a public world of common meanings is thrown into doubt, a paradox that Hume struggles to avoid.[11] If discrete perceptions are the only things that are actually present to the mind, the status of the entire external world as apprehensible or even as existent, not to mention that of other persons or indeed the thinking subject's own "self," becomes problematic. The ramifications of this theory become yet more pronounced if the philosopher adjoins, as Hume does, the additional assumptions "that every distinct perception, which enters into the composition of the mind, is a distinct existence, and is different, and distinguishable, and separable from every other perception, either contemporary or successive" (T. 259) and that "there is no object, which implies the existence of any other if we consider these objects in themselves" (T. 86). The rather startling idea of the mind that results is that it "is a kind of theatre, where several perceptions successively make their appearance; pass, re-pass, glide away, and mingle in an infinite variety of postures and situations" (T. 253), a view whose profoundly skeptical implications are apparent.[12] Hume insists on these assumptions, which are latent in Locke, with much greater rigor, and he draws what would appear to be appropriate conclusions. If every perception of the mind is indeed a distinct existence, and if we do not apprehend any necessary or stable connections or patterns among them, then not only is much of what ordinarily passes for knowledge about the world called into question, but even

[11] Cf. Antony Flew, *Hume's Philosophy of Belief* (London: Routledge and Kegan Paul, 1961), esp. p. 23.

[12] As were similar implications of the sophist Protagoras's "perceptualism" to Plato; see his *Theaetetus*. Cf. Eric A. Havelock's comment: "The pragmatism and empiricism of Protagoras would have won sympathy from Hume"; *The Liberal Temper in Greek Politics* (New Haven: Yale University Press, 1957), p. 18.

the capacity of experience, as conceived in empiricism, to yield such knowledge is thrown into doubt.

These assumptions have a kind of axiomatic status for Hume; they are presented as if unprovable in any other sense than their alleged reflective self-evidence. Yet well-known and distinctive arguments in Hume's philosophy of the understanding may be seen as flowing from them, as the skepticism that Locke dexterously avoids becomes manifest.[13] The program that emerges in those parts of Book I of the *Treatise* on which Hume's reputation as an extreme skeptic has rested is to show how these initial premises, when rigorously applied, are inadequate to support our most universal and commonplace beliefs— in particular, the fundamental beliefs concerning self, substance, and causation that Descartes had justified by reference to innate ideas and that Locke managed to retain despite his rejection of Cartesian rationalism. The Lockeian method, pursued consistently, appears to lead to conclusions about the fundamental problems of knowledge that are quite at odds with Locke's own; indeed it leads, at the epistemological level, to the skepticism about knowledge of fact and value that constitutes the notorious thrust of one whole aspect of Hume's philosophy.

The importance of the other, more psychological and more positive aspect of Hume's theory of the understanding, however, has been recognized by most recent commentators and is emphasized below. What is sometimes called Hume's "philosophy of belief" consists of his attempts to analyze why it is that this skepticism is as a matter of fact untenable in ordinary life and how it is that people generally maintain their common-sense beliefs even in the absence of logical justification; the "mitigated" skepticism that Hume finally embraces accommodates this larger perspective on human nature. In the rest of this chapter I consider more closely several different facets of Hume's account of "human understanding": the skeptical analysis, the psychological naturalism that is developed in consequence, and the intervening "skeptical crisis" in which the philosopher takes stock of the course of his inquiry and deliberately reorients it from "abstruse" epistemological speculation toward the broader problems of belief and

---

[13] For comments on the determinative force of Hume's perceptualism and of his denial of "interconnectedness" among perceptions, see Alfred North Whitehead, *Adventures of Ideas* (New York: Macmillan, 1954), pp. 283-84. Cf. also David Pears, *The Naturalism of Book I of Hume's Treatise of Human Nature* (London: Oxford University Press, 1976; reprint from the *Proceedings of the British Academy*, vol. 62), p. 5. The difficulties that Hume's philosophy encounters as a result of his uncritical acceptance of the "theory of ideas" is a main theme in Barry Stroud, *Hume* (London: Routledge and Kegan Paul, 1977).

conduct. The development of Hume's philosophy along these lines exhibits similarities to that of other skeptics, ancient and modern, for whom a conviction of the limited capacities of human reason has likewise led to a new interest in, and respect for, the sources and strength of belief among ordinary people as well as the social values, customs, and institutions that rest on a foundation provided by such belief.

2. KNOWLEDGE, BELIEF, AND FICTIONS OF THE IMAGINATION

The *Treatise* opens with the fundamentally Lockeian assertion (expressed in somewhat different terms) that all our "simple ideas" are derived from, correspond to, and represent the more original "simple impressions" of our experience, and that many of our "complex ideas" are likewise fainter reflections of previously received "complex impressions" (T. 3-4). Hume alludes to more active mental operations, which receive attention later, by which the complex ideas that figure in much of our thinking are generated within the mind from combinations of simple ideas; and, in suggesting unidirectional causality from impressions to ideas, Hume omits the special case—which also acquires importance later—of certain passions (a kind of impression) that are occasioned by previous ideas. The thesis advanced in the opening section nevertheless informs much of the program, both epistemological and ethical, of the *Treatise* as a whole: however the mind may manipulate the materials it has at its disposal, it cannot entertain the thought of, or coherently conceptualize, anything that is not ultimately reducible to distinct impressions.

Hume recognizes several sorts of impressions, the sole original data of our thoughts. There are first of all "impressions of sensation," a category that includes pleasures and pains as well as impressions of the qualities of material objects. A more distinctive feature of Hume's philosophy is the second category, "impressions of reflexion," in which he includes the "passions, desires, and emotions," and he suggests that it is these impressions that "principally deserve our attention" (T. 7-8, 192).[14] That these two faculties, sensation and reflection—or "our outward or inward sentiment," as he also calls them—provide "all

---

[14] Locke calls the "desire of Happiness, and an aversion to Misery," and by implication the other impulses that Hume calls passions, "innate practical Principles" rather than ideas, which of course in Locke's view are not innate. By thus excluding them from the realm of ideas, Locke tends to exclude them from, or to overlook their role in, thought. That Hume gives the passions a prominent place as data that are operative in the understanding sets him apart from Locke and forms the bridge between his study of

the materials of thinking"[15] is the first major tenet of Hume's account of the understanding. It is established on the basis of a small amount of introspective evidence and appeals to readers for confirmation, a procedure whose weaknesses are evident; it is in effect a premise of Hume's philosophy, a foundation on which his subsequent analyses are based.

In the second section of Part 1 Hume states his intention of continuing his investigation by beginning with ideas and proceeding thence to impressions, a plan that reflects the method Hume adopts throughout "Of the Understanding": taking as working assumptions the dicta that every simple idea is a "copy" of a simple impression, and that every complex idea may be reduced entirely to simple ones, Hume proceeds to consider certain key ideas that appear problematic and to seek the impression(s) on which they ultimately depend.[16] This method leads to Hume's most interesting philosophical positions when it is applied with full rigor to the three great ideas—those of substance or external object, personal identity, and necessary connection—that Locke, although working with similar assumptions, had left largely intact. Before examining these positions,[17] however, we must take note of Hume's divergence from his stated program and of the broadening of his philosophy of mind beyond his initial framework.

The simple, reductionist method laid out in the opening section is almost immediately deferred by Hume's recognition of various other faculties of the mind, an account of which supplements the analysis of mental contents or perceptions in Hume's theory of knowledge. In section 3 of Part 1, for example, Hume introduces memory and imagination as faculties by which ideas are brought to awareness in the mind, the imagination being the faculty by which all thought except simple recollection takes place. Hume's psychological interest in describing the operations of the various "propensities" or modes of activity in accordance with which the imagination works on and arranges its ideas is most conspicuous in his doctrine of the association of ideas, which dominates much of the first two books of the *Treatise*. Locke added to the fourth edition of his *Essay* a chapter on association,

---

the understanding and that of the passions specifically in Book ii. See Locke, *Essay* i.iii.3.

[15] Hume, *Enquiries* (i), p. 19.

[16] See Norman Kemp Smith, *The Philosophy of David Hume* (London: Macmillan, 1949), pp. 216-18, on the structure of Book i of the *Treatise*. Hume's procedure encounters the risk of circularity, rejecting ideas that do not meet the standard for which they might rather constitute contrary evidence.

[17] Personal identity will be taken up in chapter iii below.

in which he emphasizes chance or customary connections of ideas, in contrast to "natural Correspondence" among them, as a principal source of errors, prejudices, and hence needless disputes.[18] Hume, however, takes over the notion of association and, elaborating a set of principles descriptive of its operation, treats it as a normal function of the mind and as the most satisfactory way of accounting for all our thinking. The youthful Hume felt that in his principles of association he had found the central key, analogous to Newton's gravity, to his science of human nature: "Here is a kind of ATTRACTION, which in the mental world will be found to have as extraordinary effects as in the natural, and to show itself in as many and as various forms" (T. 12-13); and in his *Abstract* he claimed association as the most glorious of all his "new discoveries in philosophy."[19]

Hume attempts to explain many kinds of mental phenomena—including, in Book II, the operations of the passions—on the basis of association, which was later in the century to be adopted by Hartley and other British psychologists as their central hypothesis. Hume himself, however, became dissatisfied with the adequacy of this mechanism for explaining all that he had originally expected of it; and association plays a greatly diminished role in the *Enquiry*.[20] The importance of Hume's early introduction of the doctrine of association as a way of describing the usual operations of the imagination, however, lies in his acknowledgment of an autonomous and innate faculty of the mind whose active contribution to the arrangement of the primary data was to be at least as important to his theory of the understanding as is the analysis of the perceptions themselves.

Hume's treatment of association is only his most prominent and systematic effort to delineate various mental operations to which perceptions are subject. So much that is distinctive in Hume concerns such operations that his theory of "mental activities" may be regarded as the central focus of his philosophy of the understanding or indeed of human nature as a whole.[21] Hume's endeavor to account for the

[18] Locke, *Essay* II.xxxiii.5.

[19] Hume, *An Abstract of a Treatise of Human Nature*, ed. J. M. Keynes and P. Sraffa (Cambridge: Cambridge University Press, 1938), p. 31.

[20] Cf. Smith, *Philosophy of Hume*, pp. 71-72, 531, for criticisms of Hume's doctrine of association. Although Hume later de-emphasizes association, some of the more interesting conclusions to which his analysis of it leads will be discussed in chapter III below.

[21] See Robert Paul Wolff, "Hume's Theory of Mental Activity," in *Hume: A Collection of Critical Essays*, ed. V. C. Chappell (Garden City: Doubleday, 1966), pp. 99-128. Fred Wilson, "Hume's Theory of Mental Activity," in *McGill Hume Studies*, ed. Norton et al., pp. 101-20, offers a useful corrective to the common view that Hume's association

origin of the ideas of time, and similarly of space, for example, illus-
trates what he finds to be the necessity of abandoning at an early stage
his original claim that every simple idea is derived from a precedent
impression—or at least the necessity of modifying it substantially. Five
consecutive notes played on a flute give us the idea of time, although
there is no sixth impression—either of sensation or of reflection—to
which this idea specifically corresponds. The ideas of time and space
depend on certain precedent sense impressions, but they arise not
directly from any impression but from the "manner" in which the
mind perceives (T. 36); they are thus in a sense contributed to experience by the mind.

An even more fruitful element enters into Hume's account of the
understanding when he discusses the nature of abstract ideas. Hume
begins by accepting Berkeley's view that there is in fact no such thing
as a general or abstract idea but rather only "particular ones, annexed
to a certain term, which gives them a more extensive signification, and
makes them recall upon occasion other individuals. . . ." Hume argues
that a general or abstract word evokes a particular idea and along
with it an "attendant custom" by which the imagination "surveys"
or "runs over" a series of resembling particulars represented by the
general term; or it arouses at least an habitual "readiness" so to
"recall" whatever particulars are required by our present purposes (T.
17-22). So-called general ideas are thus reducible to sets of particular
ideas united by whatever resemblances the mind picks out among
them, but they depend in addition on a quite definite "customary" or
"habitual" activity of the mind, which on appropriate occasions is
able to summon up in consciousness as many particulars as it requires
among which it has previously noted some resemblance. Custom and
habit (terms that Hume uses for the most part synonymously) thus
enter the *Treatise* as fundamental mental processes, integral not only
to patterns of thought but also to the formation of basic concepts.
Custom becomes the most important category of Hume's philosophy,
playing a decisive part not only in his analysis of the understanding
(where it is closely allied to association) but also in his account of
emotional and moral life and finally in his political science as well.

Hume in this way quickly expands his initial contention that human

---

is a determined and therefore passive process, arguing that for Hume a person can
choose to exercise some control over associational impulses or habits, including causal
ones. "Propensity" is Hume's favorite term for the various active dispositions or functions of the mind, such as association, custom, and belief; it is a Newtonian word and,
like Hume's reference to "attraction" above, suggests the source of inspiration of this
part of his work.

thought is to be explained by an analysis of the distinct perceptions of which it is composed. The prominence that he gives to association exemplifies the interest in psychological processes that becomes increasingly conspicuous as the *Treatise* advances; he soon finds himself speaking of the "manner" of perception and of "customs" and other mental "propensities" as fundamental components of the understanding. Locke occasionally refers to the active powers of the mind working on its materials, but he does not provide any detailed treatment of these active faculties. Not only does Hume give them a proportionately greater share of his attention, but his hope that mental propensities and activities would prove to be susceptible of orderly description generated much of his early confidence in the possibility of an improved science of human nature.

Hume then, like Locke, begins his study of the understanding by attempting to identify the various elements of which our thought is composed; and the most distinctive feature of his account is the greater emphasis he places on the role of mental processes and propensities. For both philosophers this classificatory endeavor serves as a prelude to the analysis of human knowledge, its nature and grounds, with the determination of its appropriate limits forming the principal objective of the enterprise. Further similarities between the two may be seen in the outcome of this analysis, but certain differences, which may at first glance seem minor, point to the major epistemological novelties that distinguish Hume's philosophy from that of his predecessor.

Locke's purpose, as he tells us at the outset, is "to enquire into the Original, Certainty, and Extent of humane Knowledge; together with the Grounds and Degrees of Belief, Opinion, and Assent,"[22] and he adheres to this dichotomy throughout. Knowledge is asserted to arise when the mind "certainly perceives, and is undoubtedly satisfied of the Agreement or Disagreement of any *Ideas*."[23] Locke's analysis of knowledge in this strict sense, which occupies the first thirteen chapters of his fourth book, concludes that certainty is to be had only through intuition, that is to say, direct intellectual insight or apprehension of self-evidence, and through demonstration, or a chain of reasoning whose individual steps may be reduced to the ground of intuitive evidence. Applying these criteria, Locke usually speaks as though the appellation knowledge properly pertains only to mathematics and to analytic or verbal truths, and he proclaims that *"universal Propositions, of whose Truth or Falshood we can have certain Knowledge,*

---

[22] Locke, *Essay* i.i.2.
[23] Ibid. iv.xiv.4.

concern not *Existence*."[24] Judgment, on the other hand, is said to be the faculty by which we "presume" even when we cannot directly "perceive" the agreement or disagreement of our ideas, and thus attain belief, opinion, or assent to the probable truth or falsehood of propositions when certainty is not accessible.[25] Locke usually holds that all inferences and general propositions concerning matters of fact—that is, all our supposed knowledge of the external world beyond those ideas of sensation of which we are immediately aware—fall into the latter category of probable opinion rather than into that of knowledge or certainty.

Had Locke adhered consistently to this classification, his empiricist line of analysis might have led him to the kinds of skeptical conclusions that Hume, who started with much the same scheme, actually reached. Instead, through lack of rigor at certain key points and through a notably generous interpretation of the capacity of intuition, Locke failed to achieve (or chose to avoid) the dramatic break with rationalism that Hume found to be the only logical outcome of his method. Universal causality, the existence of God, the independent existence of objects, the thinking self: all these fundamental cognitive tenets that were to appear problematic in Hume's analysis managed to survive Locke's dismissal of innate ideas and to maintain in an only slightly shaken way their status as matters about which we might claim assurance. Their respective published views on religious and related ethical questions are perhaps the most conspicuous point of difference between Locke and Hume that is obviously attributable to their epistemological divergence. Hume's more deeply skeptical version of empiricism provides the basis for his quite different political philosophy as well, in ways that will become apparent.

The map of human reasoning that results from Hume's exploration of "mental geography" is similar to Locke's, although his subsequent allocation of different sorts of propositions to the various epistemological categories contains important differences. Like Locke, Hume proposes to reserve the term knowledge for those conclusions of reason to which we may ascribe absolute certainty or necessity; all else is belief or opinion. Hume likewise restricts the field of knowledge to those relations that "depend entirely" on the ideas that we "compare together" in our minds and thus to propositions whose opposites are inconceivable. Knowledge, then, falls into two categories: by direct intuition we apprehend the relations of resemblance, contrariety, and

[24] Ibid. IV.ix.1.
[25] Ibid. IV.xiv.4, IV.xv.

degrees in quality among ideas in our mind, and by demonstration we attain knowledge of proportions of quantity and number, as exemplified in the exact sciences of arithmetic and algebra (T. 69-73).

All other kinds of judgments that we make are, in contrast, matters of belief or opinion rather than knowledge. In this category Hume includes all judgments regarding taste and value, which, originating as they do in feeling, are not properly regarded as matters pertaining directly to the understanding at all and are reserved for treatment in Book III of the *Treatise*. Otherwise the category of belief includes all our reasonings and judgments concerning matters of fact, which in Hume's classification constitute at best "probable knowledge" in contrast to "knowledge" in the strict sense.

Under the heading of probability fall propositions involving the other three of the seven possible relations that, according to Hume, may unite the ideas or objects of which we are conscious. The relations that enter into our reasoning about matters of fact differ from those that pertain entirely to our ideas in that they purport to refer to objects independent of our minds. Two of them, identity and situation in time or space, are characteristic of perception itself rather than of reasoning, since they are apprehended through the "mere passive admission of the impressions" of objects that are "immediately present to the senses" (T. 73); direct perception of relations can lead to erroneous judgments because the problematic nature of the connection between an impression and the object it represents (T. 190-91) always leaves open the possibility of illusion. By this accounting, then, we are left with the sole relation of causation, which in Hume's analysis emerges as the essential element in all our reasoning about objects or matters of fact beyond those impressions that are immediately present to us (T. 74). Only application of the relation of cause and effect, that is to say, enables us to go beyond what is present to us, or beyond those instances of which we have had experience, and to formulate and believe general propositions about matters of fact, or propositions regarding future (and non-experienced past) events. Hume promises that he will "endeavor to explain fully" the nature of the causal relation before leaving the subject of the understanding, a promise that leads to the most celebrated part of his philosophy.

First, however, Hume briefly reformulates his classification of human reasoning in terms that he claims are more in accordance with common usage and hence more convenient. Although it is correct to divide all reasoning into knowledge and probability, and although all inferences from experience belong strictly speaking in the latter category, nevertheless it may be granted that there are certain beliefs about matters of fact that we hold with such assurance that to call them merely probable would seem overly contentious: that all men must die, and that the sun will rise tomorrow, are Hume's examples of causal arguments or inferences that, though they go beyond our experience, are commonly assumed to "exceed probability, and may be receiv'd as a superior kind of evidence." He therefore proposes a revised threefold division of human reason: *knowledge* refers to demonstrative arguments founded on the comparison of ideas; *proofs* to causal arguments that, resting on apparently constant and universal experience, are (in effect) "entirely free from doubt and uncertainty"; and *probabilities* to conjectures "still attended with uncertainty" (T. 124).[26] This revision may be seen as a concession to the "common signification of words" on Hume's part: "proof" is simply a special case of "probable knowledge" or opinion in the larger sense, and the assurance it yields is not that of the intuitions and demonstrations that constitute certain knowledge. It is at least conceivable that the sun will not rise tomorrow, in a way that it is not conceivable that the Pythagorean theorem should fail to hold true. On the other hand, Hume's radical exclusion of all arguments regarding matters of fact and experience from the category of knowledge dictates that he make this explicit distinction, within the realm of experiential reasonings, between those beliefs that in fact are accompanied by a kind of psychological certainty and those that are consciously held as only probable. This distinction thus raises the question of the nature of belief and of the conviction that attends some beliefs that cannot be justified as certain or necessarily true under strict logical analysis, an issue that becomes inescapable in Hume's further investigations of human understanding.

Hume's analysis of causation, together with his lengthy discussion of the nature of belief, occupies nearly the whole of the third part of Book I of the *Treatise* and Parts 4 through 7 of the first *Enquiry*. This is the portion of his philosophy in which his skepticism is most strikingly evident, insofar as he concludes that the belief in causation itself, and accordingly the logical operation of causal inference, cannot be rationally validated or justified but remains a "mere" belief leading to probabilities or "proofs" but never to knowledge. And since it is only by means of the causal relation, or the supposition of regular connections between "the present fact and that which is inferred from it," that we can ever reason about matters of fact "beyond the evidence

---

[26] Also Hume, *Enquiries* (I), p. 56n. Cf. Locke, *Essay* IV.xv-xvi.5.

of our memory and senses,"[27] the doubts that he raises about the standing of this relation appear to remove the possibility of any certain knowledge of fact or existence. In his analysis of causation, Hume usually speaks as though he has in mind relations between physical objects, such as the transmission of motion from one billiard ball to another; but it should be remembered that the same analysis pertains to causation in the social sciences, with respect to moral and political objects, as well. It is the limitations of our understanding in this area that set the terms of Hume's practical political teachings.

Hume begins his inquiry into the "idea of causation" by "tracing it up to its origin, and examining that primary impression, from which it arises" (T. 75). He first disposes of the possibility that there is anything discernible in either of the objects that we regard as cause and effect, taken separately, that produces these ideas. Any object may, in certain circumstances, be identified as a cause or an effect, but there is no perceptible common property in the objects we so classify; all the properties in an object to which we attribute causal influence on a particular occasion are equally present in it when we do not regard it as a cause. Causation then cannot be imputed as a matter of direct insight into the nature of things themselves but is rather a relation between objects that we observe in experience.[28] Hume then identifies two of the characteristics of this relation between cause and effect as contiguity in time and space and priority in time of the one to the other; remote causal connections are always linked by a chain of successive causes (T. 75-76).

Sensible succession or sequence is, in Hume's view, the only observable feature of particular relations that we call causal; yet when considered alone, these criteria are not adequate, since we do not regard every sequence of contiguous objects as causally related. The distinctive feature of the causal relation, it appears, is that we take the connection between cause and effect to be a (somehow) necessary one: similar causes must be followed by similar effects. But this supposed necessity of causal sequences, however, which is the foundation of all our inferences from events of which we have had experience to those of which we have not, does not, like contiguity and succession, seem to be an immediately perceptible relation. Hume therefore turns his attention to this problematic idea of necessity, the crux of the causal relation; the analysis of causation is transformed into the quest

[27] Hume, *Enquiries* (I), pp. 26-27.

[28] It follows from this that no one can infer the causal antecedents or the causal properties of a newly presented object through an examination of its other features or apart from its relations to other objects, as Hume emphasizes; ibid., p. 27.

for the impression underlying the idea of necessary connection (T. 77).[29]

In treating causation Hume attempts to account for a relation that exists among our ideas insofar as they are supposed to refer to objects having real existence. All thought (he claims) begins with the impressions of what is present to us; beyond these we have, in memory, the ability to recall past impressions as they appeared to us and, in imagination, the capacity to associate the ideas derived from our impressions as we please. But causation alone forms the basis of all our reasoning concerning matters of fact in which we make a transition from a present impression to the idea of an object—whether an anticipated effect or a presumed cause—that was not, or has not yet been, present to us but of whose reality we are convinced. How are we able to make such transitions, given Hume's basic assumptions that all ideas are separable and that none in itself implies the existence of another? A first answer is clear: " 'Tis therefore by EXPERIENCE only, that we can infer the existence of one object from that of another. . . . We remember to have had frequent instances of the existence of one species of objects; and also remember, that the individuals of another species of objects have always attended them, and have existed in a regular order of contiguity and succession with regard to them" (T. 87). It is our remembrance of the "constant conjunction" of the objects we call cause and effect that, along with contiguity and succession, seems to be their distinctive characteristic: causation is a relation we learn to ascribe to certain sequences of objects whose regularity we have discerned in experience, a relation we then project with confidence on to instances, such as those in the future, of which we have no experience.

This point clarifies the nature of the causal relation, but it has not significantly advanced Hume's quest for the impression underlying the idea of necessity. Constant conjunction does not indicate anything new in any particular causal relation as such but only multiplies the instances of the contiguity and succession that he has already identified: "From the mere repetition of any past impression, even to infinity, there will never arise any new original idea, such as that of a necessary

---

[29] At this point in the *Treatise* Hume pauses to brush aside Locke's inadequate treatment of causation, which Locke did not identify as the basis of all probable inferences or reasonings about real objects and events and in which he failed to find the great stumbling block for empiricism that it became with Hume. Locke asserts that we have intuitive knowledge of the general necessity of causes and takes for granted the corollary of the uniformity and regularity of nature. His remarks on causality are scattered through the *Essay*; cf. ii.xxi.4, ii.xxvi.1, iv.iii.10-16, 25, 28, 29, iv.x.3.

connexion" (T. 88); and so the search for the putative impression assumed to underlie any genuine idea continues. Meanwhile there is more to be said about the nature of the causal inference and the belief that it generates.

The criterion of constant conjunction draws attention to the role of experience in our identification of cause and effect relations; but is there a rational justification for holding beliefs about the future (or about the past, beyond what is contained in memory) or for making universal statements on the basis of our experience, which obviously comprises only a limited number of cases in the past? This would be so only if we had reason to suppose *"that instances, of which we have had no experience, must resemble those, of which we have had experience, and that the course of nature continues always uniformly the same"* (T. 89). Put another way, all our beliefs about the future and all general factual statements are logically justifiable only as conclusions of syllogisms whose tacit major premise affirms that the future will resemble the past or that nature exhibits universal causal regularity.[30] Such an assumption is necessary to validate even the probable status of our causal reasoning. But the truth of such an assumption can certainly not be demonstrated: "we can at least conceive a change in the course of nature," and, as Hume consistently maintains, *"whatever we can imagine, is possible"* in the sense that its negation can never be affirmed with certainty (T. 89, 250). Thus experience is a trustworthy guide to "probable knowledge" only insofar as we make an assumption that is itself the very question at issue; we are justified in our particular causal reasonings only if we assume the truth of universal and regular causality. "Thus," says Hume, "not only our reason fails us in the discovery of the *ultimate connexion* of causes and effects, but even after experience has inform'd us of their *constant conjunction*, 'tis impossible for us to satisfy ourselves by our reason, why we shou'd extend that experience beyond those particular instances, which have fallen under our observation" (T. 91).

Such a skeptical conclusion respecting the most fundamental form of human reasoning about events in the external world is the outcome of epistemological analysis. Hume has exposed a tacit premise, if not cast doubt on the validity, of the whole of what is now termed inductive logic (in the exploration of which Hume is a pioneer). But this nevertheless is only the starting point, in a sense, of Hume's investigation of the understanding. For it is undeniable that people do universally engage in the kind of reasoning that the philosopher is unable to justify

[30] Cf. Flew, *Hume's Philosophy of Belief*, pp. 82-84.

by reason, and that they make with the utmost confidence the assumptions that they must make in order to do so. The philosopher must ask why and how this can be so; and for this question to be answered a broader view of human nature must be taken. Before completing his analysis of the idea of necessary connection that is at the heart of causation, therefore, Hume devotes seven sections of the *Treatise*, and a corresponding section of the *Enquiry* entitled "Sceptical Solution of These Doubts," to an investigation into the nature of belief and the autonomous role that it appears to play in thought.

Whenever we make an inference from a present impression to the idea of an object that is not present, the processes of our thought operate in accordance with the principles of association that Hume has already discovered in the imagination. These associative transitions, however, can generate two different sorts of ideas: those that we regard as fictions (in the sense of untruths), however clearly envisioned or potentially existent the idea of the object may be in our minds, and those to which we give our assent, or in whose real existence we actually believe (or hold to be probable). "I therefore ask," says Hume, "Wherein consists the difference betwixt believing and disbelieving any proposition?" (T. 95). No difficulty arises with regard to propositions that are intuitively or demonstratively true, where the truth depends on the directly perceptible relations of the ideas themselves; the question about belief arises with respect to inferences regarding matters of fact, where the contrary is always conceivable and hence possible.

Hume's answer to this question is one for which we have been prepared. Since the same idea may, in different circumstances, be regarded as fictitious or as representing something existent, Hume concludes that it cannot be any special characteristics of certain ideas that determine our belief in them. The difference between incredulity and belief lies in the *manner* in which we conceive the two kinds of ideas, which Hume seeks to explain in terms of the greater "force and vivacity" that attend an idea that arouses belief; and, assuming that any inferential chain culminating in a belief must begin with an impression, he defines belief as "A LIVELY IDEA RELATED TO OR ASSOCIATED WITH A PRESENT IMPRESSION" (T. 96). Subsequently, in the Appendix to the *Treatise*, Hume seems to abandon this mechanical view of the transference of force from one perception to another; there he simply calls belief a "peculiar *feeling* or *sentiment*" that modifies, or attends, or determines the manner in which we apprehend certain ideas (T. 623ff.). On either formulation, it is clear that to account for the phenomenon of belief, the philosopher must abandon logic in favor of psychology—two modes of inquiry that are in any case never far removed in Hume's philosophy.

Hume now sets out to find the determining factors of belief itself, especially our frequently strong belief in facts causally inferred from experience. Under what circumstances do we find ourselves believing in the existence or the probability of something we have never seen? Hume conducts a variety of mental experiments in order to discover how ideas can be enlivened by their relation to already-vivid impressions; he arrives at the conclusion that it is only the repetition of "a number of past impressions and conjunctions" of a similar nature that regularly produces an inclination in us to believe in an inference from a present impression. Furthermore, in the Appendix, Hume retains the doctrine that the special feeling constitutive of belief normally arises from the operation of mental customs, or the facility with which the mind is able to make transitions among ideas that it has regularly found to be associated together. We thus find our way back to the constant conjunction that constitutes one of the objective criteria of a causal relation, but we are now examining its psychological efficacy in producing that "manner" of conception that is the essence of belief. Custom appears to be the factor responsible for producing belief: "When we are accustom'd to see two impressions conjoin'd together, the appearance or idea of the one immediately carries us to the idea of the other" (T. 102-103). Custom or habit is the characteristic mechanism by which the imagination is passively "carried" from one perception to others in more or less orderly sequences. Custom, which together with association constitutes the most usual basis on which ideas are united in our thought, is here called on to explain the particular mental state of belief as it is manifested in the inductive inferences of which all our reasoning about "matters of fact and existence" consists. "Objects have no discoverable connexion together; nor is it from any other principle but custom operating upon the imagination, that we can draw any inference from the appearance of one to the existence of another" (T. 103).

Now inference founded on observed conjunctions is the basis not only of scientists' endeavors to identify obscure causal relations among complex phenomena but of all our everyday reasonings as well; and Hume recognizes that ordinarily custom operates, producing transitions in our minds, without conscious reflection on our past experience. A lifelong experience of various kinds of regular sequences of objects that we have learned to regard as causal has produced in us a general habit of expecting that "*instances of which we have no experience, must necessarily resemble those, of which we have*" or that "*like*

objects, plac'd in like circumstances, will always produce like effects."
The tendency for habitual transitions to be generalized from particular
cases explains how we are able to ascribe a causal relation (and to
make inferences in which we believe and in accordance with which
we are prepared to act) on the basis of a single particularly striking
experiment or experience (T. 104-105). We have so frequently observed regular patterns of repetition of cause and effect that we have
developed a general propensity to assume universal causality in all
phenomena that bear any resemblance to those with which we are
familiar. Thus, in the course of his investigation into the nature of
belief, Hume confronts the general causal maxim, so fundamental that
other philosophers (such as Locke) had regarded it as a matter of
intuitive certainty; and he finds that it, too, is grounded in custom and
formulated, like all general ideas, from a multitude of particular cases
of customary transition: "The supposition, *that the future resembles
the past*, is not founded on arguments of any kind, but is deriv'd
entirely from habit, by which we are determin'd to expect for the
future the same train of objects, to which we have been accustom'd"
(T. 134). The order, or causal regularity, of nature, which is the premise
that validates all inferences to future or remote past events and all
general statements of fact, is thus only our most universal article of
belief, arising like all beliefs from imaginative impulses explicable in
terms of custom.[31]

Having in this examination of belief laid the psychological groundwork for his solution of the problem of causation, Hume returns to
his analysis of the idea of necessary connection. The nature of the
impression from which this idea is derived is now evident. We cannot,
by any contemplation of a cause and its effect, perceive the causal
agency that unites them, and the repetition of similar sequences does
not present any new impression to our senses; and yet, in our observation of such sequences, we become aware of a new impression in
our own minds: "For after we have observ'd the resemblance in a
sufficient number of instances, we immediately feel a determination

---

[31] The problem of causation involves two issues, the universal necessity of causes
(every event has a cause) and causal regularity (the same cause always produces the
same effect). Hume for the most part deals with the latter issue, but our natural belief
in the order of nature extends to both. Lewis White Beck, "A Prussian Hume and a
Scottish Kant," in his *Essays on Kant and Hume* (New Haven: Yale University Press,
1978), p. 120. Hume himself and commentators on Hume generally emphasize the
presumptive resemblance of the *future* to the past; but this implies also that the *past*
resembles the present—an assumption that underlies all our beliefs about the past other
than what we actually remember having experienced.

of the mind to pass from one object to its usual attendant, and to conceive it in a stronger light upon account of that relation. . . . Necessity, then, is the effect of this observation, and is nothing but an internal impression of the mind, or a determination to carry our thoughts from one object to another" (T. 165). Hume's famous doctrine, which has appeared paradoxical to many, that necessity "is something, that exists in the mind, not in objects," rests on his conclusion that an impression of reflection rather than of sensation underlies the idea of necessary connection, which is at the heart of causation. A specific propensity of the imagination, activated by custom, generates the distinctive feature of causation and our belief in the validity of causal inferences. We recall Hume's early remark that it is "the impressions of reflexion, *viz.* passions, desires, and emotions, which principally deserve our attention" (T. 8). This statement seemed (rightly) to indicate Hume's primary interest in moral subjects and hence in the passions, which he examines at great length in Book II; but it acquires additional significance when it emerges that a cognitive idea such as causation rests as well on an internal impression, that the "determination" of the mind to make a certain kind of transition with sufficient force to carry belief along with it is likewise a "feeling" or "sentiment," as Hume calls it in the *Enquiry* as well as in the Appendix to the *Treatise*, whose source is within us.[32]

Hume concludes his discussion of causation with two definitions of cause, suggestive of the dualism between philosophical skepticism and psychological naturalism that pervades his work. As a "philosophical relation" causation is mere uniform sequence of similar objects, grounded in observed frequency of incidence. As a "natural relation," however, causation includes the idea of necessity that we (the observers) bring to it and the liveliness of conception that elicits our belief: "A CAUSE is an object precedent and contiguous to another, and so united with it, that the idea of the one determines the mind to form the idea of the other, and the impression of the one to form a more lively idea of the other" (T. 170).[33] Both these definitions, which together serve to refute those critics who have interpreted him as denying the reality of causation, are important for Hume's philosophy. Although he asserts that apart from experience we can have no idea of causes and

[32] D.G.C. MacNabb offers a modern, "Wittgensteinian" interpretation of Hume's conclusion that the necessity of connections lies not in things but in us or in our way of thinking about things; *David Hume: His Theory of Knowledge and Morality* (Hamden, Conn.: Archon, 1966), pp. 108-10.

[33] See J. A. Robinson, "Hume's Two Definitions of 'Cause'," in *Critical Essays*, ed. Chappell, pp. 129-47.

effects and that in our imagination, or considered a priori, "any thing may produce any thing" (T. 173, 247), nevertheless Hume accepts, as he believes any reasonable person must, the principle of causation as a working assumption. In fact he goes on in other sections of the *Treatise* and the *Enquiry* to discount the possibility of miracles, free will, and chance insofar as these concepts are at variance with the maxims of universal causality and uniformity. What he has done is to deny the strictly logical justifiability of causal inference, pointing out that all inductive arguments depend on an assumption of the uniformity of nature that is only a deeply held (but unprovable) belief derived from habit or custom, and that the idea of necessity that we bring to our reasoning about facts is a function of certain propensities of our imagination. Particular causal relations are objectively nothing but observed patterns subject to continual reconfirmation by the test of future experience. When with respect to such relations our experience has been uniform, we may, in Hume's terminology, speak of inferences whose probability we take to be so high that they may be regarded as "proofs"; nevertheless, any reasoning about matters of fact, resting as it must on nondemonstrable premises, can be accorded the status merely of belief or opinion, and the conviction it elicits must be ascribed to the operations of our imagination rather than to our rational faculties.

We may now turn to the other main topic on which Hume encountered difficulties that led, as had his analysis of causation, both to skepticism and to a fruitful search for alternatives. This is the question of the existence of the external world—the problem of justifying our ordinary convictions regarding both the independent existence and the continuous identity of the objects that we apprehend by means of our senses, or in Hume's terms our confidence that our impressions of sensation represent (more or less accurately) such objects. Hume seems to have recognized the difficulties and skeptical implications in this issue, which seems to be logically prior to that of causation, as an afterthought; he devotes to it only two sections of the *Treatise*, and in the *Enquiry* there is only a brief reference to it in his concluding skeptical summation. It is important that we consider the matter, however, since the problem of identifying stable, independent objects, like that of ascribing causal relations, poses a far from trivial difficulty when it arises as an aspect of the scientific enterprise in the social rather than in the physical field. The problem of our knowledge of objects existing independently of our minds, moreover, figures equally with that of causality in Hume's account of his skeptical crisis, which constitutes a focal point for the reorientation of his philosophy in the direction of naturalism and an explicitly moderate form of skepticism.

Hume raises this problem in the final part of Book I of the *Treatise*, which is concerned as a whole with the skeptical implications of his findings with respect to the understanding.[34] He comes to the issue of the reality of the external world directly from some reflections on his previous analysis of causation, and it is clear from the beginning that an analysis of our belief in independent objects is going to result in a similar failure of logical justification juxtaposed to an acknowledgment of the tenacity of the belief itself. His opening words are: "Thus the sceptic still continues to reason and believe, even tho' he asserts, that he cannot defend his reason by reason; and by the same rule he must assent to the principle concerning the existence of body, tho' he cannot pretend by any arguments of philosophy to maintain its veracity." In the same vein he suggests that the more interesting question is *"What causes induce us to believe in the existence of body?"* rather than the unanswerable *"Whether there be body or not?"* (T. 187). Hume begins, however, with an epistemological analysis of the claims involved in the supposition of external objects before proceeding to an investigation of the psychology of belief.

Recalling that the senses apprehend only those impressions that are present to them, and that reason cannot independently inform us of matters of fact, Hume argues that it is only through some imaginative process that we can and do make inferences from certain of our perceptions to the continuous identity and the independent existence of the objects represented by them. He then identifies the qualities of those perceptions to which we attribute objective existence as either "constancy" (unchangingness from one appearance in our senses to another) or "coherence" (a regular pattern of alteration), both involving resemblances that we note among successive perceptions. Constancy and coherence in objects, like contiguity and succession in causal relations, are thus identified as observable features of phenomena to which we ascribe a continuing existence. The supposition of objectivity is consistent with such observations, and in conjunction with the supposition of causation it is consistent with many features of our experience that seem otherwise inexplicable (T. 195-96). The

[34] Here as elsewhere Locke brusquely bypasses the skeptical implications that seem implicit in his theory of ideas. After rejecting the traditional doctrine of substance, he is forced to contrive a new category of "sensitive Knowledge," to supplement the intuitive and the demonstrative, by which we are said to know of the real existence of external objects. *Essay* IV.ii.14, IV.iii.5, IV.xi.11.

existence of the external world, independent of ourselves, thus seems a perfectly plausible and noncontradictory hypothesis. We do not in practice, however, entertain this supposition as a hypothesis but rather as a belief so strong that it is rarely if ever genuinely suspended; and so Hume turns his attention, in characteristic fashion, to the operations of the imagination through which this belief is generated.

He begins by recalling a feature he had discovered in the course of his earlier investigation of our ideas of space and time: "The imagination," he says, "when set into any train of thinking, is apt to continue, even when its object fails it, and like a galley put in motion by the oars, carries on its course without any new impulse" (T. 198). This principle is at work, in Hume's view, in our tendency to perceive a greater degree of coherence and uniformity in the objects that appear to our senses than they often display under more exact scrutiny; and he suggests that our propensity to suppose a continuing existence in objects might in part be derived from this kind of imaginative impulse. But this principle seems "too weak to support alone so vast an edifice, as is that of the continu'd existence of all external bodies" (T. 198-99); in any case, the principle is a general one that needs refinement in order to be applicable to this particular problem.

Two additional features of the imagination play a part in the more detailed analysis that ensues. The first is the operation of the relation of resemblance, which Hume has previously discussed as one of the three principles governing the association of ideas. Resemblance evidently contributes to our attribution of identity to perceptions that display a certain constancy despite the fact that each is a separate and distinct existence: "When we have been accustom'd to observe ... that the perception of the sun or ocean, for instance, returns upon us after an absence or annihilation with like parts and in a like order, as at its first appearance, we are not apt to regard these interrupted perceptions as different, (which they really are) but on the contrary consider them as individually the same, upon account of their resemblance" (T. 199). Later Hume argues that resemblance is the "most efficacious" of relations with respect to our ideas both of identity as a property of interrupted but similar perceptions and of their real and continuing existence (T. 203).

Resemblance, however, is supplemented by another mental propensity that Hume introduces here for the first time: "Nothing is more certain from experience, than that any contradiction either to the sentiments or passions gives a sensible uneasiness, whether it proceeds from without or from within; from the opposition of external objects, or from the combat of internal principles" (T. 205). There is such a contradiction, Hume says, between the identity that we imaginatively ascribe to a succession of resembling perceptions and their interruption, or their separate existences as distinct impressions. In this situation "the mind must be uneasy," and it "will naturally seek relief" (T. 206) by sacrificing one of the two opposing principles; in fact it disposes of the disturbingly transient nature of perceptions by creating what Hume calls a "fiction of a continu'd existence" (T. 209). Because this fiction is always closely related to a present impression, or to a lively idea in the memory, it obtains sufficient vivacity to compel the belief we habitually accord it. Hume's provocative use of the term "fiction" in this context, as well as his statements to the effect that we "feign the continu'd existence of all sensible objects" (T. 209), is not of course intended to suggest that this belief is false, a claim for which he has no grounds, but only, as with universal causation, that it is unjustifiable by reason. The fiction of external and continuous existence (like that of personal identity later and the causal connection too, although Hume does not use the term in the latter connection) is a mental construction that the imagination imposes on certain perceptions, thereby fixing cognitive patterns and creating order in experience, which might otherwise, on Hume's perceptualist premises, appear as mere flux. These mental fictions are thus in a sense analogous in the cognitive realm to the artifices by which order is created among our feelings and actions in the moral and social realms, as we shall see.

This analysis, then, adds three more factors to the initial suggestion regarding the mind's inertial propensity to unify and perpetuate its perceptions: these are the force of resemblance, a propensity to eliminate the uneasiness of discontinuity by "feigning" objects, and an account of the vivacity necessary to the phenomenon of belief that characteristically accompanies our conception of objects. As was the case with causation, furthermore, Hume points out that our lifelong experience of a substantial amount of constancy in our sense impressions, notwithstanding interruptions, creates in us a general habit of belief in objects that we extend to all such impressions, even in the absence of personal experience of their continuing resemblance over time. All philosophical systems that have tried to account in some rational way for such fundamental beliefs have proved inadequate; Hume, by contrast, is left with what he is compelled to regard as mental fictions, useful (no doubt) and accompanied ordinarily by strong belief, which, though explicable, can never be justified by argument.

In this way Hume pursues to their inescapable conclusions his two major epistemological investigations into the suppositions of regular causation and independent objects that underlie all our thought about the world. Before following him in the directions indicated by these conclusions, we may briefly restate the crux of the argument. The problem, Hume says, is that "what we call a *mind*, is nothing but a heap or collection of different perceptions, united together by certain relations"; furthermore, "as every perception is distinguishable from another, and may be consider'd as separately existent; it evidently follows, that there is no absurdity in separating any particular perception from the mind; that is, in breaking off all its relations, with that connected mass of perceptions, which constitute a thinking being" (T. 207). When philosophers reflect on the contents of their minds, they find nothing present but perceptions, and no necessary foundation for the connections among them and the inferences beyond them that are clearly involved in what passes for knowledge during every waking moment. This conclusion would seem to entail the most extreme skepticism were it not for another observation that stands beside the first— that "almost all mankind, and even philosophers themselves" (T. 206), in fact hold the opinions that are here subjected to critical analysis. Philosophers begin their investigations with the aim of clarifying and justifying the fundamental beliefs of mankind; the fact that justification is not always forthcoming through the philosophers' methods does not constitute a conclusive ground for rejecting these beliefs, which in any case does not appear to be possible. What does seem to be in order, in Hume's view, is a change in the nature of the inquiry, a decisive shift from epistemology to psychology, which as we have seen has been a constant tendency in Hume's work on the understanding.

Although such a redirection of attention has fruitful consequences, however, it is perhaps not entirely satisfying. Must the philosopher discard any hope of validating—and thus of criticizing—beliefs? All beliefs are on the same footing before the psychological enterprise: they are simply explicable; and such a skeptical reorientation seems to negate the philosopher's principal ambition, the discovery of grounds for preferring some beliefs to others. The conclusion of Book i of the *Treatise* is that our most fundamental and universal sorts of inferences about matters of fact are not susceptible of rational justification, although there is nothing that all people believe more strongly. Belief without grounds is *mere* belief; such an analysis constitutes the essence of philosophical skepticism. At this point we must follow Hume through a turning point in his philosophy, as he finds his way beyond a position that might have crippled his philosophical hopes to the moderate skepticism to which he adheres consistently thereafter.

3. The Skeptical Crisis and Its Outcome

Hume embarked on his philosophy with great ambitions of presenting a comprehensive new system, one that would incorporate and enlarge upon promising recent discoveries.[35] His study of the "understanding," however, which was intended to serve as the foundation of the whole projected science of human nature, culminated in skeptical doubts that seemed to threaten the whole enterprise. This apparent impasse provoked the famous skeptical crisis that Hume describes at the close of Book I in the most vivid autobiographical passage of the *Treatise*; here he portrays his own response to his skeptical doubts and tentatively formulates his proposed solution.

Hume's mature position is reflected in the more cautious and dispassionate *Enquiry*. Here his earlier grandiose intentions with respect to the analysis of the understanding are reduced to a claim to have delineated "mental geography"; his proud discoveries concerning the association of ideas are virtually abandoned; and his inability to find rational grounds for causal inference elicits the following conclusion:

> These ultimate springs and principles are totally shut up from human curiosity and enquiry. . . . The most perfect philosophy of the natural kind only staves off our ignorance a little longer: as perhaps the most perfect philosophy of the moral or metaphysical kind serves only to discover larger portions of it. Thus the observation of human blindness and weakness is the result of all philosophy, and meets us at every turn, in spite of our endeavours to elude or avoid it.[36]

Calm admissions such as this are characteristic of Hume's later writings; in the more candid *Treatise*, however, we are permitted a glimpse of the not always tranquil process of intellectual discovery through which the mature and moderate position was achieved.

Are his discoveries regarding the understanding such as to warrant the continuation of his investigations into the other fields he had originally projected? Hume considers his situation: "Methinks I am like a man, who having struck on many shoals, and having narrowly escap'd ship-wreck in passing a small frith, has yet the temerity to put out to sea in the same leaky weather-beaten vessel, and even carries his ambition so far as to think of compassing the globe under these disadvantageous circumstances" (T. 263-64). His "past errors and perplexities" lead him to doubt the adequacy of his methods to his task; more important, his conclusions so far, insofar as they are trust-

---

[35] Hume's early enthusiasm is reflected in the Introduction to the *Treatise* and in his *Abstract of a Treatise of Human Nature*, p. 31.

[36] Hume, *Enquiries* (I), pp. 30-31.

worthy, serve only to accentuate the "weakness, and disorder of the faculties" by means of which the scientific enterprise was to have been pursued. This reflection, Hume says, strikes him with "melancholy" and even "despair," feelings that are intensified by the "forelorn solitude" of his pursuit of philosophy (T. 264). The abstruseness and paradoxical nature of his reasoning separate him from ordinary people, and his criticism of their systems earns him enmity from other philosophers. Looking to himself he finds only "doubt and ignorance"; support and encouragement are not forthcoming from any source.

Hume here recounts—with stylistic affectation but intellectual seriousness—his personal experience of a typical crisis confronted by skeptics at a certain point in their development. It seems contradictory that reason should disparage reason, and the reasoning that throws all claims to knowledge into doubt eventually returns to cast doubt on its own validity. "Can I be sure," Hume asks, "that in leaving all establish'd opinions I am following truth; and by what criterion shall I distinguish her, even if fortune shou'd at last guide me on her footsteps?" (T. 265). Earlier Hume had criticized the philosophers' inclination to delight in "whatever has the air of a paradox, and is contrary to the first and most unprejudic'd notions of mankind" (T. 26); yet no philosopher's conclusions were more paradoxical (or so it appeared) than those at which Hume arrives. It is difficult to see how his discovery that all the operations of the understanding are "founded on the imagination, or the vivacity of our ideas" can be certainly known or justified: "After the most accurate and exact of my reasonings, I can give no reason why I shou'd assent to it; and feel nothing but a *strong* propensity to consider objects *strongly* in that view, under which they appear to me" (T. 265). This final recognition of the place of habit and feeling in thought, and of the problematic status of all propositions about matters of fact, must to some degree undermine retrospectively the arguments on which it is based.

Contradictions such as these in skeptical reasoning exemplify a typical "debacle of reason" encountered by skeptics—the realization, in Hume's words, that "the understanding, when it acts alone, and according to its most general principles, entirely subverts itself" (T. 267). The ancient Pyrrhonists to whom Hume alludes in the *Enquiry* acknowledged this paradox of dogmatic skepticism and sought to refrain from any positive statements; skeptics of religious inclination have often seized upon this debacle as the occasion for turning to faith or revelation.[37] Hume, however, despite the skeptical outcome, remains

[37] Cf., for example, Blaise Pascal, *Pensées,* trans. W. F. Trotter (New York: Modern Library, 1941), pensée 434, p. 143. The term "debacle of reason" is used by Richard

too much committed to his study of human nature to withdraw from the pursuit of his philosophy, and he is not tempted by the fideist alternative. It is a reorientation, and not a surrender, of reasoning that he undertakes, and his eventual resolution of the crisis provides the underpinning for a new stage in his philosophical development.

The skeptical doubts prescribe caution at the very least, however, and before Hume can advance his inquiries he reviews the difficulties facing him. These pertain generally to the tenuous status and dubious trustworthiness of the imagination, which Hume has identified as the faculty on which all our mental operations are based: "No wonder a principle so inconstant and fallacious shou'd lead us into errors, when implicitly follow'd (as it must be) in all its variations" (T. 265-66). Hume seems to have at least two things in mind with this admonition. In the first place, as he points out, "Nothing is more curiously enquir'd after by the mind of men, than the causes of every phaenomenon" (T. 266); yet Hume's analysis has established that it is precisely causes, in the sense of the ultimate principles of connection among things, that we cannot know. Furthermore, this impossibility of insight into the nature of causality, besides frustrating a natural intellectual aspiration, opens the way to a multitude of specific erroneous ascriptions of causation; for a variety of imaginative factors may interfere with the reservation of this category to cases of carefully observed and consistently uniform sequences. More inclusively, the imagination, which underlies *all* reasonings and inferences, must be the source generally of erroneous beliefs as well as of true judgments. There is a sense, Hume says, in which all our inferences about matters of fact are illusory, insofar as we suppose necessary connections among things when in fact the necessity lies, so far as it can be discerned at all, in ourselves. We could not of course get along without such "illusions," or "fictitious" suppositions, but the question remains, "how far we ought to yield to these illusions" (T. 267). The imagination, through similar operations, generates errors, superstitions, and fantasies as well as scientific conclusions. How can Hume draw a clear line between undesirable credulity and reasonable belief? This distinction is important: "Nothing is more dangerous to reason than the flights of the imagination" (T. 267); and yet since reliance on reason alone appears to be self-defeating, we are left with no choice other than Pyrrhonian doubt or acceptance, in some degree, of the products of our imagi-

---

H. Popkin in the Introduction to his edition of Pierre Bayle, *Historical and Critical Dictionary* (Indianapolis: Bobbs Merrill, 1965), p. xxvii.

nation. Drawing a line between reasonable and unreasonable beliefs, and justifying his principle of differentiation, is thus a problem for Hume, the solution to which is not evident at this point.

Hume's philosophy thus far, then, appears to contain disheartening implications for the fulfillment of his aims. This circumstance, along with the general skeptical doubt regarding his capacity to philosophize at all, leads Hume to find himself surrounded by the "deepest darkness" of the skeptical crisis and the apparent debility of mental faculties (T. 268-69).[38] This appears to be the outcome of the philosopher's reasoning, and reasoning does not itself offer any hope of a cure. It is at this moment that Hume reaches a turning point, grounded in a personal resolution of his intellectual impasse: "Since reason is incapable of dispelling these clouds, nature herself suffices to that purpose, and cures me of this philosophical melancholy and delirium" (T. 269).

How does nature effect her cure? Hume relates how he emerges from his study, plays backgammon, converses with friends, and immerses himself in affairs of life where speculative doubts have no place. "Here I find myself absolutely and necessarily determin'd to live, and talk, and act like other people in the common affairs of life" (T. 269). Hume presents his personal experience of a distinction, often mentioned by skeptics, between the solitude of the study, where the contradictions of reasoning thrive, and the ordinary affairs of life, where people are observed to get along for the most part following the unexamined "general maxims of the world" (T. 269). The contrast between these two settings stimulates the philosopher to a set of observations that form the nucleus of a resolution of the conflict. Hume had earlier noted, with respect to the practical untenability of a paradoxical conclusion of his philosophy, that "Nature, by an absolute and uncontroulable necessity has determin'd us to judge as well as to breathe and feel" (T. 183). Total skepticism is therefore a position that, although plausible in the study, is not in fact maintained by anyone, including the philosopher, with any real conviction. The fact that all our reasonings appear to be founded on nothing more substantial than custom does not, even in the philosopher, result in a complete suspension of judgment concerning causation. Hume, in this respect following a line of thought previously recorded by ancient

[38] That Hume's crisis was genuine is suggested in his letter of [March or April 1734] to [Dr. George Cheyne], in *The Letters of David Hume*, ed. J.Y.T. Greig (Oxford: Clarendon Press, 1932), vol. 1, p. 17. This letter is notable for Hume's comparison of an overdose of solitary speculation to religious "fanaticism," given his opinion of the latter phenomenon.

skeptics,[39] concedes the obvious fact that he as well as other people assent to what appears to be evident and grants that assent or belief is implied in action. Not only does he continue to believe, but also he comes to the realization that the nonrational sources of belief actually constitute its strength: *since* he continues to believe, despite his inability rationally to justify doing so, "he may safely conclude, that his reasoning and belief is some sensation or peculiar manner of conception, which 'tis impossible for mere ideas and reflections to destroy" (T. 184). Skeptical doubts appear to the philosopher as a kind of "malady" that recurs periodically and that "can never be radically cur'd" (T. 218); yet the philosopher finds it possible to stand aside from the paradoxes, emerge from the study, and mix in society, where the necessity of action and belief strikes him forcefully enough to cast his former reasonings in an entirely new light.

The relief that the philosopher finds outside the study points to an important feature of Hume's philosophy as a whole—its constant interest in the opinions and behavior of ordinary people, to which he frequently appeals in opposition to abstract doctrines.[40] Philosophers by virtue of their speculative endeavors are inevitably set apart to a degree from those whom Hume calls the "vulgar," who do not reflect on their beliefs. Yet philosophers in their isolation are apt to spin their abstruse reasonings into systems that, although plausible in the rarefied atmosphere of the study, bear little relation to the beliefs that are held without. Hume, who generally resists this temptation, now looks on it with redoubled suspicion. Although genuine philosophers must maintain a critical distance from ordinary belief, they must never overlook the fact of such belief and its frequent though problematic tenacity. Rejecting the ingenious doctrines concerning "*occult qualities*" proposed in the "antient philosophy," for example, Hume argues that intellectual sophistication of this kind is as misleading as the unreflecting errors of the vulgar. All men, he says, seek "indifference," by which he means something close to the ancient skeptics' ataraxy or peace of mind in their cognitive grasp of things. Dogmatic philosophers attain this state through complex conceits, the vulgar through unreflecting "stupidity," and "true philosophers" through moderate skepticism; of these three possibilities, "the true philosophy ap-

[39] Cf., for example, Cicero, *Academica*, trans. H. Rackham (Cambridge: Harvard University Press, 1972) II. 38, p. 517.

[40] The most familiar example of this in Hume's political philosophy occurs in "Of the Original Contract": one argument against contractualism as the basis of political legitimacy lies in its counterintuitive quality, the fact that most loyal subjects of states would not acknowledge its truth even if the doctrine were presented to them.

proaches nearer to the sentiments of the vulgar, than to those of a mistaken knowledge" (T. 222-24). Hume's philosophy, here as later in his moral and political doctrines, will not lightly repudiate what is firmly grounded in ordinary belief, judgment, and feeling.

Hume began with an examination of certain fundamental beliefs that are commonly held to be true, and he discovered that this presumed "knowledge" depends, at its foundation, on certain irreducible beliefs; further inquiry revealed, however, that whereas rational justification for these beliefs is lacking, their psychological status as basic components of human nature stands out all the more vividly. The philosopher thus becomes a psychologist; but at the same time, acknowledging a similarity to the "vulgar" in this respect, he acquiesces in the necessities of common human nature and adheres to skepticism in a moderated form. The opinions held by "children, peasants, and the greatest part of mankind" will continue to be matters for reflection and scrutiny in the philosopher's hands, yet he will continually be reminded that "all of us, at one time or another" share the situation of "the unthinking and unphilosophical part of mankind" (T. 193, 205). It is the prompting of nature and the force of custom rather than reason that underlie the inferential faculty—for philosophers no less than for the "generality of mankind" (and even animals!).[41]

Hume accordingly turns to nature as his guide, the nature that is exemplified in the ordinary beliefs and common affairs of the life of those who do not trouble themselves with skeptical doubts and the contradictory presumptions of reason. In methodological terms this new departure means that Hume decisively recognizes the necessity of expanding his philosophical program from epistemology to human nature as a whole, in which the rational features appear to be inextricably connected with nonrational ones. Not only does all our reasoning rest on certain psychological propensities and habits; philosophers themselves, recovering from the temporary paralysis of mind induced by the skeptical debacle, eventually return from "amusement and company" to the renewal of their studies because they find themselves "naturally *inclin'd*" to do so: "I cannot forbear having a curiosity to be acquainted with the principles of moral good and evil, the nature and foundation of government, and the cause of those several passions and inclinations, which actuate and govern me" (T. 270-71). Since philosophizing itself is revealed to be the product of a certain inscrutable inclination, philosophers must attend to this and similar dispositions in themselves and in others; and so psychology

[41] Hume, *Enquiries* (I), p. 106.

and even social science are indicated as a close adjunct of an account of the understanding.

Substantively this reorientation has important consequences as well, leading to a positive philosophy of naturalism (allied to a now mitigated skepticism) following close upon the most debilitating doubts. Hume's skeptical crisis is resolved, at least tentatively, not only in the sense that he discovers new directions for his intellectual efforts but also insofar as his philosophy yields practical rules for the direction of life. Nature becomes a practical guide as well as a universe of facts to be explored; the forms of belief that under epistemological scrutiny appear as the *mere* belief of skeptical criticism are now acknowledged as a positive faculty, and common opinion, in the absence of rational alternatives, acquires a certain presumption of trustworthiness. The "honest gentlemen" whom Hume recognizes as his fellow citizens and backgammon companions—men who, "being always employ'd in their domestic affairs, or amusing themselves in common recreations, have carried their thoughts very little beyond those objects, which are every day expos'd to their senses"—are not properly objects of disdain on the part of the philosopher; rather, "I wish we cou'd communicate to our founders of systems, a share of this gross earthy mixture, as an ingredient, which they commonly stand much in need of" (T. 272). Such approval of common-sense beliefs and of the natural propensities of ordinary people marks the new element in Hume's system, saving him from both the paradoxes of extreme skepticism and the aloofness of overly abstruse philosophical systems.

Acquiescence in the ways and beliefs of common life, however, carries with it another potential hazard: the loss of any standard of judgment with regard to received opinions and the ensuing passivity of relativism. This was a perennial tendency in skepticism in the past: the Pyrrho of legend is said to have regarded complete suspense of judgment on all questions combined with full external acquiescence in the established ways of his community as the appropriate stance of the philosopher. Thoroughgoing naturalism, combined with conventionalism in social affairs, takes the existence of any phenomenon as its own justification; and philosophers who pass from the explanation of the observed operations of human nature to approval of them as appropriate may forfeit any possibility of criticism, thereby abandoning the more significant aspect of their calling. Hume declines to go so far: he always maintains a strong sense of his separateness from other people as well as of his fundamental similarity to them, and his tendency to approve of ordinary beliefs is restricted to a presumption in their favor, always tempered by a certain critical distance. In the midst of the resuscitation of his spirits in the tangible affairs of social life he adheres to the basic conviction of his philosophy: "In all the incidents of life we ought still to preserve our scepticism" (T. 270), a motto that, although addressed hopefully to all, continues in practice to set the philosopher apart.

The distinctive position of mitigated or moderate skepticism advocated by Hume thus displays two different facets. Recognizing as practically untenable the doubts concerning reasoning in their extreme form, Hume acknowledges nonrational sources of belief as appropriate and useful faculties for the conduct of life; yet his philosophic suspension of judgment is not so complete as to render him wholly indifferent in the face of opinion. Whereas extreme skepticism turns back on itself and crumbles before everyday experience, Hume urges that a moderate skepticism, in alliance with a not entirely uncritical naturalism, represents a viable position. Hume thus adopts two guides: nature, which ensures that speculation does not diverge too far from the necessities of life, and philosophy (including philosophical criteria for inferential reasoning that serve to refine impulsive belief), whose pursuit signifies a confidence in the importance of thought despite its limitations and inhibits the skeptic's periodic temptation to succumb blindly to the promptings of temperament or environment.[42] Of the two guides it is not clear which has priority. Hume's recognition that he, but not the others, is attracted to philosophy would suggest that philosophy itself is ultimately subordinate: in the end Hume justifies his philosophizing only on the ground that he *feels* inclined to it.[43] His continuing frequent defenses of the value of mitigated skepticism, on the other hand, make it clear that his position is one of self-conscious detachment: "Human Nature is the only science of man" (T. 273), but the scope and tenacity of human nature do not preclude a critical appraisal on the part of the philosopher. The balance that Hume tries to sustain between these two guides is a tenuous one, and the nature of that balance, on the foundations of his empirical science of human nature, determines the quality of his political philosophy.

4. Aspects of Hume's Naturalism

The term naturalism used in connection with Hume's philosophy refers, in the first place, to the view of human nature as an integrated

[42] Cf. Smith, *Philosophy of Hume*, pp. 131-32, where skepticism is asserted to be the subordinate of the two guides.

[43] Richard H. Popkin, "David Hume: His Pyrrhonism and his Critique of Pyrrhonism" in *Critical Essays*, ed. Chappell, p. 84. Popkin (in this respect following Kemp Smith) offers what may be called an extreme naturalistic interpretation of Hume, attributing to him the view that we cannot help succumbing to all the promptings of nature.

whole that Hume develops following his discovery that key problems of epistemology are insoluble within the limited framework of the theory of perceptions. Hume's psychological naturalism is grounded in his conclusion that cognitive problems are overcome in practice through the operation of nonrational, natural mental processes whose interaction with rational ones is continuous, inescapable, and on the whole benign. Further, this naturalism involves a tendency to regard human nature so delineated as part of nature in a broader sense, in which all normal organisms are understood as being well suited, in their capacities, to their environments and coexistent in a general system of fundamental harmony. Just as Hume's philosophy of human nature explicitly denies what had previously been regarded as a radical distinction between the rational and the irrational, so it also tends to repudiate any claim of discontinuity between human nature and the rest of organic existence, as may be seen for example in the curious *Treatise* chapters on animals.[44] It is on this basis that Hume studies the phenomena of human mental and moral life, utilizing the methods and logic of inquiry by which any investigation of experience of any sort must be conducted.

Naturalism thus pertains to more than a materialist metaphysic or an empiricist methodology for Hume's positive doctrines. The concept nature for Hume—as for others, like Montaigne, who have turned to it in search of a guide in their skepticism—carries the normative connotations of a lingering and, in Hume's case, fully secularized teleological outlook. The study of human nature promises to reveal, in its discovery of the most basic or normal attributes and operations of understanding and behavior, an appropriate guide for the conduct of life in addition to what is generally the case in fact. Hume's naturalism, complementing his skeptical assessment of the potentialities of reason, conceives of human nature as being nonetheless, and for the most part, well adapted for the satisfaction of its needs and for the fulfillment of its natural ends—although Hume, in contrast to some of his contemporaries, declines to invoke providential design as the source of this harmony. This orientation must be understood as representing a basic philosophical conclusion, one to which Hume adheres as a general presumption even while retaining, in his mitigated skepticism, the possibility of detachment and tentative criticism.[45]

---

[44] Hume, *Treatise* I.iii.16, II.i.12; II.ii.12; also *Enquiries* (I), sec. 9.

[45] Cf. Carl L. Becker, *The Heavenly City of the Eighteenth-Century Philosophers* (New Haven: Yale University Press, 1965), p. 66. But Becker is mistaken about Hume: despite his scientific outlook Hume nevertheless retains a normative meaning of "nature," with connotations of philosophical approval of what is natural beyond the word's descriptive meaning as "normal." Such naturalism at times even appears teleological

Naturalism of this sort motivates and pervades the further studies of human nature that Hume undertakes on the foundation of his skepticism, and similar assumptions inform the moral and political investigations that grow out of these. Although Hume's subsequent analysis of the elements of human nature and later of politics contains a significant scientific or empirical component, the normative implications of his naturalism persist as a complement to the limitations prescribed by his skepticism, forming a basis on which he can continue to philosophize with the expectation that his philosophical efforts will serve practical ends. I shall return to the practical import of Hume's political philosophy in the final chapter, following a closer examination of his psychology and political science. In this section, however, I adumbrate several of the themes in which Hume's naturalism in its broad sense manifests itself, remembering that the central question posed by an alliance of this sort between skepticism and naturalism concerns the delicate balance between the philosopher's passive acceptance and his capacity for criticism of the basic features of his subject matter.

The interpretation of Hume as (in some degree) a "naturalist" has become a common theme among recent scholars. In this respect they follow the work of Kemp Smith, who regarded Hume's doctrine of belief—the "positive teaching of Book I of the *Treatise*"—as outweighing the notorious negative or skeptical teachings on which previous commentators had frequently dwelt. Although Kemp Smith, on a more balanced view, seems to have exaggerated the subordination of reason to the passions in Hume's philosophy, thus neglecting or discounting the persisting element of critical skepticism, his emphasis on the constructive role of sentiment as a natural component of mental life—both cognitive and moral—has undoubted validity.[46] We have

---

in its largely implicit suggestion that the observation of nature reveals standards of appropriateness. See also Basil Willey, *The Eighteenth Century Background* (Boston: Beacon Press, 1961), pp. 110-35. Hume discusses the meanings of "natural" in the *Treatise*, pp. 473-75. David Fate Norton, *David Hume—Common-Sense Moralist, Sceptical Metaphysician* (Princeton: Princeton University Press, 1982), has emphasized the differences between Hume and contemporary providential naturalism, especially that of Hutcheson and Reid.

[46] Smith, *Philosophy of Hume,* pp. 43-44. See also his earlier article, "The Naturalism of Hume," *Mind* N.S. 14 (1905): 149-73, 335-47. See also Charles William Hendel, Jr., *Studies in the Philosophy of David Hume* (Princeton: Princeton University Press, 1925). I follow the interpretation offered in these pathbreaking works to a significant extent. Norton, *David Hume,* offers the most searching critique of Kemp Smith's "subordination thesis" while equally rejecting the older Reid-Green interpretation of Hume as an extreme skeptic and subjectivist. The balance that Norton strikes has Hume maintaining a skeptical stance in "metaphysical" or scientific questions while giving greater (though not exclusive) weight to sentiment or common-sense judgments in ethics.

observed the line of thought by which Hume comes to focus on the problem of belief and in particular on the tenacity and universality of certain basic beliefs that defy rational justification yet must underlie all reasoning concerning matters of fact. The further topic to be considered here is Hume's effort both to distinguish the fundamental ontological beliefs from others and in a way to validate the psychological (though not epistemological) certainty that normally attends them.

In the *Treatise* Hume, seeking to grasp the nature of the difference between an idea to which we assent and one that we hold to be fictitious, concludes that the former "*feels* different" from the latter, and that belief in general is "something *felt* by the mind" (T. 629), a matter of "sentiment" comparable to the taste that determines our aesthetic judgments (T. 103). In the *Enquiry* belief, like the passions of love and hatred, is spoken of as "a species of natural instincts,"[47] a more or less spontaneous consequence of the mind's being placed in certain circumstances. Hume thus characterizes belief in terms that seem promising for further psychological analysis. The difficulty is that from this perspective all belief appears to rest on the same non-rational footing, belief in the existence of perceived objects and in causal relations as well as in the most "vulgar" superstitions and erroneous convictions. Can a distinction be drawn, on Hume's principles, between acceptable and unacceptable beliefs? Hume certainly did not intend to disparage or reject the forms of belief on which inductive reasoning depends, and he experienced great frustration at being misunderstood to have denied the reality of causal relations or even to have claimed that we cannot "know" causes and effects. In one of his infrequent answers to his critics Hume argues that we can have a kind of "moral certainty" about such propositions as "all Men must die" and "the Sun will rise To-morrow"—propositions that no one ever doubted.[48] Belief, or the capacity for genuine assent to propositions such as these, yields the conviction we require in order to act effectively in the world. But surely all kinds and cases of merely subjective certainty cannot have an equal status in the eyes of the philosopher, and he therefore must find some means of differentiating appropriate beliefs from inappropriate ones, legitimate belief from unwarranted credulity.

Hume's answer to this problem is found in his doctrine of natural

[47] Hume, *Enquiries* (I), pp. 46-47.

[48] Hume, *A Letter from a Gentleman to his Friend in Edinburgh*, ed. Ernest C. Mossner and John V. Price (Edinburgh: Edinburgh University Press, 1967), p. 22. Cf. also Hume, letter of [February 1745] to [John Stewart], *Letters*, vol. 1, p. 187.

beliefs, in which he grants a special status to two fundamental forms of belief—in external objects and in causality—and attempts to provide grounds for restricting assent with respect to matters of fact to propositions founded on these most basic convictions. All belief is a product of the imagination working according to certain principles; all beliefs, therefore, are "natural" phenomena (in one sense of the word), and their occurrence can in principle be explained. Having granted this, however, Hume takes the further step of distinguishing imaginative principles that are "natural" in the additional senses of being "permanent, irresistable, and universal" from those that are "changeable, weak, and irregular." As a philosopher rather than as a psychologist he argues that the former are to be approved as salutary and necessary—"the foundation of all our thoughts and actions, so that upon their removal human nature must immediately perish and go to ruin" (T. 225)—whereas the latter are to be subjected to criticism.

This doctrine, by which Hume seeks to differentiate the belief in the external world and the belief that the future will resemble the past from other beliefs, is not without its difficulties. It is not clear what it would mean for human nature to "go to ruin," unless Hume has in mind the Pyrrhonian doubt that philosophers experience in the study when they do temporarily attempt to suspend all belief. It is not clear whether Hume means to justify only those beliefs that are literally "unavoidable" and "universal": this standard poses a formidable empirical difficulty, and in any case Hume himself knows of peasants who do not seem to believe consistently in universal causality (T. 132). The two basic beliefs are strongly, even instinctually held, presumably by everyone (most of the time); yet it may be that other and in Hume's view erroneous beliefs are no less vivid in the minds of their adherents or indeed any less frequently encountered.[49] In the larger perspective of Hume's philosophy, the most important questions arise concerning religious beliefs, many of which Hume regards as lying at the heart of deplorable "superstitions" and "fanaticism,"[50] and beliefs in the extravagant ideas on which dangerous political ideologies are built.

[49] Ronald J. Butler, "Natural Belief and the Enigma of Hume," *Archiv für Geschichte der Philosophie* 42 (1960): 73-100.

[50] Hume, "Of Superstition and Enthusiasm," *Works*, vol. 3, pp. 144-50. Cf. also Hume, "The Natural History of Religion," *Works*, vol. 4, in which he asserts the naturalness of polytheism and of belief in miracles and special providences, at least among "barbarous" peoples. A steady view of entirely regular causality appears to be a refined and rare philosophical achievement, at least with respect to unusual occurrences. On this subject see Terence Penelhum, "Hume's Skepticism and the *Dialogues*," in *McGill Hume Studies*, ed. Norton et al., pp. 253-78.

In both religion and politics the reasonable person, in Hume's view, apportions belief in accordance with the evidence and the rules of inductive logic that depend on the "natural belief" in uniform causality and the regularity of nature. But the standards by which this stance is more "natural" than the various kinds of deplorable credulity remain imprecise in Hume's philosophy.

These difficulties point up the fact that Hume is here proposing a standard of validity in reasoning, one that is founded on a normative criterion of what is natural and therefore beneficial for human beings. Speaking of the fact that an irrational belief in "spectres" can be forceful and coherent, Hume argues that reasoning about such fictions of the imagination is natural "in the same sense, that a malady is said to be natural; as arising from natural cause, tho' it be contrary to health, the most agreeable and most natural situation of man" (T. 226). Hume the philosopher *approves* the basic beliefs in objects and causality, although in his terms they are no more founded in reason, or *rational*, than other widespread and psychologically similar beliefs—in spiritual entities, for example—that are to be rejected unless they can be adequately supported by probable reasonings that ultimately rest on the two approved beliefs. Hume argues that these beliefs are natural in the sense of being most fundamental to our mental constitution and thus inescapable; but it is difficult to avoid the impression that the *nature* being appealed to here includes a standard of suitability and usefulness with respect to human needs that reflects a philosophical choice.

The doctrine of natural beliefs in the *Treatise* pertains to the fundamental forms of cognition and inferential reasoning about perceived phenomena. Analogously defended natural beliefs may later be seen to underlie Hume's moral philosophy as well, although he does not enunciate an explicit doctrine to this effect. Moral judgments (as we shall see) have their source in feelings and generally in the basic sentiment of approval that we normally experience at the prospect of human happiness. On the conscious level, the reasons that we can give for our moral judgments come down finally to the basic belief, corresponding to natural feeling and not further rationalizable, that happiness is a good and an appropriate object of our actions. In a similar vein Hume remarks that it is only our fundamental conviction "that human life is of some importance" that saves us from despair in view of our mortality,[51] a sentiment reminiscent of Hume's decision to put aside his debilitating Pyrrhonism upon finding it to be at variance with

[51] Hume, "The Sceptic," *Works*, vol. 3, p. 228.

his natural inclinations. Thus in the practical as in the cognitive sphere Hume endorses those forms of belief that, arising from what he regards as the most basic natural impulses, appear necessary to life itself.

Hume's naturalism is likewise manifest in his program to study "human nature" as an integrated whole. The formulation of this program involved the recognition that what Locke denoted by "understanding" in reality embraces other facets of human nature than this term implies, and it culminates in Hume's consequent rehabilitation of the passions and related nonrational human attributes. In a large view the most conspicuous difference between the great works of Locke and of Hume is the far greater attention Hume gives to the passions and to moral theory built on a detailed study of the passions; in this decisive respect the influence of Hutcheson, with his moral sense theory and corresponding interest in the sentiments, seems evident. Books II and III of the *Treatise* are explicitly devoted to these subjects; and even in his initial classification of the contents of thought, Hume includes "passions and emotions" in the category of "impressions of reflection," thereby integrating them directly into the framework of the understanding as a type of mental contents. Feelings mingle throughout with sense impressions as objects of awareness for Hume as they do not for Locke.[52]

Furthermore, "feeling" in the sense of intensity of conception or as any of a number of mental "propensities" enters Hume's epistemology at two crucial points: to characterize the difference between impressions and ideas and to account for the phenomenon of belief. The term "feeling" is applied to imaginative in addition to emotional capacities in ways that are central to Hume's account of the "understanding," and the integration of affective with rational processes is thus thoroughgoing. His psychology is therefore decidedly not, as has been charged, characterized by a stark opposition between understanding and passion, reason and desire.[53]

When Locke occasionally turns his attention to nonideational features of human nature, he tends in a traditional way to think of such things as appetites and desires, instinctual "Principles of Actions" of which he says that if "left to their full swing they would carry Men to the overturning of all Morality"; moral rules, far from growing out of men's natural propensities, are said to be devised by man's reason to serve as a "curb and restraint" on his desires.[54] Locke in this way

---

[52] Locke's interest in the passions is small in the *Essay*; cf. II.xx.

[53] See Roberto Mangabeira Unger, *Knowledge and Politics* (New York: Free Press, 1975), pp. 38ff., 299, for this hackneyed and misleading view.

[54] Locke, *Essay* I.iii.13.

retains to a substantial degree the rationalist and ultimately Christian view of human nature as divided into higher and lower faculties, a fact that explains his awkward effort to preserve a demonstrative ethics in the midst of his empiricist epistemology.[55] Hume rejects such a dichotomy between reason and feeling as untenable in explaining the principles of the understanding, showing how Locke's ideal of clear thinking has to rest on a foundation in the "lower" reaches of the imagination. He proceeds to recognize in this nature that underlies reason—a nature that includes the irreducible passions as well as the active principles of the imagination—a largely satisfactory guide both in our cognitive and in our moral life. Reference has already been made to the three sections in the *Treatise* in which Hume compares human reasoning and passions with those of animals, finding differences of degree only. An apparently discordant note in this theme is struck when we find a section entitled "Of curiosity, or the love of truth" instead of another animal section where we expect one, at the close of Book II, Part 3. Far from demonstrating that human beings are differentiated from the rest of nature by a special desire and capacity for truth, however, this section in actuality explores the natural or instinctual (and nonrational) pleasures attaching to mental activity of all sorts, thus confirming Hume's naturalism. Hume may be said to replace the older dualism with a different one, in which a naturalism founded on the unity of human nature is opposed to the skeptical possibility, open to philosophers, of suspending belief and thus overcoming the tendency of the "vulgar" to equate uncritically their belief with certainty.

Hume's view of the unity of human nature accounts for the tendency in his philosophy to reduce problems of epistemology and of ethics to issues of psychology, a tendency that is productive for his intended science of human nature and of morals but that threatens to vitiate any standards of critical evaluation. It is important to recognize this tendency in Hume's work, but it is also necessary to note its limits: Hume's naturalism never quite loses a normative dimension that distinguishes it from modern scientific behaviorism, in which, for the study of human beings as for physics, the term nature has no other signification than the totality of what exists, subsumed in what is taken to be a universal network of causality. Human nature is indeed the object of Hume's scientific study, pursued through the methods that properly govern all reasoning regarding matters of fact. But there

[55] Cf. Shirley Robin Letwin, *The Pursuit of Certainty* (Cambridge: Cambridge University Press, 1965), pp. 43-44.

remains the other sense in which nature provides the skeptic with guidance in choosing standards of right reasoning and of moral value from among the actual tendencies of the human imagination and judgment.

The line of inquiry that pointed toward the explanation of mental processes in terms of physics had been pioneered in radical fashion in the previous century by Hobbes and Descartes, who had both been led from traditional philosophical problems by way of psychology to what appeared to be their ultimate grounding in physiology. Of the two, Hobbes was the more radical in his programmatic reduction of the whole of the mind to a material basis, thus avoiding the Cartesian problem of the mode of interaction between body and mind, and in this he was followed by later British psychologists, including Hume. Descartes, despite his claim regarding the rational autonomy of the mind, had been an influential investigator of biological physiology, which proved to be a more promising approach to the study of perception and the passions than Hobbes's physics. Descartes's view that perceptions are to be understood as stimulations of the nervous system was taken for granted by later proponents of the theory of ideas, such as Locke; Descartes moreover originated the criterion of "liveliness," on a physiological foundation, to differentiate sense perceptions from the dreams and illusions that are excited by the "fortuitous course of the animal spirits" through the nervous system.[56]

Hume acknowledges the validity of this line of investigation, with its implication that all mental phenomena are finally explicable in terms of biological or physical operations, but like Locke he was not inclined to pursue it. Hume at one point embarks briefly and reluctantly on an "imaginary dissection of the brain," invoking a Cartesian model of "animal spirits" (T. 60-61); but generally he restricts his science of the understanding to psychology, delineating the principles of the imagination without further efforts at materialist reduction. The "ultimate cause" of sense impressions is said to be "perfectly inexplicable" (T. 84); perceptions are treated as simply arising within us in certain circumstances, according to rules whose discovery is his main concern. Hume typically treats epistemological problems as psychological ones—quickly passing from the question of the justification of inductive inference, for example, to the broader questions of why we make such inferences and the source of the accompanying belief.

[56] René Descartes, *The Passions of the Soul*, art. 26, in *The Philosophical Works of Descartes*, trans. Elizabeth S. Haldane and G.R.T. Ross (Cambridge: Cambridge University Press, 1970), vol. 1, p. 343.

But he resists the next step toward a thoroughgoing behaviorism; more a moralist than a physiologist, Hume shows his primary concern to be the suitability and utility of the principles of human nature that he observes rather than their material foundation. In this respect he reveals himself to be more a disciple of Shaftesbury than of Hobbes or Descartes in the field of psychology as well as in his assessment of human nature as a whole. Shaftesbury, criticizing not so much the accuracy as the point of Descartes's physiological analysis of the passions, sought to integrate the study of the affective part of human nature with that of other human potentialities to the moral ends of self-knowledge and regulation of conduct.[57] With this program of recruiting psychology to inform the study of ethics, Shaftesbury founded the tradition of British moral philosophy to which Hume acknowledges his debt in the Introduction to his *Treatise*.

Hume claims to be offering a science of human nature, and much of his work is devoted to the elucidation of the psychological facts of the mind and the regular patterns of operation that it exhibits. He was not tempted to pursue more precise studies of the human material constitution principally because such efforts did not promise to contribute to the more normative naturalism and moral theory for which this science was to be the groundwork. The outcome of his descriptive study of mental life is a view of the wholeness or unity of the human psychic constitution that is occasionally disrupted only by the skeptical capability of the philosopher. His psychology itself, moreover, is pervaded throughout by a concern with the question of the adequacy of our faculties to our needs and our aspirations, a question that is posed in the terms of skeptical doubt; Hume's largely affirmative resolution of this question completes the naturalistic outlook that develops out of his empirical premises and unified view of human nature.

Hume's positive philosophy of naturalism, like Montaigne's and that of others in the skeptical tradition, culminates in a judgment affirming the general appropriateness of human nature to human needs and our legitimate purposes, modestly conceived though these may be. Hume's conviction of the adequacy of our faculties, in contrast to Locke's goal of the mastery of nature for human "convenience,"[58] is grounded in a more passive view of human adaptation to the environment and a more diffident sense of our proper role in the world. Nature overcomes the paralysis of extreme skepticism, permitting the

[57] Shaftesbury, "Soliloquy or Advice to an Author," Part 3, sec. 1, in *Characteristics of Men, Manners, Opinions, Times*, ed. John M. Robertson (Indianapolis: Bobbs Merrill, 1964), vol. 1, pp. 191-93.
[58] Locke, *Essay* II.xxiii.12.

philosopher like ordinary people to carry on in the daily affairs of life, restoring the normal balance between a speculative capacity to doubt and an instinctual propensity to believe and judge despite doubts. Philosophers find in themselves a rationally unjustifiable propensity toward certain beliefs, which nevertheless seem to serve well enough as a basis for their probabilistic reasoning about the world. This unaccountable fact leads Hume to his most teleological statement of the status of human beings in nature: "Here, then, is a kind of pre-established harmony between the course of nature and the succession of our ideas; and though the powers and forces, by which the former is governed, be wholly unknown to us; yet our thoughts and conceptions have still, we find, gone on in the same train with the other works of nature."[59] Though we cannot know, as we believe, that the future will resemble the past, the fact that our experience has been uniform in key respects suggests that our belief, and the custom in which it is grounded, should be regarded and accepted as a reliable guide. The "subsistence of all human creatures" in fact seems to be due to a kind of beneficence in nature, which has met our most fundamental needs with instinctual responses that, being involuntary, are "infallible" in their operation. Practical experience rather than logic provides all the justification that is necessary for the "sentiments" or "propensities" underlying our reasoning about causes and effects;[60] might not the same hold true for other aspects of our imaginative and affective nature?

Hume's naturalism is completed when he passes from the epistemological introduction to the moral philosophy that is constructed upon it, in which the psychological doctrines of the first two books of the *Treatise* provide not only a basis for an analysis of moral judgment and motivation but also a generally satisfactory underpinning for ethical practices and political institutions. Hume's ethical theory is his primary concern—"a subject that interests us above all others" (T. 455); and the subject of morals is one that, in his view, can be treated adequately only from the perspective of the unified conception of human nature that it has been his aim to present. The opening section of Book III, "Of Morals," recapitulates the central

---

[59] Hume, *Enquiries* (I), pp. 54-55. Although he appeals in this passage to the "wisdom of nature," Hume ironically dismisses the concept of final causes, as he does more systematically in the *Treatise*, p. 171. The harmony or wisdom of nature remains mysterious.

[60] A. J. Ayer emphasizes the pragmatic quality of Hume's justification of induction; *Language, Truth, and Logic* (Harmondsworth: Penguin, 1971), p. 74. See also Noxon, *Hume's Philosophical Development*, p. 159.

positions of Hume's philosophy of the mind and the passions and offers a sustained argument against those philosophers who, postulating a marked dichotomy in human nature, assert "that virtue is nothing but a conformity to reason." Hume reaffirms his contention that reason, which has to do with the "discovery of truth or falsehood," pertains only to the discovery of certain relations among ideas. Morality on the other hand is a topic that pertains to the practical side of life, its conclusions being such as to "excite passions, and produce or prevent actions" (T. 456-58), and thus it cannot be within the exclusive province of reason. Later we shall look more closely at Hume's account of the faculty of moral judgment, which he finds to be located, like belief in general, in the sphere of "feeling" that underlies and cooperates with the rational faculties. Here it should be noted that this introduction to moral theory recalls an earlier—and famous—passage that contains Hume's best-known affirmation regarding naturalism as a normative position.

In the course of his analysis of the passions Hume calls into question the favorite philosophical commonplace regarding the "combat of passion and reason" and the "suppos'd pre-eminence" of the latter above the former as a circumstance conducive to virtue. Hume's intention is not so much to reverse the priority as to deny the appropriateness of "combat" as a description of the usual relation between these two facets of our nature. With respect to volition, to be sure, reason must be regarded in the final analysis as subordinate, since the impulse that constitutes the will arises directly from an "emotion of aversion or propensity [by which we] are carry'd to avoid or embrace what will give us . . . uneasiness or satisfaction." The fact of this gulf between reasoning, whose "proper province is the world of ideas," and motivation to action, whose immediate source lies in the passions, leads Hume to make his well-known though perhaps overstated claim that "Reason is, and ought only to be the slave of the passions, and can never pretend to any other office than to serve and obey them" (T. 413-15). This statement occurs in a discussion of the nature of the will, and it does not imply that reasoning always takes place under the influence of desire or any other passion. It does, however, express vividly Hume's characteristic emphasis on the primacy of the nonrational elements in human nature, specifically indicating the role of the passions as the final determinant of choice and will in practical life, including the sphere of moral judgment. It might also be taken, furthermore, consistently with Hume's philosophy of mind as a whole, to signify the general dependence of all reason ultimately on "sentiments" or "propensities" that are, like the passions, irreducible elements of our nature.

Interpreted in the context of the *Treatise* as a whole, however, the subordination of reason to the passions ought not to be exaggerated: interaction would be a more accurate description of their normal relation, which Hume portrays as mutually supportive. Just as imaginative factors supplement the bare comparison of ideas in thought, so reason plays a role that can be significant in the direction of the will: the passions of desire or aversion arise from the "prospect" we have of the pleasure or pain associated with a given object; and this prospect, being an idea, is generated or modified by chains of reasoning about the objects involved—a fact that leads Hume to assert that an impulse to action may be "directed" by reason even though it does not immediately "arise" from it (T. 414). Thus in judgment and in action, just as less obviously in reasoning itself, there is reciprocity and cooperation between rational and affective factors, a wholeness in human nature that dictates the necessity of considering all its various attributes together as a basis on which to reach an understanding of the more controversial issues of morals and politics.

The most striking thing about this passage, however, is of course not the statement that reason "is" but the additional assessment that it "ought only to be" at the service of the passions. This rare example of normative language in the midst of Hume's "science" of the passions and motivation has attracted much attention, in part because it has been taken to be a logically unwarranted intrusion. But more positively it may be interpreted and emphasized as the clearest revelation of a major theme of his philosophy as a whole.

Criticism has started from the ironic fact that it is Hume himself, in another section of the *Treatise*, who gives the classic statement of the often-repeated argument that propositions containing "ought" can never properly be "deduced" from propositions containing only "is." Criticizing theories that contend that morality consists in certain rationally perceptible relations, Hume argues that the new term "ought" in ethical statements signifies a "new relation or affirmation" for which new reasons must be given beyond the statements of fact that they may follow, an argument that leads directly to his discussion of the "moral sense" (or certain distinctive moral sentiments) as the faculty responsible for the transition (T. 469-70). Those who have interpreted this widely influential argument to signify a radical dichotomy between factual and normative statements, and who understand a tacit "therefore" in the "slave" passage, have regarded Hume as breaking his own rule and as having committed what in ethics has been called the "naturalistic fallacy" of elevating a fact directly into a value without justifying the special status of the latter.

Hume may be defended, on the other hand, in various ways—on the grounds that he is simply making the logical point that factual propositions can never strictly "entail" normative ones and that he did not mean that facts cannot be relevant to, and constitute at least part of the grounds for, moral judgments; and that the "ought" part of the passage in question is not intended to follow logically from the fact of the subordination of reason but constitutes an additional as-sertion partly based on the first but logically independent of it and adding a substantial new dimension to the analysis.[61] It is most cer-tainly not Hume's intention, moreover, as a kind of precursor of Weber, to assert that a special gulf exists between "fact" and "value." In Hume's philosophy, as we have seen, all perceptions are separable, and connections among our ideas are supplied, in all crucial instances, by the imagination rather than by reason. The most important general point of Book I of the *Treatise* is that inductive inferences cannot be *logically* justified—that is, that a new proposition of *fact* cannot be "deduced" from other propositions containing "is" or "was." Yet we make such inferences, as we must, and Hume certifies the assurance we feel in so doing as arising from a perfectly legitimate, "natural" faculty of belief. There is no special reason why an analogous faculty of assent should not validate transitions from "is" to "ought," and, as we shall see, this turns out to be the case in Hume's ethical theory: the "fact" of utility underlies the quality of goodness or rightness in an act or state of affairs that the observer ascribes to it on the basis of a feeling of approval, just as the observer brings the feeling of necessity to a causal sequence. This parallelism between the logical and the ethical parts of Hume's philosophy constitutes its main overall unity. In both cases the conclusion is naturalistic: human nature pro-vides the bridge between received impressions and judgment, and the philosopher, noting how nature compensates for the default of logical necessity, finds these mental transitions to be justifiable for all practical purposes.[62]

[61] A. C. MacIntyre, "Hume on 'Is' and 'Ought'," in *Critical Essays*, ed. Chappell, pp. 240-64, argues that the facts of human needs, desires, and wants form a necessary bridge between "is" and "ought" in Hume's as in Aristotle's and indeed in any sub-stantive doctrine of ethics having reference to human happiness. Thus, although he denies logical entailment, Hume may be held to have admitted the validity of a peculiar form of inference from facts to values. Cf. also J. Kemp, *Ethical Naturalism: Hobbes and Hume* (London: Macmillan, 1970), p. 46.

[62] Cf. Lewis White Beck, " 'Was-Must Be' and 'Is-Ought' in Hume," *Philosophical Studies* 26 (1974): 211-28.

Although Hume's skepticism questions the rational basis of putative connections among things of all sorts, his positive philosophy recognizes in the unity of human nature—of the passions and reason—the appropriate basis not only for judgments and action but also for thought (causal reasoning) itself. This solution to the skeptical dilemma rests on Hume's express approval of the observed relation between reason and the passions: the "slave" passage thus expresses, epigrammatically, a normative position that grows out of his science of human nature and, interpreted broadly, is central to his philosophy as a whole. Hume's adoption of this position, the reasons for which will become clearer when we turn to his moral philosophy, constitutes the essence of his naturalism. Hume's science of human nature, which is in its early stages compelled to recognize the close connections between reason and feeling, culminates in an acknowledgment of the propriety of its normal manifestations. Hume's doctrine regarding human nature not only provides a basis for a science of moral phenomena but serves as a foundation—and is acknowledged to be a proper and adequate foundation—for a normative moral theory as well.

This completes our survey of the epistemological foundations of Hume's skepticism, the ensuing skeptical crisis, and the naturalistic resolution of his doubts in which he both determines to proceed with his projected science of human nature, with special attention to what he recognizes as its inescapable though nonrational features, and accepts this nature at least tentatively as a guide for living, as the only apparent alternative to the debilitating skepticism he experiences in the solitude of speculation. It is important that the skeptical crisis comes where it does in the *Treatise*, following the initial investigations of our presumed knowledge of the external world and of the causal regularity that unites the objects of our awareness but preceding the later books of psychological and ethical theory that Hume proceeds to construct on assumptions that are grounded only in belief. Naturalism is an appropriate characterization of the ensuing positive philosophy, but it must be remembered that the skepticism thus tentatively overcome in the pursuit of science and an acceptance of nature is never wholly eclipsed. Though nature is the agency that compensates for the deficiency apparent in reason alone, the naturalistic cure must be regarded as provisional. Hume's final position is that skepticism should be maintained, not only in philosophy but "in all the incidents of life"—a skepticism that is only "mitigated," and not replaced, by naturalism.

CHAPTER III

Hume's Science of Human Nature

1. The Study of Human Nature

Thomas Reid, an influential opponent of Hume's skepticism, found it
ironic that Hume should promise a new science, when "the intention
of the whole work is to shew, that there is neither human nature nor
science in the world."[1] The prospect of a philosopher who apparently
denied the necessity of causes and the reality of the material world
making any positive contributions to the study of human affairs appeared paradoxical to those for whom Hume's philosophy was simply
the modern epitome of skepticism. This view, however, misunder-
stands or overlooks important features of Hume's work.

In the first place, although a certain mitigated skepticism pervades
Hume's investigations, the extreme Pyrrhonist skepticism that disturbed readers like Reid is only a moment in the whole. The skeptical
crisis at the close of Book I of the *Treatise* never manifests itself again
as a genuine problem, and it is resolved in ways that permit Hume to
view the matters considered in the succeeding books in a new and
fruitful perspective. The import of the skeptical doubts is that reason
alone is insufficient to provide justification for our fundamental beliefs,
and that therefore the philosopher must range more widely over the
whole of human nature. This suggests that the scientist of human
nature would do well to pay close attention to the nonrational foundations of thought and belief. The weaknesses of reason, however, do
not render it an entirely useless instrument, nor does the clarification
of the nature of belief result in its complete suspension. Such constructive assumptions as the causal regularity of nature and the stability
of objects may at least be provisionally accepted as the basis for scientific observation and prediction, even if they are acknowledged to
rest ultimately on such factors as habit and imagination. It is in this
spirit that Hume passes from his "solution" of the skeptical doubts
to other areas of inquiry, and the reader of Books II and III of the

[1] Thomas Reid, *An Inquiry into the Human Mind*, chap. 1, sec. 5, in *The Works of
Thomas Reid*, ed. Sir William Hamilton (Edinburgh: MacLachlan and Stewart, 1863),
vol. 1, p. 102.

Treatise discovers that the intellectual despair of the Pyrrhonist moment is successfully overcome.

A second point concerns what may be inferred to have been Hume's intellectual growth.[2] The exuberant talk of "a compleat system of the sciences, built on a foundation almost entirely new" (T. xx) is found in the Introduction to the *Treatise*, Hume's earliest work. These ambitious claims are not repeated in the *Enquiry*, and Hume's references to the possibility of political science in his later essays are generally tempered with cautious disclaimers. It is plausible to suppose Hume to have happened upon the logical difficulties that gave rise to his skepticism in the course of his investigation of the mind, which he had intended to serve as the basis for what was to be principally a science of morals. These doubts temporarily obstructed his projected plan of study, and even after they were resolved the skepticism persisted in mitigated form as an underpinning and as a limiting framework for the subsequent investigations, which were not, however, without substantial positive results.

Since Reid's response is, however, a natural one to the Humean combination of skepticism and science, it may be well to suggest at the outset some of the residual aspects of the skeptical analysis as they pertain to the scientific enterprise. Hume finds that the general causal maxim is merely a matter of deep belief, and that specific causal arguments, the probability of whose truth varies with the extent and uniformity of the experience on which they are based, depend on this belief. If we assume the truth of the general maxim, as any scientist does, causality may be cautiously ascribed to those relations (and only to them) in which uniform sequence has been observed in a number of similar cases, the "probability" of the argument increasing with the frequency of similar (and the scarcity of dissimilar) observations. But although causal judgments may legitimately be made in the case of such sequences, it must always be remembered that in no way can the nature of the causal relation itself be perceived or understood, or indeed "explained" in any sense other than description in terms of lawful or regular behavior. Anything can conceivably cause anything, and no one can legitimately claim the sort of insight that would permit identification of causes (or effects) in the absence of carefully registered

[2] There is virtually no evidence on the composition of the *Treatise*. Kemp Smith's effort to show that Hume wrote Book II before Book I is compatible with the view suggested here that Hume's discovery of the skeptical difficulties occurred in the course of a scientific enterprise whose ambitions were gradually reduced. See also James Noxon, *Hume's Philosophical Development* (Oxford: Clarendon Press, 1973), on the waning of Hume's early rationalist or scientific ambitions.

experience. Similar criteria may be formulated for the correct identification of objects that are taken to have real existence independent of the observer. Hume's epistemological preliminaries indicate the essentially skeptical basis for the scientific outlook that has in general received the name of positivism.[3]

These Humean contributions to scientific methodology appear in a stronger light when they are applied to the moral rather than to the natural sciences. In his discussions of causation Hume generally speaks as if he were considering a relation supposed to exist between physical objects; but the problematic status of the causal nexus and the methodological rigor that Hume urges must attend the correct ascription of causality appear more vividly in the case of the social or political sciences, for example, than in physics. Hume's original perceptualist premises, and his subsequent account of reasoning with respect to "matters of fact and existence," make no provision for any distinction between these two kinds of science: the phenomena of human conduct are, for the purposes of reasoning about them, "matters of fact" of the same sort as any other. But do we actually believe in universal and regular causality as strongly and in the same sense in the realm of moral as of physical events? Hume does not raise the question whether the "natural belief" that the future will resemble the past (on which all inductive inferences depend) extends to the mental and social in addition to the material world, and yet such a belief (which rests, in part, on a conviction of uniformity in human nature and motives) is requisite to support a social science analogous in form and credibility to the natural sciences. Similarly it appears that the problems regarding the existence and identification of the moral and social "objects" among which we are to seek causal relations pose difficulties that are far from trivial. Thus all Hume's skeptical analyses take on new significance when considered in the light of a projected moral and social science; and the propensity for belief that easily overcomes doubts with regard to the regularity of the course of physical nature would seem to be a somewhat more tenuous source of support in the world of moral phenomena.

Hume's proposed science of human nature is a science of "moral topics"—of mental life, of behavior both individual and social, and

---

[3] In associating the term "positivism" with Hume, and in using it to denote the prevalent outlook of modern science, I follow Alfred North Whitehead, *Adventures of Ideas* (New York: Macmillan, 1954), p. 160. That modern (logical) positivists have, focusing exclusively on a limited number of his doctrines, recognized Hume as a precursor by no means implies, however, that this term is *generally* adequate as a label for Hume's philosophy.

of the workings of moral and political institutions—and it is with regard to this project that we must consider the skeptical provisos that emerge from his epistemology. To proceed with such a science, one must take the assumption of uniformity (or determinism) in moral affairs as a working hypothesis—or as a mental "convention," rigidly adhered to;[4] and one must understand causality in the same way as in natural science, as carefully observed sequential regularity, rigorously resisting the temptation, more frequent here no doubt than in physics, of claiming to apprehend causal relations in the absence of such observation. In view of the complexity and apparent variability of moral and political life one may suspect that fewer if any "proofs" will be forthcoming, and that in this field a science will have to be one exclusively of "probabilities" based on cautious appraisals of conflicting or inadequate evidence. The tentativeness of all such probable conclusions, furthermore, might well remain a matter of conviction rather than a mere logical tenet.

Even amid the confidence of his Introduction Hume hints at these difficulties. Since we cannot know the "ultimate original qualities" of human nature any more than we have direct insight into the relations of things generally, we must restrict our conclusions to those drawn from experience—from "careful and exact experiments, and the observation of those particular effects, which result from its different circumstances and situations" (T. xxi). A "peculiar disadvantage" that attends moral in contrast to natural philosophy, moreover, is the fact that purposive experiments often cannot be made, both because of the nature of the phenomena being studied and because of the intrusion of the observer, whose preconceptions and aims would preclude the formation of any "just conclusion" (T. xxii-xxiii). The difficulty of contriving experiments presents a formidable obstacle to the scientist who is committed to the view that only carefully registered regularities can provide grounds for conclusions about causality, although this difficulty does not, in Hume's view, constitute any difference in principle between natural and moral science. In lieu of planned experiments Hume acknowledges that he must undertake "a cautious observation of human life" (T. xxiii)[5] as he encounters it in various contexts, a procedure that in practice means a heavy reliance on introspection for

[4] A. J. Ayer, *Hume* (New York: Hill and Wang, 1980), pp. 75-76, refers to Hume's determinism in his moral science as a "convention"—one that I argue is analogous in the theoretical sphere to the artifices that Hume analyzes and recommends adherence to in his ethics.

[5] Hume does not distingush between experiments and observation, both of which are included in his "experimental method."

his psychological and moral investigations and on history for his political science.

Although within these recognized limits there seems to be no reason to doubt that substantial achievements can be made, the methodological guidelines that arise from Hume's analysis of the mind serve generally to reduce the claims and confidence that were associated with science in his time.[6] It is true that by clarifying the nature of scientific knowledge, skeptics like Hume have typically sharpened the focus of scientific investigation even while reducing its scope. It may also be said that Hume's recognition of the force and scope of non-rational factors in the mind, although it raises salutary doubts about the potentialities of reason, is not at all incompatible with a properly conducted scientific enterprise;[7] indeed, by identifying such nonrational factors as an important object of systematic study, it may, as in Hume's own case, have the effect of furthering the discipline of psychology and the social sciences based on discoveries in this field. Hume wishes merely to urge caution and the appropriateness of a skeptical outlook in the face of a scientific spirit that in his view is too often prone to exaggerate its claims and become enthralled in the "chimerical systems" that have characterized philosophers in all times and places (T. 273). He pursues his researches, unlike some of his contemporaries, with both lessened ambitions and modesty in the face of the unsatisfactory record of scientific endeavors in the past.[8]

With these considerations, Hume leaves the negative aspect of his skepticism in abeyance, and, drawing on his previous analysis of causal reasoning, he proceeds to affirm the possibility of a scientific approach to "moral topics." There are three famous arguments in his philosophy that reveal that Hume, in his role as a scientist as well as in the ordinary affairs of life, firmly adopts and adheres to the belief—whose truth he contends cannot be demonstrated—that the future will resemble

[6] Hume was not alone in his effort to apply the Newtonian or "experimental" method to moral affairs. He was unique mainly in the restricted nature of the conclusions to which it led him. Careful observation of the world led others, including Newton himself, not only to the discovery of laws of nature but also to the conviction of design and proofs of a beneficent Creator. See Duncan Forbes, *Hume's Philosophical Politics* (Cambridge: Cambridge University Press, 1975), chap. 1.

[7] Cf. Victor Brochard, *Les Sceptiques Grecs* (Paris: Imprimerie Nationale, 1887), pp. 375-79.

[8] Thus I would question the emphasis of Thomas H. Huxley, *Hume* (New York: Appleton, 1897), pp. 66-70, who welcomes Hume as a prophet of modern science; and Peter Gay, *The Enlightenment: An Interpretation*, vol. 2: *The Science of Freedom* (New York: Knopf, 1969), p. 334, who assimilates Hume to the prevailing scientific optimism of the eighteenth century.

the past and that the course of nature continues uniformly the same. The essay on miracles in the first *Enquiry*, in addition to its subtle treatment of religious faith, concerns Hume's deliberate adoption of the scientific point of view, with its necessary supposition of regular causality together with methodological exclusion of allegations to the contrary and systematic distrust of reports of extraordinary events. Equally striking as a revelation of the scientific Hume is his assertion "that what the vulgar call chance is nothing but a secret and conceal'd cause" (T. 130). Philosophers, he says, must rigorously assume that every event has a cause and that causal relations are absolutely uniform. When faced with apparent irregularities, as when a medicine fails to produce its usual effect, or with seemingly "chance" events, philosophers retain their belief in causality: "chance" becomes a term applied to situations in which the putatively operative causal ties are too complex to permit accurate prediction of particular cases, although sustained observation may even in such cases yield probabilistic statements based on the weighing of opposite "chances," a procedure that presupposes the regularity of presumed though not specifiable causes.[9] Everyone has a natural propensity to believe in the necessity of some kinds of causes, corresponding to the more conspicuous uniformities in experience: no one doubts that the sun will rise tomorrow, or that everyone will die. The philosopher universalizes this principle, rigorously assuming the existence of causes and regularities even where none are obvious, and where the "vulgar" may resort to loose talk of "chance" and "miracles"—exceptions to the usual rule of uniformity. Hume in this manner identifies himself with the philosophers in contrast to the vulgar, deliberately taking up the standpoint of the scientist with its frequently critical attitude toward common opinion.

In the sphere of human affairs, however, Hume finds that assumptions and methods acceptable in the physical sciences are controversial for reasons other than the complexity and the obstacles to experimentation that are presented by moral and social phenomena. Hume defends the possibility of a science of human behavior chiefly in sections of the *Treatise* and *Enquiry* entitled "Of Liberty and Necessity," where he argues that the philosopher "must apply the same reasonings [that are appropriate in physical science] to the actions and volitions of intelligent agents."[10] All human behavior and action, from the operations of the individual mind to the complex events of social and political life that can be observed or recalled from history—all of these

---

[9] Hume, *Enquiries* (I), sec. 6; *Treatise* I.iii.11, pp. 124-30.
[10] Hume, *Enquiries* (I), p. 88.

display sufficient regularity that the scientist may reasonably make the same assumption of universal causality and necessity that is made in physics and proceed on the same basis to the collection of data, the inductive reasoning, and the formulation of probable generalizations that will constitute a science of human nature. Only on such a view, at any rate, is any philosophical comprehension of human affairs possible.

The immediate stumbling block in the way of this scientific approach was the doctrine of free will that had traditionally been juxtaposed, and widely defended, against the deterministic notion of "necessity" governing voluntary actions. Hume argues that if the "necessity" posited by the application of the concept of causation to human actions is understood correctly, as either "the constant conjunction of like objects, or . . . the inference of the understanding from one object to another,"[11] then, he asserts, all people have always demonstrated by their thought and behavior that they take for granted the existence of necessity in human as much as in physical events. The confusion surrounding this dispute arises from the erroneous opposition of the term "liberty" to necessity as the latter idea is understood in Hume's analysis. Hume accordingly distinguishes the "liberty of spontaneity," or the freedom to act in accordance with one's will without external coercion or constraint, and the "liberty of indifference," or the capacity to perform acts that are free of causal determination. The first of these sorts of liberty, which Hume contends the defenders of human liberty ought to be concerned with advocating, is perfectly compatible with universal causation; indeed, the regular determination of actions by the will, and of the will by other factors of character and circumstance, is one important aspect of the causal uniformity on which a science of human nature would be founded. It is only the liberty of indifference—the conceivable possibility of performing an act wholly unconnected in a perceptible and regular way with antecedent circumstances—that Hume rejects (T. 407).[12]

Those who have upheld liberty in the sense of the agent's freedom

[11] Ibid., p. 97.

[12] Hume does not go into the questions raised by what he calls the "liberty of spontaneity." In the *Treatise* he calls it that liberty "which is opposed to violence," and in the *Enquiry* he suggests that it is "universally allowed to belong to every one who is not a prisoner and in chains"; *Enquiries* (I), p. 95. Hume thus implies that only physical coercion interferes with this kind of ("negative") liberty. He does not raise such troublesome questions as whether a poor person is less free than a rich one or a mentally ill person less free than a healthy one, nor does he distinguish between actions for which the agents have reasons and those (such as impulsive or habitual actions) for which they do not.

to choose courses of action independently of precedent circumstances have, according to Hume, misunderstood the nature of causal connections. Assuming that necessity is a perceptible relation among objects, and failing to "feel" any such constraint in the exercise of their own faculty of choice, they have concluded that they are free (not determined) in their actions. Causal necessity, however, is (as Hume has shown) nothing more than the mind's tendency to make convincing inferences from one object to another on the basis of observed regularities; and so necessity in the moral sphere refers simply to the correct inferences and predictions that we can (or could, with sufficient information) make on the basis of experience from observable circumstances or from the known character of agents to their opinions and behavior. The thesis of necessity or causality rests on the same footing in the human as in the physical world: it refers to the observation of uniform sequences among the objects of our awareness and the habitual propensity by which we generalize from and accord belief to these regularities with sufficient force that they serve as the basis of our own expectations and behavior. "The necessity of any action, whether of matter or of mind, is not, properly speaking, a quality in the agent, but in any thinking or intelligent being, who may consider the action."[13] Thus from the point of view of reasoning about human affairs, it is beside the point that agents may experience choice or freedom from constraint in their actions. The necessity of the actions consists only in the fact that a "spectator"—and especially the scientist of human nature—may "commonly infer our actions from our motives and character" (T. 408); and the scientist proceeds on the assumption that this is always possible in principle. The epistemological foundation of the social sciences is therefore identical with that of the natural sciences, both disciplines conceived as seeking to identify the causes of events through the careful observation of regularities among perceived objects, without any claim to penetrate more deeply into the nature of necessity than the recognition of the psychological facts of habit and belief that make all reasoning possible (T. 171).

Hume's analysis of causation, with its rejection of "insight" (T. 400), permits at least the possibility of a social science; whether such a project is practicable depends on the extent and the significance of the specific regularities that careful observers of human affairs are actually able to discover and on the adequacy of their observational techniques to the kinds of information and the degrees of probability they hope to achieve. Hume, who regarded himself as only a pioneer

[13] Hume, *Enquiries* (I), p. 94n.

in this venture, went on to formulate a number of experimental hypotheses in the fields of psychology, morals, and politics, some of which we shall examine in due course. As a prior step, however, he presents some arguments in favor of the prima facie credibility of his enterprise through appeals to common-sense notions of the uniformity of human life. Hume's most general contention in this respect is that all of us, throughout our lives, proceed on an assumption of uniformity in human affairs that probably equals that which we expect to find in (nonhuman) nature. Our conviction regarding the value of the "experience, acquired by long life and a variety of business and company, in order to instruct us in the principles of human nature, and regulate our future conduct,"[14] rests on the supposition that social experience reveals uniformities and makes possible adequate inferences about human behavior. Social intercourse of any sort involves continuous, barely conscious expectations regarding the opinions and actions of others, expectations that we usually find to be justified in practice. Our tendency to accept the testimony of other people, the source from which most of our opinions are derived, depends on our experience of certain regularities—both truthfulness and consistent patterns of deviation from truthfulness—in the reports we receive. Our belief in the efficacy of rewards and punishments reflects our application of causal reasoning to human motivation. The more deliberate reasoning that enters into all the calculations and decisions of political and economic life simply replicates in a more careful way the inferential habits of everyday life. The concept of "necessity" conceived in this manner "indeed mixes itself so entirely in human life, that 'tis impossible to act or subsist a moment without having recourse to it" (T. 405).[15]

Although we undeniably engage in such reasoning in the ordinary course of our lives, however, it is also true that we often meet with much that strikes us as new or unexpected in our relations with other people. The diversity and unpredictability of particular cases, however, ought not to discourage the social scientist any more than it does the physicist. The continual variations in the weather do not lead us to doubt the regularity of the laws of physics, even though their opera-

---

[14] Ibid., p. 84.

[15] Hume argues that the doctrine of necessity is in fact essential to a common type of moral judgment: we blame a person less for an evil act performed "hastily and unpremeditately" because we assume that it does not reflect a vicious or dangerous character, an assumption that rests on our conviction of regular patterns of motivation and continuity of character in individuals (T. 412).

tions in particular cases are not always "easily discoverable";[16] and in the same way the differences we encounter in the character and behavior of individuals need not prevent us from formulating generalizations about human beings or about classes of people that are as useful as those achieved in the various branches of natural science. Hume's philosophy seeks to "account for a few of the greater and more sensible events" of human experience, leaving aside the endless variability of particulars as "dependent on principles too fine and minute for her comprehension" (T. 438). But in elucidating general patterns such a science can hope to achieve the precision characteristic of explanations of natural phenomena of comparable complexity and experimental difficulty.

Regular causation in human behavior is not the only assumption that must be made by the aspiring scientist of human nature. The operative principles of human nature must in addition prove, like those of Newtonian physics, to be both few and simple if they are to be susceptible of scientific comprehension (T. 282). In the association of ideas Hume hoped he had found the Newtonian "attraction" that would economically explain a great range of mental phenomena, and subsequently in his moral philosophy he expresses the hope that a large variety of moral duties can be traced to a small number of "original instincts" or motivational principles, appealing to the same maxim of the economy of nature (T. 473).[17]

This extension of a concept of physics into the psychological and moral sciences would appear to be a condition of the development of the latter along the same lines as the former, which was Hume's hope in the *Treatise*. Unlike causal regularity, however, which is a necessary assumption for inductive reasoning, the maxim of simplicity appears to be simply a hope or hypothesis whose status must await the conclusions of research. There is a risk, however, that such preliminary hypotheses may distort the observations or bias the selection of evidence that is intended to test them, and it is possible that Hume, in the Newtonian enthusiasm of the *Treatise*, may be guilty of methodological indiscretions of this sort.[18] The model provided by physics quickly occupies the opening provided by Hume's provisional sus-

[16] Hume, *Enquiries* (I), p. 88.

[17] The principle of natural parsimony or economy of causes is Newton's first rule of reasoning in philosophy, found in his *Principia*, Book III. Hume refers to it in the *Treatise*, p. xxi, and in the *Enquiries* (II), p. 204. For its importance in his political philosophy, see Forbes, *Hume's Philosophical Politics*, pp. 83-86.

[18] Reid, *Inquiry*, in *Works*, vol. 1, p. 103; Reid was one of Hume's first serious critics in this as in other respects.

pension of his skeptical doubts, and many of the positive doctrines of the *Treatise* (especially in Book II) display both a mechanistic simplicity and an air of certainty that seem odd for a skeptic, even when their tentative and empirical status is clear.

This positivity occasionally leads Hume to adopt a methodological incredulity that seems almost contradictory in view of his logical tenets as well as detrimental to his doctrine. Uniformity in the course of nature (including human nature) and the resemblance of the future to the past are as much conditions—or necessary hypotheses—in the human as in the natural sciences; and only such uniformity as is manifest in relatively simple causal relations is amenable to scientific comprehension. Apparent irregularities must therefore be disregarded as illusory when they cannot be accounted for in terms of causal laws that are compatible with the whole system of such laws; or else the system as a whole must be modified so as to account for the discrepancies. The economy of the scientific enterprise as a whole, however, dictates that the scientist's attention be oriented in the first instance to those phenomena and relations that seem most significant because most general; and in order to pursue inquiries into these objects without distraction the scientist must disregard or even reject as incredible alleged particular evidence that appears to be at variance with the usual course of his observations. Accordingly we find Hume advancing the following argument:

> Should a traveller, returning from a far country, bring us an account of men, wholly different from any with whom we were ever acquainted; men, who were entirely divested of avarice, ambition, or revenge; who know no pleasure but friendship, generosity, and public spirit; we should immediately, from these circumstances, detect the falsehood, and prove him a liar, with the same certainty as if he had stuffed his narration with stories of centaurs and dragons, miracles and prodigies. And if we would explode any forgery in history, we cannot make use of a more convincing argument, than to prove, that the actions ascribed to any person are directly contrary to the course of nature, and that no human motives, in such circumstances, could ever induce him to such conduct.[19]

The scientist infers a "course of nature" in human motives from a certain number of observations and thenceforth is no more willing here than he would be in physics to admit testimony of "miracles," although strict adherence to Hume's epistemological principles should

[19] Hume, *Enquiries* (I), p. 84.

dictate that discrepant reports be considered as possible disconfirmations of previously formulated laws and never rejected out of hand.[20]

Hume's position in this passage may seem surprising for a skeptic until we remember that he has resolutely put aside his skeptical doubts and adopted the point of view of the scientist. The question is rather whether or not such a methodological program is the most appropriate one for an inquiry into the complex fields of moral and political life. Although it is true that there could be no science of human nature at all if there were no regular relations to be ascertained, it is nonetheless arguable that the scientist would be more prudent to maintain a higher degree of sensitivity to diversities and discordant data than Hume sometimes seems prepared to do. Hume's systematic discounting of the testimony of religious enthusiasts, from a distrust of their motives, is well known from his essay on miracles; and this principle leads to plausible results in historical research, as in his skeptical account of Joan of Arc, where an admittedly "marvellous" event is ascribed as much as possible to ordinary (that is, mundane and nonmiraculous) motives.[21] Likewise, Hume's incredulity regarding the genuineness of the extraordinary poems of Ossian was vindicated in the event, which led him to reflect that testimony associated with "national Prejudices" should also be systematically mistrusted.[22]

Apparently successful applications of Hume's method, however, do not entirely obviate the potential dangers for the student of human affairs in neglecting or rejecting the unusual. Hume can scarcely bring himself to believe that Sparta, as described in the ancient literature, actually existed;[23] and the self-imposed strictures that he says would lead him to discredit reports of people "exactly of the same character with those in *Plato's Republic* on the one hand, or those in *Hobbes's Leviathan* on the other" (T. 402) may possibly impede his appreciation

[20] A. E. Taylor, "David Hume and the Miraculous," in his *Philosophical Studies* (London: Macmillan, 1934).

[21] Hume, *History of England*, chap. 20, vol. 2, p. 389.

[22] Hume, "Of the Authenticity of the Poems of Ossian," *Works*, vol. 4, pp. 415-24; and letters of 19 September 1763, to the Rev. Hugh Blair, and 18 March 1776, to Edward Gibbon, in *The Letters of David Hume*, ed. J.Y.T. Greig (Oxford: Clarendon Press, 1932), vol. 1, pp. 398-99; vol. 2, pp. 310-11. See also Ernest Campbell Mossner, *The Life of David Hume* (Austin: University of Texas Press, 1954), pp. 414-17, and *The Forgotten Hume: Le Bon David* (New York: Columbia University Press, 1943), pp. 89ff., for accounts of the Ossian episode.

[23] Hume, "Of Commerce," *Works*, vol. 3, p. 291. Cf. Rousseau's remark, of his adversaries: "Que ne donneroient-ils point pour que cette fatale Sparte n'eût jamais existé?" *Oeuvres Complètes*, ed. Bernard Gagnebin and Marcel Raymond. Bibliothèque de la Pleiade (Paris: Gallimard, 1964), vol. 4, p. 83.

of a range of phenomena of some significance in the field of politics. Hume is therefore vulnerable to criticism for overconcentration on what he takes to be the most normal or usual patterns in moral life to the neglect of events and potentialities that in history are most interesting precisely because they are out of the ordinary. Our suspicions, in any case, are certainly aroused by Hume's suggestion that we can understand the life of the ancient Greeks and Romans by studying the modern English and French: "Mankind are so much the same, in all times and places, that history informs us of nothing new or strange in this particular. Its chief use is only to discover the constant and universal principles of human nature, by showing men in all varieties of circumstances and situations, and furnishing us with materials from which we may form our observations and become acquainted with the regular springs of human action and behaviour."[24] The question does not concern the factual truth of this view but its usefulness as a methodological maxim for the social scientist. Although an assumption of some degree of uniformity (at some level) in his subject matter is necessary for any scientist, Hume's science of human nature may be said to bear the marks of his restriction of attention exclusively to what appeared to him to be central and usual in experience, to those fundamental respects in which both individuals and societies manifest similar features rather than to the more noteworthy differences that may be observed to arise on the substratum of a common "human nature."

Hume's assumption of uniformities in human nature, and his confidence that the study of history would bear out this view, may be regarded as skeptical at least with respect to any speculative scheme of historical alteration in the characteristics of mankind. Repudiation of claims of insight of this sort was not particularly remarkable in the middle of the eighteenth century: the decisive challenges to the older degenerative view of the human condition had already been made, and the great "scientific" systems of historical development lay in the future. Hume's rejection of any "miraculous" changes—including prospective, revolutionary changes—in human affairs does, however, have important practical implications for his political philosophy, which will be examined in the final chapter. The variability in events, prac-

---

[24] Hume, *Enquiries* (I), p. 83. Forbes defends Hume against charges of being "unhistorical" and insensitive to cultural diversity, with comments on this passage; *Hume's Philosophical Politics*, pp. 115-19. See also S. K. Wertz, "Hume, History, and Human Nature," *Journal of the History of Ideas* 36 (1975): 481-96; and Christopher J. Berry, *Hume, Hegel and Human Nature* (The Hague: Martinus Nijhoff, 1982), chap. 4, on Hume's view of the constant principles of human nature.

tices, and institutions that Humean science considers must be accounted for in terms of patterns observed in experience alone; and in history as in physical nature, experience can be a meaningful cognitive and practical guide only on the assumption of its deeper underlying uniformity.

Thus Hume is able, notwithstanding his skeptical doubts, to resume the scientific study of human nature that had been his first ambition on the assumptions that he self-consciously adopts for the purposes of this enterprise. The doctrine that ensues is extensive and logically ordered: it begins with an individual psychology that is especially concerned with the operations of the imagination and the passions; the study of the individual gradually yields insights regarding the sources of social influence on the individual mind, an analysis of which contributes a collective dimension to the science; and the psychology leads naturally to a science of morals that includes both an inquiry into the motivation of moral judgments and an analysis of the kinds of ends sought and the reasons that enter into ethical justification. These various investigations together constitute the foundation on which Hume builds his political science, the culminating achievement of the system. Out of such a wide field I shall examine only certain topics, ones that appear to have special significance or implications for political science. In the remainder of this chapter I scrutinize several topics in Hume's psychology, bearing in mind that Hume, in making psychology the central discipline on which to base moral philosophy, was a leading practitioner of what in the eighteenth century was a common approach to an understanding of human affairs.

One might surmise that a political science arrived at in so systematic a fashion might be more detached or objective than one born, like so many of the great works of political philosophy, in the heat of controversy.[25] The extent to which this is true is a question that we must defer until we come later to consider Hume's more practical political views and the connection between these and the conclusions to which he is led by his more speculative scientific treatment of moral and political problems. The case of Hobbes, moreover, suggests that there is no clear dividing line between speculative and controversial origins of political works. Hume may be said to resemble Hobbes most among English philosophers in his systematic impulse and in his effort to place his political science in a general science of human nature; in this respect he resembles Hobbes more than Locke, for whom the philos-

[25] Cf. Robert McRae, "Hume as a Political Philosopher," *Journal of the History of Ideas* 12 (1951): 285-90.

ophy of the *Essay* notably does not culminate in a social science or a turning toward history. The importance of the continuities in Hume's epistemology, his ethics, and his political science underscores the differences between him and Locke in his treatment of the Lockeian issues of psychology and epistemology as well as in his more general orientation toward moral and political questions.

2. PRINCIPLES OF THE IMAGINATION

The imagination is Hume's comprehensive term for all the operations of the mind by which ideas are joined together into thought; it is the seat of all those dispositions or active principles in the mind with which he finds it necessary to supplement the theory of ideas as mere copies of sensory impressions in attempting to account for our thought and beliefs about the world.

Hume's first main interest in analyzing the imagination is the association of ideas, in terms of which he thought he could describe the usual way in which the mind unites ideas or passes from one to another in trains of thought. In the course of Book I of the *Treatise*, however, the focus of his attention shifts to the phenomenon of belief as the most interesting problem facing him. By what processes and criteria does the mind accord the status of truth (or probable truth) to some of the ideas, or inferences, to which it is led by the association of ideas while acknowledging others to be "fictions" or improbable in different degrees? The same operative components of the imagination serve in Hume's scheme to explain all the conclusions to which the mind is carried, whether believed or not, and whether or not they meet philosophical standards of valid inferential reasoning.

Hume's psychology is ostensibly an empirical discipline that attempts to describe all kinds of mental operations in terms of as economical a model as possible; but Hume as a philosopher of the logic of causal inference is also concerned to develop a standard for distinguishing scientifically valid from fallacious or "erroneous" reasonings that arise from similar and equally "natural" psychological processes. Hume's logical investigation reveals that the belief that generally attends, and ought to attend, causal inferences must be admitted to rest on a nonrational foundation. Such inferences are, in a sense, "mere beliefs," irreducible facts about our nature—or more precisely, facts of our imaginative faculty. It is, however, just such facts about our imagination that frequently lead us to what, from the scientific point of view, are erroneous beliefs, fanciful associations, and illogical convictions. Hume's skepticism culminates in an acknowledgment of the "imaginative" foundation of all thought, which, although fruitful for a comprehensive naturalistic psychology, results in a continual tension for the philosopher who, as scientist rather than skeptic, wishes as Hume does to preserve some standards of correct reasoning. It may be said by way of anticipation that the tension between scientific logic and psychology in this part of Hume's philosophy is analogous to that between his ethics and his moral psychology later, where he is concerned to point out what he takes to be correct grounds of moral judgment even while he surveys the whole range of actual moral beliefs and their psychological origins.

In studying the imagination Hume (like most of his contemporaries) directs his attention first to the mind of the individual taken in isolation. The inquiry comes in due course to recognize the impact of social factors in determining the contents of any individual's beliefs: Hume is appreciative of the fact, as we shall see when we examine the workings of custom, that the great bulk of anyone's beliefs is obtained not from one's own direct experience but from the testimony of others, and in other respects as well the individual in Hume's final analysis appears highly susceptible of social influence. The role of society, however, is explored subsequently to, and on the foundation of, the analysis of the individual mind, and I follow Hume in this order of presentation. It is in Hume's psychology, furthermore, that he is compelled to rely mainly on introspective evidence, no wider range of data being available in the way, for example, that history offers extensive materials for his political science. This methodological limitation compels Hume in his psychology more than elsewhere to make the assumption that all people are similar in the important relevant respects, and that the things he finds on reflection to be the case in himself can be generalized as features of human nature as such.

Hume's theory of the imagination begins, unfortunately, with certain ambiguities of terminology, partly traceable to inconsistencies in ordinary usage: sometimes, he says, imagination is opposed to memory, sometimes to the faculty of demonstrative and probable reasoning (T. 117-18n; cf. 265). Generally for Hume all mental processes except immediate perception (the direct apprehension of ideas and impressions) and memory are imaginative; the imagination is the faculty responsible for all the active processes by which ideas are combined in trains of thought, with the exception of their accurate recollection in the form and order in which their generative impressions were originally received. The distinction between imagination and memory, however, is not so clear in practice as in definition. The memory after all can err, deviating from the original order it is attempting to recall, and people (who cannot recover the original impressions for comparison) have no way of ascertaining when their memory is failing them, when they are in fact "imagining things" when they think they are remembering (T. 85). Hume also says that memories are distinguished from products of the imagination by their usually greater vividness, but this criterion is not definitive. The vividness of memories fades with time, and after a long period the individual may be in doubt as to whether he is remembering or imagining. Likewise "an idea of the imagination may acquire such a force and vivacity, as to pass for an idea of the memory, and counterfeit its effects on the belief and judgment" (T. 86). Noteworthy problems are posed, both in everyday life and in the special sphere of political argument, by the propensity of the imagination to acquire sufficient vividness to override or blend with memory: in his essays on political ideologies and in his *History* Hume is well aware of the common human inclination to idealize a remembered past, or to contrive (and then believe in) a fictional past, from which are then drawn motives for action or confused reasoning respecting the present or future.[26] This is an issue, however, that Hume does not develop in detail, although his psychology provides a framework for so doing.

In Hume's first introduction of the term, the imagination appears, in contrast to the memory, as the faculty of arranging ideas in the mind at liberty or of generating fictions. At first Hume seems to intend this characterization to correspond to the ordinary usage in which a fiction is an idea of something not found in experience; thus "fables" and "romances"—flights of fancy—are mentioned as typical products of the imagination (T. 10). But further reflection suggests that "fiction" here must be taken broadly to include the sense in which Hume later speaks of our concepts of object, causal connection, and self as fictions contributed by the imagination to the passively registered sequences of received impressions. In this way we arrive at the larger meaning of imagination to which Hume is led as a consequence of his analysis of our inferential faculties, in which it is regarded as the source of all our mental processes except immediate awareness and accurate memory. It is in this large sense that Hume discovers the imagination to be governed by certain principles of association, to which I shall turn later. All our thinking about the past (insofar as it goes beyond the bounds of our personal experience), all our thinking about the present

---

[26] James Noxon, "Remembering and Imagining the Past," in *Hume: A Re-evaluation*, ed. Donald W. Livingston and James T. King (New York: Fordham University Press, 1976), pp. 270-95. For criticisms of Hume on this issue see John Passmore, *Hume's Intentions* (London: Duckworth, 1980), pp. 93-97.

excluding our immediate impressions, and all our thinking about the future without exception—all this is the product of characteristic operations or tendencies that together make up the imagination.

The principal problem for Hume both as a scientist and as a philosopher interested in estimating the scope of human rationality is stated most clearly in the *Enquiry*: "Nothing is more free than the imagination of man; and though it cannot exceed that original stock of ideas furnished by the internal and external senses, it has unlimited power of mixing, compounding, separating, and dividing these ideas, in all the varieties of fiction and vision." Since the imagination, among these possibilities, can produce a false "appearance of reality" that may be deceptive, the question becomes: "Wherein, therefore, consists the difference between such a fiction and belief?"[27] Hume answers the factual question in terms of "vivacity" of conception, the special *feeling* that accompanies the ideas we take to represent reality in contrast to those we consciously entertain as fictional or hypothetical. But, since deception is a continual danger, the philosophical question remains concerning the criteria by which a given idea (or inference) generated in the imagination *ought* to be believed. Whereas the psychologist may simply identify the essence of belief with a sentiment, the philosopher— as one whose enterprise among other things depends on some criterion of validity in reasoning—must also consider the trustworthiness of the faculty of belief.

The imagination is the faculty by which discrete ideas are combined to form compound ideas and trains of thought. Although Hume sometimes speaks of the imagination as being "at liberty" to arrange its materials in an apparently free or capricious manner, he holds that it operates for the most part in accordance with a few discernible rules— the principles of association. The operation of these principles, however, is general: erroneous as well as valid reasonings, colorful fantasies as well as the most careful judgments, are all the products of a single faculty and the same set of operative principles. This circumstance seems to eliminate any clear-cut dichotomy between the mind's "fictions," insofar as this term denotes a creative deviation from experience, and the "fictions" that underlie causal reasoning. "Nothing is more dangerous to reason," Hume says, "than flights of the imagination, and nothing has been the occasion of more mistakes among philosophers." Yet the same faculty that is the source of such "flights" is necessary for all reasoning: the "conjunction of cause and effect" is itself a kind of "illusion" of the imagination; and so the question

[27] Hume, *Enquiries* (i), p. 47.

for the philosopher becomes "how far we ought to yield to these illusions" (T. 267). This is the major issue that Hume raises at the end of the epistemological part of the philosophy, prior to passing on to a consideration of the passions and the more obviously nonrational aspects of human nature. Although, as we shall see, he lays down guidelines for proper causal inference, the problem is one that is not ultimately escapable. The effects of the imagination are pervasive in mental life; although for the most part people seem to succeed in adequately distinguishing fact and fantasy for the usual purposes of everyday life, it is also plausible to suppose that there is a borderline area of natural confusion between the two realms, and that people all too readily on occasion succumb to "illusions" and "flights of fancy" in ways that the philosopher may find disturbing. Hume's problem is to distinguish necessary beliefs from superfluous ones, the salutary from the dangerous, to avoid "flights" of the imagination while recognizing that a certain amount of trust in it is the only alternative to total skepticism.

Recognizing that in the absence of any special faculty of rational insight it is the imagination that generates all our reasonings, Hume's psychology is sensitive to the sources and the typical directions of what the philosopher regards as deviations from legitimate inferential reasoning. Hume mentions several such sources of error, any of which would seem to promise interesting results to more extended analysis than he gives them. There is the principle, for example, that "assent to those images which are presented to our fancy" is a source of pleasure. The assent stimulated by causal reasoning is only one possible type; poetical fictions, although they are not believed in the same sense, nevertheless produce a kind of assent and thus "give an equal entertainment to the imagination" (T. 121). Another such principle concerns the uneasiness that the mind experiences in the presence of two apparently contradictory appearances and the consequent propensity of the imagination to generate "fictions" that serve to resolve the contradictions (T. 206). Hume utilizes this principle, as we have seen, to explain the origin of the concept of object, which is one of the most fundamental and natural of such "fictions." More widely applied, however, this principle can be the source of needless beliefs: Hume, for example, criticizes the concept of "substance" and the other "occult qualities" postulated by the "antient philosophy" as "unreasonable and capricious" and as useless for a scientific understanding of the world. Such fictions, however, appear to have a similar epistemological status as that of "necessary connection," all of them arising from the tendency of the imagination to "feign something unknown and invisible" in order to bestow regularity and coherence on its perceptions (cf. T. 219-22).

The study of such philosophical "fictions," like the study of dreams and fantasies of all kinds, is important because it reveals the distinctive propensities of the imagination and some of their aberrant manifestations (T. 219). As another example, Hume points out how the tendency to ascribe identity to a series of related perceptions, beyond the specifiable relations (such as succession in time) that constitute their only objective link, can yield notable philosophical "mistakes"; indeed, "seemingly trivial principles of the imagination" account for such grandiose systems of thought as Shaftesbury's (Platonic) vision of the providential harmony of nature (T. 254n)—a speculative system or world view of the sort from which far from trivial practical implications may be derived. Hume's attitude toward such imaginative flights is ambivalent. They are important data for the scientist of human nature, being all natural, that is, explicable in terms of the principles of his psychology; yet throughout his treatment of them Hume occasionally adopts the critical point of view that rejects certain of the products of the imagination as "absurd" in favor of the other, equally imaginative propensities of the mind that constitute the basis for correct causal reasoning. To see more clearly how Hume manages to make this distinction, we must turn to his doctrine of the association of ideas, which represents his most systematic effort to develop a scientific psychology.

Hume believed he had found in the doctrine of the association of ideas the potential "Newtonian" key to the human understanding. Locke had briefly treated association with respect to the origins (especially the social origins) of errors and "madness," contrasting the connections of ideas that are due to chance or custom with their "natural correspondence" to which it is the proper function of reason to adhere.[28] Hume in contrast attempts to develop, in association, a model for explaining all patterns of thought, including fantasies and conscious fictions on the one hand and inferences pertaining to reality on the other. He begins by examining the operations of the associative processes within the mind of the individual taken singly rather than treating them as the (generally deleterious, in Locke's opinion) consequence of custom and emulation—although, as we shall see, his analysis subsequently makes a large place for what may be called the social dimension of imagination. Hume believed that certain principles

[28] John Locke, *An Essay Concerning Human Understanding*, ed. Peter H. Nidditch (Oxford: Clarendon Press, 1975) II.xxxiii.5.

by which discrete perceptions are joined in the mind could be described systematically, and he devotes much of the first book of the *Treatise* to their elucidation; in Book II he expands the doctrine to include association of impressions of reflection as part of his theory of the passions, and much of his account of moral motivation and of political beliefs in Book III is based on these theories.[29]

Given the prominent place of this doctrine in the *Treatise*, its severe curtailment in the *Enquiries* poses a difficulty of interpretation for students of Hume's philosophy.[30] Even in the course of the *Treatise*, Hume's main attention may be seen to shift from association itself to the phenomenon of belief, and this he concludes cannot be explained merely in terms of mechanical associations of ideas but requires an account of the special feelings that accompany certain of them, producing assent. In the first *Enquiry* these feelings acquire virtually the status of autonomous instincts and are made the central theme of that work. The second *Enquiry*, finally, is to a greater degree than the third book of the *Treatise* concerned with the criteria rather than with the psychological motivation of moral judgments, and there is therefore less scope for application of the associational doctrine in that work.

There is, therefore, no reason to conclude that Hume ever repudiated the doctrine, although he may well have gradually lost some of his early conviction that he could explain all thought in this manner; it may be, as Kemp Smith argued, that he came to incline more to the "moral sentiments" school of thought, whose influence eventually overcame that of the physical model to which he had at first been attracted. It is nevertheless important to consider Hume's associational psychology as he applies it to both ideas and the passions. Some of the problematic phenomena of the imagination for which Hume attempts to account in terms of association raise questions that are crucial for Hume's practical philosophy. Some of them contain important implications for his political science, and many of the moral and political doctrines of Book III of the *Treatise* are formulated in terms of the models of the mind and the passions set out in the first two books. The second *Enquiry*, although it is more widely admired

---

[29] See especially Hume's effort to account for rules of property in *Treatise* III.ii.3, especially the notes. Although the institution of property as a whole is justified by its utility, specific rules are ascribed to imaginative factors (at least in part), either because utility is indifferent as between possible rules, or because the facility with which the mind can learn and apply the rules is itself a factor that enhances their utility.

[30] See Elie Halevy, *The Growth of Philosophic Radicalism* (Boston: Beacon Press, 1966), pp. 9-10, on how associationism later merged with Benthamite utilitarianism and radicalism.

as an ethical work, is in fact less interesting as a work of political science precisely because it is not related so systematically to a psychological doctrine as is Book III of the *Treatise*, and it lacks the larger work's detailed efforts to account for specific political phenomena and beliefs by reference to the previously delineated psychology. The philosophical question regarding the validity of certain kinds of reasoning, finally, is answered in terms of a distinction among the types of association, and it is to this problem that I turn now.

The doctrine of the association of ideas is announced early in the *Treatise* as a sequel to Hume's premise that the only materials of our thought are distinct ideas and impressions. It would seem that trains of thought would be random and hence chaotic if chance alone were operative in uniting these discrete elements; the fact that "the same simple ideas" "fall regularly into complex ones," however, implies the existence of some "uniting principle" among them. Hume contends that three such principles account for all the multitudinous connections among the ideas that we entertain in our imagination, both the combination of several simple ideas into a complex one and trains of ideas that follow one another in definite sequences. These principles are resemblance, contiguity in time or place, and cause and effect, of which Hume affirms that the last is the most extensive in its influence as well as the basis of all reasoning concerning matters of fact (T. 10-12).

These three principles of association are innate propensities or dispositions—"*original* qualities of human nature, which I pretend not to explain" (T. 13) but the effects of which may be described. As dispositions of the mind, the principles of association express merely the tendencies according to which ideas are joined. The imagination retains some freedom (in the sense of unpredictability) in combining ideas, though it tends to do so within the outlines suggested by the three principles, which may be thought of as "a gentle force, which commonly prevails" (T. 10), even in dreams and the most extravagant reveries of the imagination. The explanatory force of the doctrine is weakened by Hume's occasional reaffirmations of the irregularity that was one of his initial defining characteristics of the imagination: thought, he says, "may leap from the heavens to the earth, from one end of the creation to the other, without any certain method or order" (T. 92). Nevertheless, Hume's psychology proceeds with the conviction that the operations of the mind will, within limits, prove amenable to scientific description, even if absolute precision is not attainable. The importance of this project arises from the fact that in Hume's philosophy all relations among the objects in the world are, subjectively considered, "nothing but a propensity [of the mind] to pass from one idea to another" and that "whatever strengthens the propensity strengthens the relation" (T. 309). I shall consider shortly Hume's account of our belief in causal inferences through the strong imaginative propensity to associate the idea of an effect with that of its cause; and later we shall see how the imagination interacts with the passions, imaginative connections serving to stimulate our feelings and our estimations of things. The world as understood and evaluated by human beings is, in Hume's psychology, one in which all the relations among things are generated by the imagination, working according to roughly explicable rules. It is on the basis of this discovery that Hume eventually delineates the typical features of humans as moral and political beings.

I now return to Hume's endeavor to find criteria of "right" reasoning that, as a scientist, he is concerned to counterpose to the comprehensive view of the imagination, which in itself reinforces the skeptical point of view: all the propensities of the imagination seem to be on the same footing, all equally natural, and there is no self-evident way in which those that yield the careful causal inferences appropriate to science have any higher status than, or indeed are readily distinguishable from, those whose influence is responsible for the wildest fantasies or the most egregious errors in our imputation of causality to events in the world. Hume's solution to this difficulty is to ascribe a special status to association by cause and effect, in distinction to the other two principles, and to insist that the scientific method (or "philosophical reasoning") is to be defined by its exclusive reliance on this mode of thought, insofar as it generates propositions about matters of fact that go beyond the immediately given. The basis for this distinction is established in the final analysis in connection with Hume's deliberate adoption of a skeptical "rule of life," which must include a rule of reasoning for the factual judgments that he cannot avoid making.

All three modes of association have their appropriate uses, in different degrees and combinations. Some poetry, for example that of Ovid, depends chiefly on the relation of resemblance; Milton's effort to portray a lengthy train of causation, on the other hand, constitutes a defect in the aesthetic effect of his poetry. The connecting principle of narrative history is principally contiguity, in both time and place, although that history is more "useful" that attends to causes and effects as well. The principle of causation, however, is not only the most usual and most forceful mode of association in our reasoning; it is also "the most instructive; since it is by this knowledge alone we are enabled to control events and govern futurity."[31] The relations of resemblance

[31] Hume, *An Inquiry Concerning Human Understanding*, ed. Charles W. Hendel

and contiguity would appear to underlie important classificatory functions in our reasoning that Hume does not fully examine; and the relation of causation, moreover, draws on them insofar as ascription of causality requires that we have noticed instances of proximity and succession between the members of classes of resembling objects. The causal relation, however, characterized by the element of necessity in the connection, is asserted to be a distinct form of imaginative association, the only one, normally, by which the mind is led from a present object to the idea of one never actually experienced, whether past, present, or future, in such a manner that one experiences a conviction of its probable existence. This relation, in other words, is at the root of the inferential faculty by which we reason concerning reality and arrive at conclusions regarding the existence of things in accordance with which we are prepared to act.

Hume contends that the relation of causation is in fact the strongest and most frequently exercised of the three principles of association; it is habitually utilized by everyone in everyday life as well as, more self-consciously, by scientists and historians in their efforts to discover the less obvious operations of causes in the natural and moral worlds. Its proper, as opposed to its everyday, application, however, is a crucial issue on which Hume temporarily leaves his descriptive psychology for a critical excursion into the field of logic. To distinguish the causal relation as the sole foundation for correct philosophical reasoning is an arbitrary choice on the part of a skeptic like Hume, fully aware that the basis in the imagination on which this principle rests is identical to that underlying the other two principles—whose fitting use, we gather, lies in the sphere of poetry and other "fanciful" activities of the mind. The decision to restrict "right reasoning" about matters of fact to causal inference must in the end be justified pragmatically, as the means by which we may best "govern futurity" and achieve our practical ends. In this justification the philosopher finally appeals to common opinion and the desires of ordinary people.

The special status that Hume wishes to confer on causal association and careful induction may be a difficult goal to achieve in practice, however, as a result of various kinds of interference and erroneous tendencies originating with the other two principles or deriving from other fundamental propensities of the mind. Hume's analysis of the imagination provides a model for the explanation of errors as well as of right reasoning, and it simultaneously points up the difficulty of

(Indianapolis: Bobbs-Merrill, 1955), p. 34; on Ovid, p. 33; Milton, p. 38. This edition provides material that Hume cut from the last edition of his essays that he prepared for publication.

sustaining the logical distinction that Hume seeks. Philosophers, Hume says, allow three different sorts of probable inference to be the sole "reasonable foundations of belief and opinion" in reference to matters of fact not immediately apprehended or remembered (T. 143). These three types of probability are all equally based on the causal relation and on the basic beliefs that the future will resemble the past and that every event has a cause. The distinction pertains to three possible sources of uncertainty that may accompany different sorts of inferences, in accordance with which the philosopher must carefully apportion the degree of probability in every case. Uncertainty may arise from the limited number of observed cases, from a contrariety in the available evidence (assumed to be the result of the simultaneous action of contrary causal agencies), or from imperfect resemblance among the objects or events whose sequential regularity is being placed in evidence (T. 130-32); reasoning in which any of these conditions is present can yield only probable, though scientifically valid, conclusions. Besides these "reasonable" grounds of inference, however, there is a variety of natural and common ways in which the imagination can deviate from strict "philosophical" standards. Hume's analysis of "vulgar" errors is intended both as a description of tendencies manifested frequently in the thought of ordinary people and as a critical examination of pitfalls in what purports to be scientific argument.

The first source of errors is the failure of the imagination to keep its causal associations always distinct from the other two kinds and to reserve belief, or attribution of real existence, to conclusions of the former. Contiguity or resemblance between two ideas may "augment the conviction of any opinion, and the vivacity of any conception" in a way for which there is no scientific justification. Hume's example with respect to contiguity pertains to a pilgrim whose faith becomes more zealous following a visit to the Holy Land: "A man, whose memory presents him with a lively image of the *Red-Sea, and the Desert, and Jerusalem, and Galilee,* can never doubt of any miraculous events, which are related either by *Moses or the Evangelists.*" The "lively idea" of the locale "encreases the belief by encreasing the vivacity of the conception" of the events alleged to have taken place in the vicinity, though without adding to their causal evidence (T. 110-11). A strikingly ironic example of the opposite kind of error is Hume's suggestion that people's belief in the eternal rewards of heaven has little actual effect on their conduct: the rewards, being remote, are faint in the imagination, although this feature is irrelevant to their alleged causal relation to present good behavior (T. 114-15). The implicit conclusion (contrary to the usual opinion of enlightened thinkers of Hume's day) is that religious sanctions are unnecessary to morality, even for the common people, because the reasoning of ordinary people is so universally fallacious.[32]

Such intermingling of relations can also have harmful results when causality is precipitately imputed to a relation in which resemblances are deceptive, a circumstance that can attend more erudite matters. One of Hume's aims in his essay on population, for example, is to dispel the illusion that the practice of infant exposure contributed to depopulation; he finds that the actual effect of this custom was the opposite and argues accordingly that enlightened condemnation of infanticide must rest on other grounds, but at the same time he notes the psychological source of the tenacity of this common belief.[33] In a similar vein Hume attempts in his economic writings to expose the fallaciousness of the commonplace views that the extravagance of courts is necessarily a drain on national wealth, and that austerity is a condition of prosperity.[34] Again resemblances are deceptive—and a dangerous though natural basis for causal arguments. Philosophers must learn that causality in political matters is often obscure and contrary to first impressions, and they must discipline themselves to resist the impulsive claims of direct insight that characterize the "vulgar."

Hume also warns against another tendency, namely, that "when objects are united by any relation, we have a strong propensity to add some new relation to them, in order to compleat the union" (T. 237). This propensity, which yields psychic "satisfaction," is clearly related to the mind's impulse, which we have noted previously, to generate "fictions," such as the concept of an object, in order to resolve or account for apparent contradictions in perceptions and to overcome the accompanying "uneasiness." Hume identifies the Cartesian concept of the soul as such a fiction (*not* an especially useful one, in his view) that has resulted from feigning a conjunction in space, and hence substantiality, in addition to the more obvious relations of contiguity in time and causation among our thoughts. Hume here points to the tendency of the mind to seek to create order among the discrete perceptions with which it is presented, an important feature of human

[32] For other arguments against the alleged importance of religion in upholding morality see Hume, *Dialogues*, pp. 220-22.

[33] Hume, "Of the Populousness of Ancient Nations," *Works*, vol. 3, pp. 396-97. This essay is a classic, pioneering effort in scientific demography, with attention to problems of historical evidence.

[34] For example, see Hume, "Of Refinement in the Arts," *Works*, vol. 3, pp. 302-303; "Of Commerce," *Works*, vol. 3, p. 294; and *Enquiries* (II), p. 181.

nature generally, some of the implications of which in his moral philosophy will be emphasized later. All the various mechanisms of the imagination serve this ordering function in one way or another; the problem here is that the mind seems prone to connect phenomena with more ties than the skeptical philosopher can see good grounds for, or than the scientist finds useful. The natural desire for holistic knowledge of ties among things and the imagination's readiness to satisfy this desire constitute the psychological sources for the doctrinaire impulse in politics against which Hume directs much of his later political and historical writing, whereas it is the mind's ordering propensity that is responsible for the rules and artifices of the moral world of which Hume decisively approves. In both the cognitive and the moral spheres the philosopher must draw a line between the proper and the excessive functioning of the imagination.

Difficulties surrounding the ascription of causality and its correct application in inferential arguments exist even apart from the problem of interference from the other two principles of association. A fact or an experiment, for example, that is recent may have more influence on belief than one that is remote in time, due to its greater force in the imagination, although its evidential value is no greater. Likewise, an inference that can be drawn immediately produces a stronger conviction than a "long chain of connected arguments, however infallible the connexion of each link may be esteem'd" (T. 143-44). These examples illustrate how conviction varies, according to Hume's psychology, with any imaginative mechanism that stimulates liveliness of conception; whereas it ought, according to the canons of his scientific logic, to follow the philosophical understanding of the nature of causation exclusively.

Another discrepancy between these two standards, one to which human nature is "very subject," concerns the origin of "prejudices" in the rash formulation of general rules (T. 146-47), along with the related problem of analogy. Causal reasoning depends on generalization, insofar as present cases must be assimilated to previously observed sequences involving members of general classes of objects. Since it infrequently happens that we have observed past instances involving objects exactly like those with which we are presently confronted, we must be able to pick out relevant resemblances, calculate their degrees, and apportion our present estimates of probability accordingly. The generalizing capability is connected with the tendency to associate ideas by their resemblance; the difficulty is to prevent the imagination from rushing to unwarranted generalizations, or "prejudices," and from invoking such inadequately supported classifications in causal inferences. Likewise Hume notes that reasoning by "analogy," in which imperfections in resemblance between the objects being compared are acknowledged, detracts from the probability of causal arguments (T. 142). In the *Enquiry*, however, he remarks that "all our reasonings concerning matter of fact are founded on a species of Analogy," since resemblances are never perfect.[35] Indeed on Hume's epistemological principles it is not possible to draw a firm line between fanciful or unfounded analogies (such as, most notably, he believed he discerned, and rejected, in the design argument of natural religion) and resemblances that provide a valid basis for causal reasoning, just as no clear criterion can be stipulated for distinguishing spurious "prejudices" from valid empirical generalizations. This then is a "new and signal contradiction in our reason," one that Hume as a skeptic relishes (T. 150). Prejudices in this sense of reasoning from irrelevant resemblances nevertheless are real and have detrimental consequences in political life: Hume attempted (without great success) to uphold his consistency, in his *History*, in defending Charles I while condemning James II in opposition to the usual ideological lumping of them together because they were of the same family.[36]

A final aspect of causal reasoning in which it appears to be impossible to set down rules for unambiguously distinguishing truth from error concerns the criterion of regularity. The "philosophical" analysis of causality as uniform sequence dictates that the relation be ascribed only where regular conjunctions have been observed, and that probability be proportioned to the number of identical cases (and infrequency of contrary cases) observed. Common sense, however, infers a causal relation from a few experiences or even from a single particularly vivid one: a child correctly concludes from one painful instance that fire burns. Hume can attribute this capacity to the generalizing or rule-following propensity of the mind: a lifetime of experience of regularities in nature produces a habit in us of expecting such regularities and of imputing them even in the absence of numerous experiments (T. 131). But although Hume acknowledges the occasional salutary effects of this habit in everyday life, he cannot justify it as a correct mode of reasoning: the too-hasty ascription of causality, or a general inference drawn from a single instance, is one of the most common pitfalls of the human understanding. Yet Hume cannot lay down a precise rule informing us how many cases should be taken to

---

[35] Hume, *Enquiries* (I), p. 104.
[36] Hume, letter of 30 November [1756], to William Strahan, in *Letters*, vol. 1, p. 235.

constitute adequate ground for belief, just as he cannot specify the degrees of resemblance that are appropriate for a causal generalization. He advocates a philosophical habit of suspending judgment and carefully proportioning belief to the evidence available. But such methodological caution involves a partial curtailment of natural tendencies of the imagination that not only are the condition of any reasoning at all but also whose indulgence seems to be the ordinary and largely indispensable practice of people in the "common affairs of life."

Hume does stipulate eight rules of inductive logic "by which we ought to regulate our judgment" (T. 173-76, 149). He advances, that is, a normative standard of right reasoning, embodying the methodological presuppositions of empirical science, in the midst of his psychology; or, seen in another light, he proposes a kind of logical artifice, steady adherence to which promises order and control in our cognitive life.[37] These rules are said to be "extremely difficult in their application," since most phenomena in nature, and even more so in the moral sphere, are surrounded with a great "complication of circumstances" that render it difficult to identify correctly the effective cause of an event from among its numerous antecedents. The difficulties involved both in establishing the criteria of and in practicing correct reasoning, however, are explicable ultimately in terms of the more general conclusions of Hume's philosophy, in its denial of any possibility of direct insight into the nature of causation or into any particular causal relations and in its recognition of the unity of the psychological processes underlying all mental activity. It is accordingly with a strong sense of the need for caution that Hume carves out a scientific foothold in the midst of his skepticism and at the same time establishes the basis for his distinction between wise and vulgar reasoners.

Although Hume later reduced his claims for association, he never lost his interest in the development of a descriptive psychology centering on the imagination. The phenomenon of belief eventually came to be the principal object of his attention, both because it appeared to pose the most interesting psychological issue and because, more broadly, the problem of credulity and false belief holds such obviously significant practical implications. To what extent do people's actual beliefs tend to correspond to that restricted class of inferences that the philosopher admits as "reasonable" conclusions about matters of fact? An estimation of the reasonableness of ordinary people in this respect is clearly a significant matter for Hume's subsequent understanding of moral and political phenomena.

---

[37] See Noxon, *Hume's Philosophical Development*, pp. 81-84. Cf. also Hume, *Enquiries* (I), p. 107n., for criteria of superior reasoning or strength of understanding.

Of all the perceptions and combinations of perceptions that occur in our minds, some are accompanied by a conviction of their real (or probable) existence and some are not; and in the case of those in which we believe, there may be more or less good grounds for so doing. A person generally believes in the reality of his immediate impressions and in the objects represented by the ideas of his memory, in consequence of the liveliness or force of conception that accompanies these perceptions. The phenomenon of belief becomes problematic in the case of objects neither directly apprehended nor remembered—that is, ideas of things of which a person has had no direct experience, whether their existence is supposed to have been or to be in the past, present, or future. The mind generates such ideas, along with fanciful ideas and fictions of all kinds, by means of the principles of association, through trains of thought that always begin with some perception drawn from experience. Since belief, upon analysis, appears to be nothing other than the feeling of a certain force accompanying some ideas, the problem becomes one of discovering the various sources of this "vivacity" in the imagination; and Hume's answer is that association by the relation of cause and effect, grounded as it is in a strong habit of expectation of regularity, is the usual—and the only trustworthy or valid—source of vivid and credible ideas of nonpresent things. At this stage Hume, while recognizing belief as an unanalyzable feeling, attempts to account for its production in mechanistic terms: past frequency of repetition of a given conjunction, for example, is said to strengthen proportionally one's belief in its future occurrence (as, philosophically, it increases its probability) through its strengthening of the associative habit of the imagination.

By the end of Book I of the *Treatise*, however, Hume seems to grow less confident of his ability to account for belief systematically in terms of putative quantities of "force" generated by discrete operations of the imagination. The fundamental belief that the future will resemble the past, common to all people, does not seem derivable from experience in this way; and the equally unavoidable belief in independent existence (objectivity) that people confidently attribute to certain of their perceptions does not prove susceptible of explanation in terms of the associational scheme. These two "natural beliefs" appear to constitute autonomous or innate propensities of human nature; and the later Hume tends to speak more of the "sentimental," even "instinctual," quality of all belief rather than of quanta of "vivacity" as the determining factor.[38]

Hume's development in this respect thus corresponds to his partic-

---

[38] See Hume, *Enquiries* (I), pp. 48-49; also *Treatise*, Appendix, pp. 628-29.

ular mode of resolution of the skeptical crisis and his discovery of the naturalistic basis on which he comes to see the whole of human capabilities as founded. His science of human nature, however, although it is grounded in this recognition of the instinctual quality of the most fundamental tendencies of the mind, requires tools for more precise analysis, and especially for the explanation of variations among people and their beliefs, of the sort offered by the more "mechanistic" doctrines of his earlier psychology; and Hume's studies of moral and political life continue to draw on both the theory of association and the larger doctrine of mental "propensities" as a model for explaining particular forms of behavior and belief. The basic instinct of belief works through the imagination, where it is subject to a variety of influences that are the proximate causes of specific convictions, even if the basic tendency toward belief is a fundamental datum. The study of these particular causes of belief becomes in Hume's model the study of the various sources of vivacity, productive of conviction and hence (sometimes) of volition, in the imagination.

The most common type of belief is that which accompanies causal inference from a present impression to the idea of a nonpresent object (its cause or effect), and in this case the source of the necessary vivacity is the habit of expectation that grows in us from repeated experiences of similar conjunctions in the past. It is such customary transitions or associations in the imagination, facilitated by a general expectation of regularity, "which peoples the world, and brings us acquainted with such existences, as by their removal in time or place, lie beyond the reach of the senses and memory" (T. 108). This explanation of legitimate belief suggests at the same time some characteristic difficulties. There is the problem of the single particularly vivid experience that overrides custom and engenders a precipitate imputation of causality, sometimes justifiable but perhaps more often not, and the impossibility, in the absence of further evidence, of distinguishing; problematic cases of this kind might prove frequent in political life, where evidently important experiences are not repeatable and where extraordinary events are indeed held to teach significant lessons. Fallacious reasoning of another sort results from the tendency of the habitual mechanism to perpetuate erroneous judgments, the force of our customary associations leading us to disregard or misperceive contrary evidence. In a general way our formed habits concerning the "system" of expectations that, Hume suggests, "we are pleas'd to call a *reality*" (T. 108) may induce us to overlook novel and discordant phenomena. The possessor of such an imagination as Hume describes is on the one hand vulnerable to the undue influence of special vivifying influences and on the other hand firmly set, as a rule, in the cognitive ways dictated by his normally preponderant associative habits; such a person is thus prone to two opposite sorts of erroneous judgment.

Hume regards habit as the decisive element in the greater part of people's lives—cognitive, emotional, and moral—an insight to which he is brought through consideration of the doctrine of association. But although habits are formed in response to repeated experiences, effective repetition is not always of the sort on which the scientist relies in formulating a causal law; habits of belief and action acquired through social emulation and education provide the basis for much of moral life, as we shall see in the next section. And habit, in the sense of customary linguistic usage, forms a key element in Hume's largely undeveloped theory of language. According to Hume all meaningful complex ideas may be broken down into the simple ideas, derivable from impressions, that compose them. He recognizes, however, that when we use words for such complex ideas as government, church, negotiation, or conquest, "we seldom spread out in our minds all the simple ideas, of which these complex ones are compos'd." It is rather through learned habits of usage that we "may avoid talking nonsense on these subjects" and on others like them—that is, virtually the whole of those subjects embraced by our moral and other abstract vocabularies. Entire habits of thought about such subjects may be "reviv'd by one single word" and recalled through association (T. 23). If habit in the form of our education in a native language underlies our ability to use words correctly, however, it also explains typical abuses of language. Terms that on Hume's theory of meaning are unintelligible can be used consistently and with conviction through custom, and frequent repetition seems to endow them with a "secret meaning" (T. 224).[39] It is usual, Hume remarks, for people to "talk instead of thinking in their reasonings" (T. 62), and furthermore, "we find few disputes, that are not founded on some ambiguity in the expression."[40] These observations provide a starting point for the analysis of both political ideology and religious rituals—phenomena that Hume classes together partly for reasons connected with the psychology of belief.

Belief aroused by frequency of relevant experience, so far as it is a psychological reality, is a fortunate one, since it corresponds to Hume's philosophical ground for causal inference. More generally, however,

---

[39] Hume, *Enquiries* (I), p. 22, for his theory of meaning. Hume's remarks on language recall some more frequently expressed concerns of Hobbes; see Frederick G. Whelan, "Language and its Abuses in Hobbes' Political Philosophy," *American Political Science Review* 75 (1981): 59-75.

[40] Hume, "Of the Dignity or Meanness of Human Nature," *Works*, vol. 3, p. 151.

belief is constituted by the special "liveliness" that attends some ideas (T. 96), and from this it appears that any of a variety of factors may serve as an enlivening agent of ideas, of which the habit of causal association is only one. In this connection Hume turns a critical eye to the role of religious ceremonies and imagery: the adherents of "that strange superstition," Roman Catholicism, claim to "feel the good effect of those external motions, and postures, and actions, in inlivening their devotion, and quickening their fervour, which otherwise wou'd decay away, if directed entirely to distant and immaterial objects" (T. 99-100).[41] All immediate impressions, in Hume's account, are lively, and any of them can potentially transfer its liveliness to an idea somehow associated with it. We have seen how associations based on contiguity and resemblance can interfere with causality, distorting inferential reasoning through just such an infusion of inappropriate liveliness. In the example just cited Hume touches on the potentiality of symbolism—a type of resemblance—in enhancing certain ideas, making them more attractive and tenacious in the mind, even if not always sufficing to establish belief in them. By the same token, an abstract argument, however philosophically valid, may fail to win genuine assent precisely because it is too far removed from any sensible impression. Hume, pondering the outcome of his skeptical reasonings, is forced to recognize that the "effort of thought disturbs the operation of our sentiments, on which the belief depends" (T. 185). The Humean philosopher, as psychologist, is aware of the reasons why superstitions of various kinds are likely to have more adherents than his own moderate skepticism; and he must accordingly reconcile himself to the limited impact his doctrines are likely to have in the face of received beliefs.

In the face of the psychological fact that belief is a matter of sentiment or force of conception, Hume attempts to define and uphold a philosophical standard of careful inductive logic. He also draws an implicit distinction, however, within the class of unreflective people who simply follow the dictates of their imagination. He frequently suggests that, since causal association and the inferential habits drawn from experience are in fact the strongest forces in the imagination, ordinary people as a rule succeed quite well in their causal reasoning, at least for most of their everyday purposes, and that the various errors

---

[41] Hume, *Enquiries* (I), p. 51, where the same example is used. Although there is no reason to suspect that Hume may have been favorably disposed toward Roman Catholicism, it may be noted that he also refers to the skeptics as "that fantastic sect" even while seriously presenting one of their arguments (T. 183); and his psychology in these passages confirms the effectiveness of the "strange" rituals.

to which the imagination is prone do not have such frequent or serious practical consequences as might be feared. He does, however, employ the term "madness" to denote the state of abnormal susceptibility to the unphilosophical promptings of the imagination, and especially to the propensity to acquire belief in those productions of the imagination that most people succeed in recognizing as fictions. The imagination, in one of its aspects, is a faculty that can associate ideas at its pleasure, "feigning" whole patterns that have no basis in experience except the separate simple ideas out of which they are composed. Such creative mental activity can be pleasurable, the source of poetry as well as of our daydreams and "fancies," though as Hume points out the "mixture of truth and falsehood in the fables of tragic poets" generally succeeds in satisfying the imagination without procuring belief (T. 121-22). The problem is that the liveliness that excites and pleases the imagination can on occasion be of the kind that tends to produce belief; indeed, Hume says, " 'tis difficult for us to withold our assent from what is painted out to us in all the colours of eloquence; and the vivacity produc'd by the fancy is in many cases greater than that which arises from custom and experience" (T. 123). The border is indistinct between the innocent pleasures of "fancying" and the "folly" of incautiously succumbing to the force of eloquence and "poetic" fictions. This border is of course all the harder to defend inasmuch as even legitimate beliefs rest, in the final analysis, on certain definite kinds of fictions generated in the imagination. Hume finds that common sense for the most part agrees with philosophy in adhering to experience and induction, and that "madness" therefore can meaningfully be held to denote severe deviations from the normal distinction between reality and fiction. The work of the philosopher in this respect is to uphold the healthy instincts of ordinary people while continuing to offer refinements in the sphere of correct causal reasoning.

I close this discussion with a consideration of Hume's general assessment of the human capacity to experience—and to exercise some critical control over—the feeling or manner of conception constitutive of belief.[42] The philosopher, accepting the two natural beliefs and certain rules of logic, determines to apportion belief cautiously and according to the evidence. The deviations from this standard that constitute the errors of the "vulgar" could, it seems, take either of two forms. People may be overly incredulous, withholding belief from arguments that in the philosopher's view have a significantly probable

---

[42] The ability of a "reasonable" person to control his feelings and to suspend or withhold belief is discussed further in section 4 of this chapter.

status and should therefore serve as a basis for reasonable action. Incredulity may result from the fact that ordinary people, confronted by apparently chance happenings and the complexity of events, do not rigorously assume the truth of the causal maxim. Incredulity of this sort may lead to bewilderment in the face of an abstruse scientific explanation, or it may induce a resort to the opposite extreme, the quest for explanation in terms of "miracles" or extraordinary causal agencies. Insufficient belief may result in general from any failure of an otherwise valid line of reasoning to enliven the imagination, and as a consequence of this particular weakness of human nature philosophers may expect on occasion to find themselves making proposals or warning of foreseen consequences by means of arguments that fail to arouse conviction.

Generally, however, Hume suggests that the opposite problem is more frequently encountered. The imagination is an active and impressionable faculty, readily stimulated by a large variety of influences; and anything that enlivens it may tend to produce the feeling of belief. All mental activity, furthermore, belief prominently included, is pleasurable in itself (T. 122). Human beings are therefore fundamentally credulous beings; there are psychological reasons, beyond the simple necessity for some belief in order to live, why skepticism is found so rarely outside philosophical circles.[43] As the phenomenon of belief emerges as the central issue of Hume's epistemology, so credulity becomes an important problem for his practical philosophy. In an intriguing section of the *Treatise* entitled "Of curiosity, or the love of truth," Hume presents several arguments ostensibly to explain the motivation of the philosopher's quest for truth. But, relying on psychological insights of the sort just discussed, he does not succeed in showing why truth should be more satisfying than fiction or myth. Intellectual curiosity is compared with hunting and gaming, in which pleasure is derived more from the excitement of the pursuit than from the attainment of the end, and he repeats his opinion regarding the natural pleasure attending liveliness in the imagination (T. 451-53).[44]

[43] Cf. Edmund Burke, *A Philosophical Enquiry into the Origin of our Ideas of the Sublime and Beautiful*, ed. James T. Boulton (Notre Dame: University of Notre Dame Press, 1958), p. 18, for a similar assessment of human credulity based on a view of the pleasure accompanying belief. Burke carries the implications of this observation into his political theory; and like Hume he sees in it principally a source of health for the body politic, although he does not advocate the maintenance of philosophical skepticism as a counterweight to it. Hume admired this work: letter of 12 April 1759, to Adam Smith, in *Letters*, vol. 1, p. 303.

[44] Another skeptic, Montaigne, also compares the pleasures of mental activity with those of the chase, and he goes on to tell an anecdote of Democritus' preference for a

Elsewhere Hume refers to excessive credulity as the most conspicuous weakness of human nature (T. 112).

Although the philosopher's role is a critical one with respect to the beliefs of ordinary people, however, Hume nevertheless attaches a positive value to human credulous propensities for the most part, in accordance with what I have called his naturalism. The basic beliefs in cause and object are of course viewed as thoroughly healthy instincts, and in any case the philosopher as much as anyone is bound, outside the study at any rate, to uphold them. Beyond this the philosopher will attempt to distinguish between reasonable and unreasonable beliefs, employing the criteria derived from the analysis of the logic of inductive inference. A skeptic like Hume, however, must admit to a certain degree of arbitrariness surrounding his criteria of "reasonableness" as well as to the natural strength of those imaginative factors that tend to impinge on it. In the end, therefore, he recognizes the desirability of adapting his practical teachings to the realities of human nature, his moderate skepticism always tempered by respect for what is instinctual and customary.

3. THE SOCIAL CONTEXT OF THE UNDERSTANDING

Thus far I have been examining Hume's psychological doctrines as they pertain to the individual considered in isolation from others and as they deal with mental processes that are operative in thought of all kinds. The basic principles, for example those of custom and association, are regarded as innate in the individual, and they manifest themselves equally whether one is assimilating personal experience or participating in the collective beliefs of a group, and whether one is reasoning about physical or moral objects. I now turn to Hume's view of the social character of human nature and his observations on the social influences that are frequently operative on the individual's mind. Since I am still concerned, generally speaking, with Hume's theory of the imagination, this section will continue to emphasize belief—both the social sources of belief and the special qualities of collectively generated or perpetuated beliefs. I also consider some of the ways in which typical phenomena of the imagination are commonly manifested in moral and political life, and I shall conclude with a consideration of Hume's doctrine of personal identity.

---

complicated though false explanation of a strange occurrence to the simpler and less interesting true one. Michel de Montaigne, "Apology for Raymond Sebond," in *The Complete Essays of Montaigne*, trans. Donald M. Frame (Stanford: Stanford University Press, 1957), p. 378.

The transition in the study of belief and the imagination from the individual to the social context marks the beginning in Hume's philosophy of the analysis of moral life that is his principal concern, for which the study of human "understanding" is intended to be a preliminary. Before Hume is fully equipped for this enterprise, however, it is also necessary for him to develop a systematic theory of the passions to complement that of the understanding. This program occupies Book II of the *Treatise*, and in form it parallels his treatment of the understanding, beginning with an analysis of the passions of the individual and then gradually extending its observations into the realm of collective behavior. I examine pertinent aspects of Hume's theory of the passions in the following sections before turning to the doctrines of his moral and political theory. Even while he is engaged in his study of the understanding, however, Hume is led to a variety of insights into the dynamics of social life, and I follow the order of Hume's work in considering what may be called the collective dimension of his doctrine of the imagination at this stage.

Hume begins, like Locke and most of his contemporaries, with an analysis of the individual, tacitly assuming the methodological adequacy of this approach for a full understanding of human affairs. From this starting point, however, he nevertheless finds his way to a deep appreciation of the social dimension of experience, to the extent that he may be judged to have largely compensated for whatever defects attend his initial bias. In carrying through the Lockeian program Hume in the end undermines Locke's methodological individualism and with it, to some degree, the moral and political individualism that often appears to be its natural concomitant.[45] This line of development, moreover, follows ultimately from Hume's skeptical positions in epistemology, since it is these that lead to his distinctive psychology of belief, which in turn indicates the pervasive force of habit and custom in human life. Hume's recognition of the fundamental importance of custom in the operations of the imagination leads him naturally to a consideration of social life as a locus of experience generative of both mental and behavioral habits; meanwhile, his denial of any special faculty of rational insight, together with his active view of the imagination, leave the individual quite susceptible to the influence of others in the formation of his beliefs and character. In this way Hume arrives, having laid an extensive

---

[45] See Steven Lukes, *Individualism* (Oxford: Basil Blackwell, 1973), esp. chaps. 11, 16, 17.

foundation, at the "moral topics" and the study of politics in which his philosophy culminates.

The impact of social life on the individual is first suggested by the recognition that, of the ideas and beliefs that compose the mental stock of the average person, only a fraction are derived from personal impressions or remembered from personal experience of the objects represented in his imagination. The bulk of them, as Hume points out, are received from and believed on the testimony of other people (T. 117); hence the nature and validity of testimony must fall under the scrutiny of the philosopher of human nature.

The force of testimony is grounded, on the face of it, in the habit-forming propensity that Hume regards as fundamental to the imagination.[46] It is the repetition in experience of successive objects that normally generates the habit of causal association, and it is the forcefulness of conception arising from an established mental habit that accounts for belief. Repetition of testimony, however, has an effect in the imagination similar to that of frequency of perception of conjoined objects; and ordinarily the repetition of a certain combination of related ideas is more frequently encountered in testimony than in one's actual observation of events. This may be the case with regard to our beliefs about the behavior of physical objects, from which Hume draws most of his examples in describing the basis of causal reasoning in experience; certainly testimony, oral or written, and not direct experience is the source of the great majority of our beliefs about history, and it would seem to play a significant role in the formation of most of our ideas and beliefs in ethics and politics. In Hume's psychology a "custom of imagining" a given relation can be as efficacious as a "custom of observing" it in producing belief (T. 222), and as a result of habituation in the use of language the imagination can pass immediately from words to ideas, without always pausing to reflect on their meaning (T. 93). These two features of human nature, together with the force of repeated testimony, explain the prominence that the role of social communication of ideas acquires in Hume's system.

The double question of the force and the trustworthiness of testimony provides an example of the dualism between analysis and criticism in Hume's philosophy. As a scientist of human nature he seeks to describe the characteristic elements of mental and moral life; as a philosopher he attempts to differentiate among these features between

---

[46] See Hume, *Enquiries* (I), p. 43, for the clearest characterization of habit or custom as a psychological principle.

the salutary and the harmful, those that will be cultivated or guarded against by the "wise" in contrast to the "vulgar."

Why are people so apt to be influenced by testimony—to believe what they are told? Repeated testimony acquires at least some of its force from our normal propensity to develop habits, which in turn intensify our conceptions; this process is operative whether the repetition is deliberate, as in the case of education by precept and rote, or simply the informal consensus of opinion to which we are exposed on most subjects. Most people tend to give credence to testimony, however, even when it is not repeated, and society is normally characterized by mutual trust among its members, at least with respect to their reports to one another on matters of fact, and where common sense sees no obvious motive for deceit. Hume at one point defines the common human weakness of "credulity" as a "too easy faith in the testimony of others," pointing out that belief often exceeds the judicious limits prescribed by our uneven experience of the trustworthiness of reports; indeed, he asserts that people have "a remarkable propensity to believe whatever is reported, even concerning apparitions, enchantments, and prodigies, however contrary to daily experience and observation" (T. 112-13). Hume's psychological explanation of this points to the fact that the words of testimony are the "images" as well as the effects of the ideas that putatively cause them (T. 113). Resemblance, that is, "fortifies" causal inference in a philosophically illicit fashion, a fact that should lead to special caution in the reception of reports.

With respect to a standard for evaluating testimony, the *Treatise* offers only the brief suggestion that it is only "our *experience* of the governing principles of human nature, which can give us any assurance of the veracity of men" (T. 113). This point is elaborated later in the essay "Of Miracles" that Hume incorporates into his first *Enquiry*, where, laying down the general rule that "a wise man . . . proportions his belief to the evidence," he inquires whether one could ever have grounds for believing testimony of a "miracle." Here Hume acknowledges that "there is no species of reasoning more common, more useful, and even necessary to human life, than that which is derived from the testimony of men, and the reports of eye-witnesses and spectators." Testimony compensates for the limitations of our personal experience of facts and events; but testimony itself is a kind of experience, to which careful reasoners must apply the same rules of inference that they habitually utilize:

It will be sufficient to observe that our assurance in any argument of this kind is derived from no other principle than our observation of the veracity of human testimony, and of the usual conformity of facts to the reports of witnesses. . . . Were not the memory tenacious to a certain degree; had not men commonly an inclination to truth and a principle of probity; were they not sensible to shame, when detected in a falsehood: Were not these, I say, discovered by *experience* to be qualities, inherent in human nature, we should never repose the least confidence in human testimony.[47]

The wise person assesses the credibility of testimony by carefully considering such factors as the character of the informant, likely motives other than truth-telling, and the special circumstances of the case, so far as they are known. In this essay Hume argues that there are special reasons to distrust the evidence of religious devotees with regard to alleged miracles; elsewhere he points out that our whole supposed knowledge of history depends on our having no reason to suspect systematic deception on the part of "Printers and Copists" (T. 146). These conclusions, and others like them, depend on causal reasoning on the basis of our experience of moral rather than of physical phenomena: we seek regularities and estimate probabilities with regard to testimony as well as to everything else, always making the assumption that permits us to engage in any reasoning at all—that the course of nature, including human nature, continues uniformly the same. Here as elsewhere the philosopher simply seeks a more rigorous application of the principles supplied by common sense.

Nevertheless, reliance on testimony, however necessary it may be, is a great source of mistaken and even harmful beliefs. Credulity, Hume says, is a conspicuous weakness of human nature; and testimony may be the source of misreported facts or of whole arguments containing unphilosophical inferences from facts. Communication of ideas among the members of a society, by testimony and by sympathy, and reinforced by repetition, provides a substitute for autonomous reasoning for most people most of the time. This state of affairs, which seems inescapable, may be deplored up to a point; but the most reasonable response for the philosopher is to recognize the unavoidable limitations on autonomous reason and direct his critical efforts to where they seem most urgently needed. The natural disposition to accept reports and opinions from others is, after all, an essential component of people's sociable nature, and although credulity has its dangers, the tes-

[47] Ibid., pp. 111-12.

timony of others remains the only possible source for much of the information we require in order to live; here as more generally, total skepticism is an untenable position. Hence Hume checks his initial impulse to condemn credulity out of hand and instead moves toward a positive philosophy of belief in moral life that parallels, and is derived from, the same kind of analysis as that in which his epistemology culminates. This process may be discerned in his views on education.

Although Hume does not have a developed doctrine of education, or prescriptions beyond his general advocacy of the proper use of reason, he is attentive to the importance of the systematic social transmission of belief as a determinative factor in moral life. Here also Hume's views may be seen as a revision of Locke's, with respect both to the inescapable importance that Hume attaches to this facet of the formation of beliefs and to his evaluation of its influence. Locke dealt with the association of ideas primarily in terms of erroneous associations, which he attributed mainly to the influence of social custom; and he regarded education, insofar as it is a manifestation of custom, as likely to be partisan and factious, promulgating narrow views contrary to a correct view of the facts as well as to genuine interest.[48] Locke, however, did not come to Hume's eventual realizations that custom is not so easily dispensed with and that reliance on testimony is an unavoidable circumstance of human life. Hume regards as inescapable many of the features of the understanding in which Locke saw merely defects in right reasoning, and as a result his criticisms are less sweeping and his view of education less radical.

It is perhaps here, in fact, that Hume stands in greatest contrast to Locke, despite the apparent similarities of their philosophical aproaches. Causation and hence all inferential reasoning are resolved into forms of customary association, and Hume emerges from total skepticism with an acceptance of custom as the "great guide of human life";[49] accordingly he is led not only to an awareness of the necessity of habit or custom as a component of the understanding but also to a generally positive evaluation of it as a "natural" and usually salutary process, only the excesses and occasional vagaries of which require critical modification. This is Hume's position with respect to the understanding of the individual; the same position is extended, by way of his analysis of our reliance on testimony, into his account of the social dimension of reasoning and belief; and a central issue of Hume's moral

---

[48] Locke, *Essay* II.xxxiii.18; I.iii.22-26. It is Locke's criticisms of customary education that impel him, unlike Hume, to look into alternative methods.

[49] Hume, *Enquiries* (I), p. 44.

philosophy pertains to his analogous analysis and evaluation of the place of custom in the determination of moral value and conduct, as we shall see.

Hume prefaces his comments on education in the *Treatise* with a refinement of his psychology of belief. Ordinarily, repeated experience provides the basis for our inferential transitions from a present impression to the idea of its cause or effect. If, however, "a mere idea alone . . . shou'd frequently make its appearance in the mind, this idea must by degrees acquire a facility and force; and both by its firm hold and easy introduction distinguish itself from any new and unusual idea" (T. 116). This process provides the foundation for the observable force of education, which may thus be characterized as the more or less systematic introduction of lively ideas directly into the imagination.

This account, which is simply an elaboration of Hume's general view of testimony and its relation to belief, leads to some strong assertions concerning education: "All those opinions and notions of things, to which we have been accustom'd from our infancy, take such deep root, that 'tis impossible for us, by all the powers of reason and experience, to eradicate them; and this habit not only approaches in its influence, but even on many occasions prevails over that which arises from the constant and inseparable union of causes and effects" (T. 116). In Hume's normative account of the understanding, the causal relation is imputed and believed on the basis of a habit of association built up through experience of regular sequences of objects. In the absence of direct experience of objects, or prior to such experience, however, habits of thought and belief can be implanted in the mind through instruction, and these habits are no less forceful, drawing as they do on the same capacities of the imagination, than those that are not mediated by testimony. Everyone is educated, receiving and absorbing a great number of opinions and beliefs about many things before he is in a position to have direct experience of them; furthermore, any one person's experience of things is limited, and we must hold opinions about many matters that we cannot hope to confirm by observation and experiment. Such inevitable reliance on testimony leads Hume to assert that "more than one half of those opinions, that prevail among mankind, [are] owing to education, and that the principles, which are thus implicitly embrac'd, over-ballance those, which are owing either to abstract reasoning or experience" (T. 117). Hume concludes, somewhat ironically, that education is an "artificial" rather than a "natural" cause of belief; and in the case of received opinions as with testimony generally, Hume seeks to uphold a critical standard, maintaining in experience and probable inference alone the philosopher's proper mode of cognition. But his final observation is that education in reality is "built almost on the same foundation of custom and repetition as our reasonings from causes and effects" (T. 117); its force, against which philosophers may on occasion try to set themselves, has a firm foundation in Hume's psychology and in his skepticism.

In the preceding account education is treated as equivalent to instruction by repetition of words and arguments, as in the deliberate manner of formal education. Elsewhere, however, Hume usually treats education in a more general sense, as embracing all the informal means by which a society transmits ideas among its members and from one generation to another, thus achieving the broad like-mindedness or homogeneity of opinion constitutive of a community and requisite for smooth and orderly social interaction. Education in this sense is nearly equivalent to social tradition, as in the usage of Strabo, whom Hume quotes approvingly to the effect that "all is custom and education": the great bulk of our opinions are received or customary opinions, and custom operative at the social level is the principal determinant of character.[50]

Education in this broad sense is also the means by which values, as well as opinions about matters of fact, are disseminated and passed on: Hume recognizes that motivation to just actions for people in a "civiliz'd state" arises principally from the fact that they have been "train'd up according to a certain discipline and education" (T. 479). A full discussion of Hume's assessment of moral education will be deferred until we come to consider his moral philosophy as a whole, although it appears that custom would play an even greater role in molding an individual's beliefs about values than about facts, at least those facts whose confirmation lies within the realm of the individual's potential experience. Intermediate between moral values and opinions of fact lies the extensive sphere of manners, where Hume attributes great force to people's habit-following propensities: it is through a consideration of manners, he says, that we principally learn "the great force of custom and education, which mold the human mind from its infancy and form it into a fixed and established character."[51]

Most of Hume's observations on the social effects of habit are scientific in nature, and there is no question about his view of its factual importance. His remarks notably lack, however, the tone of

[50] Hume, "Of National Characters," *Works*, vol. 3, p. 247n.

[51] Hume, *Enquiries* (I), p. 86. Locke regards all moral conventions with suspicion, as "fashions," always a probable source of false values and bad habits, to be corrected by philosophy and a carefully managed education; *Essay* II.xxviii.12; II.xxi.71.

hostility that usually accompanies Locke's observations on the admittedly great influence of the "law of fashion" and similar customary phenomena. Even when Hume deplores a specific custom, he maintains a neutral attitude toward custom as such,[52] and more often he moves from an acknowledgment of the necessity of custom and habit in society to approval of its usual effects. In this respect Hume may be interpreted as presupposing a model of human beings who are more satisfactorily socialized than in the case of Hobbes, for example, and conceived also, in contrast to Locke, as being less in need of breaking out of the bonds of custom and received opinions.

Such a fundamental view, in any case, emerges from some basic doctrines of Hume's philosophy: the psychological principles with which he fills the gap left by his rejection of rational insight are of the sort taken over and developed further by later observers and proponents of a sociable and traditional human nature. The pleasurable social impulse of "imitation," for example, which both Burke and Smith regarded as "one of the strongest links of society," is a derivative of Hume's analysis of custom as generative of opinions and manners.[53] In his essay treating of the "moral causes" of the formation of national characters Hume himself speaks of the natural imitativeness of the mind as a factor in the communication of both passions and ideas, and of the "sympathy or contagion of manners."[54] In some circumstances, it is true, the operation of these factors can be discordant: religious and ideological factionalism (including what Hume calls "parties from *principle*"), and the ensuing intolerance, are traced to the fact that the mind "always lays hold on every mind that approaches it; and as it is wonderfully fortified by an unanimity of sentiments, so is it shocked and disturbed by any contrariety."[55] These psychological principles, however, more often provide Hume with a means of explaining the cohesive ties of societies, with which he is generally more concerned. They are to a large degree elaborations of his early, more

---

[52] Cf. Hume, *History of England*, chap. 29, vol. 3, pp. 161-62. The "prevailing force of custom" explains the survival of remnants of the older European code of honor in modern times, in particular the practice of dueling. On a more political subject, Hume attributes the resistance of early Stuart Parliaments to royal demands for increased taxation partly to the inertia of habit, in the face of sound reasons for change. "Habit, more than reason, we find in everything to be the governing principle of mankind." *History of England*, chap. 50, vol. 5, pp. 3-4.

[53] Burke, *Sublime and Beautiful*, p. 49. Cf. Adam Smith's portrayal of a person's sensitivity to the opinions and feelings of others, *The Theory of Moral Sentiments* (Indianapolis: Liberty Classics, 1976) III.2, pp. 208-31 and passim.

[54] Hume, "Of National Characters," *Works*, vol. 3, pp. 248-49.

[55] Hume, "Of Parties in General," *Works*, vol. 3, p. 131.

mechanistic, accounts of the operation of association and repetition in the imagination, as well as of his constant attention to the central role of habit in human nature.[56]

More will be said later about the passions and sympathy: here we may confine our attention to education conceived as a determinant of modes of thought rather than of behavior, or as the vehicle for the transmission of ideas rather than of passions as such. In this connection we may speculate on a theme that is only implicit in Hume, to the effect that the force of testimony and received opinion is likely to be especially great with respect to moral and political topics. The ideas that we contemplate and arrange in thinking about such matters, if they are to be meaningful in Hume's terms, must in principle be reducible to their component impressions, the discrete units of sensory data and feeling from which they are derived. Common political objects, however, when subjected to etiological analysis, prove to be extraordinarily complex; hence most of the time political discourse would seem to provide a case of words used consistently and more or less intelligibly through habits of speech and verbal association, without any resolution of complex into simple ideas except infrequently, and perhaps usually as a mode of criticism. It will be recalled that Hume offers "government" and "conquest" as examples of subjects on which we "may avoid talking nonsense" through linguistic habits rather than through any summoning up of the many distinct perceptions involved in the complex ideas (T. 23). This capacity, necessary as it seems to be, however, is a potential source of suspect reasoning in the eyes of the philosopher, and the problem of meaningless "jargon" has its roots in the inability of the imagination to sustain precision in its handling of abstract and complex ideas.[57]

The ideas of political objects, which we conceive unclearly and denote imperfectly by means of language, are complex in another way as well: many of them are resolvable, in Hume's terms, into impressions of both sorts—impressions of sensation insofar as they have material-objective referents, and impressions of reflection insofar as they also contain passionate and evaluative elements. Although most of Hume's examples have to do with our thinking about physical objects, his system clearly accommodates both emotional ideas, drawn from internal impressions such as hatred or desire, and complex ideas

---

[56] G. H. Sabine, "Hume's Contribution to the Historical Method," *Philosophical Review* 15 (1906): 17-38, argues that the "corporative" view of society, a central premise of later conservatism, was a natural extension of Hume's psychology of habit and belief, which thus eventually succeeded in abolishing the theoretical individualism from which it was derived.

[57] Hume, *Enquiries* (I), p. 21.

in which these are united with ideas of external objects. Moral ideas are generally of this last type, seldom lacking an element of affection or approbation (or their opposites) intermingled with images of the material features of the thing or event in question. The philosopher may attempt to distinguish and analyze these components in particular instances, but Humean psychology suggests that the affective elements are inextricable from the ideas of the qualities of external objects in most of our thinking about complex entities. Hume does not explore this issue at length, but he provides the ingredients for a psychology of political opinions in which the role of education would undoubtedly loom large as a determinant especially of this "sentimental" component of ideation. Moral ideas, not to mention moral beliefs and arguments, are of such a complexity, and of their nature expressive of experience so beyond the reach of the single individual, that their generation through education rather than through independent reasoning must be regarded as normal—and this for reasons over and above those that explain the force of repeated testimonial evidence for beliefs about all kinds of things.

Hume's attitude toward education parallels that which he maintains toward belief: just as he seeks to define the precarious boundary between reasonable belief and dangerous credulity, so he seeks to distinguish the baneful influence of testimony and indoctrination from their more usually beneficial and often inescapable effects. The dangers are apparent, as in the case of liars, "who by the frequent repetition of their lies, come at last to believe and remember them, as realities; custom and habit having in this case, as in many others, the same influence on the mind as nature, and infixing the idea with equal force and vigour" (T. 86). Elsewhere he notes the similar effect of the frequently repeated lie on the hearer as well (T. 117). The problem is the same in both cases: the suggestibility of the imagination, its dependence on experienced patterns, including those whose source is moral experience or testimony, and the fact that belief is nothing other than a vividness of conception engendered in a normally passive agent in the course of experience. Lies of course are an important component of experience, of equal force with truthful reports unless contradicted by other experience, which is not always likely to be available to the individual in the case of complex moral or historical questions. It is therefore not surprising that Hume has been accused of having been led by his skepticism and psychology to an unrealistic picture of people as being "excessively" influenced by education and propaganda.[58] His

[58] Norman Kemp Smith, *The Philosophy of David Hume* (London: Macmillan, 1949), p. 378.

appreciation of this side of human nature, in any case, reinforces his commitment to a skepticism that might permit a measure of criticism, moderated, however, by the awareness that false belief is simply a faulty product of the same mental tendencies that produce reasonable belief, and that one can no more abolish the influence of education than one could do without belief itself.

I turn now from education to several specialized topics in Hume's psychology as they manifest themselves in social life. His treatment of prejudice, first, may be regarded as a stage in a reevaluation that was taking place among certain of his contemporaries. This word originally connoted, as it does today, error or injustice perpetrated through hasty and fallacious reasoning. In Hume's own time, however, some Englishmen were beginning to question the Enlightenment's commitment to thoroughgoing rationalist criticism and even to declare themselves proud of their prejudices, seeing in them a beneficial and even necessary support of social stability and morality.[59] Although Hume's elevation of habit and sentiment over reason probably contributed to the development of this peculiar sensibility, he himself speaks of prejudice only in the usual pejorative sense. In the case of an individual, as we have seen, Hume explains prejudice as misapplication of the otherwise necessary general rule-forming tendency of the imagination; a prejudice is an inference drawn too hastily, either from an insufficient number of instances or from instances displaying insufficient resemblance (T. 146-54, 374). Hume points out, however, that the unreflective habits by which the imagination arrives at prejudices are of the same sort that underlie correct causal reasoning, and he acknowledges that no one is in a position to seek experimental confirmation for every opinion that one adopts for one's practical purposes. People's everyday reliance on inferences that must appear hasty to the philosopher is an inescapable fact of life; and although a critic might attempt to expose as "prejudices" those generalizations for which there is contrary evidence, he could scarcely set out to cure people of their generalizing propensity altogether.

Prejudice in Hume's sense can be a social as well as an individual phenomenon, since the members of any community have most of their experience mediated through the testimony of one another and even receive many entire beliefs through social transmission. Social influence can thus reinforce and extend the rule-forming tendency of the individual's imagination and provide it with specific contents. Prejudices

[59] See H. B. Acton, "Prejudice," *Revue Internationale de Philosophie* 6 (1952): 323-36.

expressed as judgments, moreover, are succinct verbal formulations and therefore lend themselves to direct communication more readily than do full accounts of the experiences from which they are drawn; and when they accumulate the force inherent in frequent repetition, and the liveliness of personal testimony, their influence is formidable.[60] As an example of social prejudice in the *Treatise* Hume mentions pejorative national stereotypes, a subject on which as a Scot he was always sensitive (T. 146-47). On the other hand he examines, more positively, the way in which the operation of the same kinds of general rules that produce prejudices also make possible the insinuation, the saving of appearances, and the indirect intimations that constitute what is called "good-breeding" in polite society (T. 150-51). Here Hume touches on the realm of morals, where effects of the rule-following propensity, no longer called "prejudice," are discovered to lie at the root of some of the most important facets of moral judgment and behavior, as we shall see in the following chapter. In his account of the understanding, however, Hume contents himself with the skeptical observation that the same mental habits that produce prejudices must be brought to bear, when necessary, to correct them. This is a task that the philosopher will undertake with some caution: although Hume never says, with Burke, that prejudices are to be cherished, the import of his philosophy as a whole is equally to the effect that wise reasoners should seek the "latent wisdom" in the prejudices of ordinary people and take a modest view of their capacity to correct these opinions.[61]

Another theme in Hume's psychology that pertains to the social nature of human beings is the dualism between the inertia and restlessness that compete for predominance in the human understanding. Hume portrays the imagination sometimes as a sluggish faculty, firmly set in patterns of habitual association, and sometimes as an active and lively faculty capable of far-ranging and unpredictable vagaries. These two pictures, which derive from the ambivalence in Hume's account of the imagination as a fundamentally rule-abiding or fundamentally creative or volatile faculty, are of significance to the future political scientist, even before Hume develops a parallel view of our affective nature: at stake is an understanding of human beings as primarily

[60] Hume acknowledges the force of rumors in *A True Account of the Behavior and Conduct of Archibald Stewart, Esq.; Lord Provost of Edinburgh, in a Letter to a Friend*, in *The Ironic Hume*, by John Valdimir Price (Austin: University of Texas Press, 1965), p. 154.

[61] Edmund Burke, *Reflections on the Revolution in France*, in *The Works of the Right Honourable Edmund Burke* (Boston: Little, Brown, 1865), vol. 3, pp. 346-47.

conservative, stable beings who derive satisfaction from routine modes of thought and action, or as prone to visionary undertakings or innovative ingenuity.

Of these two poles it is the former that Hume usually emphasizes and that on the whole receives the most support from his psychological principles. The associative rules of contiguity and resemblance would seem to have the effect of confining most speculations to the near and familiar, whereas that of causation normally tends to direct attention to observable sequences of experience. The disposition to generalize from apprehended particulars and the facility with which customary transitions among ideas repeat themselves in the imagination serve to inhibit people's ability to envisage the unaccustomed or to attain intellectually satisfying comprehension of novelties. The habits born of repetition, including the basic habit of expectation that the future will resemble the past, tend to restrict belief to the tangible objects of experience while relegating utopian suggestions to the faint and tenuous realm of fantasy.

In opposition to this picture, however, stand several distinctive tenets of Hume's psychology. Since all ideas are separable and related in no necessary way, the imagination has the liberty to join them "in what form it pleases" (T. 10) and thus to engage in flights of fancy whose distinction from reality is not always plain. Various adventitious factors may temporarily displace habit as the source of conceptual vivacity and hence belief, affording undue influence in the imagination to extraordinary events or conjunctions of ideas, thus detracting from ordinary people's ability to engage in correct causal reasoning and rendering them susceptible to belief in "miracles" or departures from ordinary experience. It is to such factors that Hume typically attributes the erroneous reasoning, undue credulity, fanaticism, and other phenomena that in the eyes of the skeptical philosopher are the characteristic shortcomings of the human understanding.

The normal and far more usual picture, however, is the first one: people in their mental as in their practical lives are largely creatures of habit, and accordingly the philosopher, for whom right reasoning about matters of fact arises from the careful recording of experience, confirms the trustworthiness of the usual origins of belief. It is noteworthy that Hume does not identify the novel and the startling as sources of aesthetic pleasure,[62] nor does his analysis of curiosity point to any special attraction to the new or unusual. In apparent contradiction to earlier statements about the mind's proclivity to constant

---

[62] As Burke was later to do: *Sublime and Beautiful*, p. 31 and passim.

motion, he concludes Book II of the *Treatise* with the assertion that the sudden alteration of objects "gives uneasiness" and that it is the stability of a firmly believed idea that principally satisfies our nature (T. 453). This is why skeptics are so rarely met with, and why Hume agrees with Burke that "men are much more naturally inclined to belief than to incredulity"[63] while, however, emphasizing that belief is generally a product of custom, the great guide of life, and not of imaginative leaps.

I have been considering in this section a variety of ways in which Hume's philosophy of the understanding moves from its individualistic inception to a view of the sociable nature and the social sources of mental formation in human beings. In this connection I conclude with mention of his doctrine regarding personal identity, or the idea of the self, which he concludes after analysis to be a "fiction," on the same order as the fictions of necessary connection and continuing objects, by which the imagination habitually postulates unities among its perceptions and thus orders its experience.

Hume's epistemological atomism must not be forgotten: all impressions are discrete entities, and every complex idea may be resolved into simple ones that are conceivably separable and distinct. His dictum that "every thing in nature is individual" (T. 19), moreover, might seem to include the unity and identity of conscious agents as well, inasmuch as his analysis of impressions and ideas seems to proceed on the assumption of a continuous mind as the locus of these units of perception. Here as elsewhere, however, Hume's epistemological analysis eventually leads him into paradox. His quest for a distinct impression underlying the idea we sometimes claim to have of our "mind" or "self" is fruitless, and the perceptions we have of the phenomena associated with a given mind do not display the constancy or coherence that is generally requisite for an ascription of objective and continuing existence. The mind appears to be nothing but its various contents, "a heap or collection" of ephemeral and distinct perceptions, along with the imaginative propensities and habits that unite and fix certain of them in patterns of thought (T. 207). Since impressions appear spontaneously and inexplicably in the mind, and since the habits that govern our mental transitions are to a large degree formed through our exposure to the recurrent features of our environment, we seem to be left with a picture of the cognitive agent as a passive receptor of stimuli, lacking any strong sense of continuous identity that might be counterposed to the flux of experience.

---

[63] Ibid., p. 18.

Some indication of the potential moral and political significance of this doctrine may be offered by way of justification for raising what might seem a technical issue of epistemology. Liberal thought before Hume had characteristically drawn on a philosophy of mind that took the individual's private consciousness as its starting point and as its measure of possible knowledge. This philosophy, proceeding introspectively, tended to assume the reality of a well-defined ego or conscious self, which, as with Descartes's rational soul, might be treated as the most certain of all existents or, as with Hobbes' system of passions, might be viewed as an autonomous center of desire and volition. In either case the presence of an undoubted and consistent ego provided the basis for a view of the mental and emotional self-sufficiency of the separate, private individual, which in turn served as the preliminary to the analysis of economic and political life as a matter of the pursuit of interests and of contractual arrangements undertaken by such individuals. The concept of individual interest itself, central to liberal theory (and present in Hume as well, as we shall see in the following section), presupposes a continuous conscious self that can reflect on its own potential future states. In this light Hume's doubts about the reality of the "self" assume significance as yet another way in which his skeptical probings lead him to conclusions whose implications, at least, are at odds with the usual doctrines of the (broadly liberal) tradition to which he at first sight seems to belong.[64]

Hume's analysis of the self follows his skeptical doubts about the external world, and his method is similar: any intelligible idea of a continuous and identical entity constitutive of our self must be traced to some distinct impression or to a set of impressions that displays such constancy or coherence that it becomes plausible, as in the case of external objects, to maintain a fiction of an underlying real existence. Philosophers such as Descartes trace personal identity to the mind or soul, which they characterize as an "immaterial substance"; but they have failed, in Hume's view, to account for this concept in terms of distinct perceptions. Nor is it necessary to suppose this concept of a mind or soul as that in which the several perceptions belonging to a

[64] Descartes, doubting everything except his own existence as a thinking being, inferred from the hats and coats that he saw from his window that other people were passing in the street; *Discourse on Method* III, and *Meditations* II, in *The Philosophical Works of Descartes*, trans. Elizabeth S. Haldane and G.R.T. Ross (Cambridge: Cambridge University Press, 1970), vol. 1, pp. 100, 155. In Hume's case it is his *own* self for his belief in which he cannot discover any good ground. He does not doubt the existence of other people, any more than of any of the objects of his perception. Humean skepticism, unlike Cartesian doubt, has the tendency of dissolving individuality.

particular conscious agent are located; our perceptions appear to us, Hume argues, in a way that is ultimately inexplicable, but they may be apprehended without any necessary thought of their being located or inherent in any special entity (T. 232-37). Another common argument alleges the necessity of a rational faculty (a soul) to explain the fact of consciousness, on the ground that the generation of thought and awareness through the mere motion of matter is inconceivable. But Hume dismisses this as a classic example of a claim of insight into a causal relation of the sort that his analysis of causation declares to be untenable. "To consider the matter *a priori*, any thing may produce any thing"; and since the factual question of the causes of consciousness does not appear to be readily amenable to investigation by experiment or observation, it is an issue on which philosophy should refrain from making pronouncements (T. 246-50).

Do we then have experience of any impressions constitutive of the problematic idea of our self, and if not, in what does personal identity consist? Hume concludes that he can discover no specific and constant perceptual element corresponding to this idea; the mind, rather, "is a kind of theatre, where several perceptions successively make their appearance; pass, re-pass, glide away, and mingle in an infinite variety of postures and situations" (T. 253), amid which, Hume says, "I never can catch *myself* at any time" as something distinct from the other things of which he is conscious (T. 252). Hume now finds himself in a familiar situation: epistemological analysis having failed to find grounds for a commonly held notion, he must still come to terms with the fact that we do nonetheless entertain a strong and usually ineradicable sense of our personal identity, which in common opinion serves as evidence for there being such a thing as a self. Here then as with causation and objectivity Hume makes his characteristic transition to psychology, attempting to account—with reference to propensities of the imagination—for a belief that, although not strictly justifiable by reason, may nevertheless be a useful and appropriate feature of our nature. Hume invokes familiar principles, most notably the tendency of the imagination to confound a series of related perceptions into a unity and generate a fiction of real and continuing existence to create order in its perceptions. This fictional identity or self is a product mainly of the memory, the faculty by which we recall and reflect on our past perceptions and which represents them as linked together in the network of relations in which the imagination originally associated them. Without memory a conscious agent would be in effect nothing more than a "bundle or collection of different perceptions," succeeding each other in a meaningless flux (T. 252); memory, by fixing some of these perceptions in recoverable patterns, provides us with such sense of continuous personal identity as we have (T. 260-63).

How strong, in general, is this sense of identity? The prevalence and tenacity of the belief in "self" might suggest that, like causation, it is a "natural belief," vivid and inescapable. Yet Hume speaks of claims of real personal identity as "confusion" and a "mistake" (T. 254), and the ingenuous tenor of his introspective reports suggests that his skepticism on this issue is a matter of genuine conviction. Elsewhere Hume remarks that in ordinary life the ideas of "self" and "person" are "never very fix'd nor determinate" (T. 189-90); and in his last philosophical work he still writes persuasively of the usual weakness of the sense of self in the face of experience.[65]

Hume's doctrine of the self, notorious as one of the principal components of his skepticism, has been more severely criticized than his other main positions.[66] I have, nevertheless, chosen to place some weight on it, both as another illustration of the development of Hume's philosophy from its epistemological to its moral stage and as a telling indicator of the generally passive view of cognitive processes that pervades Hume's psychology. It bears, moreover, on the theme of the individual's receptivity to the influence of the social environment: on Hume's account an individual's concept of himself would be inextricably bound up with his social and other memories and with those ideas that he has absorbed from communication with other people. These would include (perhaps prominently) the ideas that the person receives regarding other people's opinions of him—that is, his reputation. Reputation in turn is, in Hume's psychology, an important cause of the passions of pride and humility (T. 316), which likewise can figure significantly among the perceptions that are peculiarly one's own, when one reflects on oneself. Thus may social influence play a role in determining a person's very sense of identity, as well as the bulk of a person's ideas concerning other subjects.[67]

A due estimation of the relation of this doctrine to Hume's moral and political philosophy, however, requires that we consider the principal difficulty raised by commentators. This is the apparent inconsistency between Book I of the *Treatise*, where Hume seems to deny

[65] Hume, *Dialogues*, p. 159.

[66] For example, Terence Penelhum, "Hume on Personal Identity," in *Hume: A Collection of Critical Essays*, ed. V. C. Chappell (Garden City: Doubleday, 1966), pp. 213-39. Hume expresses dissatisfaction with his treatment of personal identity in the *Treatise*, Appendix, pp. 633-36.

[67] Annette Baier, "Hume on Heaps and Bundles," *American Philosophical Quarterly* 16 (1979): esp. 293-94.

any rational meaning to the idea of self, and the two subsequent books, where on several occasions he refers uncritically to this idea (cf. T. 286, 317) and employs it in elaborating some of the main doctrines of his theory of the passions and morals. It plays a key role in particular in Hume's account of the important psychic mechanism of sympathy—which figures prominently in his moral psychology—as well as in his analysis of such indirect passions as pride and in the concept of property.

A degree of tension or inconsistency on this issue no doubt does exist in the *Treatise*, although some of Hume's later characterizations of the idea of the self seem compatible with the treatment in Book I (e.g. T. 277): Hume does, generally, in his discussion of the passions and morals seem to take for granted a stronger sense of self-consciousness than is allowed for in the previous analysis. It is noteworthy, however, that Hume utilizes the idea of self in Books II and III primarily in connection with his doctrine of sympathy, whose application constitutes, as we shall see, one of the principal respects in which Hume's basic understanding of humans is as sociable and not egoistic beings. Hume thus somewhat paradoxically draws on the notion of self for the purposes of a moral psychology that emphasizes not autonomous selfhood but the communicability of feelings among the members of a group or society and the fundamental human disposition to be receptive, both affectively and imaginatively, to the experience and testimony of others. My concern in considering Hume's skeptical position on the self at this stage is its place in his overall portrayal of the human understanding as susceptible of social formation. Since there is no distinct individual mind but only perceptions associated in various patterns, individual identity seems more dependent on experience, including socially instilled habits of thought, than might otherwise be the case. Insofar as Hume then goes on to speak as though the self were a reality, in connection with sympathy, in order to arrive at a similar conclusion regarding the sociable dimension of awareness and personality in the affective sphere, the contradiction would appear to be less detrimental to the interpretation of Hume's main teaching than might be supposed.

I would affirm, however, that the doubts Hume raises on this issue stand as evidence of the degree to which his analysis takes him beyond the unquestioningly individualistic assumptions that form his epistemological point of departure. A person whose understanding is of the kind described by Hume is not so much the self-reliant individual associated with the politically liberal tradition that has historical affinities to philosophical empiricism but is rather a creature of imagination and mental habits, a significant portion of whose mental contents—including those bound up with his own identity—are received by testimony, precept, and other modes of social communication. The words such a person uses receive their meaning from public usage, in which the individual gradually learns to participate through education.[68] Although the two most fundamental mental habits—the expectation that the future will resemble the past and the belief that external objects exist when unperceived—are formed by constant experience in each individual separately, the great majority of specific customary associations and beliefs about causes and objects are mediated through the testimony of others. That the individual inhabits a world of wholly private events has seemed to some to be a corollary of the perceptualist theory of knowledge that Hume adopts; yet the question he raises about the self suggests that the individual's sense of identity, depending as it does on the manner in which elements from personal experience are related in memory, is in practice determined at least in part by the patterns and vividness with which the individual's ideas are endowed in the process of social intercourse. Much depends, for one who characterizes himself as a "bundle of perceptions," on the content and arrangement of those perceptions; and from such a *tabula rasa* the prevalence of custom and received opinion is at least as plausible an outcome as autonomy. Hume's evaluation of this propensity of human nature becomes fully manifest only within the context of his moral theory, in which the principles of psychology that we have been considering find their most important application.

4. Passion, Volition, and Reasonableness

The study of the passions forms a bridge in Hume's comprehensive science of human nature between his analysis of the understanding and that of morals. The distinctions among these different areas of inquiry are not hard and fast, in accordance with Hume's view of the fundamental unity of human nature: the operations of the imagination by which Hume explains cognitive activities play an important role likewise in accounting for affective processes; and Hume's broad view of the passions includes such features of human nature as the motivation of the will and the faculty of approbation, which form the transition to moral psychology and the analysis of the source of moral

[68] Cf. Antony Flew, *Hume's Philosophy of Belief* (London: Routledge and Kegan Paul, 1961), pp. 46-47.

judgments. In the *Treatise*, however, a doctrine of the passions is presented as a discrete unit in Hume's science of human nature, and in this and the following sections I consider several topics from within this division of his philosophy. As was the case with the imagination, I shall emphasize those doctrines that are of greatest consequence for his political science and especially for those parts of the ensuing moral theory that pertain to the political virtues. Although we are no doubt bound, in light of modern psychology, to see defects in this part of Hume's philosophy, it nonetheless has its strong points as well, illuminating certain issues; and in any case it, as well as his account of the understanding, constitutes the essential underpinning for his moral and political theory.[69] I follow Hume's presentation again in beginning with the passions as manifested in the individual, moving thence eventually to their social context and influence.

The passions occupy a distinct place in Hume's theory of mental contents as "impressions of reflection." As such they are immediate elements of consciousness, irreducible and unanalyzable, although Hume believes that their typical operations and the circumstances of their occurrence are susceptible of scientific description. It is characteristic of Hume's philosophy that from the outset he integrates the passions closely into his general view of the normal operations of the mind, alluding in his very first mention of them to their relations with ideas and thought processes (T. 7-8). Even while Hume is engaged in his epistemological investigations it becomes apparent that the role of this particular set of perceptual elements is important, extending into the logical foundation of what had been taken by other philosophers for purely rational thought. All belief is or involves a kind of feeling or sentiment (Hume does not call it a "passion," but its status seems similar), and on such belief depends all our reasoning about matters of fact or existence. Human beings emerge from this analysis of the understanding as fundamentally creatures of feelings and impulses, whose powerful ratiocinative capacity is itself grounded in instinct as well as circumscribed by a variety of nonrational dispositions. If the term passion is used, as Hume occasionally uses it, as equivalent to feeling and inclusive of all our instinctual dispositions, then passion may be regarded as the fundamental category of human nature. Even if passion is taken in the restricted sense to cover only the particular impulses with which Hume deals in his systematic account of the

[69] That Hume did not recast his doctrines of the passions as an *Enquiry*, as he did with his theories of the understanding and of morals, may be taken as evidence that he also was less satisfied with this part of his philosophy. Some of Hume's later views on the passions may be found in the second *Enquiry* and in his essays.

passions, it remains a broad category, including all the dynamic forces operative in the active and evaluative spheres of human life. On either view the passions are at least as deeply rooted in the constitution of human nature as the rational faculties with which they cooperate.

The passions have been a frequent philosophical theme ever since the classical moral treatises of Aristotle and Cicero, on which most subsequent ones have drawn.[70] Skeptics have acknowledged the large influence of the passions as well as of custom in human life in consequence of the weakness of reason; naturalists have regarded the passions as complementary to or integrated with the rational faculty, in opposition to the dichotomous view of human nature propounded by rationalists and theologians. In the early years of the eighteenth century Shaftesbury and Hutcheson opposed the currently dominant rationalist systems of ethics, locating the "active principles" of human conduct in the passions, to which they regarded the rational faculty as subordinate. These thinkers were mainly concerned to modify the earlier Hobbesian analysis of the constituent elements of our passionate nature, rejecting Hobbes's stark egoism for a more amiable and sociable interpretation, to which they added a new account of moral feeling.[71] Hume carried this program to the famous conclusion that reason's proper place is as the "slave of the passions": not only do the passions exercise a pervasive influence in human nature, but in addition they are found, from the point of view of the naturalist and the moralist, to provide a viable and appropriate foundation for moral life and ethical values as well.

Although Hume was working within an influential philosophical tradition, his own strongly stated conclusion was provocative. The word passion was ordinarily used, then as now, to signify "some agitation of mind, which is opposed to that state of tranquility and composure, in which a man is most master of himself."[72] Reid notes that Hume's much broader usage of "passion," to include calm and reflective emotions and indeed every principle of action, renders his assertion that reason must be subordinate to passion in willing and acting much less paradoxical than it first appears. Hume's deliberate extension of the category is integral to his philosophy as a whole,

[70] Hume acknowledges the inspiration of Cicero (*De Officiis*) and Aristotle (*Ethics*) in a letter of 17 September 1739, to Francis Hutcheson, *Letters*, vol. 1, pp. 34-35; and in the *Enquiries* (II), pp. 177, 264, 318-19.

[71] See Shirley Robin Letwin, *The Pursuit of Certainty* (Cambridge: Cambridge University Press, 1965), pp. 34-36; and Smith, *Philosophy of Hume*, p. 43.

[72] Thomas Reid, *Essays on the Active Powers of the Human Mind*, Essay III, Part 2.vi, in *Works*, vol. 2, pp. 570-75.

providing a way of accounting to the satisfaction of the skeptic for the conspicuous fact that people carry on their reasonings and beliefs in the absence of logical justification, as well as of explaining the many more obviously nonrational features of human conduct. In order to make plausible his extended sense of the passions, Hume draws several distinctions, of which the most fundamental is that between "violent" passions and "calm" ones; this distinction is important both to his analysis of volition and to his normative view of what it means to be a "reasonable" person within the premises of his philosophy, topics to which I turn in the rest of this section.

Hume's account of volition, alluded to above in connection with his naturalism, must be considered in greater detail, since it is at the root of his analysis of all the active capacities of human beings, including the faculty of moral judgment. Action of any sort is ordinarily motivated or stimulated by an "aversion or propensity" by which we are led to "avoid or embrace" any object from which we have a "prospect of pain or pleasure" (T. 414). Now in Hume's system pleasure and pain, when experienced, are impressions of sensation, but the "prospect" we may have of them is an idea, which is associated in our imagination with an idea of some object; ideation and thought thus enter into the process of motivation. The "aversion and propensity" (or "desire") that directly influence the will, however, are passions and thus "original existences" (T. 415) that appear within us. All the active principles of conscious life—evaluative judgment, choice, and voluntary action itself—are thus distinguished from mere reflection and the movement of ideas in the imagination by the additional presence of certain feelings; and it is the feeling, rather than whatever ideas may also be present, that Hume identifies as the motivating force.

The issue that Hume makes central in the analysis of motivation concerns the role of reason in determining or influencing the will. Although he holds that it is some passion that in the final analysis is determinative, the place Hume makes for reason permits him to define a standard of "reasonableness" of conduct in the very same section of the *Treatise* where the more often commented upon "slave" passage may be found.

Reasoning for Hume consists in an awareness of relations among ideas in the imagination—either their direct comparison through juxtaposition, or inferences from one to another through association. Although the imagination may envisage action, it lacks in itself the additional element of emotion that, responding to the ideas of pleasurable or painful objects conjured up by the imagination, stimulates an active impulse toward such objects. Hume's science is concerned generally with conscious agents in whose minds passions and ideas mingle; and in his psychology the feelings that stimulate action, although they are distinct elements, do not operate in isolation from processes of reasoning. Hume does recognize a category of passions said to be instinctual (T. 417, 439), including such impulses as hunger and love of life, whose operation is either constant or stimulated without conscious thought of their objects. The occurrence of most of the passions, however, is occasioned in Hume's account by the prior existence in the mind of ideas, which themselves are the products of thought and inference. It is reasoning, that is, that discovers and defines the objects that the passions then pronounce good or evil, desirable or undesirable. Given a certain inclination of emotion or desire, moreover, the reasoning faculty may come into play to specify the exact nature of potentially gratifying objects and to discover the means of their attainment. The intellectual endeavor is properly restricted to the identification of objects and of causal relations on the basis of experience and probability; but its conclusions, so far as they extend, may be efficacious in directing—by clarifying the objects of—the passions. By revealing the precise attributes of an apparently attractive object, or the difficulties (or costs) involved in achieving it, or the probable consequences of its attainment, reason may generate new ideas that arouse the passion of aversion, which then counteracts or redirects the previous desire. The imagination, on the other hand, may alight in its meanderings, or in its deliberate exploration of a particular object, on ideas that have the effect of arousing some new volition. In these ways the imagination or reason may be said to guide, even if it does not directly "influence," the will.

Hume notes that we often experience indecision in our feelings toward different objects, indecision that may be resolved by an exercise of thought, and that our occasional emotional agitations and desires can be cooled and modified by reflection. Experiences such as these lead to the commonplace moralizing about the "combat of passion and reason" and to the precept that everyone is "oblig'd to regulate his actions by reason" (T. 413). These experiences are not incorrectly reported, according to Hume, but the usual analysis and conclusions are inaccurate. The heterogeneity of reason and the passions in Hume's psychology precludes reason's having any active power that might compete with that of the passions; "nothing can oppose or retard the impulse of passion, but a contrary impulse" (T. 415), and so our sense that reasoning counteracts passion is in part an illusion. A truer statement of the case would be that our reasoning brings to our attention a set of ideas other than the original object of our passion, that these new ideas in turn stimulate "contrary passions," and that it is these passions that serve to negate or modify the original passion.

At this point Hume introduces his (imprecise) distinction between the calm and the violent passions as a way of accounting for the common experience just described (T. 417).[73] A violent passion is the "disorder in the soul" or perturbation that the word passion connotes in ordinary language. Calm passions, on the other hand, operate with such tranquillity in the mind that they are often mistaken for reason, although under closer scrutiny they are found equally to be impressions of reflection, or feelings. Violent passions are more intense, in that when present they tend to predominate in the agent's consciousness, although their influence is usually sudden and ephemeral. Their intensity, however, is not equivalent to strength, in the sense of a tendency always to determine the will; violent passion can yield to a process of reasoning and thence to a calm passion, which then exercises the paramount influence over the will in the long run. Later, Hume argues that the strength or weakness of a passion, as opposed to its calmness or violence, depends mainly on the extent to which it has become habitual (T. 419).

Although Hume implies that any particular passion, or most of them, can manifest itself in either form at different times, he does mention certain of the instinctual passions—benevolence, resentment, love of life, and kindness to children—as examples of normally calm ones (although in the following paragraph he points out that resentment, at least, can sometimes be violent; T. 418). Another example of a calm passion is the "general appetite to good, and aversion to evil, consider'd merely as such" (T. 417). Hume here may be alluding, as some have thought, to a moral impulse or sentiment of reflective approval or disapproval that an agent can oppose to the precipitate impulses to action aroused by the more violent emotions;[74] and indeed this is the role that "calm passion" plays in Hume's moral theory. The "good" here may be taken, however, in the more narrow sense in which Hume often uses it, to refer to the agent's view of his own happiness; on this reading Hume is positing a eudaemonistic impulse that operates in individuals regularly and calmly, along with the other calm instincts, and that serves as a general principle of motivation that

---

[73] This distinction appears to be adopted from Hutcheson; cf. *A System of Moral Philosophy* i.i.6-7, in *Collected Works of Francis Hutcheson* (Hildesheim: Georg Olms, 1969), vol. 5, pp. 9-12. See Hume, letter of 10 January 1743, to Francis Hutcheson, in *Letters*, vol. 1, p. 46.

[74] Smith, *Philosophy of Hume*, p. 167.

is opposed on occasion by more violent and "sensible" emotions, including desires with respect to specific objects of proximate or transient pleasure. Generally speaking, the distinction between the calm and violent passions is one of constancy and intensity, the best candidates for distinctive membership in the "calm" category being such constant but unobtrusive instincts as "love of life." The calm passions are also often associated with more sustained reflection or reasoning, which is made possible by their comparative lack of intensity and which guides them toward their often more remote or more enduring objects.

In connection with his account of motivation Hume presents three variants of a normative model of reasonableness in individual conduct. Although reason cannot directly influence the will, it can influence and indeed govern the passions that do determine the will. As the faculty of ideation, reason always plays a role in pointing out potential objects of action, and as the faculty of more or less elaborate causal inference to remote objects, it can constitute a significant part of the prelude to judgment and volition. Thus, although no desire, Hume says, can be in itself contrary to reason, there are two senses in which "any affection can be call'd unreasonable": "First, When a passion, such as hope or fear, grief or joy, despair or security, is founded on the supposition of the existence of objects, which really do not exist. Secondly, When in exerting any passion in action, we chuse means insufficient for the design'd end, and deceive ourselves in our judgment of causes and effects" (T. 416). The function of reason in the process of motivation may be termed instrumental, but its role is a large one, for in its activity of identifying objects and the causal relations in terms of which the real or probable existence of certain objects is held to be contingent on that of others, reason supplies the mind with the ideas of all its potential objects of desire and action, together with their probable consequences. All passions except certain instinctual ones such as hunger are aroused by certain objects outside the agent, objects supposed to be real, or anticipated to be real in the future; all volition and action are likewise exercised toward real objects and by means of real objects. Therefore all the passions and action are related to judgments concerning objects and causes that are the province of reasoning, and the validity of these judgments, in accordance with Hume's criteria of correct inductive inference, provides a standard for estimating the reasonableness of conduct. More is involved here than the mere calculation of means to ends. The correct identification of objects, especially complex and nonpresent ones, can be a difficult process; and the scientific attitude to causality assumes that all objects are related to others in endless and necessary but not easily ascertainable patterns. Reasonable action is thus characterized by the accuracy of the reasoning that attends the establishment of the relevant facts of a matter prior to the exercise of the will.

The second variant of the model of reasonableness, closely related to the first, pertains to the prevalence of the calm over the violent passions. The calm passions, Hume says, have been mistaken for "reason" by philosophers who have sought to describe motivation in terms of a conflict between reason and passion. This error arises from the fact that the calm passions are steadier and less agitating, but also because they do in fact tend to be associated with more extensive reliance on reasoning than do the violent ones. A violent passion is defined in terms of its turbulence, but it may be observed to be stimulated as a rule by some proximate object of desire or aversion, without the interposition of reasoning. The calm passions, in contrast, are both more reflective and typically oriented to more distant objects (T. 419). Any passion manifested in association with a process of deliberation would presumably be calm, in the sense that it could not be so intense as to displace all other mental contents; and any passion directed toward a remote object would therefore be relatively calm, since it is only by inferential reasoning that we acquire ideas of such objects. This relation explains why people acting under the influence of calm passions are regarded as acting "reasonably": they are indeed more likely to be exercising their reason, even if passion determines their will in the end. A reasonable person is one who reasons more, and in a scientific fashion, surveying extensive chains of causes and effects with cautious precision, and who accordingly is more often possessed by calm than by violent passions.[75]

Such people are reasonable, finally, because they are in this way led to act more in accordance with their "interest" (T. 418), a term Hume here uses to signify a larger or true interest, in contrast to momentary desires people may indulge under the influence of more violent emotions.[76] One's interest is one's "greatest possible good," "the greatest and most valuable enjoyment" (T. 416, 418), or those objects that together constitute a person's long-range happiness, and not necessarily those objects that arouse present desire. It is only by reasoning that one can discover the remote objects that are part of this larger interest, and it is only through the cooperation of reasoning and the

[75] Rachel M. Kydd, *Reason and Conduct in Hume's Treatise* (New York: Russell and Russell, 1964), pp. 115, 132ff., and passim.

[76] See below in chapter IV, section 2, where the concept of "true interest" appears in Hume's moral theory as equivalent to utility.

calm passions that the impact of present objects and violent emotions is counteracted in the determination of volition.

This model of "reasonable" motivation and action has clear normative content in addition to being a description of a particular psychological state. Hume's preference is explicit, as when he equates this state with "what we call strength of mind" (T. 418). Elsewhere he affirms that anyone—or any sensible person—would prefer to be of a "cool and sedate temper" rather than of extreme "*delicacy of passion*" or susceptibility to emotional agitation;[77] and in another passage he characterizes genuine happiness as consisting, among other things, in a "just moderation" of the affections.[78] People in actuality experience and exhibit the two sorts of passion in different degrees, or in alternation; no single statement about motivation accurately accounts for the variation that we find: "Men often act knowingly against their interest: It is not therefore the view of the greatest possible good which always influences them. Men often counteract a violent passion, in prosecution of their distant interests and designs: It is not therefore the present uneasiness alone, which determines them."[79] Hume's doctrine that it is always passion that determines the will does not therefore commit him to any single or simple view of motivation. He does, however, emerge with a fairly definite idea of what constitutes a desirable type of character—the reasonable person, who has obvious affinities to the "wise" or "philosophical" person, characterized by a healthy "tincture" of mitigated skepticism, to whose judgment Hume frequently appeals, and who reappears later in Hume's moral theory as a person who grasps the value of, and adheres to, the artificial or "reflective" virtues over more immediate promptings of desire.

We confront here an effort on Hume's part to assess and evaluate various facets of human nature that emerge in his psychological analysis, just as in his study of the imagination he attempts to delineate certain restricted aspects of association and belief as the proper standard of right reasoning. The outlines of an analogous standard may be discerned in these passages with regard to our volitional nature, and we shall observe a similar process in Hume's moral theory; in all these fields Hume develops related philosophical norms out of the data of human nature. In the present case he clearly conveys his philosophic disapproval of the indulgence of the violent passions, which like undue credulity (a similar indulgence of unreflective feeling) we may assume

[77] Hume, "Of the Delicacy of Taste and Passion," *Works*, vol. 3, p. 91.
[78] Hume, "The Sceptic," *Works*, vol. 3, pp. 220-21.
[79] Hume, "Dissertation on the Passions," *Works*, vol. 4, p. 162; also *Treatise*, p. 418.

is characteristic of the "vulgar," although its roots in human nature are shared by all alike. The prevalence of the "calm passions," in contrast, implies self-control or moderation, and hence a steady pursuit of those long-range objects that constitute one's true interest, with minimal distractions from ephemeral emotions and proximate objects. This calmness in the conduct of individuals is analogous, furthermore, both to the social order that is attained by observance of what he later calls the artificial virtues and to moderation in political action, both of which he also distinctly approves, as we shall see. The long-term social happiness promoted by justice, which in turn is upheld by moderate legal governments, depends in the final analysis on "calm" and reasonable people who will support these institutions.

The possibility of self-control that Hume endorses here, involving the deliberate suppression of impulse in favor of reflection and calm feelings, is also analogous to his advocacy elsewhere—in connection with his mitigated skepticism—of circumspection in reasoning and judgment. Hume's psychology often portrays the thinking agent as the passive recipient of perceptions, in whom belief simply occurs as the product of a certain feeling that arises from the circumstances in which the mind is placed; indeed Hume has been credited with grasping the alleged logical impossibility of "deciding to believe" (or not to believe).[80] This view does not seem quite correct, however, since Hume recommends that we "proportion [our] belief to the evidence,"[81] and his distinction between the "wise" person and the credulous "vulgar" is based on the former's ability either to grant or to withhold assent in accordance with philosophic criteria. A wise person, in other words, is able to refrain from succumbing to the promptings of a vivacious imagination in favor of careful reasoning, in much the same way that reasonable people overcome impulse and take a larger view of their interest.[82] In both cases, of course, the suspension of inclination eventually yields to judgment or volition.

Hume may appear here to be sponsoring a model of "rational" conduct conceived in terms of the deferred gratification and personal utility-maximization that were later to be formalized in liberal economic doctrine and related forms of political theory, and there is no doubt that such a model grew out of the psychological tradition to which Hume belongs. Hume's contribution, however, makes clear the

[80] Bernard Williams, *Problems of the Self* (Cambridge: Cambridge University Press, 1973), p. 148. See *Treatise*, p. 624, for the best evidence for this interpretation.
[81] Hume, *Enquiries* (I), p. 110.
[82] See J. A. Passmore, "Hume and the Ethics of Belief," in *David Hume: Bicentenary Papers*, ed. G. P. Morice (Austin: University of Texas Press, 1977).

limits of rationality in this "rational" model, emphasizing the fact that the self-control in question, although it is connected with the exercise of reason and reflection, is in the end a product of the balancing of certain passions or desires against others. However much reason may bring a wider range of objects to our attention, it is finally by virtue of a "feeling" that we choose one over another. The "ultimate ends of human actions" cannot be accounted for by reason but only, rather, naturalistically, by their "accord or agreement with human sentiment and affection."[83]

Hume's model of reasonable conduct does, however, exhibit the fundamental difficulties of the more formal models. How far is it "rational" (or reasonable) to postpone gratification, to forego immediate in favor of remote objects of happiness? How long is one's "long-range" interest?[84] How long ought one to think about trains of causality and consequences before finally yielding to feeling and exercising the will? The irremediable fallibility of our reasoning, Hume warns, ought to inhibit our efforts in practical affairs to look very far ahead.[85] More generally, it is apparent that these difficulties in the practical sphere are analogous to that facing the skeptical philosopher in the theoretical one. The skeptic, through sustained epistemological analysis, arrives at a total suspense of judgment and belief, unable to justify even probable reasoning about elementary matters of fact; but this impasse is overcome in life through instinctual propensities to belief, whose operation is then selectively justified by naturalism. Similarly it is the moderate skeptic, the epitome of the reasonable person, whose inclination to reflection is more conducive to the prevalence of the calm over the violent passions; and here also the "mitigated" quality of the skepticism is important: if it were total, it might just as readily bring about either a paralysis of the will or its uncritical acquiescence in immediate impulse. Moderate skeptics, though they reason extensively and cautiously, act and judge in the end because they acknowledge and accept the facts of their own affective nature, just as they are aware of the passionate element in the conduct and the values of others. The contradictions in the concept of "rationally self-

[83] Hume, *Enquiries* (II), p. 293.

[84] In Hume's theory the tendency of the imagination to be stimulated (and of desire to be provoked) by near more than by equivalent remote objects provides a rough psychological analogue to the economist's assumption that it is rational to discount (at some rate) future benefits in assessing their present value. Thus, although the reasonable person *considers* future objects, the natural tendency of the imagination is not wholly opposed to rationality (in this sense) and needs only occasional correcting.

[85] Hume, "Of Commerce," *Works*, vol. 3, p. 287.

interested behavior," like those in the skeptical crisis, although they are not resolved by reason, do not commonly arise in life because reason is only one of the basic features in human nature considered in its entirety.

Although Hume alludes, then, to the notion of "interest" in this section of the *Treatise*, his political science, as we shall see, can be interpreted only to a limited degree as a doctrine grounded in self-interest, just as his view of motivation is in general far from being one of egoistic calculation. The "rational" possibility is, in both these contexts, an abstracted one, and it is one that Hume does indeed seem to favor—at least when the alternative is stated in terms of succumbing to "violent passion." There are, however, other potentialities in human nature, to some of which I now turn in considering Hume's survey of the passions and his treatment in this sphere of the fundamental operations of sympathy and custom.

5. Hume's Analysis of Particular Passions

Hume brings to his study of the passions in Book II of the *Treatise* the same paradigm of the scientific enterprise that marks his approach to the imagination, hoping to account with a simple and comprehensive scheme for the whole range of emotional phenomena (T. 281-82). He pursues this project in three stages: by enumerating the basic passions and describing the circumstances in which they manifest themselves; by showing how various passions are related successively through association; and by showing the interaction and reciprocal influence of passions and ideas in the imagination, or the way in which the two types of association (of ideas and feelings) can "assist and forward each other" (T. 284) as individuals apprehend and react to objects.

Hume believes that such a simple explanatory science of the passions is possible on the explicit assumptions that the fundamental passions and their operative principles are "original qualities" in human nature rather, for example, than variable products of environment and training, and that human nature displays uniformities in this respect (T. 280-81). The *Treatise*'s uncritical acceptance of the truth of these postulates is less pronounced when Hume later turns to political and historical studies and finds there how great a diversity of effects must be traced to his few and simple psychological principles. Even within the *Treatise* Hume's initial framework for treating the passions proves to be inadequate, however, and, as was the case with the doctrines of ideas and association in the imagination, it is modified and supplemented as he proceeds. The first two parts of Book II are the most crudely mechanistic part of the *Treatise*;[86] the most important supplemental element is sympathy, which, following its unheralded introduction,[87] evolves to play a prominent role in Hume's moral psychology and the view of human sociability that, with respect to the passions as to the imagination, eventually displaces the original individualism. Even if much of the analysis of the passions does prove unsatisfactory, however, it provides the context for an important segment of Hume's theory of human nature, and it contains substantive observations that are of significance in the subsequent moral theory. In this section I therefore examine in a critical fashion several issues in this part of Hume's philosophy.

Hume begins by dividing the passions into two categories, direct and indirect, both of which are said to "arise immediately from good or evil, from pain or pleasure" (T. 276). Later Hume discovers a third category—the instinctual passions—that constitutes an important exception to the kind of motivation implied in the phrase just quoted. Both the direct and the indirect passions "arise" from pleasure and pain in that they appear in us consequent upon an idea of a pleasurable or a painful object; the occurrence of these passions, that is, can be systematically related to certain circumstances, or causes, and it is these that Hume sets out to analyze. I follow Hume's order of presentation by considering first the more complicated indirect passions, of which Hume identifies four main examples and which he examines as correlative pairs: pride and humility, love and hatred; benevolence, anger, compassion, malice, and envy also receive some attention. All these passions are indirect in that, in addition to "causes" in the form of precedent ideas of good and evil, they also have "objects," namely, the idea of oneself in the case of pride or humility and of some other person in the case of love and hatred. The indirect passions occur as a result of the association in the mind of an appropriate "cause" and an "object" in what is portrayed as a routine and mechanical process. The scheme is compact and symmetrical, if limited in the view it permits Hume to take of human emotional potentialities; and it defines precisely Hume's analytical project, which is the discovery of what sorts of things cause or stimulate the various passions in us.

Hume begins with the passions of pride and humility, feelings that are experienced when the idea of some good or bad thing comes to

[86] Smith, *Philosophy of Hume*, pp. 74-76.
[87] Sympathy appears first in the *Treatise* II.i.11. It is not itself a passion but a special mental mechanism functional in the generation of certain passions.

be associated in the imagination with the idea of oneself.[88] Hume affirms that these are the most commonly experienced passions, but beyond this it is not clear that there is any special significance in the fact that he chooses to give the first place in his study to pride.[89] It is not an overriding passion, nor does it play a dominant role in his political philosophy, as it does, for example, for Hobbes; and although in some of his essays Hume explores the ways in which pride and humility can be oriented to different sorts of objects in aristocratic and commercial societies, he does not, in the manner of Montesquieu, develop systematically a typology of different regimes based on the characteristic motivating principles of their citizens. In assuming the frequent incidence of pride (and humility) in individuals, however, Hume may be said to take for granted the prevalence of private am- bition and to that extent to discount the possibility of a society based on what some of his contemporaries called civic or republican virtue (or selfless dedication to public objects), at least in its more rigorous versions. That pride is given priority over love (in Hume's broad sense of this term), furthermore, may generally count as evidence of the egoistic dimension in Hume's theory of human nature.

Another noteworthy point is that in Hume's treatment humility and pride lack any substantial connotation of moral virtue or vice; that is, these qualities lack the status that they have traditionally had in Christian systems of ethics and are analyzed simply as passions, normal features of human nature that arise naturally in certain situations (cf. T. 600).[90] Indeed, the valuation attached to these passions has, for the most part implicitly, been reversed: moral virtue, or reflection on one's own generous actions, is said to excite pleasure and hence pride in us, a fact that Hume defends as proper (T. 297-98). Elsewhere he argues that pride arising from a favorable opinion of one's rank, dignity, or character is an important inducement to moral virtue;[91]

---

[88] On the problematic status of the self, see above, section 3 of this chapter.

[89] Cf. Annette Baier, "Master Passions," in *Explaining Emotions*, ed. Amelie Rorty (Berkeley: University of California Press, 1980), pp. 403-23. Pride is said to be a master passion, one by which reason "ought" to be ruled as a "slave," since the desire associated with it is a self-sustaining or "conservative" desire to keep the things or qualities that cause it. This thesis, however, seems to be inconsistent with Hume's association of pride and ambition: pride in what we have can spur us to seek *more* of the same, or the anticipation of pride can motivate action (see below).

[90] Cf. Hume, *Enquiries* (II), p. 314n. Cf. also Pall S. Árdal, *Passion and Value in Hume's Treatise* (Edinburgh: Edinburgh University Press, 1966), pp. 20, 25.

[91] Hume, "Of the Dignity or Meanness of Human Nature," *Works*, vol. 3, pp. 150-51.

and due pride later appears (briefly) in Hume's moral theory as a natural virtue in its own right:

> But tho' an over-weaning conceit of our own merit be vicious and disagreeable, nothing can be more laudable, than to have a value for ourselves, where we really have qualities that are valuable. The utility and advantage of any quality to ourselves is a source of virtue, as well as its agreeableness to others; and 'tis certain, that nothing is more useful to us in the conduct of life, than a due degree of pride, which makes us sensible of our own merit, and gives us a confidence and assurance in all our projects and enterprizes. (T. 596-97)

Pride moreover renders individuals ambitious, and ambition, when properly channeled into efforts to excel in a particular profession, is a quality generally beneficial to society.[92] It is true that the rules of "good-breeding" (components of artificial virtue) restrain the expression of pride and indeed enjoin a certain appearance of humility in polite society, just as the rules of justice restrain the pursuit of self-interest (T. 597-98). But in both cases it is only excessive manifestations of these natural impulses that must be checked.

Hume's generally favorable attitude toward pride (and his correlative conception of humility as the subjective response to failure, deprivation, or low estate) follows from his enumeration of its usual causes, which are for the most part objects or qualities of personality on which society places a positive value. An individual is likely to receive pleasure, and hence feel pride, in an association of himself with socially esteemed objects such as wealth, virtue, or an enterprising spirit. This fact is not fully intelligible in Hume's system until he discusses the nature of sympathy and the social "contagion" of feeling by which emulation and sensitivity to the feelings of others are explained as motives of action. Enough has already been said, however, concerning the force of education and social communication to suggest that Humean individuals are far from autonomous in their modes of

---

[92] Hume, "Of National Characters," *Works*, vol. 3, p. 246n. Hume remarks that it is preferable to err on the side of over- rather than under-valuation of our own merit: "Fortune commonly favours the bold and enterprizing" (T. 597). Hobbes had treated pride as a natural passion, but one that had to be overcome by an acknowledgment of equality, in accordance with the ninth law of nature; *Leviathan*, chap. 15. Adam Smith was subsequently to treat pride generally as a vice; *Theory of Moral Sentiments* VI.iii, pp. 400-421. Hume's comments are therefore not commonplaces. Their inspiration seems partly classical, insofar as due pride is seen as promoting the cultivation of excellence of character, and partly modern, insofar as it is associated with the spirit of individual enterprise.

evaluation of objects; the same must hold true for the self-directed passions of pride and humility that depend on such evaluations, which are therefore in this sense social as well as egoistic phenomena.

Although, in keeping with his hopes that a science of human nature might reveal the operation of a few uniform principles, Hume says that "in all nations and ages, the same objects still give rise to pride and humility" (T. 281), he does call special attention to several different causes that appear to reflect the influence of different sets of social norms. In a section on property and riches he remarks that it is this that "most commonly" produces pride (T. 309), a view that, it may be thought, reflects the assumptions of a commercial or bourgeois milieu. He mentions only in passing the "personal merit" and achievements that might figure in a liberal estimation of due pride (T. 281, 303). He devotes far more attention, however, to qualities such as wit and taste, family and descent, and a sense of honor and rank that seem to reflect a more aristocratic ethos (T. 297, 307-309, 598-99).[93] Some of this may be attributed to Hume's acquiescence in the customary values of modern European monarchies, as characterized by Montesquieu; some is due no doubt to the classical inspiration of his psychology and moral theory, for example, his approving reference to "courage, intrepidity, ambition, love of glory, magnanimity, and all other shining virtues of that kind" that arise from healthy self-esteem (T. 599-600). Notwithstanding his allusion to Alexander in this context, however, Hume's paganism stops short before the "suppos'd virtue" of military heroism, which he views as arising from excessive pride and ambition (T. 600-601). Pride must yield to the values of peace and order, which his political philosophy generally emphasizes.

In his survey of the causes of pride Hume mentions two factors that deserve special attention in light of their possible implications for politics as potential sources of political discord, since the pride-causing objects in both cases are at least problematic as sources of general social benefit. In neither case does Hume draw out these implications, in keeping with a general weakness of his political theory in regard to its sensitivity to sources of conflict and antagonism.

As mentioned, Hume gives a good deal of attention to family and descent as a cause of pride (or humility), apparently ranking these as

[93] Acknowledging the importance generally accorded to descent, Hume comments, "I doubt that our morals have not much improved since we began to think riches the sole thing worth regarding." Letter of 12 April 1758, to Alexander Home, *Letters*, vol. 1, pp. 274-77. Cf. also his appeal to "nobility, gentry, and family," in connection with an attack on stock-jobbing, in "Of Public Credit," *Works*, vol. 3, p. 367.

of equal or greater importance than property. Hume's interest in the family is constant though always somewhat in the background: his moral theory, for example, is built around the distinction between "natural" virtues that operate spontaneously among members of a familial or other closely knit group and the "artificial" virtues of a larger society; his conjectural account of the origin of the artificial virtues and of government is expounded in terms of an evolution from familial to more extended social groups. In all these topics there is a latent tension between the affective ties characteristic of a family and the more extended, legal ties that supersede but do not wholly replace them in a larger society—between family pride and family duty and broader social obligations. I shall return to this problem in discussing Hume's ethics, of which his observation on family pride may be taken as an anticipation, only noting here the possibility that this form of pride may occasion motives that are at variance with the requirements of justice.

The other problem in Hume's treatment of pride is what may be called a Hobbesian one in which again Hume fails to probe as deeply as he might into sources of conflict, even if they are regarded as normally latent ones. Although for the most part he adheres to the simple formula that any agreeable object related to oneself can be a source of pride, Hume does at one point make certain very important qualifications: "that the agreeable or disagreeable object be not only closely related, but also peculiar to ourselves, or at least common to us with a few persons"; and that the agreeableness of objects is generally estimated "more from comparison than from their real and intrinsic merit" (T. 291). These observations, along with the assertion that men are "every moment" comparing themselves with others (T. 292), are as close as Hume comes to an understanding of pride as a function of preeminence or as associated with a desire for preeminence among one's fellows, and hence a source of endless striving and tension; or as typically caused by prestigious objects or goods that are intrinsically scarce, and hence objects of relentless competition in which most people are inevitably disappointed and "humiliated." Hume is aware of the degree to which people live in one another's eyes, but sympathy rather than emulation becomes his principal category for analyzing this fact of social life, and therefore, despite the suggestions offered here, he does not (like Rousseau, for example) develop a theory of social disorder or alienation based on the common propensity to feel pride and humility.

Related to this issue is the psychology of power, the sense of which was for Hobbes the principal source of pride. Hume defines personal power instrumentally, as the probability through voluntary actions of attaining some desired object; he adds that insofar as the envisioned object is regarded as pleasurable, so the possession of power provides an anticipatory pleasure and hence is generally a cause of pride in its possessor (T. 311-15). A weakness of this analysis is that in its terms one cannot desire or enjoy power for its own sake but only as a means to some other end; and Hume does not explore the psychological process by which a means can become an end in itself. Wealth is a type of power in Hume's sense, but he does not recognize the ways in which wealth can be abstracted from its potential objects and become a source of actual rather than anticipatory pleasure for its possessor. More significantly, Hume treats "authority over others" as a form of power, pleasurable therefore only insofar as it is conceived instrumentally. He does note that the "vanity of power" is "much augmented by the consideration of the persons over whom we exercise our authority" (T. 315), implying a special pride attaching to power over persons. For the most part, however, desire for authority would motivate a person such as Hume describes only as a means of accomplishing some other end; the love of domination, and pride of power as such, are psychological possibilities that he neglects.

The passions of love and hatred are presented as parallel to pride and humility in their manner of operation, being likewise indirect, occasioned by an agreeable or painful idea in association with some person other than oneself. It has been pointed out that Hume's sentiment of love is genuinely altruistic and not a transferal of self-love to another or a regard for the usefulness to ourselves of another person, as in the accounts of some psychological associationists.[94] Love of another, on the other hand (and all of this applies, *mutatis mutandis*, to hatred as well), cannot be a free and unqualified affection for the other person as such but is seen as contingent on a "cause," the idea of some pleasant quality or circumstance associated with the person. The very "indirect" nature of these passions, which renders them analyzable in terms of cause and object, means that they cannot be more deeply seated than the specifiable relationships on which they depend.

Love and hatred, in Hume's scheme, must have as their "objects" specific individuals, and presumably individuals of whom the agent has a fairly distinct idea, since the passions are occasioned by the

---

[94] E. B. McGilvary, "Altruism in Hume's *Treatise*," *Philosophical Review* 12 (1903): 290-91. "Self-love" is technically not a possibility within Hume's scheme of the passions (T. 329).

constellations of ideas in the imagination. From this follows the important conclusion that "there is no such passion in human minds, as the love of mankind, merely as such, independent of personal qualities, or services, or of relation to ourself" (T. 481). This passage occurs in Hume's discussion of the origins of justice, which he consistently declines to attribute to any such diffuse passion as the love of one's fellows in general; although, as we shall see, by a broad interpretation of the effects of sympathy, and in the second *Enquiry* by the postulation of a general sociable instinct, he accomplishes much the same purpose. Another corollary of this principle would seem to be the impossibility of any such feeling as love of the public, or of one's country, as such, or love of any abstraction. The attachment of citizens to the state in Hume's political theory is grounded in interest and in a sense of moral obligation toward the laws but not in public spiritedness, civic virtue, or the like, conceived as a special feeling or passion. Likewise, Hume recognized the phenomenon of patriotism, and his psychology includes several principles, such as the force in the imagination of the close-at-hand and the accustomed, that could be brought to bear on it. But his restriction of love to feelings toward persons means that this emotion can be related to country only mediately, through the love of one's prince (T. 330), or perhaps through love of one's fellow citizens individually, when they are mentally associated with agreeable ideas of one's country. These ideas—in Hume's terms the "cause" of the passion—would be the more efficacious as they are more distinct and vivid, a fact that would undoubtedly lead Hume to agree with Burke that attachment to country must be mediated through the ideas of certain of its specific or local attributes.[95] These observations may be applied in reverse to hatred, the strength of which in Hume's account would seem to increase as its cause and object acquire greater specificity and vividness in the imagination. Xenophobia would have a place in his scheme, since he treats fear as a passion connected with uncertainty; but it is not clear how he could explain hatred as a forcible motive with respect to unknown, remote, or abstracted objects.

Hume's analysis of the indirect passions suffers both from the scheme of double association and from the symmetry he postulates between the two basic pairs, both of which are aspects of his model and its scientific economy. Not only, for example, must the passions have specific causes, but moreover opposite passions, such as love and hatred,

[95] "Men are vain of the beauty of their country, of their county, of their parish" (T. 306). Pride in country is mediated by attachment to a more familiar locality, in accordance with the effect of the relation of contiguity on the imagination.

must therefore have opposite causes and opposite effects—a consequence that appears naive in the light of more modern views of emotional ambivalence as the normal state of affairs. Nor could Hume readily explain how some people find pleasure in hatred, or in humiliation, since both these passions arise in his model from an idea that is supposed to be painful.[96] Perhaps the most questionable claim to which Hume is led by his insistence on symmetry stems from his view of the parallelism of causation between pride and love (cf. T. 391-92). Those objects that produce pride when associated with oneself produce love when associated with another: hence the remarkable fact that Humean individuals derive satisfaction from the riches, power, and high rank of others and feel esteem or love for their possessors (T. 357). The argument here draws in part on the doctrine of sympathy, the mechanism by which the emotions of one person—for example, the (putative) happiness of a rich man—are communicated to and shared by others. This kind of psychological argument, moreover, was later expanded by theorists such as Smith and Burke to explain generally why distinctions of social rank and wealth are so universally pursued and accepted.[97] It may be objected that such analyses uncritically take for granted an inegalitarian social order normally deferential and harmonious, although on the other hand they may be credited with accounting for the real and frequent fact of deference, often overlooked by theories that assume the universality of self-interest and competition. Hume at any rate scarcely considers the possibility that one person's wealth might arouse envy and hatred in others rather than esteem (cf. T. 595), and thus his political theory omits this whole dimension of potential discord and conflict. One is inclined to venture the comment that Hume's understanding of the phenomenon of hatred is generally limited, a shortcoming that may be observed, for example, in his assimilation of hatred to contempt: one "hates" the poor and the mean in that one feels "uneasiness" in contemplating the painful object, the poverty or low estate, associated with them (T. 357-58). Contempt such as this is undoubtedly a genuine feeling; but

[96] Cf. Árdal, *Passion and Value*, pp. 24, 114-15. See Hume's brief discussion of "irregular appetites of evil [toward oneself]," including the agreeableness of a "prospect of past pain" and even "malice against ourselves" under certain conditions, such as when we feel "remorses for a crime" (T. 376). Hume is of course aware of phenomena that he has difficulty fitting into his scheme.

[97] See Smith, *Theory of Moral Sentiments* I.iii.2, pp. 112-25. The same line of analysis is found less systematically in Burke. Thus could empirical psychology be applied to conservative social theory.

Hume dwells on it to the neglect of other and more virulent—and politically more ominous—forms and causes of hatred.

The analysis becomes more complicated in Hume's regrettably brief discussion of malice and envy. He begins his treatment of these distinct passions by recalling the principle of the imagination that "*objects appear greater or less by a comparison with others*," which explains why the amount of pleasure or pain we take in various objects is also determined by relative considerations (T. 375-76). This principle, when applied to the indirect passions, yields a view of a characteristic oscillation in our feelings that qualifies the previous analysis of love and hatred: the idea of another's wealth or power may produce esteem in us insofar as we sympathize with that person's happiness, or humility as we reflect on our own comparative deprivation, or a combination of both. Such mixed emotion as this, however, does not explain the precise sources of envy and malice—the "unprovok'd desire of producing evil to another, in order to reap a pleasure from the comparison" (T. 377)—which also have to do with the imaginative operation of comparison. Malice and envy appear to be alternative responses that one can (unaccountably) experience, instead of esteem, in the presence of another's happiness and in opposition to the tendency to share in that happiness through sympathy. Beyond this Hume says only that malice and envy arise from comparisons of our own position with that of others who are near and similar to us: a common soldier envies his corporal but not the more remote general, whom he presumably esteems (T. 377). The operation of these discordant passions is thus confined to proximate contexts, whereas the more harmonious ones extend over a broader range, thereby reducing the scope of potential social conflict.

Hume's treatment of the direct passions, along with those he calls "instinctual," is confined to one brief section of the *Treatise*. This allotment of space, however, is disproportionate to the relative importance of these passions in conduct and in the moral theory to which Hume turns in Book III and later in his second *Enquiry*, where it is only this portion of the larger doctrine of the passions that is retained. The direct passions, like the indirect, are "founded on pain and pleasure," in that they are occasioned by a precedent idea of some attractive or disagreeable object, but they arise immediately upon the idea of such an object (or cause) without the interposition of the additional idea of some person (T. 438). Of the six that he lists—joy and grief, hope and fear, desire and aversion—Hume says that only hope and fear merit attention, the operation of the others being readily evident.[98]

[98] Hume does not discuss the moral feelings, approbation and blame, in his enumer-

His treatment even of hope and fear is too brief, however, at least from the point of view of political science, since both these passions would appear to have extensive ramifications for political beliefs and behavior.[99] Hope and fear are occasioned by the idea of a pleasant or painful object whose existence is taken to be probable but not assured, their intensity varying with the imagination's estimation of the probability. The most interesting point that Hume makes is the asymmetry of the two passions—the fact that uncertainty is much more likely to arouse fear than hope. Human nature seems to be "in general pusillanimous," more readily supposing an unknown, novel, or startling object to be evil than good, and reacting to surprise with fear. On further analysis Hume relates this propensity to the more general disposition in human nature, which we have previously seen operative in the imagination, to experience uneasiness in the face of any abrupt disturbance in regular and habitual patterns of expectation:

> The suddenness and strangeness of an appearance naturally excite a commotion in the mind, like everything for which we are not prepar'd, and to which we are not accustom'd. This commotion, again, naturally produces a curiosity or inquisitiveness, which being very violent, from the strong and sudden impulse of the object, becomes uneasy, and resembles in its fluctuations and uncertainty, the sensation of fear or the mix'd passions of grief and joy. This image of fear naturally converts into the thing itself, and gives us a real apprehension of evil, as the mind always forms its judgments more from its present disposition than from the nature of its objects (T. 446).

A similar uneasiness, provoked by the inconstancy in our experience of sensible things, leads the imagination to frame and to believe in the "fiction" of independent objects as a way of resolving the "contradictions" and creating order in its perceptions. Hume does not point to any characteristic mechanism by which the mind moves analogously

---

ation of the direct passions; when he invokes them in his moral psychology, however, they clearly have this status.

[99] The treatment of fear again raises questions of comparison between Hobbes and Hume. Hume's, in addition to being briefer and less forceful, does not serve so centrally as a foundation for political motivation, nor does Hume pay any special attention to the fear of violent death. Cf. Hume, *An Abstract of a Treatise of Human Nature*, ed. J. M. Keynes and P. Straffa (Cambridge: Cambridge University Press, 1938), p. 30. Fear figures in Hume's account of the origins of superstitious religion, but it takes second place to the natural varieties of fallacious reasoning; see Hume, "The Natural History of Religion," *Works*, vol. 4, pp. 319, 352-53. On Hume's personal attitude toward death, see Boswell's famous deathbed interview, printed in Hume, *Dialogues*, pp. 76-79.

to resolve the uneasiness of fear. It is clear, however, that his analysis here reveals a uniformity that appears to be a fundamental property of human nature; and the effect of the artificial virtues, whose defense is the central theme of his political theory, is the creation of a social order that diminishes uncertainty as much as possible in this sphere of life. The parallel dispositions of both the imagination and the passions to thrive on regular habits, and the unpleasantness of the disorder produced by disruptions in mental patterns, provide more evidence for Hume's general thesis that custom is (and should be) the great guide of life.

Following his enumeration of the six main direct passions Hume adds the following:

> Beside good and evil, or in other words, pain and pleasure, the direct passions frequently arise from a natural impulse or instinct, which is perfectly unaccountable. Of this kind is the desire of punishment to our enemies, and of happiness to our friends; hunger, lust, and a few other bodily appetites. These passions, properly speaking, produce good and evil, and proceed not from them, like the other affections. (T. 439)

This passage defines what is best regarded as a distinct set of instinctual passions within the category of the direct passions, of which four examples are given. On a former occasion as well Hume refers to "certain instincts originally implanted in our natures," listing benevolence, resentment, love of life, and kindness to children (T. 417). Of these, "benevolence" may be taken to include the "desire of happiness to our friends" in the quoted passage, although the latter formulation (correctly) suggests that Hume regards particular and not general benevolence—benevolence, that is, to immediate acquaintances—as a direct impulse. Likewise the "desire of punishment to our enemies," or revenge, corresponds to the instinct of "resentment" mentioned in the earlier passage (cf. T. 366-68). Hume thus recognizes six impulses that he calls instincts: particular benevolence toward friends and loved ones, and its opposite, revenge or anger; kindness to children; and the "bodily appetites" such as lust, hunger, and love of life.[100]

These instincts are "unaccountable" in the sense, apparently, that their etiology cannot be explained in Hume's usual manner, in terms of the "prospect of pleasure or pain" that constitutes the "cause" of all the other passions. The instinctual passions function like the other direct passions in that they arise in us spontaneously in the presence of certain kinds of objects, or in consequence of the ideas of these

---

[100] Cf. Hume, *Enquiries* (II), pp. 201, 301.

objects in the imagination. The instincts, however, "proceed not from" good and evil: the transition from the idea to the passion is not mediated by any accompanying anticipation of pleasure and pain, and hence the impulse to action that may be generated by these passions cannot be attributed to a fundamental propensity in voluntary agents to seek what they take to be the former and avoid the latter. Nevertheless, Hume says, these passions "produce good and evil," by which he appears to mean that their gratification immediately produces, or leads to subsequent states that may produce, sensations of pleasure or pain in the agent. We have noted previously how the operation of another instinctual propensity—that of natural belief—provides relief from uneasiness, and how the exercise of any of the active powers of the imagination is pleasurable; and so it is not surprising that the operation of the instinctual passions is naturally a source of satisfaction, even though they are not stimulated by a precedent idea of prospective pleasure.

Hume's fragmentary account of the instinctual passions has attracted attention from those primarily interested in his moral theory, the examination of which may be briefly anticipated here. On the one hand Hume inquires into the standard or criterion by which moral judgments are justified, and on the other he concerns himself with moral psychology or the motivational sources in human nature of moral judgments and conduct. This latter part of Hume's moral philosophy is of course closely connected to the preceding analysis of the passions; and Hume, although he has a normative doctrine of ethics, remains deliberately close to the psychological realities in terms of which the moral standards he advocates are presented as feasible for people as they are. The doctrine of the instinctual passions, and especially Hume's analysis of benevolence, has important implications for the theory of moral motivation, to the extent that in the end the human moral capacity in general is reduced to a fundamental disposition of human nature, in much the same way that all our cognitive endeavors are found to rest on the basic instinct of belief.

Hume recognizes a class of moral virtues that he calls "natural," in the sense that our tendency to act and to judge in accordance with them is spontaneous and unreflective; in this class are such virtues as generosity and affection to one's immediate family and acquaintances and kindness to children. Moral virtues such as these are manifested as the direct expression of certain of the instinctual passions, of which the most important is undoubtedly benevolence, which as I have suggested Hume portrays in the *Treatise* as particular benevolence, or "limited generosity" toward close relations and friends.

As a moral and political philosopher, however, Hume is more interested in the origins and content of what he calls the "artificial" or reflective moral virtues, such as justice, whose application is necessarily more extensive, impersonal, and according to general rules. With respect to the artificial virtues, the role of the instinctual passions becomes problematic. If the impulse of benevolence (and likewise resentment or anger) is restricted and partial, it clearly cannot serve as a psychological basis for justice, whose nature is to treat friends and strangers alike by the same rules of equity; and indeed generous (and more obviously, hostile) impulses can in some circumstances interfere with the dictates of justice. In the *Treatise* Hume accounts for the sources of justice by a variety of factors in addition to benevolence, including self-interest, sympathy, and the assurance of reciprocity provided by the existence of government. In the second *Enquiry*, however, there is a marked change in emphasis, and an important addition, to the moral theory of the *Treatise*. Here Hume argues in effect that a fundamental and general sociable instinct must be understood to underlie all moral distinctions, even those that ostensibly are founded on a reflective estimation of utility, and accordingly he adds to the list put forward in the *Treatise* an instinct that he variously calls "humanity," "fellow-feeling," or the "natural sentiment of benevolence," where benevolence is regarded as being far more extensive in scope than is implied in the *Treatise*.[101] The *Treatise*'s elaborate attention to a mixture of motives and to political circumstances in the analysis of the artificial virtues is more interesting, because more problematic and complex, than the *Enquiry*'s approach, and it is considered in the following chapter. If, however, the argument of the *Enquiry* is correct in its basic point that even the artificial virtues in the final analysis rest on a certain irreducible and disinterested tendency to approve of the happiness of others, then this tendency must take its place as another fundamental feature of human nature in the list of instincts in Hume's classification of the passions.

6. The Social Dimension

I now turn, following these remarks on Hume's treatment of particular passions, to some of their implications for motivation and action and especially to their manner of operation in a social context. Here again there are illuminating parallels between Hume's theory of the under-

---

[101] "Benevolence" is used in the *Enquiries* (II) mainly to denote a moral virtue (that is, a quality or character trait of which we approve) but occasionally also to denote a feeling or instinct, as in the *Treatise*. In the latter sense it is used synonymously with "fellow-feeling" and "social sympathy"; see Hume, *Enquiries* (II), secs. 1-5 and Appendices 1 and 2.

standing and that of the passions, parallels illustrative of his manner of overcoming the skeptical crisis through acceptance of certain basic qualities of human nature. This development in Hume's doctrine leads, in the case of the passions as of cognition and belief, to a generous assessment of social influence and sociability, which is the topic of this section.

Just as in his analysis of knowledge Hume begins with the individual mind as the seat of consciousness, the receptor of discrete perceptions united by the imagination, so here Hume begins with the individual conceived as the potential possessor of the various discrete states of awareness (impressions) called passions or feelings, which may be observed to occur in certain circumstances and to bear certain relations to one another. The two parts of Hume's psychology are connected in several ways, for example, in his conclusions that all factual knowledge rests on an instinctual propensity or sentiment of belief, and that reasoning through the medium of enlivened ideas easily and frequently interacts with the passions. In addition, Hume in both parts of his psychological investigation comes upon what may be called the social dimension, or certain issues in the beliefs or feelings of individuals that are inexplicable without reference to the social environment from which initially isolated percipients are found to derive many of their perceptions and toward which much of their reasoning and most of their emotional responses are directed. The exploration of this side of human nature was evidently not part of Hume's plan prior to Book III, which is on "morals" or social life as such; but as we have already seen with regard to the imagination, the logic of his analysis at many points in his ostensibly individual psychology points to the influence of social factors on the mind of the individual, even more so, as one might suppose, in the analysis of the passions than of the understanding. The operation of many of the passions is unintelligible apart from relations between the agent and other people, and in this sense the passions are data of the moral world, closely linked to the study of moral values and social institutions that constitutes Hume's explicitly "moral" philosophy. Hence even while he examines the several passions as distinct phenomena, Hume has frequent occasion to refer to sociable and moral features of human nature, which prepare the ground for the final book of the *Treatise*. I consider in particular the egoism-altruism ambivalence in Hume's doctrine of volition, the nature of sympathy, and the idea of natural sociability in Hume's science of human nature.

One of the two principal schools of British moral philosophy in the decades prior to Hume's writing had become deeply involved in the study of moral psychology, and the most prominent debate within this tradition concerned the thesis that "self-love" constitutes the sole motive of human actions and moral judgments.[102] Those who (following Hobbes) regarded all affections and motives as "interested" or "selfish" may be said to have maintained a doctrine of psychological egoism, or egoistic hedonism, since pleasure and pain were generally held to be the exclusive objects of an agent's desire and aversion. Writers on the other side of this debate called attention to the plurality of passions and impulses that activate people, including such "disinterested" affections as benevolence and pity, which they argued could not be reduced to forms of self-love. This psychological controversy, with its obvious implications for ethics, provided a context that Hume acknowledges in his second *Enquiry*, where he unequivocably repudiates the "selfish" thesis.[103] His own account of volition in this respect has, however, been a matter of dispute, especially as it appears in the *Treatise*, where some passages render an egoistic reading plausible.

It is clear that Hume regards the desire of one's own pleasure, immediate or distant, as the most usual influencing motive of a person's will, and we have seen how he uses the term "interest" to signify those objects of calm and sustained desires that are conducive to an agent's greatest happiness in the long run. Those who have attributed an egoistic psychology to Hume, however, take him to hold that the desire of pleasure constitutes the *sole* motive of all voluntary action.[104] This interpretation rests on Hume's assertion that all the passions (with the brief exception of the "unaccountable" instincts) are "founded on pain and pleasure" (T. 438), meaning that it is a view of a prospective pleasure or pain that occasions the passions, and on several passages in which a strong relation is suggested between pleasure and pain and the passions of desire and aversion, which in turn seem closely linked to volition (T. 314, 414, 439, 574). A close reading, however, suggests that although desire of pleasure may be the "chief spring" of action, it is neither an invariable nor the exclusive source of motivation. The egoist interpretation is damaged if some passion other than desire and aversion could motivate the will, or if desire and aversion could in

[102] See Thomas Hill Green, "Introduction to the Moral Part of the *Treatise*," in Hume's *Works*, vol. 2, pp. 21-23. The other main tradition in British ethical writing was the rationalist school represented by Clarke and Wollaston. In the late seventeenth century the rationalist approach appeared as the only alternative to Hobbism; but beginning with Shaftesbury the new doctrine of the "moral sense" and "disinterested affections" came into prominence, to be developed by Hutcheson, Butler, and Hume.

[103] Hume, *Enquiries* (II), pp. 295ff. (Appendix 2).

[104] Green, "Introduction," pp. 31-32, 50, and passim; also C. E. Vaughan, *Studies in the History of Political Philosophy before and after Rousseau*, ed. A. G. Little (New York: Russell and Russell, 1960), vol. 1, p. 309.

certain situations pursue objects other than the agent's own pleasure and pain. Evidence that Hume regards both of these as real potentialities of human nature is found in his observations on the instinctual passions, and it is on the comparative importance attached to these that much of the interpretation of Hume's psychology appears to depend.

In discussing the "influencing motives of the will" Hume speaks of "exerting any passion in action" (T. 416), as though *any* passion could conceivably activate volition, although desire and aversion are his usual examples of passions that do so. He specifically includes a set of "instincts" among the "calm passions" that are said to be able to produce, retard, or prevent action; and subsequently he speaks of the passion of resentment toward the perpetrator of an injury, "which makes me desire his evil and punishment, independent of all considerations of pleasure and advantage to myself" (T. 418). Two points stand out in this passage. First, a passion that Hume treats as an instinct (and thus not "founded on pain and pleasure") is invoked as a source of volition, and volition moreover that is not directed to and may be at odds with the agent's own pleasure. Second, revenge is here defined as "desire of evil" to an enemy, suggesting that although Hume may indeed often treat volition in terms of "desire," the desire that he means can be oriented toward objects other than the agent's pleasure. In particular, a person can desire certain objects to which his relation is instinctually or naturally determined—that is, "by the original formation of our faculties" (T. 437).[105] It thus appears that the instincts, whether or not they are conceived of in the terminology of desire and aversion, constitute a source of motivation that cannot be classified as egoistic hedonism; and although Hume's example here is of resentment, there is every reason to suppose that its correlative, benevolence, operates in a similar fashion. Hume then recognizes a class of instinctual motives, whose operation is not mediated by ideas of personal pleasure or advantage, and a corresponding class of objects to which they are oriented, despite the brevity of their treatment in the associational framework of the *Treatise*.

Opponents of the egoist thesis have not only drawn attention to this kind of motivation but have in addition emphasized the role of benevolence as constituting a substantial "altruistic" aspect of Hume's view of human nature.[106] This interpretation appears to be vindicated by Hume's second *Enquiry*, where he indisputably maintains a doctrine

[105] Hume, "Dissertation on the Passions," *Works*, vol. 4, p. 139.
[106] McGilvary, "Altruism," is the principal work.

of general benevolence as the ground of all moral feeling. Its advocates, however, not only see substantial continuity between the *Treatise* and the *Enquiry* on this issue; more important, they argue that emphasis on the instinctual passions is warranted in light of Book III of the *Treatise*, where Hume's moral theory revolves around the feelings of approbation and blame. These, though different from any of the passions discussed in Book II, are closely related to the instincts (especially particular benevolence and resentment) in the case of the "natural virtues"; and Hume's central issue of accounting for such "artificial" virtues as justice is couched in terms of the need to overcome the spontaneous action of these instinctual passions and to reorient them toward general objects. The passions of benevolence and resentment, like the moral sentiments of approbation and blame, are disinterested in the sense that they are not occasioned by, and do not aim at, an idea of a person's own happiness. What may seem to be a disproportionate emphasis on the former in the interpretation of Book II, then, is justifiable in light of other parts of the work, especially the moral and political philosophy that Hume builds on the study of the passions.[107]

The attribution to Hume of pure psychological egoism, furthermore, overlooks a distinction that is of importance for moral psychology—that between the pleasure and pain that provoke or accompany action, and the agent's idea of his own prospective pleasure or pain as the end or goal of his action. The doctrine of egoism holds that an agent's voluntary actions are motivated by a desire for what he takes to be his own pleasure or happiness, however reflective and sophisticated his understanding of this may be. Hume's frequent use of the terms pleasure and pain in connection with the passions, and especially with the principal volitional passions of desire and aversion, may create the impression that this is his position; the indirect and direct passions are described as "arising from," or as being "founded on," ideas of pleasure and pain, which are regarded as the occasioning "causes" of these passions and thence, in some cases, of volition. But Hume never argues that a person's own foreseen pleasure is the *end* of his passion or, as a rule, the end of willed actions. The indirect passions (pride,

---

[107] Green rejects the passages on benevolence as Butlerian intrusions into an otherwise egoistic philosophy; "Introduction," pp. 46-47. Leslie Stephen also felt that it was somehow illogical for Hume, as an "atomist" and an intellectual ancestor of the egoistic utilitarians Godwin and Bentham, not to resolve all motives into selfish ones; *History of English Thought in the Eighteenth Century* (New York: Harcourt, Brace, and World, 1962), vol. 2, pp. 85-88. Egoist interpretations must come to terms with the problematic status of the self in Hume's larger philosophy.

humility, love, and hatred) arise from an idea of a pleasurable or painful object, and the experience of these passions is accompanied by a pleasurable or painful feeling; but one does not feel pride or love for the sake of pleasure. Love (and hatred) moreover are literally selfless passions for Hume, the idea of the self not being involved, and they are said to be followed frequently by benevolence (or anger) toward the person who is their "object," that is, by a desire for the other's happiness or hurt without regard for the agent's own (T. 367). The direct passions of desire and aversion are likewise occasioned by pleasurable or painful ideas, which thus in a sense are the motive force or cause of the ensuing action; but again, we do not always act in order to receive the pleasure or to avoid the pain, and not with an eye toward our own pleasure or pain exclusively. The instinctual passions, finally, do not even "arise" from an idea of pleasure and pain, although Hume says their gratification may as a consequence "produce" such sensations in us, just as the fulfillment of any natural impulse is satisfying quite apart from any ideas or objectives the agent may have had in view. Hume generally explains volition and action by reference to the motivating influence of a passion, most often desire; desire, however, like the other passions, arises within a person as a natural feeling in response to a variety of objects, which appear as its "causes." These objects may be mediated in our imagination by pleasurable ideas, which thus frequently enter into volition; but as a conscious goal of action one's own prospective pleasure is only one among the various natural propensities or objects of desire.[108]

This distinction is only implicit in the *Treatise*, although it is a plausible reading.[109] Hume, however, devotes to its clarification an Appendix to his second *Enquiry*, emphasizing that the pleasure we get from the satisfaction of any passion is to be distinguished from the objective we pursue in satisfying it—whether it be a bodily "appetite," a direct passion like benevolence or anger, or an indirect one such as pride or love. The "natural propensities" that lead people to pursue certain goals are autonomous and distinct features of our nature, not

---

[108] "Indeed no philosophical writer has ever stated more forcibly than Hume the important ethical principle that pleasure is conditioned by desire and not *vice versa*." Smith, *Philosophy of Hume*, p. 338; also pp. 140-41, 163.

[109] Butler had already argued that a motive that consciously aims at pleasure must be differentiated from one that incidentally produces pleasure in the agent through the fulfillment of some other end, or through the gratification of a natural impulse. See Joseph Butler, *Fifteen Sermons*, in *The Works of Joseph Butler*, ed. W. E. Gladstone (Oxford: Clarendon Press, 1896), vol. 2, Preface and Sermon 11, esp. pp. 21-25, 188-201. Hume acknowledges Butler in the Introduction to the *Treatise* and (apparently) in his *Inquiry Concerning Human Understanding*, ed. Hendel, pp. 23-24n.

resolvable into "self-love." Among them Hume finds such impulses as benevolence and anger, either of which may clearly be pursued without consideration of self, and indeed to the neglect of our "ease, interest, or safety."[110]

This distinction also finds an application in Hume's comments on economic motivation, an issue historically associated with the doctrine of egoistic hedonism, which through the work of Bentham and others became an axiom of classical political economy. Hume himself does not link his concept of "desire" to a special drive to accumulate material goods or wealth as a fundamental attribute of human nature. Although he occasionally speaks of "avarice" or the "love of acquiring" as autonomous passions,[111] Hume more often attributes such activity to the intrinsic, natural pleasure derived from the exercise of mental faculties, a topic that he discusses most fully in the section on "curiosity" (T. II.iii.10). Hume classifies "business" together with hunting, gaming, and the practice of philosophy itself as activities that give satisfaction through challenging and stimulating the mind but that are not typically undertaken as deliberate means to future pleasure or profit (T. 352, 451-53). "Business and action fill up all the great vacancies in human life," Hume says (echoing Pascal), and are therefore pleasurable in themselves and not simply the means to an end;[112] likewise in one of his economic essays Hume attributes the systematic profit motive of merchants to the operation of the general "craving" of the mind for "exercise and employment" in a particular environment.[113] This analysis, which pertains to entrepreneurial or otherwise mentally engaging economic activity, provides a valuable corrective to the crude view of economic interest as simple material gain sometimes attributed to classical liberalism, and it qualifies the instrumental rationality, discussed above, that Hume endorses.[114] The point to be

[110] Hume, *Enquiries* (II), pp. 301-302. See also p. 298, where Hume attributes purely egoistic theories to "that love of *simplicity* which has been the source of much false reasoning in philosophy." Hume in the *Enquiries* relinquishes his claims to be developing a science of human nature, which depended (he thought) on assumptions of simplicity. Instead he claims to be upholding the distinctions "marked by common language and observation."

[111] See Hume, "Of Commerce," *Works*, vol. 3, p. 295-96, for his clearest statements on the social advantages of harnessing avarice and on the need of profits to "arouse men from their indolence." See Albert O. Hirschman, *The Passions and the Interests* (Princeton: Princeton University Press, 1977), pp. 37, 54.

[112] Hume, "The Sceptic," *Works*, vol. 3, p. 220. Cf. *Treatise*, p. 352.

[113] Hume, "Of Interest," *Works*, vol. 3, p. 325.

[114] Cf. Peter J. D. Wiles, *Economic Institutions Compared* (New York: John Wiley and Sons, 1977), pp. 17-19, on motives or incentives to work over and above "Benthamite" ones.

made in the present context, however, is that volition, in Hume's account, is not invariably directed to the attainment of the agent's calculated future pleasure.

It is of course true that for Hume the indulgence of any passion is in a sense an expression of the self conceived as a natural organism with innate emotional capacities, just as it is true that satisfaction often accompanies their usual operation with respect to their appropriate objects. But a man who for these reasons regards all passions and motives as varieties of "self-love" is simply using "a different language from the rest of his countrymen," a probable sign of a deviation from truth in the study of human nature.[115] An analysis of the ends of voluntary actions reveals diverse motives, including both egoistic and altruistic ones, and everyday experience provides plentiful evidence of both.

Hume's account of motivation is thus not monistic, nor is any particular passion or drive accorded an overriding importance in the determination of conduct. In surveying the various potentialities I have concentrated on pointing out nonegoistic elements in the theory, in the face of the influential contrary interpretation, in order to restore a balanced view. The pursuit of private interest nevertheless remains a very important motive, perhaps the one most commonly encountered in social life; at one point Hume states that generally predictable results may be obtained in devising political institutions if one makes the assumption, false in fact, that this is the sole motive of action.[116] Hume's more central account of justice and allegiance as types of moral virtue, on the other hand, and of the necessity of artificial rules serving in part to offset the effects of natural virtues such as private benevolence, is not fully intelligible except in light of the other dispositions of human nature as well.

Hume's account of sympathy, like that of motivation, has obvious implications for his moral psychology, which is taken up in the next chapter. Here I consider sympathy as a general psychological mechanism as it is described, for the most part, in Book II of the *Treatise*, where it constitutes the principal element in the social dimension of the theory of the passions. Hume calls on sympathy to explain such feelings as esteem for the wealthy and powerful, the love of fame, and compassion—phenomena of people's affective and active life that bear on their relations with and feelings toward other members of society.

---

[115] Hume, "Of the Dignity or Meanness of Human Nature," *Works*, vol. 3, pp. 154-55; and *Enquiries* (II), p. 298.

[116] Hume, "On the Independency of Parliament," *Works*, vol. 3, pp. 117-18. See David Miller, *Philosophy and Ideology in Hume's Political Thought* (Oxford: Clarendon Press, 1981), pp. 105-106, for a discussion of this passage.

Sympathy appears in the *Treatise* as an element in the mental machinery by which Hume seeks to describe the manner in which the discrete data of consciousness—ideas and impressions—are joined in patterns of awareness and feeling. Like belief and the principles of association, sympathy is a mental mechanism, disposition, or habit that exercises a selective and enlivening influence on certain ideas, helping to determine the "manner" in which we apprehend them. More specifically, sympathy is a technical term for a psychological process by which passions are communicated from one person to another with sufficient force that the recipient or spectator comes to share, or feel, the passion in question. Sympathizing with others is therefore analogous in the sphere of emotions to the reception of testimony in the case of ideas and beliefs, with the qualification that it is more usually a passive process: a sympathetic feeling, like feelings generated in other ways, appears as an all but involuntary—though perfectly conscious—response to certain "causes." Hume does not raise the question whether one can deliberately withhold a sympathetic response in the same way one can critically reject or withhold assent from testimony, when the objects that usually occasion it are present.[117] Compliance with the requirements of what Hume terms the artificial virtues (such as justice), however, sometimes involves control over immediate sympathetic responses, in the sense of refraining from acting on them, as we shall see in the following chapter. The greater involuntariness of sympathy renders it, if anything, a stronger force in social communication, and hence in education, than testimony; and I shall take note of some of the conclusions Hume draws from this fact. We must first, however, consider more precisely the manner in which sympathy is said to operate.

We apprehend the existence of a particular passion in another person, Hume says, by observing the "external signs in the countenance and conversation, which convey an idea of it." When, on the basis of our experience, we judge the signs to be clear and sufficient, we believe in the reality of the passion in the other. In sympathizing, however, we not only entertain an idea of another's emotions, but we actually feel these emotions ourselves: "This idea is presently converted into an impression, and acquires such a degree of force and vivacity, as to become the very passion itself" (T. 317). Such a reconversion of an idea into the impression it represents seems an unlikely occurrence

---

[117] This point should be qualified by mention of eloquence, whose impact Hume explains in terms of the deliberate sympathetic conveyance of emotions from the speaker to his audience; Hume, "Of Eloquence," *Works*, vol. 3, p. 166. Cf. *Treatise*, pp. 426-27.

with respect to ideas of sensible objects, but it appears to be a plausible way of describing mental processes in the case of feelings. We can actually begin to feel sick simply by thinking about it, "from the mere force of the imagination" (T. 319), and by a similar process a person first notices and then shares in the mood of the those around him, as when "a good-natur'd man finds himself in an instant of the same humour with his company" (T. 317). The problem of explaining how an idea can be so "enlivened" as to be felt as an actual impression is solved by reference to a distinct mental process of association. Hume first points to the always-present impression of one's self, which is always "lively" and therefore increases the "vivacity of conception" of any object "related to ourselves" (T. 317). Next Hume argues that there is such "resemblance among all human creatures" that "we never remark any passion or principle in others, of which, in some degree or other, we may not find a parallel in ourselves." (We would have to have noticed a fundamental resemblance between the other person and ourselves and between the "external signs" of that person's passion and similar signs of remembered passions of our own, before we could have inferred the existence of a particular passion in the other person in the first place.) On the basis of these resemblances we can, sympathetically, "enter into the sentiments of others, and embrace them with facility and pleasure" (T. 318). More technically, the peculiar resemblance among human beings in respect of their feelings is the "relation" that permits the lively impression of one's self to be associated with and to infuse its vivacity into the idea one has of another's passion, thereby transforming it into a similar feeling in oneself. Hume thus accounts for the complex mental phenomenon of sympathy in the usual terms of his psychology; it is a propensity of the imagination reducible to the association of distinct ideas and impressions.[118]

Several special features of sympathy should be mentioned before we turn to some of its applications. Since sympathy is simply a mechanism of the imagination, one might suppose that it would enable people to share indifferently in any passion to whose external signs in another

[118] The term "sympathy" is used in *Enquiries* (II) but with a different meaning: it is equivalent to "fellow-feeling" or "benevolence," and it denotes a basic instinctual capacity to identify with the happiness (not *any* passion) of others, and at the same time to approve of it and of what causes it. It is thus a moral faculty and no longer merely a psychological principle. I follow Árdal, *Passion and Value*, pp. 45, 134ff., in treating sympathy as the more precise technical term that it usually is in the *Treatise*. See also Philip Mercer, *Sympathy and Ethics* (Oxford: Clarendon Press, 1972), esp. chap. 2.

they are exposed, whether pleasant or painful, direct or indirect; sympathy in this case would have no particular moral direction but would cause us indifferently to share in the anger of an aggressor as readily as in the fear of a victim, in the pride of the powerful as readily as in the humility of the poor. Instead Hume portrays sympathy as operating in a more selective fashion, without, however, specifying the nature of the selective principle; later he accords to sympathy a role in his theory of moral motivation that would be impossible if it were indiscriminate.

The role of sympathy as a principle of emotional communication is limited in another way as well. The sympathetic generation of a passion in us is said to take place when we receive the idea of the passion in another person by the observation of its external signs. This formulation suggests that we can sympathize with the feelings only of people who are in our presence, or at least of people of whose circumstances we have received an exact enough description to enable us to form a distinct idea of their affective state; we could not sympathize with general categories of people or with persons who are remote from us. Some degree of resemblance between ourselves and the other must be apprehended before sympathy can have an effect at all, and the intensity of the sympathetic response varies with the degree of resemblance. Hume adds that the same holds true for degrees of proximity, which also helps to determine the facility of the imaginative transition (T. 316-18).

Although sympathy therefore is efficacious, in varying degrees, only within a limited range, Hume makes clear the importance of sympathy in his view of human nature as a whole by emphasizing the continuous and manifold nature of its role in experience. Human emotional life is presented as founded on sympathy almost to the same extent that our cognitive life is founded on the analogous imaginative impulse of belief, with which it is compared (T. 319-20);[119] one difference, however, is that sympathy is connected exclusively with social life, whereas individuals can (though they do not ordinarily) arrive at belief entirely on their own. Hume's method of presenting the passions at first may suggest that they, like reasoning, are simply the movements of an individual mind; but he later emphasizes that they are frequently "con-

---

[119] Smith emphasizes the parallel: belief is the imaginative process by which certain ideas are enlivened to the point that we take them to have real existence; sympathy is the process by which the idea of a passion in another is enlivened to the point that we actually experience it ourselves. Though they are not perceptions, Hume occasionally refers to both belief and sympathy as "sentiments." See *Philosophy of Hume*, pp. 149-51, 170, 221.

tagious" (T. 605) and that many of them, at least, are usually mediated by sympathy: "No quality of human nature is more remarkable, both in itself and in its consequences, than that propensity we have to sympathize with others, and to receive by communication their inclinations and sentiments. . . . Hatred, resentment, esteem, love, courage, mirth and melancholy; all these passions I feel more from communication than from my own natural temper and disposition" (T. 316-17).

On a Humean account of the self we may be said to *be*, as conscious agents, nothing more than the sum of our perceptions, arranged and enlivened in certain patterns. That many or most of our passions—one entire category of our perceptions—are generated through sympathy suggests the importance of social communication in determining our individual consciousness and characters. At one point, moreover, Hume states that sympathy is operative with regard to "opinions" as well as "affections" (T. 319): it is not clear how any other kind of idea than that of a passion could actually be "converted" into an impression, although Hume may intend to suggest that the sharing of opinions, which takes place by means of verbal communication, may be furthered by sympathy insofar as opinions are generally maintained in conjunction with some sentiment susceptible of a sympathetic response (cf. T. 373, 393). Reasonings, sentiments, and ideas of sentiments are all intermingled as perceptions in Hume's picture of the imagination, all subject to the same principles of association and capable of communication. In this perspective sympathy is one of several devices by which Hume seeks to explain the fact that our passions, like our beliefs, are more often than not characteristics that we hold in common with others.

Hume draws on sympathy to explain three specific affective phenomena in Book II of the *Treatise*, in addition to its most important application in the moral psychology of Book III. The first of these is "esteem for the rich and powerful," which has been noted as one of Hume's illustrations of the passion of love, along with its social implications. Such esteem, however, cannot on a closer view be satisfactorily accounted for simply by the conjunction of the idea of an agreeable object with that of a particular person (its owner) to whom it is related. Power, and likewise wealth (a form of power), are not agreeable objects in themselves but please only insofar as they are imagined to be convertible into desirable objects. We esteem a rich man (Hume says), however, without having any idea of how he spends his money or indeed even knowing that he is miserly and not likely to acquire what we take to be the "pleasures and conveniences of life"

(T. 360). Hume accordingly considers the possibility that the esteem is stimulated by the agreeable idea of an *"expectation of advantage"* to ourselves from the rich or powerful person; but this (egoistic) hypothesis fails the test of experience (T. 360-61). Hume therefore turns to the principle of sympathy, by which "we enter into the sentiments of the rich and poor, and partake of their pleasure and uneasiness." This sharing of their feelings produces real joy or uneasiness in us, which by a process of association is connected with the similarly agreeable or disagreeable feelings of love or contempt, which in this way are intensified. Sympathy in this case simply supplements the associational mechanism by which Hume accounts for love or esteem in general; nevertheless, its influence is, in Hume's view, of paramount importance in explaining our experience and the prevalence of this form of love (T. 362). Psychological facts such as this, it may be added, are of practical significance for ethical theories, such as Hume's, that take the general happiness of society as their standard of approval: that the happiness of the great or the wealthy tends to be disseminated by sympathy—rather than to provoke the unhappiness of envy—might well be invoked as a step in an argument justifying social inequalities, although this is a conclusion that Hume does not himself draw.

A second application of sympathy pertains to the explanation of pity or compassion, which Hume treats as a separate indirect passion. Pity resembles benevolence in its desire for another's happiness, but it differs in following upon the observation of the other's grief or misery (unlike benevolence, which has no such ideational "cause") and in that it can be directed toward "strangers, and such as are perfectly indifferent to us" (T. 369). These facts suggest that pity is to be explained in terms of sympathy, by which we share in the feelings of the miserable, including their desire to have their miseries alleviated; and Hume finds additional confirmation of this hypothesis in the fact that "pity depends, in a great measure, on the contiguity and even the sight of the object"—factors that normally enhance the operation of sympathy and related imaginative processes (T. 370). This account of pity reveals some of the difficulties of the egoistic interpretation of Hume's psychology: sympathy involves the impression of our "self," but this impression serves the function of enlivening the idea of another's pain, allowing us to experience it. We do not project ourselves into the other's place and then imagine how we would feel; we are therefore not actually thinking of ourselves while pitying another.[120]

Hume's account of pity is clear, although difficulties emerge when

---

[120] Cf. Árdal, *Passion and Value*, pp. 134ff.

it is considered in the context of other doctrines. Hume never discusses, for example, the exact relation between compassion and contempt, which like the former is said to be generated by a view of a painful object ("poverty and meanness" [T. 357], for example) associated with another person. Evidently the sight of poverty may alternately—or unpredictably—evoke either pity or contempt in the spectator; Hume implies that a fuller measure of sympathy is what determines the response to be one of pity rather than contempt, but his theory is finally indeterminate here.[121] Another difficulty concerns Hume's failure to differentiate adequately the causes of pity from those of its opposite, malice or "a joy in the sufferings and miseries of others," unrelated to hatred and revenge in the same way that pity is unrelated to love and benevolence (T. 372). Hume readily accounts for malice (and likewise envy) by reference to the imaginative principle of comparison, by which, after a view of another's pleasure or pain, we reflect on our own enhanced opposite situation (T. 593-94). Pity for the poor and esteem for the rich depend on sympathy, whereas their contraries, malice and envy, arise in the absence of this tendency of emotional communication and sharing of feeling, and when the principle of comparison, which functions as a mental process in a sense antagonistic to sympathy, is operative (T. 594). Hume devotes more attention to the two former passions, and his general emphasis on the prevalence of sympathy in psychic life suggests that he takes these to be the more usual reactions to the circumstances of others. The alternative possibilities, however, particularly the passion of envy, have often been regarded as very serious matters in moral and political life, and Hume's psychological doctrine may be faulted for failing to explore their manifestations more extensively.

The final application of sympathy to be considered is taken from the section in which Hume first introduces it, a section on "the love of fame," or the manner in which pride and humility arise "from praise and blame, from reputation and infamy" (T. 320), a topic whose implications extend throughout many parts of Hume's work. Pride arises, in the first analysis, from the association in the imagination of a pleasing object with the idea of oneself. It is observable, however, that people also take pride in the manifest favorable opinions that others entertain of them and are humiliated by the opposite. Hume first suggests that reputation is usually a secondary source of pride, which serves to reinforce and intensify pride that we already have or could have from other objects. We do not ordinarily receive pleasure

---

[121] Hume, *Enquiries* (II), p. 248n.

from praise in respect of objects or qualities we know we do not possess but only for those things that would give us pride independently; and we do not receive satisfaction from the approbation of all persons indiscriminately but only of those whose judgment we respect, as though the favorable opinion of others pleases us only when it coincides with our own (T. 321-22). In this light the praises of others appear to be simply a source of confirmation for the imaginative process by which we would be led to feel pride in any case: in a favorable opinion we detect a judgment of fact that corroborates our own cognitive assessment of our circumstances.

The love of fame, or sensitivity to the sentiments of others concerning us in general, however, goes deeper than such reinforcement of our own self-directed feelings. Although Hume never retracts his point that praise does not give pleasure if it is inconsistent with facts known to us (but cf. T. 324), nevertheless it is clear that pride aroused through sympathy is an autonomous passion, stronger perhaps than any other form of pride. Hume suggests that an isolated individual might experience pride following upon his attribution to himself of certain agreeable qualities, a picture that conveys a kind of emotional self-reliance that might be characterized as a form of egoism. But such self-satisfaction in practice is weak, since "men always consider the sentiments of others in their judgment of themselves" (T. 303). Anyone who lives in proximity to others is heavily dependent on communication from them for a large proportion of his perceptions, including many of those that he applies to himself. So great is the usual force of this communication that even such an ego-oriented passion as pride apears to lack independent resources:

> Our opinions of all kinds are strongly affected by society and sympathy, and it is almost impossible for us to support any principle or sentiment, against the universal consent of every one, with whom we have any friendship or correspondence. But of all our opinions, those, which we form in our own favour; however lofty or presuming; are, at bottom, the frailest, and the most easily shaken by the contradiction and opposition of others. . . . Hence that strong love of fame, with which all mankind are possessed. It is in order to fix and confirm their favourable opinion of themselves, not from any original passion, that they seek the applauses of others.[122]

A person's self-conception, then, standing in an associative relation to a variety of objects and sentiments, emerges as something strongly

---

[122] Hume, "Dissertation on the Passions," *Works*, vol. 4, p. 152.

influenced if not indeed largely constructed under the impact of communicated opinion.

Certainly those things that count as "agreeable objects" and hence potential causes of pride would for the most part be constituted as such by public opinion and not by the individual privately. Hume lists such objects as power, riches, family, and virtue (T. 320), the exact praiseworthy features of which are matters of social convention and judgment; and such sources of pride as personal beauty and grace depend even more on others' opinions. The reasoning, moreover, by which any of these objects is associated with oneself is fragile unless "seconded" by the views of others; and it is in part by comparison that all ideas, including those that serve as the causes of pride, attain the relative degree of force they have in the imagination (T. 390). Fame or good reputation, finally, is an autonomous source of pride (self-esteem) insofar as the esteem (or love) of others, sympathetically apprehended, becomes a distinct source of pleasure for us. Sensitivity to such matters is such that "there are few persons, that are satisfy'd with their own character, or genius, or fortune, who are not desirous of shewing themselves to the world, and of acquiring the love and approbation of mankind" (T. 331-32); pride on Hume's account may require support in the esteem of others (T. 316).[123] In the opposite case, Hume points out that "the principal part of an injury is the contempt and hatred, which it shews in the person, that injures us" (T. 349); the fact that a small harm, if intentional, can constitute a great injury reveals the extent to which pride and humility are social passions. That this is true is largely due to sympathy, by which the sentiments and judgments involved in the opinions of others are communicated to us with their original force and vivacity.

Hume's applications of sympathy thus make up a significant sociable dimension in his account of the passions, despite the fact that he begins, as he does in the case of the understanding, with an analysis of the mental contents of an individual taken alone. In this light it is paradoxical that proponents of an egoistic interpretation of Hume's views on motivation have found evidence for their position in sympathy and especially in the love of fame operating through sympathy. On this interpretation agents, acting only with an eye to their own future pleasure, pursue the esteem of others so that through sympathy they may subsequently enjoy the reflected pleasant sensations of the others'

[123] This may lead to a "contradiction" in the passions: the causes of one's pride may, through the principle of comparison, arouse humiliation and thence envy and resentment in others rather than the esteem that would sustain the pride. See Annette Baier, "Hume's Account of Our Absurd Passions," *Journal of Philosophy* 79 (1982): 643-51.

good opinion of them—as well as the more tangible benefits flowing from this esteem. A concern for reputation or "respectability" is accordingly said to be the principal motivation for apparently disinterested actions—the psychological basis for the whole of morality;[124] and sympathy, too, is assimilated to a fundamental egoism: we act for the happiness of others so that we may receive the pleasure that we know from experience we will, through sympathy, share with the beneficiaries of our actions.

These views seriously misrepresent Hume's positions. It is true that he sees in pride and a concern for reputation or rank an undoubted support for virtue, but these are far from being the sole sources of moral motivation; nor does this interpretation acknowledge Hume's usual distinction between the conscious end of an action and concomitant feelings: "I feel a pleasure in doing good to my friend, because I love him; but do not love him for the sake of that pleasure."[125] It also overestimates the extent to which sympathetic responses can be a matter of voluntarism and deliberate calculation. The finding of egoism even in the doctrine of sympathy is probably the consequence of reading into Hume the doctrines of subsequent writers on psychology and morals who were his disciples only in certain limited respects.[126] All Hume's discussions of sympathy rather emphasize the weakness of the individual's independent sense of self and his reliance on others both for ideas and opinions and for the passions and judgments that through sympathy are incorporated into the individual's own affective character. "The minds of men are mirrors to one another," reflecting and reverberating emotions and opinions in a manner that calls into question the mental autonomy of the individual (T. 365).

Through sympathy as through habituation and education individuals are participants in a wide array of perceptions that are distinctive not only of them but also of their community. The common evaluations of objects and shared patterns of approbation that characterize any society exhibiting the moral unity necessary to its continuance are to a large extent a consequence, in Hume's account, of these sociable factors in human nature and not the mere coincidence of a vast number

---

[124] Green, "Introduction," p. 44.

[125] Hume, "Of the Dignity or Meanness of Human Nature," *Works*, vol. 3, pp. 151, 155.

[126] Cf. Bentham's "pleasures of a good name" and "pleasures of benevolence," also called "pleasures of sympathy," in *An Introduction to the Principles of Morals and Legislation*, with *A Fragment on Government*, ed. Wilfrid Harrison (Oxford: Basil Blackwell, 1967), p. 157.

of independent individual judgments. The pleasure that people receive from the esteem and approval of others, then, is not only not the usual objective of their altruistic actions but is rather the product of a sympathetic capacity whose general effects are the opposite of egoistic. It has been observed that social conformity of belief and behavior achieved through a variety of moral rather than legal pressures has been an important theme or assumption in many liberal political theories that are ostensibly grounded in individualism.[127] Sympathy and habit—so important in many areas of mental and social life—are the terms in which Hume's theory accounts for this kind of conformity and indeed for many other aspects of moral and political life.

I have so far examined some of the ways in which Hume's theories of motivation and sympathy point to the strength and constancy of the ties that connect one person with others by virtue of fundamental propensities of human nature. In the remainder of this chapter I consider Hume's general assessment of the sociable nature of human beings, with attention to several special features of it—in particular, the distinction between intimate and wider circles of acquaintance and the social effects of habit and custom. I shall still be speaking mainly of the passions and the psychological processes that apply to them, but the analysis will parallel that which we have previously traced with respect to the understanding: common features include the concern with "enlivening" factors that arises from the assumption that perceptions influence consciousness and volition in proportion to their force and vivacity, and of course the pervasive role of habit in mental processes. That Hume appeals to many of the same factors to explain reasoning and belief on the one hand and affective phenomena on the other makes clear that these are among the most fundamental dispositions of human nature.

As suggested above, Hume joined a tradition of thought that asserted natural human sociability against a persistent Hobbesian outlook.[128] The most influential figure in this respect was Shaftesbury, who rejected theories holding that the rational consent of calculating individuals in any way explained the existence of societies in favor of what

---

[127] Sheldon S. Wolin, *Politics and Vision* (London: George Allen and Unwin, 1961), pp. 343-44. Wolin mentions Locke's "law of opinion" and Adam Smith's "impartial spectator," as well as John Stuart Mill and de Tocqueville, who deplored conformity. Thinkers of the eighteenth century were perhaps more comfortable with a view of people as sharing in sentiments and values with those around them than were earlier or later theorists.

[128] See Thomas A. Horne, *The Social Thought of Bernard Mandeville* (New York: Columbia University Press, 1978), chap. 2, on a similar French tradition.

he variously calls a "sense of fellowship," a "herding" or "combining principle," or an "associating inclination." Shaftesbury connects this associative tendency with a similarly instinctual "moral sense," by which individuals are said naturally to approve of what is conducive to the welfare of the system of which they are a part, and with a related sympathetic capacity through which "community or participation in the pleasures of others" constitutes "nine-tenths of whatever is enjoyed in life." Shaftesbury does not invoke moral propensities of this kind in order to provide a facile and complacent alternative to theories of the self-interested basis of society and morality. He notes on the contrary that " 'tis in war the knot of fellowship is closest drawn," thus initiating a line of speculation into the psychological roots of military solidarity to which Hume and other Scottish thinkers contributed. In general the alleged "herding principle" points conspicuously to tension between small solidary groups and the larger society of which they are subdivisions; the corollary of natural sociability is the tendency to "*cantonise*" or to devote one's energies and loyalty to parties, factions, particular orders, even to seditious or criminal bands, in which the associative ties are stronger than they can be among the members of a large state: "the associating genius of man is never better proved than in those very societies, which are formed in opposition to the general one of mankind, and to the real interest of the state."[129] Thus although various sociable and selfless tendencies are postulated as the positive foundation for a new understanding of morality and political society, they also provide the framework for explaining ethical and social conflict, the existence of which is not necessarily obscured by this tradition of inquiry. Hume follows Shaftesbury's lead in these respects, developing similar conclusions in the more systematic terms of his own psychology.

A human being, according to Hume, is the creature "who has the most ardent desire of society. . . . We can form no wish, which has not a reference to society. A perfect solitude is, perhaps, the greatest punishment we can suffer" (T. 363).[130] The explanation in Hume's

[129] Shaftesbury, *Characteristics of Men, Manners, Opinions, Times,* ed. John M. Robertson (Indianapolis: Bobbs-Merrill, 1964), vol. 1, pp. 75-77, 296ff. Cf. Hume's remark, also à propos of factionalism: "No selfishness, and scarce any philosophy, have there force sufficient to support a total coolness and indifference; and he must be more or less than man, who kindles not in the common blaze." *Enquiries* (II), p. 275.

[130] Here Hume appears to be inspired by his favorite moralist, Cicero: cf. *De Officiis,* trans. Walter Miller (Cambridge: Harvard University Press, 1938) I.xliii, p. 157, and xliv-xlv, pp. 161-63.

psychology for this sociability, which surpasses "any advantages they can ever propose to reap from their union," has to do first with the pervasiveness of sympathetic passions in emotional life. These remarks occur in the discussion of esteem for the rich, in which it is evident that a person's awareness of others' approbation is the source of the most intense forms of pleasure. As it stands, however, this explanation is not entirely satisfactory. Happiness may well be reinforced and disseminated through the sympathetic contagion of the pleasurable passions, but sympathy is a mechanism by which painful as well as pleasant feelings may be communicated: people may be hated instead of esteemed, and they may find themselves sharing (it might be supposed) in others' grief, fear, and humility, all intensified by the "reverberations" of mutual sympathy. Already in the section just cited we find, in fact, intimations of the position Hume was to assume in the second *Enquiry*, where sympathy is no longer a neutral psychic mechanism but a moral faculty equivalent to "fellow-feeling" or general benevolence, by which we feel an active and disinterested concern for the welfare of others, approving what is conducive to it and blaming what detracts from it.[131] In the main *Treatise* account, however, it would appear that one's inclination to society would be contingent on a problematic balance of agreeable over painful sentiments communicated through sympathy. In the *Enquiry* Hume avoids this difficulty simply by postulating sociability as one of the innate or original qualities of human nature.

The *Treatise* contains a further explanation of sociability in the terms of Hume's specialized psychological doctrine. In his study of the imagination Hume finds that mental activity as such yields a distinctive pleasure, a fact he invokes in explaining the phenomenon of "curiosity" and by extension the activity of philosophizing itself; this pleasure, as noted above, is not so much an object of conscious pursuit as it is the concomitant of the satisfaction of a natural need, just as one receives pleasure from the fulfillment of any instinctual impulse. Hume repeats this point with respect to the passions and sympathy, stating it in even stronger terms; and of course the exercise of most of the passions—and sympathy—is impossible except in company. Hume accepts an observation that for others (such as Pascal) has been a ground of pessimism—"that man is altogether insufficient to support himself"; Hume not only explains but welcomes the need for diversion as a normal and wholesome attribute of human nature:

---

[131] See Hume, *Enquiries* (II), pp. 219ff.

> To this method of thinking I so far agree, that I own the mind to be insufficient, of itself, to its own entertainment, and that it naturally seeks after foreign objects, which may produce a lively sensation, and agitate the spirits. On the appearance of such an object it awakes, as it were, from a dream: The blood flows with a new tide: The heart is elevated: And the whole man acquires a vigour, which he cannot command in his solitary and calm moments. (T. 352-53)

Every lively perception gives satisfaction, in contrast to mental torpor and boredom. This applies especially to the passions, including those (perhaps the majority of them) that are generated by sympathy in our intercourse with other people. "Hence company is naturally so rejoicing"—the sole source of an entire category of lively perceptions, our enjoyment of which results from a natural impulse of our minds (T. 353). Solitude is debilitating because it precludes the greater part of emotional life (and the whole of moral life), and the disuse of the appropriate faculties produces the misery that accompanies the frustration of any natural impulse.[132] This doctrine recalls Hume's picture of the skeptical philosopher in his study, whose capacity for sustained doubt nevertheless has its (natural) limits: although his mind is fully occupied with ideas and reasoning, eventually he too finds it necessary to acquiesce in what he learns to acknowledge as a fundamental instinct of belief, excessive resistance to which creates tension and unease. Likewise, the philosopher feels a desire to seek the company of his friends and to mix in the "ordinary affairs of life," an experience that renews his spirits for further study as well as providing new insights into human nature itself. The roots of Hume's view of human sociability, then, extend deep into his naturalism, his understanding of all the characteristic features of mental life—whether rational, emotional, or moral—as expressions of a set of basic and determinative dispositions whose appropriateness to practical life is ultimately attested.

In developing his views on sociability Hume remarks on the same distinction between the ties that unite a small and intimate group and those of a larger society that was previously noted in Shaftesbury's writings. Hume accounts for this distinction in the terms of his own psychology, and in so doing he calls attention to several phenomena, such as patriotism, that are of obvious political significance. More important, however, Hume sees in the problem of the different relations connecting an individual to small and large groups a tension that

---

[132] Cf. Hume, "Of Tragedy," *Works*, vol. 3, pp. 258-65. That the mental activity involved in the sharing of emotions gives pleasure is part of the aesthetic psychology of tragedy.

has serious repercussions later in the central moral distinction between the "natural" and the "artificial" virtues and their corresponding duties and motives. This tension is explained in terms of a principle that is basic to Hume's theory of the imagination—the claim that the forcefulness of an idea increases with the habit of frequent mental association.

We have already seen in our examination of the sympathetic mechanism that its efficacy depends on the cooperation of other imaginative processes. Hume in fact draws on all three principles of the association of ideas and on the force of habit in order to explain why sympathy is intensified with the familiarity of its objects. That we can sympathize with other people at all is due to the fact that a certain resemblance among human beings permits us to recognize the signs of a passion as well as to associate the idea of ourselves with that of the other's passion. Beyond this, the greater the resemblance "in our manners, or character, or country, or language," the stronger the sympathetic response (T. 318). The force of sympathy also varies with the relation of contiguity in space: the greater immediacy of the ideas we have of those in our proximity—our friends and neighbors—also facilitates the requisite transitions in the imagination. Hume adds the relation of causation (of which he believes blood ties are an example) as enhancing sympathy, and of course we sympathize more readily with those to whom we are accustomed by long acquaintance (T. 318). Although sympathy, then, may extend to anyone of whose feelings and opinions we become aware, its effect becomes more intense as the other person is closer and more familiar to us, achieving its greatest impact among the members of a family, in which all the enumerated enlivening factors of the imagination are operative. Nor is it only sympathy that varies in this manner. The instinctual passions (such as particular benevolence or anger) are aroused only by proximate objects, and the other passions too are strengthened or diminished in force to the degree that these same imaginative factors cooperate in their production. The usual strength of a person's pride in family is partly due to the special facility with which ideas of family can be associated with oneself (T. 307-309); and the same factors determine the usual objects of our love: consanguinity yields the strongest affection, followed by love of "our countrymen, our neighbours, those of the same trade, profession, and even name with ourselves" (T. 352). The "habitude and intimacy" of long acquaintance produce love for another person even when there is no particular "valuable quality" we associate with that person (T. 352).[133] The argument from the

---

[133] See also Hume, "Dissertation on the Passions," *Works*, vol. 4, p. 156.

pleasing activity and diversion with which society furnishes the mind, finally, is qualified to the effect that "the company of our relations and acquaintance" is more agreeable in this respect than is that of strangers (T. 353).[134]

It is one of the merits of Hume's system that he accounts for these facts by reference to the same mental propensities that he finds to underlie the operations of the understanding. Through the principles of association and especially the influence of habit the mind exercises a selective and ordering function on its perceptions, creating for itself a coherent and regular emotional environment in much the same way that it apprehends a stable physical world of continuing objects and uniform causation; it is comfortable with certain kinds of affective attachments as naturally as it believes that the future will resemble the past. In all its objects the mind, which thrives on vivacity of conception, tends to be disproportionately influenced by near objects over remote ones, the familiar over the unfamiliar. With respect to reasoning, Hume's attitude toward this propensity is ambivalent: although it may have salutary effects for everyday purposes, it is also a common source of errors in philosophical or scientific reasoning. In his account of the passions, where the same propensity leads us to sympathize more fully with those in the smaller circles of our acquaintance than with strangers in the larger society, Hume presents the fact without criticism. Problems do arise in ethical theory, where there is a tension between the impartiality demanded by certain moral rules and our natural inability to feel indifferent toward friend and stranger alike. In the next chapter we shall see how Hume assumes a critical standpoint in his moral philosophy analogous to that which he takes up with respect to the understanding, preferring the artificial to the natural virtues in cases of conflict just as he defends certain norms of correct reasoning against other natural tendencies of the imagination. It is the psychological facts I have been examining here that set the problem to which that moral distinction, central to Hume's political philosophy, refers.

Although Hume's doctrine of natural sociability is qualified in this way, he nevertheless establishes no definite boundaries to the range of affective ties: although sympathy operates most effectively within the confines of intimate groups, it is not without influence in wider

[134] For an argument on the pervasive impact of the family in Hume's philosophy, including its influence on patterns of thought and feeling that Hume takes to be fundamental, see Annette Baier, "Helping Hume to 'Compleat the Union'," *Philosophy and Phenomenological Research* 41 (1980): 167-86.

contexts. Hume, like other social theorists in his time, was interested in the phenomenon of "national character," the general similarities of culture and temperament that appear to distinguish different nations. To this problem his theory of sympathy readily lends itself, as does his emphasis on the psychic importance of custom, which renders the usual habitual and thus lively in the imagination.[135] National similarities constitute a type of resemblance among people that makes sympathetic communication among them easier (T. 318), but Hume also argues that such communication is itself an important cause of national character in the first place: " 'tis much more probable, that this resemblance arises from sympathy, than from any influence of the soil and climate" (T. 316-17).[136] Sympathy reinforces education in disseminating common opinions and beliefs throughout a society; and the communication of judgments of taste and morals would depend especially heavily on sympathy, founded as such judgments are on feelings. Hume draws on these points to explain how a particular "spirit and genius" may be "diffused" throughout a people to provide the essential background for their special cultural achievements.[137] The growth and perpetuation of a national character, however, require that members of the same community act in a similar fashion, over and above their capacity to share in one another's feelings. To explain this Hume adduces a propensity to "emulation" or "imitativeness" by which similar patterns of behavior and "manners" follow upon sympathy:

> The human mind is of a very imitative nature; nor is it possible for any set of men to converse often together, without acquiring a similitude of manners, and communicating to each other their vices as well as virtues. . . . Where a number of men are united into one political body, the occasions of their intercourse must be so frequent, for defence, commerce, and government, that, together with the

[135] Smith and Ferguson were also interested in patriotism and national ties, which they analyzed in terms of sympathy, custom, and social instinct. See Smith, *Theory of Moral Sentiments* v.2, pp. 328-43; and Adam Ferguson, *An Essay on the History of Civil Society*, ed. Duncan Forbes (Edinburgh: Edinburgh University Press, 1966), pp. 16ff.

[136] The distinction between "moral" and "physical" causes intimated here is further developed in Hume, "Of National Characters," *Works*, vol. 3. That essay seems to have been intended as a friendly criticism of Montesquieu; this *Treatise* passage reveals, however, that Hume concerned himself with this issue prior to the publication of the *Spirit of the Laws*.

[137] Hume, "Of the Rise and Progress of the Arts and Sciences," *Works*, vol. 3, pp. 176-77; cf. also the reference to the "contagion of popular opinion," p. 182.

same speech or language, they must acquire a resemblance in their manners, and have a common or national character, as well as a personal one, peculiar to each individual.[138]

By this process, as well as through a deliberate policy of education, the bonds of society at the levels of both opinion and sentiment can extend widely: manners and beliefs are quite uniform, he points out, in the empire of China.[139] Insofar as this kind of unity depends on sympathy and the passions, however, the ties among people will always be stronger in intimate groups than they can be in any national unit as a whole. Hume suggests no quantitative dividing line between large and small groups for this purpose, but tension nevertheless remains to play a part subsequently in Hume's account of the origins of government.

I turn finally in this survey of Hume's science of human nature to the function of custom or habit in determining manifestations of the passions. Hume's claims for the force of custom here, as in his explanation of belief, are large; and they are expressed in similar terms, by reference to a "*facility*" or "*tendency*" of imaginative transition as generating the usual course of conscious life (T. 422). Hume goes so far as to assert that custom can "convert pain into pleasure," which would render custom a stronger force, in a sense, than the impressions that Hume generally regards as "original qualities" of our nature and treats as though their influence in the mind were constant. That custom can constitute new sources of pleasure is due to a psychological fact that has been noted with respect to the satisfaction we derive from belief: the facility of mental transition and the "orderly motion" of perceptions produced by repetition is pleasing in itself, regardless of the quality of the ideas or passions involved (T. 423). Habituation can intensify a passion such as love or pride, or indeed stimulate these passions with regard to previously unaffecting objects. Hume offers an example of the generation of a political sentiment—love of one's city—through the settling of mental habits:

> It often happens, that after we have liv'd a considerable time in any city; however at first it might be disagreeable to us; yet as we become familiar with the objects, and contract an acquaintance, tho' merely with the streets and buildings, the aversion diminishes by degrees,

[138] Hume, "Of National Characters," *Works*, vol. 3, p. 248. On "emulation," in the sense of a combination of imitation and competition, as a special characteristic of people living under a popular government, see Hume, "Of the Rise and Progress of the Arts and Sciences," *Works*, vol. 3, p. 181.

[139] Ibid., p. 183.

and at last changes into the opposite passion. The mind finds a
satisfaction and ease in the view of objects, to which it is accustom'd,
and naturally prefers them to others, which, tho', perhaps, in
themselves more valuable, are less known to it. (T. 354-55)

Habituation such as this is in part analogous in the sphere of passions
to education through repetition and familiarization in the sphere of
ideas. Passions, however, unlike ideas and beliefs about matters of
fact, constitute their own reality; they do not purport to represent
anything outside a person's own mind, and therefore they are not
susceptible of anything like the experimental confirmation that may
be sought for beliefs regarding fact. For this reason the affective part
of one's mental constitution would appear to be more dependent on
habit than the cognitive part would be, although as we have seen
volition and conduct follow in the final analysis from a combination
of reasoning and feeling.

There are three special topics in Hume's doctrine of custom in the
sphere of the passions that may be briefly mentioned. It is habituation,
first of all, that largely determines the relative "strength" or "weakness" of passions for the purposes of their effect on volition. In Hume's
model of reasonable conduct calm passions are supposed to prevail
over violent desires or "every momentary gust of passion" (T. 419).
They may achieve this effect through the interposition of a reasoning
process that brings to view objects other than those immediately present; but the most important of the calm desires, those that motivate
our steady pursuit of our basic needs and general advantage over long
periods of time, receive their strength from their normal basis in habit.
Habit, indeed, is responsible—in self-controlled adults, in varying degrees—for the very capacity to oppose a reasoning process to a present
impulse.

Related to the concept of custom is the imagination's tendency to
follow general rules, which appears in the case of the passions as well
as in the ascription of objectivity and causation. In the affective as in
the cognitive sphere, the rule-following inclination of the mind contributes to the general disposition, which Hume derives from several
sources, to impose order and regularity on our experience and our
judgments (T. 294). We confront the array of objects that is presented
to us with certain general rules of desire and aversion, love and hatred,
and so forth, that we have acquired through the habits developed in
past experience, just as we approach the world with a deeply founded
custom of expecting regularity of causes and a multitude of other
habitual mental associations. Although such mental habits may be

broken, especially by someone of a skeptical turn of mind, all people generally depend on them for their conduct in the common affairs of life.

It is to the influence of general rules operating in the sphere of feeling and evaluation that Hume attributes the notion of social rank, which he takes to be both natural and on the whole beneficial: our esteem for rich and powerful individuals is generalized into esteem for an entire order of persons, which tends to prevail unless it is jarred by a particularly striking exception.[140] The capacity to guide our judgments and evaluations in accordance with general rules has its greatest importance for Hume's political theory with reference to his analysis of the artificial moral virtues such as justice, which require the indifferent application of rules to all members of a society. The psychological possibility of such rules is grounded in the effectiveness of the rule-following propensity of the imagination, seconded by habit and education, in counterbalancing the powerful impulses by which we tend to prefer the near and familiar to the remote and strange.[141]

A final corollary of the doctrine of habit is Hume's theory of the "predominant passion." This is a specialized doctrine stating that when two opposite passions (for example, courage and fear) are present in the mind simultaneously, the "pre-dominant" or stronger tends to "[swallow] up the inferior, and [convert] it into itself" (T. 420). Thus love may be enhanced by "jealousies and quarrels" so long as they remain minor, and courage may be bolstered by an admixture of fear unless the balance is tipped and it is overwhelmed. This phenomenon is of interest in that Hume calls attention to its role in "common artifice[s] of politicians" and especially in the efficacy of martial discipline. The predominant passion in any situation is likely to be the one most thoroughly ingrained through habit, which can be the deliberate product of training. Military discipline, together with an accentuated regularity of life and the "pomp and majesty of war," ensure that obedience and courage will predominate over other motives in soldiers, thus providing the psychological basis for the readiness—so unaccountable in egoistic interpretations of motivation—with which trained men go into combat. Habit is the fundamental fact of life in Hume's theory of human nature, and this particular illustration sug-

---

[140] See Laurence L. Bongie, *David Hume: Prophet of the Counter-Revolution* (Oxford: Clarendon Press, 1965), p. 128. The prevalence and necessity of rank, although a background assumption, is not, however, a major theme in Hume's writings.

[141] Thomas K. Hearn, Jr., " 'General Rules' in Hume's *Treatise*," *Journal of the History of Philosophy* 8 (1970): 405-22.

gests the potentialities of this natural disposition when it is directed by deliberate political contrivance.

Hume's emphasis on custom and habit thus clearly contributes to the sociable dimension of his theory of the passions. Frequently repeated mental transitions acquire facility and yield satisfaction; these facts, as applied to the passions, most of which through sympathy or otherwise pertain to our relations with other people, indicate yet another respect in which the usual patterns of any individual's mental life are inextricable from the patterns of feeling and opinion that are in a continuous process of communication throughout society. Hume first considers custom in the operations of the mind considered in isolation from other minds in his effort to account for the cognitive fact of belief in causal regularity. Even in the realm of the "understanding," however, it emerges that repeated testimony commonly serves as a kind of experience in generating customs of belief and expectation. When Hume comes to consider the effects of social custom in the realm of the passions, it stands out even more strongly as a source of shared perceptions, feelings, and hence of shared evaluations and common forms of behavior. When we leave Book II of the *Treatise*, we are firmly in the practical sphere of judgment and action, and we are just as clearly in a social world, the realm of "moral topics," as well. Hume's analysis of moral and political values and institutions that follows is firmly grounded in the science of belief, sympathy, and habit whose central tenets have been outlined in this chapter.

It is evident that the theory of the passions is central to Hume's science of human nature, providing many of the materials for his social and political theory in particular. Hume's attention to the passions follows from the epistemological criticisms that are the most noteworthy feature of Book I, being an extension of the psychology of the imagination, whose natural operations are found to compensate for the weakness of reason. This interest in the passions leads directly to the political philosophy of Book III, with its effort to explain the nature of the political virtues of justice and allegiance and the institutions that make these possible. Hume's philosophy as a whole remains one of skepticism, qualified by recognition that the actual practice of skeptical inquiry remains the province of the philosophical few. Skepticism, by revealing the insufficiency of reason and the compensatory function of belief and other "instinctual" propensities, puts feeling and habit at the center of its assessment of human nature, even though the skeptic determines to doubt and to reason, in a duly cautious manner, about the world, including the realm of human nature and society. In this enterprise it is fitting that a science of the passions forms the prelude to Hume's theory of morals and politics.

Hume's science of the passions is partly inspired by a Newtonian vision of a universe in which discrete objects subsist in observable relations to one another, relations that may be expressed as laws of motion and attraction. A century earlier Hobbes, likewise inspired by the new physics, attempted to apply a similar model to psychology and politics, and he arrived at a view of individuals and their passions as in a constant state of motion and collision. Hume offers a view of mental operations and of behavior that is tranquil by comparison. The passions especially, he says, are "slow and restive," comparable to a string instrument, whose vibrations only gradually decay (T. 441); the mind continues in its motion "as a vessel, once impelled by the oars, carries on its course for some time, when the original impulse is suspended."[142] It is perhaps the recognition of inertia that differentiates Hume's model from that of Hobbes and leads him to present a quite different picture of mental and of social life. Hume's emphasis on custom, repetition, and the force of the familiar renders his Newtonianism fundamentally conservative, the atoms naturally channeled in their motion, human beings creatures thriving on the regular patterns of habit. This model determines the character of Hume's moral and political doctrines as well, to which I now turn.

[142] Hume, "Of Eloquence," *Works*, vol. 3, p. 174. Cf. *Treatise*, p. 198.

CHAPTER IV

The Political Theory of Artifice

1. THE SETTING OF HUME'S POLITICAL PHILOSOPHY

Hume's analyses of the understanding and the passions are conceived as preliminaries to the study of "moral topics" and society, and hence we follow Hume's own intentions in seeking to grasp the significance of his theories of mental operations for the political philosophy that follows. The study of "morals" for Hume connotes investigations both into ethics, or the virtues and vices proper, and into social life generally, of which the analysis of political values, beliefs, and institutions forms a substantial portion. I have emphasized the degree to which Hume, despite his methodological individualism, is led to an appreciation of the role of social influence in the formation of an individual's beliefs, feelings, and character; education and sympathy, for example, constitute "moral" topics in Hume's broader sense of the term already, although they fall within the framework of his philosophy of mind. I now turn to the explicitly moral part of Hume's philosophy, and thus to the principles of political life, that are his chief concern.

Hume's political philosophy is contained largely in Book III of the *Treatise,* and I am mainly concerned with its presentation there. In his "Advertisement" to this book, Hume states that it is "in some measure independent" of the first two volumes and expresses a hope that "ordinary readers" will understand it (T. facing p. 455); from this, and from his subsequent efforts to popularize his moral and political views, it is evident that Hume regards this part of his philosophy as having practical implications as well as theoretical interest. Nevertheless, Hume goes on to assert that continuity exists between the doctrines of Book III and the preceding ones: "our reasonings concerning *morals* will corroborate whatever has been said concerning the *understanding* and the *passions*" (T. 455). Much of the force and interest of Hume's political philosophy stems from its integration in a more comprehensive doctrine of human nature, and especially from its grounding in the combination of mitigated skepticism and naturalism that is the outcome of his epistemological investigations. Hume's analysis of political principles and institutions makes frequent reference to such categories as belief, custom, and feeling, whose full import is intelligible only in light of the previous account of the workings of the mind. Much of Hume's analysis of political beliefs and behavior, furthermore, especially in the *Treatise,* is presented in terms of moral psychology: the solution to such problems as the nature of our sense of justice, or why people generally support political authority and obey the law, depends on materials supplied by his psychology. Thus I am concerned in what follows with the many elements of continuity that extend through the *Treatise* as a whole.

The political doctrines of the *Treatise* also contain intimations of the historical method that Hume was subsequently to pursue in his political essays and in his *History of England*: Hume's empirical political science relies for its "experimental" evidence on the two complementary disciplines of history and psychology. Hume regards history, however, primarily as "so many collections of experiments" by means of which the philosopher gains insights into the "constant and universal principles of human nature."[1] Hume eventually became a historian, and it is history alone that provides the materials for the study of the functioning of diverse political institutions that became the focus of what may be called the second phase of Hume's political theory, that which is developed in his essays. In the *Treatise,* however, appeals to historical data serve mainly to confirm the principles of psychology on which the political doctrines advanced there are principally based.[2] In this chapter I consider Hume's political philosophy as a component of his science of human nature, with only occasional glances toward the institutional and historical studies that follow.

Hume's political theory as it appears in the *Treatise* is presented as a part of a general moral theory. Although by the term "morals" Hume usually means the phenomena of social life generally, he devotes much of Book III to the pursuit of moral philosophy in a stricter sense—that is, to the study of certain types of beliefs and judgments of value that people make in the course of their social life, in particular judgments concerning what is "good" or "right," what is "virtuous" and what ought to be done and not done. Political philosophy as a branch of ethical theory is naturally concerned mainly with the analysis and justification of political values and obligations; and in fact the analysis of those virtues that are distinctively political constitutes quite a substantial portion of Hume's ethics as a whole. In particular, the moral rules falling under the two rubrics of justice and allegiance receive more attention than all other moral virtues together. Much of

---

[1] Hume, *Enquiries* (I), p. 83.
[2] Cf. John Day, "Hume on Justice and Allegiance," *Philosophy* 40 (1965): 35-36, 45.

Book III of the *Treatise*, then, and a smaller but substantial part of the second *Enquiry*, are therefore in actuality works of political as well as of broadly moral theory. The issues that Hume raises here are carried over and illustrated in his historical studies and political essays, especially as they are bound up with problems of cause and effect relations with respect to specific institutions. The investigation in the *Treatise* proceeds for the most part at a more abstract level, exploring the nature of justice and allegiance in general; Hume conducts such an inquiry on the basis of the generalized account of human nature that he has set forth in the preceding books, establishing the fundamental principles of political life by reference to the basic human needs, capacities, and mental attributes that he has already examined.

Since Hume's political theory is firmly embedded in his philosophy of human nature as a whole, a question arises concerning the autonomy of the political: what, if anything, distinguishes political life from other elements of social life, and the political virtues from moral values in general?[3] Although the structure of Hume's system indeed tends to blur such boundaries, I argue that the political in Hume's account is characterized principally by the concept of artifice, a term Hume utilizes to denote both the conventional status of certain kinds of values and institutions and the fact that such institutions achieve their ends by directing people's activities and judgments according to general rules. Artificiality is not a unique feature of political and legal institutions—the state and systems of property, for example; Hume is also interested in other types of conventions, such as a society's rules concerning sexual and familial relations and its standards of artistic taste and etiquette. Rules governing these matters are not ordinarily regarded as "political," although one of the problems raised in Hume's writings is the degree and manner in which they vary according to political regime and are therefore to be viewed as the products of political choice in a large sense; their status as artifices in Hume's system, in common with rules governing the distribution of property and authority, indicates the difficulties involved in an attempt to differentiate them from the political. Nor does Hume as a political scientist concern himself exclusively with the nature of artificial institutions or confine himself to studies of legal systems and governmental structures. In the interests of his comprehensive science of human

---

[3] Hume is, as John B. Stewart says, a less political writer than Hobbes, inasmuch as the state is not his central focus; but this is because he is a broadly social and moral theorist (like Montesquieu, Rousseau, or Smith) and not (as Stewart suggests) because he is primarily an economist; *The Moral and Political Philosophy of David Hume* (New York: Columbia University Press, 1963), p. 196. See also note 114 below.

nature, he is always alert to the sources of social rules in the rudimentary impulses of the individual mind, and the nature of the interaction and potential conflict between the realms of the artificial and the natural is an important theme in his political philosophy. It is the idea of artifice, however, that permits Hume to conceptualize these problems, and the full meaning of this idea is thus the principal question with which I approach Hume's political writings.

Hume's political theory in the *Treatise* is couched in terms of analyzing the two most important "artificial virtues"—the political virtues of justice and allegiance. The concept of artifice is applied to these topics in two ways. Justice and allegiance are necessarily manifested with reference to tangible political institutions, through which rules of conduct or laws are formulated, applied, and adjudicated in a given polity; Hume, particularly in his essays, undertakes studies of the variations among different sorts of governmental institutions and the precise nature of their operations and effectiveness in attaining various goals. More fundamental to Hume's political theory, however, is the conception of justice and allegiance as artificial sets of moral rules, in accordance with which moral agents, as members of a political community, make moral judgments, acknowledge obligations, and voluntarily regulate their conduct. Hume is interested above all in justice and the requirement of obedience to authority as moral duties or virtues, as constraints on individuals reflectively adjudged by them to be legitimate. As virtues, justice and allegiance must be analyzed as items in the larger category of moral virtues, and therefore Hume's general account of moral judgment and standards of value is applicable to them. More interesting from the point of view of political theory, however, is the way in which the political virtues differ from other moral virtues and the special problems that arise in connection with them. In particular, I examine the function of the artificial virtues in offsetting, redirecting, and indeed overcoming (in part) the spontaneous impulses of the "natural" or instinctual virtues, a theme that is central to Hume's analysis of moral life. In addition, I examine Hume's views on the role of reflection, and hence the potentiality of criticism, in the establishment of the complex rules and artifices of political life—a question that bears on the practical meaning of his skepticism in politics.

Hume's investigation of moral virtues comprises three elements, all of which provide interesting perspectives on the nature of justice and allegiance. He first examines the ends achieved by the various qualities and actions ordinarily judged favorably—the actual effects that such qualities tend to produce, whether they were deliberately aimed at or not. Second, he inquires into the sources of moral judgment in human nature as he has portrayed it, studying, that is, the motivation of value judgments and of actions undertaken in accordance with such judgments, drawing on the principles of his psychology and his accounts of reason and volition. Finally, Hume raises questions concerning the "origins" of the different virtues, the manner in which they have "arisen" and developed historically. This last question, it emerges, is meaningful mainly in the case of the artificial virtues, which because they are conventions and not spontaneous products of human nature do indeed have a history of variation and evolution over time and in different countries. This area of inquiry is important for Hume partly insofar as it sheds light on the first two questions; historical evidence yields information on the possible ends and motivational sources of moral rules and political institutions, and a thorough study of history alone can provide an answer to the question of whether human societies display any fundamental uniformities in these respects. The history of morals, moreover, increasingly came to occupy Hume's attention, and his later writings mark him as one of the pioneers of the historical age of European thought.[4] In the *Treatise,* however, with which I am mainly concerned, Hume's interest in the moral virtues is more abstract; his conclusions draw primarily on his generalized doctrines of human nature and only secondarily on an equally generalized and for the most part hypothetical account of "origins," which is invoked mainly to confirm the unhistorical science of human nature.

I have mentioned above that the uniformity and simplicity of the human mind in certain fundamental respects are assumptions with which Hume works as he elaborates psychological principles drawn from the evidence of introspection and everyday experience. At the same time, as a skeptic as well as a scientist, Hume regards these assumptions as hypotheses and not dogmas, and his reliance on experience for knowledge of matters of fact dictates sensitivity to discordant data. This same methodological tension likewise pervades his ethical theory: a scientific treatment of morals, such as he attempts to provide in his *Treatise* and second *Enquiry,* must strive for generalizations about the values upheld in human societies; at the same time the question of whether any basic moral uniformities exist at all remains open, although the ethical theory that Hume presents contains a tentative affirmative answer to this question. The historical dimension, in the case of the artificial virtues, reveals that specific moral

---

[4] Ernst Cassirer, *The Philosophy of the Enlightenment* (Princeton: Princeton University Press, 1951), pp. 226-28.

rules and political systems are the products of evolution and change, as one would expect of institutions conceived as "artifice"; but the picture presented is one of the growth of rules and values fundamentally uniform in their function, if not in their exact content, and so Hume's analysis of origins serves principally to reinforce the more central explication of the ends and psychological basis of values.

It will be noted that the issues Hume raises in his moral theory are mainly empirical ones. The psychology and history of moral virtues are obviously so; and even in the case of ends Hume for the most part sets himself the task of surveying the objectives at which moral agents aim, or the ends actually achieved through moral and political rules that may be observed in practice. This suggests that Hume's moral philosophy consists of moral science rather than of ethics—the factual study of values and their contexts rather than the philosophical defense or advocacy of one ethical or political system in preference to others.[5] This is true, however, only to a degree, and I shall dispute the common charge that Hume lacks, and even that his skeptical and analytical approach precludes, a practical or normative position in ethics and politics. The two forms of inquiry are rarely if ever completely separated in practice, and in Hume's philosophy (as in other systems) moral justification and criticism grow naturally from empirical foundations, just as his normative canon of inductive logic rests on extensive psychological foundations. Hume's effort to "introduce the experimental method of reasoning into moral subjects," however, means that observations and generalizations regarding moral practices and institutions do constitute the bulk of his work. Much of Hume's moral philosophy is concerned with moral psychology, the analysis of the sentiments that accompany and motivate moral judgments and of the ways in which feeling, reason, and habit combine to determine moral conduct; values seen from this perspective are treated as special psychological phenomena that display regularities in the same way as do other features of human nature.[6] Hume characteristically asks why people acknowledge and obey certain rules rather than why they ought to obey them, and his mode of expression throughout suggests that

[5] Hume, *Enquiries* (II), p. 174.

[6] See Leslie Stephen, *History of English Thought in the Eighteenth Century* (New York: Harcourt, Brace, and World, 1962), vol. 2, p. 76, on moral psychology and ethics. Cf. also Henry Sidgwick, *The Methods of Ethics* (New York: Dover, 1966), pp. 77ff. See Moritz Schlick, "What Is the Aim of Ethics?" in *Logical Positivism*, ed. A. J. Ayer (New York: The Free Press, 1959), pp. 247-63, for the claim that ethics ought to be subsumed under psychology; Schlick writes in a tradition of philosophy that claims Hume as one of its antecedents: see Ayer's "Introduction," pp. 4, 10, 22.

he is presenting a body of facts concerning moral and political phenomena.

Hume's political theory is thus a continuation of his comprehensive science of human nature into the sphere of morality and of the political institutions that are among the conditions of any stable and civilized society. Such values and institutions grow out of and depend on certain features of human nature previously discussed, although the more important of them are "artificial"—one or more steps removed from the immediate impulses of human nature, which they serve to check and balance. Values and the institutions through which they have historically been realized may be analyzed in scientific fashion as matters of fact, as causes and effects, in the observable course of social life.[7] In investigations such as these Hume stands as a practitioner of empirical political science, whose major contributions lie in his explorations of the moral and psychological bases of systems of justice and political regimes.

His standing as a political philosopher, however, depends in addition on his having made choices among the values and regimes that he subjects to analysis and on the force of the arguments with which he defends his preferences and renders convincing his practical conclusions. I have observed how Hume, at the turning point or crisis of his philosophical development, was confronted with the question of how to live in the face of his Pyrrhonist doubts. I characterized his resolution of the crisis as a combination of mitigated skepticism along with a naturalistic acceptance, for the practical purposes of life, of the fundamental propensities that he observed to be stronger in general than his doubts. Just as Hume elaborates certain rules of right reasoning out of the natural tendency or feeling of belief, a move which permits him to proceed with his scientific endeavors despite his skepticism, so his descriptive analysis of the moral world does not preclude his acquiescing in or deliberately adopting certain of the values he finds there as worthy and appropriate guides for living. The cautious and critical approach to opinions and judgments of all kinds that is characteristic of Hume's mature skepticism no more rules out normative and prescriptive positions in ethics and politics than it rules out a scientific commitment in reasoning about events and objects in the phenomenal world. Both these positive elements in his philosophy are reached in the same way, for which naturalism is an appropriate description. Whether or not Hume is to be credited (or blamed) for

---

[7] Frederick M. Watkins, "Introduction" to David Hume, *Theory of Politics* (Edinburgh: Nelson, 1951), pp. xi-xii.

the modern sensitivity to the distinction between factual and normative inquiries, his own philosophy exhibits no rigorous separation of facts and values, however aware Hume may have been of the logical distinction between them.[8] Although the bulk of Hume's political theory consists of matter-of-fact analysis, he finds his way, in ethics as in logic, to positions that he advocates as reasonable and tenable for practical purposes, however cautious and tentative such conclusions may be and however much he adheres for speculative purposes to a skepticism that, denying the ultimate rational justifiability of our beliefs, leaves all questions potentially open.

2. PRINCIPLES OF HUME'S MORAL PHILOSOPHY

Hume's restrictive assessment of the capacities of reason extends into ethics and the theory of value generally. Here he joins the well-known skeptics of earlier periods in one of their principal concerns, the attempt to define the status of values and moral rules in the absence of any purely rational guidelines or self-evident truths in this sphere. Hume, however, unlike some skeptics, does not evince anxiety or a sense of loss of standards in this connection, nor does he ever conjure up the prospect of moral nihilism. Indeed, since Hume never seriously doubts the reality of moral distinctions (grounded in undeniable feelings as they are), and since he did not wish to associate his theory with the views of writers (such as Mandeville) who *were* understood to have denied the existence of moral motives and actions, he does not present his treatment of ethical issues as skeptical at all. His moral philosophy, however, pursued with equanimity as it is, is premised on his view of the limited potentiality of reason and thus on the rejection of a possible rational basis for moral values.

The conviction, grounded in the prior analysis of reason, that moral qualities such as good and evil, just and unjust, and so forth, cannot be matters of knowledge and certainty can point to two different sorts of investigation. One may regard moral rules (such as the rules of justice) as conventions, established by human agreement or imposition—institutions therefore with a history and, by implication, subject to criticism and change. This is the approach that Hume adopts, in part, with the artificial virtues, which he regards as especially susceptible of such treatment. One may, on the other hand, concentrate on

[8] Cf. Stephen G. Salkever, " 'Cool Reflexion' and the Criticism of Values: Is, Ought, and Objectivity in Hume's Social Science," *American Political Science Review* 74 (1980): 70-77.

the nature of moral judgments and on the motivation of conduct as psychological phenomena: moral approval and disapproval (or from another point of view, the meanings of moral language) are explained in terms of the feelings and desires of moral agents. Hume begins his theory of morals with this latter approach: the psychology of moral judgment and the account of values as expressions of human nature represent a natural extension of the analysis of the mind with which he has hitherto been occupied. Moral psychology, moreover, provides a framework within which the whole of morality can be treated, whereas conventionality or artifice emerges as a special subject within the theory of morals generally. The artificial virtues warrant our main concern, but their special features are intelligible only in the context of Hume's more comprehensive moral theory.

Although reason gives no moral distinctions, Hume emphasizes that "there is no scepticism so scrupulous" as to deny the reality of moral distinctions, marked as they are in the language we speak.[9] The skeptical investigator finds the sources of judgment in the imagination and passions rather than in reason, but he never doubts or underestimates the strength and conviction with which they are held. People make and act on the basis of evaluative distinctions, in Hume's view of human nature, with the same tenacity with which they believe the future will resemble the past. Our moral capacity is no less natural to us, and no less founded on natural feeling, than are our basic ontological convictions; and Hume's treatment of it is parallel, combining scientific analysis and criticism with a naturalistic presumption in favor of its appropriateness for our practical purposes.

Not only is the fact of moral belief indubitable in each individual; Hume's science of morals is founded on the hope—which is substantially confirmed in the outcome—that the "principles" of moral judgment (or the kinds of things generally approved and blamed) will likewise display a certain simplicity and uniformity (T. 473). Ethical systems and judgments seem, on a superficial view, to manifest variation, even outright disagreement; but then again, so do inferences about matters of fact and predictions of the future, despite our fundamental agreement about the structure of the physical world. Hume is confident that a close study of moral beliefs will reveal an equally fundamental order in the underlying standards of judgment, however apparently diverse may be the precise content of different moral practices and popular conceptions regarding them. Hume presumes that morality, at least in its basic, normal manifestations, will, like the

---

[9] Hume, *Enquiries* (II), pp. 170, 174.

natural capacities of belief and sympathy, prove to be a coherent and salutary expression of human nature, well adapted to the satisfaction of needs and necessary to the attainment of such happiness as human society is capable of. Hume therefore, here as elsewhere, is a skeptic only up to a point; his denial of a rational basis or method of validating moral claims no more means a repudiation of morality than a similar critique leads to a rejection of the notion of causation: these possibilities serve only as speculative entertainment for the secluded philosopher. It does not even rule out the possibility that a single moral code might command general agreement and conviction, a possibility that in the first instance sets a problem for empirical investigation. Nor, finally, does it preclude ethical argument: indeed, in a way it makes ethics a more lively subject, though less likely than otherwise to issue in definitive truths. The moral skeptic like other people cannot avoid judging, and so the skeptical philosopher's task of clarifying the nature of moral judgments and rules serves as a prelude to, and even an integral part of, an enterprise of ethical advocacy.

Following a procedure similar to that by which he establishes that the basic beliefs underlying inductive reasoning are themselves founded on feeling rather than on reason, Hume begins his book "Of Morals" by rejecting the view that there are ethical truths given by reason— that rational insight into "those eternal immutable fitnesses and unfitnesses of things" (T. 463) provides standards by which the truth or falsehood of moral evaluations can be apprehended.[10] Two arguments for this position depend on doctrines established previously in the *Treatise*. Morality, first, is a practical discipline: " 'tis supposed to influence our passions and actions" (T. 457). Reason, however, consists merely in the passive comparison of ideas; it is always a passion that directly motivates the will, whether stimulating action or restraining it by checking some other passion. Now, "common experience" informs us "that men are often govern'd by their duties, and are deter'd from some actions by the opinion of injustice, and impell'd to others by that of obligation" (T. 457). Because it exhibits this active, motivational feature, Hume assimilates moral judgment to his general account of volition, concluding that it must always contain some element of what he calls passion or feeling.

The second argument pertains to the possibility that reason, passive

[10] Locke asserts the "unalterable" and "demonstrable" character of true morality; *An Essay Concerning Human Understanding*, ed. Peter H. Nidditch (Oxford: Clarendon Press, 1975), "Epistle to the Reader," i.iii.1, i.iii.13, iv.iii.18, iv.iv.7, iv.xii.8. The rationalist tradition was carried on by Clarke and Wollaston, whom Hume criticizes (T. 80, 461n.).

and contemplative as it is, might be the original source of distinctions between right and wrong, requiring only to be supplemented by passion in action. Hume's broader doctrine that feeling and not reason is the source or very essence of evaluation involves an appeal to the basic tenets of his epistemology. Using his familiar methods, Hume shows that "vice and virtue" do not fall within the province of demonstrative reason (T. 463ff.). Relations between animals or inanimate objects that are logically similar to relations subject to moral judgment when they subsist between human beings are not so judged—a point that suggests a special connection between morality and the conditions and needs of human life in addition to dispelling the notion that there is any logical necessity in ethical tenets. Moral judgment then pertains to experience: might moral distinctions be matters of fact, thus susceptible of observation and probabilistic reasoning? Hume embarks on his characteristic quest for the impressions from which moral ideas are derived and that give meaning to moral words such as "vice." A vicious act may be exhaustively described, either as a physical event or in terms of the psychological states of the persons involved; but "The vice entirely escapes you, as long as you consider the object. You never can find it, till you turn your reflexion into your own breast, and find a sentiment of disapprobation, which arises in you, towards this action. Here is a matter of fact; but 'tis the object of feeling, not of reason. It lies in yourself, not in the object" (T. 468-69). Moral judgments are made with respect to certain kinds of events and objects, whose distinguishing characteristics can be identified, a project that constitutes a large part of Hume's moral philosophy. The elucidation of the objective criteria, however, is insufficient for a full account of morality. As with the idea of "necessity" in causation, an indispensable element in a moral distinction originates in an internal impression, a sentiment in the mind of the observing and judging agent, accompanying the perception of an object with certain characteristics.[11] To this assertion Hume quickly adds, as if to forestall any excessively skeptical inferences that might be drawn from it: "Nothing can be more real, or concern us more, than our own sentiments of pleasure and uneasiness; and if these be favourable to virtue, and unfavourable to vice, no more can be requisite to the regulation of our conduct and behaviour" (T. 469). Hume shows himself to be interested equally in both the subjective and the objective dimensions of morality (as earlier he was with causality)—the feelings that enter

[11] For an interesting criticism, see Jonathan Harrison, *Hume's Moral Epistemology* (Oxford: Clarendon Press, 1976), p. 93.

into moral judgments and the observable features of the "conduct and behaviour" that both occasion and flow from them.

Hume's discussion of morality in the *Treatise* begins with moral psychology, focusing on the sentiment that determines a moral judgment and its interaction with reasoning; he then goes on, in the bulk of Book III, to survey a number of "virtues" and "vices," things generally found to be approved or disapproved, seeking among them some common feature or features that would constitute the objective "standard" or common denominator of moral good and evil. His second *Enquiry* is more concerned with the standard—identified as the quality of being "useful" or "agreeable" to society—reserving moral psychology to an Appendix. I shall follow the order of presentation in the *Treatise*, first considering certain important features of Hume's moral psychology and then passing on to particular objects of judgment, with special attention to the political virtues of justice and allegiance.

Having established that morality is "more properly felt than judg'd of" (T. 470), Hume must specify more exactly the nature and circumstances of the feeling in question. The usual names for the sentiments definitive of moral judgment are approbation and disapprobation;[12] as internal impressions, these feelings are unanalyzable "original qualities" of human nature, whose existence can be established only by appeal to common introspective experience. Certain things, however, may be said of them. Approbation is in the first place generally "soft and gentle" (T. 470), a calm passion often mistaken for (which suggests that it may typically be allied with) reasoning. Approbation accompanying the contemplation of virtue is moreover a pleasing or agreeable feeling, and disapprobation painful or "uneasy": to approve of something is to receive a kind of pleasure from it. Many things please, however, to which we do not accord any favorable moral status: the morally good pleases us in a "particular manner" (T. 471), which must be differentiated from the satisfaction we receive from other kinds of "goodness" as well as from forms of pleasure that are unconnected with evaluation.

In an effort to specify the "peculiar kind" of sentiment involved, Hume notes that we praise the good qualities even of an enemy: " 'Tis only when a character is considered in general, without reference to our particular interest, that it causes such a feeling or sentiment, as denominates it morally good or evil" (T. 472). That moral feelings

---

[12] Hume sometimes uses "praise" and "blame," although these terms would appear to have additional connotations.

are disinterested explains why they must be calm or reflective passions, experienced in abstraction from proximate objects of our own desire. Elsewhere, Hume points out that our distinctively moral feelings are marked in language by a special vocabulary: "When a man denominates another his *enemy*, his *rival*, his *antagonist*, his *adversary*, he is understood to speak the language of self-love, and to express sentiments, peculiar to himself, and arising from his particular circumstances and situation. But when he bestows on any man the epithets of *vicious* or *odious* or *depraved*, he then speaks another language, and expresses sentiments, in which he expects all his audience are to concur with him."[13] The disinterested quality of moral judgments is reflected in the words used, which carry with them an implicit exhortation or appeal to others to share our feeling.[14] The seat of moral judgment, finally, receives in common speech the name conscience or moral sense, as though it were a special faculty corresponding to a special class of feelings, whose reality is thus attested (T. 458).[15] All these points help to characterize moral feeling, whose reality and special quality must be confirmed in each individual's private experience. It is the presence of this feeling, Hume argues, that determines morality: virtue, from a psychological point of view, is *"whatever mental action or quality gives to a spectator the pleasing sentiment of approbation*; and vice the contrary."[16]

The place of reason in moral judgment is a topic to which Hume devotes a good deal of attention, in spite of his initial denial that moral

[13] Hume, *Enquiries* (II), p. 272; cf. also pp. 274, 174; and Hume, "Of the Standard of Taste," *Works*, vol. 3, pp. 266-68. It has been suggested that the *Enquiry*, in adding an emphasis on moral language to moral feelings, is a less naturalistic work than the *Treatise*; James T. King, "The Place of the Language of Morals in Hume's Second *Enquiry*," in *Hume: A Re-evaluation*, ed. Donald W. Livingston and James T. King (New York: Fordham University Press, 1976), pp. 343-61.

[14] This aspect of Hume's analysis (though scant) has been appreciated by philosophers concerned with the "emotive" meanings of ethical terms; see Charles L. Stevenson, *Ethics and Language* (New Haven: Yale University Press, 1944); and, in general, J. O. Urmson, *The Emotive Theory of Ethics* (New York: Oxford University Press, 1968).

[15] Hume does not assert that the moral sense is a real faculty, although he says that this "hypothesis is very plausible" (T. 612). In *Enquiries* (II), p. 173, he calls the faculty of moral judgment an "internal sense or feeling, which nature has made universal in the whole species." Cf. Francis Hutcheson, *An Inquiry into the Original of Our Ideas of Beauty and Virtue* II.i.1, in *The Collected Works of Francis Hutcheson* (Hildesheim: Georg Olms, 1971), vol. 1, p. 109.

[16] Hume, *Enquiries* (II), p. 289. The similarity to Hume's definition of cause as a "natural relation" is apparent. Like cause, virtue too may be seen "philosophically," as certain objective relations that usually do, and ought to, provoke the feeling, as we shall see.

distinctions are "derived" from reason. The resolution of this perennial problem carries momentous implications for the general conception and purpose of the philosophical enterprise with respect to morals, for it would seem that philosophy's right to offer any criticism or advocate any ethical position can rest solely on its claim of having reasoned more carefully about matters on which everyone holds opinions.

Hume's account of moral judgment parallels that of volition, in connection with which he offers a model of "rationality" or reasonable conduct, as we have seen. Reasoning about matters of fact may either "[excite] a passion by informing us of the existence of something which is a proper object of it," or it may "[discover] the connexion of causes and effects," thereby showing us the means to and the probable consequences of a given object or course of action (T. 459). Although moral approbation itself (like the desire that stimulates action) is a feeling, it is experienced with respect to objects, and it therefore depends on a process of reasoning for information. The usual objects of moral judgment are complex matters of human character traits and motives as manifested in social situations; moral approbation, furthermore, is expressed from a point of view of disinterest or impartiality, which requires abstraction from the particular case under consideration. For both these reasons, it is apparent that cool and careful reasoning must have a large role in guiding and influencing plausible moral judgment; evaluation, like action, can be more or less reasonable to the extent that all the relevant facts of a situation have been considered, and there is no question that Hume believes that appropriate moral standards depend, at least in part, on reasoning. "Good morals, and knowledge are almost inseparable, in every age, though not in every individual."[17] Hume clearly is concerned to defend a proper standard of morality, over and above his analysis of moral psychology, and for this accurate knowledge is a necessary if not a sufficient condition, even if fully reasoned arguments are not likely to be within the grasp of each individual on each occasion of moral judgment.

Hume argues in the *Enquiry* that a single general standard does in fact underlie all those qualities judged to be "virtuous": this is their "utility," their tendency to yield beneficial consequences for society; and it is a standard that he accepts as the proper one. Variations in specific moral beliefs may be attributed to different conceptions of social happiness, to different circumstances, or to disagreements in

[17] Hume, *History of England*, chap. 2, vol. 1, p. 74. See also Hume, *Enquiries* (II), p. 173.

reasoning about causes and consequences. Given such a standard, however, there must be reasoning; indeed, "a very accurate *reason* or *judgment* is often requisite, to give the true determination, amidst such intricate doubts arising from obscure or opposite utilities."[18] The fact that the morality of an action is ultimately constituted by the sentiment of approval in each moral agent or spectator does not preclude significant ethical argument, which in large part takes the form of establishing the exact nature and circumstances of the objects on which we are called to make a judgment. Hume suggests that a great deal of moral doubt and controversy is resolvable by reason, by a clear account of matters of fact and causation in human affairs; it is only the "ultimate ends of human actions," and choices regarding what is "desirable on its own account," that are not susceptible of argument but are determined by the fundamental needs and sentiments of human nature.[19]

Hume's insistence on the place of reason in morals points to a role for the philosopher beyond that of moral scientist and analyst. Ethical justification consists of appeals to the approbatory faculty of others by way of the scientific endeavor to point out circumstances and consequences that are not obvious at first glance; it also involves the clarification and coherent ordering of what people take as their ends. Although moral distinctions are not derived from reason, and their ultimate ends not rationally justifiable, they are nevertheless made with respect to relevant matters of fact; and it is in the enlarging of the understanding of these matters that the philosopher finds a practical, educative role. This is of course true in politics as in moral life generally, insofar as political inquiry is (as for Hume) a branch of morals, calling for the ethical assessment of political institutions and values and thus for the frequently complex empirical analyses that precede and permit any convincing evaluations.

Thus again we see that Hume's skepticism in no way leads to a renunciation of reason and the scientific enterprise, despite his modest delineation of their appropriate claims. Recognition of the complexity of the factual situations within which the real issues of ethics and politics arise, on the contrary, conduces to a normative view in which their function is emphasized.

One frequent criticism of Hume's moral theory is that it fails to indicate satisfactorily the specific quality or autonomy of moral as

[18] Hume *Enquiries* (II), p. 286.

[19] Ibid., p. 293. See Thomas K. Hearn, "General Rules and the Moral Sentiments in Hume's *Treatise*," *Review of Metaphysics* 30 (1976): 57-72.

opposed to other kinds of value judgments. Insofar as Hume argues that virtue is constituted by the pleasurable feeling a spectator has on contemplating it, he fails to differentiate it from other sorts of "good" things; even when he adds that the feeling in question is one of indifferent approval, he fails to distinguish the moral "good" or "right" from things approved in other ways, such as aesthetic beauty or qualities such as talent or good manners.[20] Hume often speaks of virtue as "moral beauty" and of moral judgment as equivalent to "taste," a feature of his philosophy in which he follows Shaftesbury.[21] The supposition that there is a firm distinction between moral virtues and other praiseworthy qualities, or between moral and other goods, however, is a modern one. Hume, who in this respect follows classical ethics, implicitly denies that there are precise boundaries between moral virtues and, for example, talents or between duties whose fulfillment is assumed to be within everyone's ability (such as truth-telling) and excellences of character (such as courage) whose voluntary status is questionable. Hume argues that all such "virtuous" qualities are similar from the point of view of our approbation of them and the praise we bestow on them; they are, moreover, justified in similar fashion in terms of their useful or agreeable tendency in social life.[22] We nevertheless have different terms for different sorts of praiseworthy qualities, even if the distinctions of feeling associated with them are not easily specified. This fact suggests the need for a complementary inquiry into the objective side of morality—an analysis of the kinds of things generally approved, together with an examination of the modes of their justification. This inquiry, as already intimated, does not any more than the psychological approach result in a rigid or logical separation of morality from other spheres of value: natural abilities, like moral

[20] Ingemar Hedenius, *Studies in Hume's Ethics* (Uppsala and Stockholm: Almqvist and Wiksells, 1937), pp. 456ff.; and Henry Sidgwick, *Outlines of the History of Ethics* (Boston: Beacon Press, 1964), p. 212; and *The Methods of Ethics* (New York: Dover, 1966), p. 220. Cf. Kingsley Blake Price, "Does Hume's Theory of Knowledge Determine His Ethical Theory?" *Journal of Philosophy* 47 (1950): 428-29.

[21] See, for example, Hume, *Treatise*, pp. 299-300, 577; *Enquiries* (II), pp. 173, 291-92; and "Dissertation on the Passions," *Works*, vol. 4, pp. 146-47. Hutcheson also treats the aesthetic and moral senses as similar.

[22] Hume, *Treatise*, pp. 606-607; *Enquiries* (II), Appendix 4. Hume thus lacks the ethical sensibility, associated especially with Kant, that there is something special and absolute about moral duties. Cf. Cicero's treatment of *decorum* and *honestum*, *De Officiis* i.xxvii, trans. Walter Miller (Cambridge: Harvard University Press, 1961), pp. 95ff. Hume was perhaps the last great modern philosopher in the Renaissance-humanist tradition, thoroughly steeped in classical ethics and looking to Cicero and Horace as the greatest exponents of civilized values—although he rejects ancient political institutions (e.g. in "Of the Populousness of Ancient Nations" and "Of Commerce").

duties, are approved because they have consequences that are similar in important respects. It does, however, yield a classification that is of interest independently of the effort to discover an autonomous sphere for ethics; and it brings us to the second part of Hume's moral theory, the investigation into the occasioning causes of the moral sentiments and the standards or common features that these objects display.

Hume asserts generally that moral judgments pertain to human character and motives (T. 477): we do not praise, or approve in a moral sense, actions performed unintentionally, however beneficial they may be; Hume also wishes to emphasize that morality is an expression of certain impulses or tendencies that people mutually recognize in their common human nature. This assertion, however, is qualified in Hume's further analysis of the virtues. We do commonly, as Hume grants (T. 517), praise or blame actions—and institutions and rules in accordance with which people act—as well as people themselves. Actions are proper objects of moral judgment insofar as we infer a motive or character from them (T. 575), as are rules and institutions insofar as we regard them as guides according to which people act or may voluntarily adapt their conduct. Motives, on the other hand, must be inferred from signs or actions, since we cannot literally "look within" another mind (T. 477). A motive, furthermore, is an object of moral judgment insofar as it represents an intention, or an habitual disposition, to perform certain kinds of actions; and so we judge the motive in accordance with a prior criterion of what kinds of actions and patterns of conduct are desirable.[23] Hume's ensuing survey of the "universal principles, from which all censure or approbation is ultimately derived"[24] focuses on classes of actions generally called benevolent and rules of conduct of the sort that constitute systems of justice. Actions and rules such as these are thus proper objects of moral evaluation, even though in a particular case we make a favorable judgment of an individual's benevolence or justice only if we believe the right motive or habitual disposition to be present in addition to the appropriate behavior; the features and tendencies of the right conduct can be stated apart from particular cases and persons. Most of the words for virtues discussed by Hume (e.g. justice) can refer to actions, institutions (rules), or the quality of a person who

[23] This is especially clear when we consider prescriptive rather than retrospective moral judgments—that someone ought to do something.
[24] Hume, *Enquiries* (II), p. 174.

tends to perform such actions and observe such rules, all of which are complementary matters for ethical analysis.

One further clarification of this point may be helpful: in the *Enquiry* Hume says that the usual objects of moral judgment are "mental qualities," including all praise- or blameworthy habits, sentiments, and faculties as well as conscious motives.[25] This formulation is in accordance with the claim, more explicit in the later work, that no clear distinction can be drawn between what are ordinarily viewed as voluntary and involuntary character traits and sources of conduct. The "mental quality" of courage is a virtue, although the voluntary status of a courageous act is sometimes doubtful, and it is usually not clear whether or in what degrees courage as a personal attribute is a matter of instinct, habit, or conscious decision. An action is not the less virtuous for Hume if its motive is habitual (as is often the case) than if it is generated by an active and reflective sense of duty. This position is attributable to the comprehensive view of human nature that I have emphasized—to Hume's account of the pervasive influence of custom in the mind, his refusal to draw a firm line between rational and affective processes, and his naturalistic inclination to regard these different faculties as mutually adapted to the satisfaction of basic human requirements.

With this contention that motives or mental qualities are the usual objects of moral approbation Hume moves to the compilation of the "virtues" to which the moral sense commonly responds. In both the *Treatise* and the *Enquiry* the result is an enumeration and analysis of various moral qualities, but there are conspicuous differences in the ways in which this material is organized in the two works. In the *Treatise* Hume proceeds directly to an extensive analysis of the artificial virtues, found in Part 2 of Book III, which is entitled "Of Justice and Injustice" but which includes lengthy sections on allegiance and the origins of government as well; the shorter and final Part 3 deals with the natural virtues and related nonvoluntary qualities such as talents. The central Part 2 of Book III, then, contains the most explicitly political doctrines of the *Treatise*, and the classification Hume adopts in the *Treatise*, with its distinction between the artificial and natural virtues, is important to his political theory; I return to these topics in the following two sections of this chapter. The immediate context of Hume's political philosophy, however, is his general theory of moral value, as its more general context is the mitigated skepticism and the psychology that unify Hume's entire science of human nature.

---

[25] Ibid., p. 173.

Before taking up in detail Hume's doctrines of justice and allegiance, therefore, I consider several further aspects of Hume's ethical doctrine, in particular the problem of a moral standard and the mode of its justification, and the extent to which Hume is a proponent of utilitarianism. Hume's positions on these matters are implicit in the *Treatise*, but they are treated more centrally and more adequately in the second *Enquiry*, making it useful to consider the formulations he defends in the later work before approaching the details of the analysis of the political virtues.

The method of the second *Enquiry* differs from that of Book III of the *Treatise* in that Hume embarks immediately on the framing of a catalogue of virtues or qualities observed commonly to be approved or blamed. This enterprise, evidently Aristotelian in inspiration, is an empirical one; Hume intends that ethics may form an integral part of his "experimental" science of human nature; in any case, since values are not derived from rational insight, Hume, surrendering the special claims of some of his predecessors, seeks to ground his speculations in a survey of common opinion and usage. He also makes it clear that the main goal of his investigation is the discovery of a standard: what (if anything) do all the things ordinarily regarded as virtues have in common, as a matter of "fact and observation"?[26]

Acceptance and advocacy of the standard discovered in common opinion as the proper ethical standard, or alternatively criticism of it, however, constitute a further dimension of philosophical endeavor. Hume does not at first give any promise that he will undertake this latter task, stating his intention simply to "account for" the undoubted moral distinctions of actual life. A survey of actual beliefs is frequently a valuable prelude to ethical and political advocacy, however, and if empirical study reveals certain universal standards of value, the step is short from their clarification to their acceptance. This is particularly true for Hume, for whom reason can guide and on occasion even correct the other propensities of the mind but cannot, independently of feeling, establish moral values, and whose naturalistic solution of his skeptical doubts characteristically involves a favorable verdict on the most fundamental impulses of human nature.

Hume's scarcely perceptible transition from descriptive to normative ethics represents a derivation (though not of course a logical deduction) of ought from is, the nature of which is to be explained both as a consistent manifestation of his skeptical naturalism and as a straight-

[26] Ibid., p. 175.

forward act of philosophical choice.[27] The faculty of assent that manifests itself in moral judgments, moreover, is analogous to the natural belief underlying inferential judgments of fact—no less rational and no less deeply seated in human nature. Hume's philosophical defense of an ethical criterion has a direct bearing on his political theory, since one of its principal applications is to the moral virtue of justice: the fact that Hume embraces an ethical position makes it possible to say that he has a theory of justice in addition to having carried out an analysis of various opinions about justice. It should be added, finally, that this distinction (though it accords with his own logic) is not emphasized in Hume's own moral writings; most of his discussion of justice and the other virtues is presented as a clarification of their actual operative features as normal phenomena of social life. Hume's normative positions in moral and political philosophy, like his standards of right reasoning, are outcomes of his analysis of the normal patterns of mental and social life, in which a limited amount of criticism and prescription is cautiously combined with acquiescence in the given features of human nature.

Besides its attention to the question of a standard, the *Enquiry* differs from the *Treatise* in its classification of the virtues. Instead of the dichotomy between artificial and natural, Hume arranges laudable qualities of character in a fourfold scheme, depending on whether they are "useful" or "agreeable" to their possessor or to others. The contents of these categories may be briefly summarized. The general terms benevolence and justice, which receive the most extensive treatment, together cover all qualities regarded as "useful to others." Benevolence here includes what in the *Treatise* appears as the primary natural virtue, signifying attachment and generosity to the immediate circles of one's family, friends, and neighbors; the "others" who are the beneficiaries of this virtue are persons who have some particular relationship (if only proximity) to us, and its "usefulness" consists in its tendency to be solicitous of the happiness of these persons. Justice on the other hand is in the *Enquiry* as in the *Treatise* the archetype of the artificial or political virtues; it consists in obeying a system of general and collectively observed rules or duties (respecting property and promises, especially), and its usefulness is to society as a whole.

As "qualities useful to ourselves" Hume has in mind such personal attributes as discretion, industry, prudence, and temperance. These

[27] See A. C. MacIntyre, "Hume on 'Is' and 'Ought'," in *Hume: A Collection of Critical Essays*, ed. V. C. Chappell (Garden City: Doubleday, 1966), pp. 240-64, who defends the philosophical respectability of Hume's derivation.

and similar qualities are "useful to," or tend over time to promote the happiness of, their possessors alone, but they are generally admired as excellences of character. Hume observes that the exact list will vary depending on the way in which "particular customs and manners" affect the usefulness of different traits in different societies.[28]

Qualities "agreeable" to their possessor include those personal characteristics, such as cheerfulness, tranquillity, and moderate pride, that are conducive to a person's own immediate rather than future happiness and that again are praised according to the values and ideals of a particular society. The principal quality "agreeable to others," finally, is "good manners" or "politeness," which constitutes that "kind of lesser morality, calculated for the ease of company and conversation."[29] The rules of politeness appear in the *Treatise* as one of the types of artificial virtue, which are all said to be "useful" or even necessary for social life as such; Hume here calls them "agreeable" rather than useful because the benefits they bring are an immediate and constant feature of their exercise rather than a future consequence.

All these qualities evidently have in common a tendency to contribute in some fashion to human happiness or well-being. Of them it is those that are "useful to others," benevolence and justice, that in most systems of ethics are held to be most important, and Hume, by his allocation of space, appears to agree with this assessment. With respect to this category, certain questions immediately arise. Who are the "others" to whom these virtues tend to be useful? Hume suggests a distinction in which justice, manifested through general rules, works to the advantage of society as a whole; whereas benevolence, manifested in specific acts of generosity and kindness, tends to benefit individuals or groups smaller than the whole of society. Further, if "usefulness" is distinguished from "agreeableness" by its tendency to conduce to the future rather than to the immediate happiness of its beneficiaries, Hume implies a further distinction within the criterion of futurity: acts of justice taken together as a system promote the advantage of society in a comparatively long temporal perspective, whereas the felicific effect of benevolent acts is more proximate. Both these issues, which are implicit in the *Enquiry* account, are important and problematic in the *Treatise*: that justice and benevolence differ with respect to the scope and the temporal range of their beneficial effects constitutes one of the grounds for their classification in the *Treatise* as opposite kinds of virtue—as the main examples of artificial

---

[28] Hume, *Enquiries* (II), pp. 241-43. See also *Treatise*, pp. 587-91.
[29] Hume, *Enquiries* (II), p. 209; also pp. 261ff.

and natural virtue, respectively. These differences between them explain the fact that they sometimes come into direct conflict with each other, a problem with theoretical implications that will be considered later. The *Enquiry* proceeds on a higher level of abstraction, where benevolence and justice are seen to exemplify the same general characteristic of being "useful to others" and thus to manifest a family resemblance as objects of a certain sort of moral approbation. The precise ways in which justice and the other political virtues differ from natural virtues such as benevolence are skirted in the *Enquiry*; in the *Treatise*, by contrast, this is the starting point and one of the principal problems of Hume's political philosophy.

The conclusion of Hume's survey of virtues is encouraging for an economical science of morals: all the qualities commonly regarded as praiseworthy do appear to display a common objective feature (in addition to the similar feeling that they all tend to arouse in the spectator). This, the standard or "principle" of moral judgment, is their effect of promoting happiness, either for someone in particular or for society generally. Often an awareness of the expected beneficial effects of a virtuous character trait or action is a conscious accompaniment of the favorable judgment, whereas in other cases a little reflection suffices to discover it. In the case of the "agreeable" virtues the happiness is aroused immediately and, it seems, without being consciously intended; in the case of the "useful" virtues happiness follows as a consequence, whether proximately (with benevolence) or more remotely (with justice). The happiness in question is not ordinarily that of the spectator who makes the favorable judgment but that of someone else, or of some collectivity of people of which the spectator may or may not be a member: an aspect of the previously mentioned disinterestedness of judgments of value is that moral agents must have a regard for the happiness of others at least as much as for their own.[30] The most important point is that all virtuous qualities are favorably evaluated in terms of their effects: they are approved as means to a desirable end, although as a rule we have a favorable feeling toward the moral quality without reflecting on its consequences in every instance. Moreover, the tendency of all the virtues is toward the same general end—the happiness of various classes of human

---

[30] Hume's theory of moral judgment is clearly not an egoist theory, although it contains the possibility of an egoistic judgment (the approbation of something conducive to one's own happiness): the case of a first-person judgment in favor of a quality useful or agreeable to its possessor, as when a person reflectively approves of and determines to cultivate thrift, or a favorable judgment of a benevolent act by the beneficiary.

beings, which by a natural impulse we contemplate with pleasure and regard as the inclusive ultimate good of life.

Hume's moral philosophy may be further clarified by raising the question of whether or in what sense he should be regarded as a utilitarian. Utilitarianism is usually presented as an ethical doctrine, one that defines the nature of the good and the right and prescribes what ought to be done. Hume by contrast is ostensibly engaged in the descriptive study of morals, attempting to discover what standards and method of justification underlie the moral judgments that people commonly make. Now the classical utilitarians usually added that there is no or little discrepancy between their normative doctrine and ordinary moral beliefs, or at least that there would be no discrepancy if the latter were suitably clarified and freed from remnants of superstition. Hume's approach is somewhat different: he seeks the underlying principles and unity in ordinary moral beliefs; he finds that what he calls the "principle of utility" constitutes the usual or normal standard of judgment; and he moves gradually from descriptive elucidation to approval or acceptance of utility as the appropriate standard, without ever affirming unequivocally a prescriptive ethical formula.

This approach to ethics is illustrative of Hume's skeptical approach in all his philosophical endeavors, displaying the typical manner in which he bypasses for practical purposes a thoroughgoing skepticism. Since reason gives no distinctions, judgments of value involve subjective feelings whose inescapably private nature might logically lead to a conclusion of ethical relativism—and of course for the skeptic there always remains a sense in which anyone's values, as assertions about his personal feelings and choices, are not susceptible of examination or refutation.[31] The subjective response, however, is not the whole of morality: moral feelings are occasioned by and result in express judgments about various objective states of affairs, which are subject to empirical investigation. Hume finds as a matter of fact not only that there is a certain uniformity of moral belief but further that the usual standard of moral value bears a direct relation to the requirements of human life and preservation. It may even be the case that fundamental moral beliefs (about which speculative thinkers raise questions) are in practice as consistent as the no more logically necessary belief in causa-

---

[31] Hume concedes that there is no "remedy in philosophy" for someone who simply lacks the normal moral feelings—someone like Rameau's Nephew (in Diderot's story), who claims to have been born without a moral sense, just as some people are tone deaf. See Hume, "The Sceptic," *Works*, vol. 3, p. 222. See also *Enquiries* (I), p. 20, where Hume considers the possibility that some people may be incapable of experiencing normal feelings. Such cases, he assumes, are rare.

tion (which no one ever really doubts); it may be that a "general opinion of mankind" on basic ethical issues may be identified (T. 552). Hume's acceptance of the standards that he finds to be the normal ones is analogous to his decision, as a skeptic, to proceed with his scientific inquiries on the basis of universal causation and induction. In both cases a practical decision supplements a theoretical position, since the enterprise of doubting can be continuous only in the study. In neither case is skepticism repudiated but only supplemented, with an eye toward questions of choice and living, by naturalism. In this perspective Hume's ethics are naturalistic: in certain of the actual inclinations of human nature he finds the proper standards of morality, which are in turn justified by their reference to the common needs and desires of human beings. The question then becomes to what degree does his naturalism lead Hume to a substantive utilitarian position?

Utilitarianism holds that actions are judged to be right, institutions just, and characters virtuous, insofar as they have the effect of contributing to the production of a "good," usually identified as the general welfare, conceived in terms of happiness or pleasure—two terms that Hume, like most of the classic utilitarians, does not try to distinguish. From what has been said it is clear that Hume regards some such pattern as characteristic of most ordinary moral judgments, and that he accepts these meanings of the "right" and the "good"; he argues explicitly that the "circumstance of *utility*" underlies, in whole or in part, all the most common moral evaluations.[32] Most virtues are qualities that are valued for their beneficial effects, which may generally be described as increases in the "happiness of mankind"; the two principal categories of virtues (benevolence and justice), in particular, fall clearly within the general utilitarian account.[33]

---

[32] Hume, *Enquiries* (II), p. 231. Bentham gives Hume the credit for opening his eyes to utility; *A Fragment on Government*, with *An Introduction to the Principles of Morals and Legislation*, ed. Wilfrid Harrison (Oxford: Basil Blackwell, 1967), p. 50n. Hume was evidently the first to use the phrase "principle of utility"; see Elie Halevy, *The Growth of Philosophic Radicalism*, trans. Mary Morris (Boston: Beacon Press, 1966), p. 11. For an interpretation of Hume as a utilitarian, see John Plamenatz, *The English Utilitarians* (Oxford: Basil Blackwell, 1958). For some reservations, see J. L. Mackie, *Hume's Moral Theory* (London: Routledge and Kegan Paul, 1980), pp. 151-54.

[33] It is doubtful whether the concept of utility applies to qualities useful (only) to their possessor. A utilitarian could perhaps develop a justification for the cultivation of such virtues in terms of their indirect effect in benefiting society, and Hume probably believed there is some such effect, at least in the case of the economic virtues such as thrift, prudence, and industry. In the *Enquiries* (II), however, Hume does not make this argument but rather appeals to the classical notion of the independent value of excellences of character and a well-balanced personality for their own sake.

There are a few important qualifications, however, that must be made in applying the label utilitarianism (a term he does not use) to Hume. In its classic form utilitarianism prescribes not simply actions that have beneficial consequences but more precisely those actions that in the given circumstances will result in the greatest general happiness, aggregating the pleasures and pains of all affected individuals. This maximization element is necessary to utilitarianism if it is to be an unambiguous prescriptive doctrine; without this specification a moral agent would have no criterion for choosing among any number of available courses of action, all of them likely to be beneficial. Hume by contrast never advocates utilitarianism as a precise practical formula, nor does he argue that conduciveness to the *greatest* general happiness constitutes part, even implicitly, of the actual standard of ordinary moral judgments; the maximization formula does not appear in his moral theory, even though it had already been suggested by Hutcheson.[34] Hume's endorsement of the principle of utility provides him with a general method of ethical justification, but it does not give him the precise means of solving specific dilemmas that arise in moral and political life, such as the central conflict between justice and benevolence, where long-range considerations of social utility as advanced through observance of rules may clash with our impulse to relieve hardship in an immediate case: Hume's solution to this problem, as we shall see, rests on other considerations. The absence of a maximization imperative also means that Hume is not confronted directly by many of the difficulties that arise within classic utilitarianism: Hume does not address, for example, the problem of whether happiness is to be maximized collectively or distributively; the problem of the scope of utilitarian obligation, both temporally and in terms of the range of ostensible beneficiaries; and the problems relating to the comparability and quantification of types and degrees of happiness necessary for the fulfillment of the injunction to promote the greatest possible good.

This last problem occupied much of Bentham's attention, and his conviction that it could be solved—and that practical morals could thus be rendered an exact science—was a condition of the reformist zeal that was the political expression of utilitarianism in his hands. We are accustomed to think of utilitarianism as an ethics of calculation, enjoining moral agents to engage in careful causal reasoning concerning probable outcomes of actions in order to discover the right practical course. Such reasoning certainly enters into ethical justification in

---

[34] Hutcheson, *Ideas of Beauty and Virtue* II.iii.8, *Collected Works*, vol. 1, p. 164.

Hume's ethical theory, but his recognition of the difficulties of establishing causality and predicting consequences in the "moral" sciences seems at variance with the assurance that Bentham exhibits and that is perhaps necessary for the practical business of reform. In any case, his doctrine does not so rigorously prescribe the achievement of the greatest possible happiness in all cases, thereby removing the need for precise calculations. Hume's position, in contrast to Bentham's, lends itself less to unceasing criticism and reform: its demands are more modest; its prescriptivist aspect is subordinate to its attempt to grasp the logic of ordinary moral judgments, which provide the naturalistic context for its standard; and it is allied with a skepticism that generally rules out claims of knowledge of the sort that would be required for definitive solutions to many moral or political disagreements. This does not mean that Hume's principle of utility has no critical bearing; it typically serves, however, more as a tool for the clarification of existing values and institutions, and the discovery of whatever usefulness they may have, than for subjecting them to the harsh test of optimality. I shall return in the final chapter to the nature of the political conservatism that is related to this as well as to other aspects of Hume's philosophy.

Another qualification of Hume's utilitarianism pertains to his doctrine that motives, in the case of voluntary actions, and "mental qualities" are the appropriate objects of moral approbation, apart from their actual consequences. Later utilitarians, concentrating on the goal of increasing social happiness, logically ascribed value only to actions that actually had this effect and to motives and habitual dispositions only insofar as they produced such actions. A strict ethic of consequences such as this is likewise well adapted to the practical needs of political reform: a determination to attend only to observable outcomes simplifies the task of judgment and keeps the moralist's attention fixed on institutions and external relations that are susceptible of manipulation. Hume adheres more closely to the ordinary moral sense in acknowledging "good intentions" and "benevolent affections" as virtuous in themselves: analysis reveals that all virtues have a "tendency" to produce happiness, but consideration of actual or probable consequences does not always enter into the mental process of judgment.[35] Inefficacious virtue, or "virtue in rags" (T. 584), remains virtue nonetheless.[36] Here as elsewhere Hume is prepared to accept the nat-

[35] Hume, *Enquiries* (II), p. 228n.

[36] Cf. D.G.C. MacNabb, *David Hume: His Theory of Knowledge and Morality* (Hamden, Conn.: Archon Books, 1966), pp. 173-74.

ural propensities of the mind as appropriate, and to this extent he adheres to naturalistic standards that are looser than those of later utilitarianism and therefore less likely to issue in negative criticisms and programmatic prescriptions.

The final qualification concerns the relation of Hume's utilitarianism to his contention that the "moral sense" (or moral sentiment) is the origin of moral distinctions and judgments. Hume stands at the juncture of these two currents in British ethical thought, which have often been interpreted as contrary positions. Bentham, in defending utility as the sole standard of morality, explicitly rejects theories of "moral sense,"[37] and modern analytic philosophy contrasts the utilitarian concept of the "rightness" of actions, defined in terms of consequent happiness, with the "subjectivist" concept, defined in terms of feelings of approval.[38] In Hume's moral philosophy, however, there is no such dichotomy: the moral sense as the inner, affective approbatory faculty constitutive of value is combined with the principle of utility as descriptive of things generally approved; the two elements are portrayed for the most part as complementary and coincident. This distinction corresponds to two of the planes on which Hume's analysis of morality proceeds: the moral sense pertains to the psychological origins or the motivation of moral beliefs and judgments, utility to the standard that underlies such beliefs. A complete view of morality, as in the parallel case of causation, requires both perspectives: a virtue, like a causal relation, consists of certain specifiable external phenomena together with a distinctive subjective state, or determination of the mind to conceive of these phenomena in a special way, on the part of an observer. Hume the skeptic and psychologist is interested in the way in which all cognitive and evaluative judgments involve certain feelings or propensities in the imagination; as a scientist he investigates the associated objective criteria—cause as regularly observed sequence, value as (usually) associated with utility. The distinction is between points of view, each appropriate in its way, the two together yielding a full account.

Such a reduction of two major ethical traditions to a methodological distinction, however, is not entirely satisfactory. There remains the question of the ultimate source of moral value: which principle—feeling or utility—is prior? Hume does not pose this question so bluntly, but it arises in his theory insofar as the principle of utility is not entirely congruent with the judgments of the moral sentiments. When Hume's

---

[37] Bentham, *Principles of Morals and Legislation*, p. 140n.
[38] A. J. Ayer, *Language, Truth, and Logic* (Harmondsworth: Penguin, 1971), p. 138.

theory is scrutinized in this light, the moral sense emerges as the more fundamental category, and it appears that his utilitarianism is derived from and depends on an affective basis, even though he holds, with respect to one important kind of conflict, that the utilitarian artificial virtues must take priority over immediate feelings.

This conclusion is evident in the structure of Hume's analysis: the peculiar feeling of approbation is the determinative or defining feature of a moral distinction; subsequently, Hume ascertains that most such distinctions are oriented to utility. The moral sense is not portrayed as a faculty that generally responds, and ought only to respond, to actions that are right because they accord with utility; Hume does not urge that approbation be apportioned in accordance with utility, as he does that belief be proportioned to the evidence. Rather, utility is found to be a frequent characteristic of qualities and actions adjudged right by the moral sense. Utility moreover is said not to be the *sole* foundation for an important class of genuine virtues—the natural virtues such as benevolence, which may conflict with virtues such as justice that *are* entirely founded on utility, a point suggesting that utility is the subordinate principle. It is true that in his theory of artificial virtue (his main addition to the previous moral sense tradition) Hume argues that, for the sake of social preservation and order, artificial rules such as the laws of justice must override contrary natural virtues or impulses that conflict with them. This can happen, however, as we shall see, only when a special feeling—a sense of duty—is developed with respect to the artificial virtues, that is, when the moral sense itself is trained or habituated so as to approve what social order requires. In the final analysis justice is a *virtue* because we *approve* it, although our feeling of approbation may well follow reflection on its utility.

Hume regards the moral sense and utility as largely complementary bases for ethics; his theory is one of reconciliation, in contrast to those of other proponents of the moral sense, who opposed utilitarianism.[39] The compatibility of the two in Hume's system is neither fortuitous nor mysterious, nor is it a ground for faith in a harmonious design of the universe. Hume's naturalism accounts for whatever harmony is manifest in the correspondence between the human mental and emotional constitution and the needs of society. In the final analysis, however, it is the moral sense that is decisive in establishing moral value, and insofar as people deliberately accept a utilitarian standard as an

[39] Stephen, *English Thought*, vol. 2, chap. 9, esp. part 4. Hutcheson also attempted to unite the two traditions, by way of providential design; see Stephen, pp. 50-51.

explicit guide to action, this choice itself must be ascribed to their fundamental moral sentiment. This conclusion emerges from Hume's answer to the query "why utility pleases," which is central to his moral *Enquiry*: why do we tend to approve, on reflection, of the general happiness, the ethical end proposed by utilitarianism? The answer must be that there is, in human nature, a "principle of humanity" that renders the happiness of others something "desirable on its own account," a general value that provides the ground for all the particular determinations of the moral sense. This "ultimate end" presupposed by utilitarianism is itself a contribution of the moral sense. Although the standard of utility, when clarified and applied through detailed reasoning, may serve to modify our moral feelings and judgments in particular cases, its work lies primarily in the sphere of clarification; utilitarianism is itself founded on an "intuition" or an instinct of the moral sense.[40]

Although Hume is accordingly a proponent of utility as an ethical—and political—standard of judgment, one must eschew the later connotations of "utilitarianism" in considering his views. Naturalism is the more fundamental category, and it is through naturalism that Hume is led to adopt utility as an appropriate practical principle. Hume's skepticism extends to the denial of purely rational justification or necessity in moral values. The further observations, however, that regularities exist among values actually held, and that moral beliefs bear a fairly clear relation to human needs and capabilities, prevent him from falling into the pure subjectivism and relativism that would have the effect of undermining morality altogether. Moderate skeptics, having provisionally adopted empiricist criteria as a basis for reasoning, can acknowledge such facts and relations in the moral world, and for the practical purposes of life they can provisionally acquiesce in the normal patterns of human nature as the guide likely to be most fitting and trustworthy. Hume thus finds his values in human nature and in history, refraining from counterposing any doctrinaire formulas to the general lines of actual moral experience. The philosopher in such a position remains aware of the epistemological status of the values to which he adheres and of course does not regard them as immune from criticism; the decision to remain close to experience in morals as in the investigation of causes, stemming as it does from skeptical diffidence, is a deliberate and ultimately tentative one. It is

[40] "Why Utility Pleases" is sec. 5 of Hume's *Enquiries* (II). For things "desirable on [their] own account" and "ultimate ends," see *Enquiries* (II), p. 293. Sidgwick similarly founded utilitarianism on "intuitionism"; *Methods of Ethics*, preface to the 6th ed., pp. xv-xxi, 423-24.

not difficult to see that such a course, although likely to be fruitful of insights into the practice of morals and politics, would be conducive neither to radical criticisms nor to visionary alternatives to experience.

3. NATURAL AND ARTIFICIAL VIRTUE

A central distinction in Hume's ethical theory is that between what he calls the natural and the artificial virtues. An examination of what is involved in this distinction not only illuminates several interesting issues of psychology and ethics; it also places us squarely in the realm of political philosophy, since the concept of artifice, especially as it is elaborated with reference to justice and allegiance, is central to Hume's understanding of the political.

Book III of the *Treatise* is organized around the classification of virtuous qualities labeled "artificial" and "natural," whereas in the *Enquiry* and other later writings Hume omits these particular terms; the basic concepts involved and the dual distinction remain, however, throughout his philosophy. In the fourfold classificatory scheme of the virtues in the second *Enquiry* the two qualities analyzed as "useful to others," benevolence and justice, exemplify respectively what in the *Treatise* are called natural and artificial virtues. The *Enquiry*'s "qualities agreeable to others" consist largely of what in the *Treatise* is presented as the artificial virtue of "good manners," whereas all those qualities either useful or agreeable to their possessor appear in Part 3 of Book III of the *Treatise* as natural virtues or praiseworthy natural abilities. Despite these differences of terminology and organization, there are no substantial changes in Hume's analysis of the various virtues in the two works. The earlier distinction, furthermore, is drawn quite clearly in the third Appendix to the *Enquiry*, where benevolence is distinguished from justice in terms of the difference between instinct and convention; Hume here summarizes most of the important points at issue between artificial and natural virtue that he develops at length in the *Treatise*. That Hume adheres to his original dichotomous view of the virtues, finally, is confirmed by a passage in his best-known political essay, where again he draws the same distinction while omitting the original labels.[41]

The artificial-natural distinction thus runs throughout Hume's moral philosophy; why then should he have abandoned this terminology in his later works? Part of the answer is that in the *Enquiry* Hume is concerned to emphasize the unity of all morality rather than distinc-

---

[41] Hume, "Of the Original Contract," *Works*, vol. 3, pp. 454-55.

tions and indeed conflicts among different kinds of virtues. All the virtues are shown to be grounded ultimately in a generalized "humanity" or "fellow-feeling," and discussion of potential tension between justice and benevolence is relegated to an Appendix. The more general answer, however, seems to be that in his more popular works Hume wishes to avoid the distractions and misunderstandings that might have been provoked by the use of technical terminology such as this. The term "artificial" as applied to justice, in particular, is one Hume realized would be troublesome, carrying the possible though unintended connotations of "unnatural," not founded in human nature, or conventional in the sense of *merely* conventional. Hume warns in the *Treatise*:

> To avoid giving offence, I must here observe, that when I deny justice to be a natural virtue, I make use of the word, *natural*, only as oppos'd to *artificial*. In another sense of the word; as no principle of the human mind is more natural than a sense of virtue; so no virtue is more natural than justice. Mankind is an inventive species; and where an invention is obvious and absolutely necessary, it may as properly be said to be natural as any thing that proceeds immediately from original principles, without the intervention of thought or reflexion. (T. 484)[42]

Elsewhere, defending his theory, Hume denies that he ever held justice to be *un*natural.[43] The meanings of "natural" and "artificial" in Hume's account of morality are the topic of this section, for which I shall draw primarily on the account found in the *Treatise*, which in this respect is the more interesting work; the distinction, however, is one that marks the whole of Hume's moral and political philosophy.

All the artificial virtues, and all the natural virtues that will concern us, are "social virtues," which manifest themselves in courses of action in some way beneficial to people other than (or in addition to) the agent. The difference between the two classes may best be approached by beginning with some observations on those virtues that Hume calls natural. In the *Treatise* Hume offers the following list: meekness, beneficence, charity, generosity, clemency, moderation, and equity (T.

---

[42] Cf. Hume, *Enquiries* (II), p. 307. See also *Treatise*, pp. 473-75, on the meanings of "nature" and "natural."

[43] Hume, *A Letter from a Gentleman to his Friend in Edinburgh*, ed. Ernest C. Mossner and John V. Price (Edinburgh: Edinburgh University Press, 1967), p. 31. Hume says that sucking is natural, speech artificial; justice is thus comparable to speech. Cf. also Hume, letter of 17 September 1739, to Francis Hutcheson, in *The Letters of David Hume*, ed. J.Y.T. Greig (Oxford: Clarendon Press, 1932), vol. 1, p. 33.

578); in the *Enquiry*, "benevolence" becomes a general heading for natural virtue, under which Hume includes such qualities as humanity, friendship, generosity, gratitude, and "natural affection";[44] love of children, gratitude, and pity are given as examples in the essay referred to above.[45] All these qualities meet with moral approbation; actions in accordance with them are regarded as "right" actions by the ordinary moral sense. Hume's investigation concerns both the apparent end or "tendency" of these virtues and their psychological source in human nature.

The sociable virtues subsumed under the category "benevolence" may in the first place be observed to have felicific consequences, in keeping with Hume's general observation in the *Enquiry* that utility enters into all moral determinations. "The happiness of mankind, the order of society, the harmony of families, the mutual support of friends, are always considered as the result of their gentle dominion over the breasts of men." A qualification is immediately suggested, however, by Hume's transition in this passage from "mankind" to "society" and thence to "family" and "friends" as the beneficiaries of these virtues. Benevolence and related virtues are directed toward securing the happiness more of close acquaintances and particular individuals— family and friends, or the needy and deserving in our immediate vicinity—than of society generally. Benevolence seeks to produce happiness or relieve distress in particular cases, and it is approved as such; it may or may not be consistent with the interests of society as a whole, and calculations regarding this larger end play no part in it. It is evidently for this reason that Hume says that utility, referring to the happiness of society, forms only a *part* of the merit of the natural virtues.[46] Although these virtues tend to have good consequences, it appears that "our approbation has, in those cases, an origin different from the prospect of utility and advantage, either to ourselves or others" (T. 604). This origin is to be found in certain immediate features of human nature.

Several of the most important of the natural virtues have appeared before in Hume's psychology as "direct passions," impressions or feelings that normally arise in us in the presence of certain objects or

---

[44] Hume, *Enquiries* (II), pp. 176-78. Also included is "public spirit," which, to be a natural virtue, however, would have to be clearly differentiated from justice and allegiance. Hume may have in mind supererogatory acts of public beneficence or philanthropy; his theory of government does not invoke "public spirit," civic virtue, or the like. Another list of natural virtues appears in the *Treatise*, p. 603.

[45] See note 41 above.

[46] Hume, *Enquiries* (II), pp. 181-82, 179, and Sec. 2, part 2 generally.

ideas: particular benevolence, love of children, compassion, and attachment to family are examples. In this perspective the natural virtues
appear to be nothing other than certain natural impulses or instincts
implanted in human nature, attended as a rule by moral approval.
Their motivation, and our favorable judgment of them, are therefore
spontaneous: "Tho' there was no obligation to relieve the miserable,
our humanity wou'd lead us to it; and when we omit that duty, the
immorality of the omission arises from its being a proof, that we want
the natural sentiments of humanity. A father knows it to be his duty
to take care of his children: But he has also a natural inclination to
it" (T. 518-19). The fact that moral duty and inclination coincide
evidently gives these virtues a special tenacity; although good consequences may be invoked in reflectively justifying benevolence, our
approval of it in practice is ordinarily an immediate response of the
moral sense, not dependent on its fulfillment of a general utilitarian
criterion and often persisting even in the demonstrable failure of an
instance of benevolence to meet this criterion.

This analysis reveals a dimension of Hume's moral theory that is
thoroughly naturalistic. The natural virtues and the ethical imperatives
associated with them, far from being opposed to desire and passion,
receive direct and constant support from the normal characteristics of
human nature. Hume's effort to delineate an objective standard of
judgment in this area is not entirely successful: "utility" is applicable
to them only in a vague way, and in any case it appears that the
feelings of moral duty and approbation that one experiences here are
independent of considerations of utility in any sense more extensive
than the immediate welfare of the person toward whom the benevolent
motive is directed. The ethical quality seems inextricable from the
motive: a natural propensity seems to yield a value directly, for which
the philosopher's criterion of utility provides only a partial explanation.[47] Hume never doubts that these qualities are genuine virtues but

---

[47] The question arises whether *all* natural, instinctual motives are (or ought to be)
morally approved. Anger and revenge to enemies, for example, which appear in Hume's
lists of instinctual passions along with benevolence and attachment to family, are moral
virtues in some societies. Perhaps these are related to courage, a natural quality or
virtue that Hume suggests has been replaced, or at least receives a different (lesser)
valuation, in consequence of the elaboration of systems of justice and other artificial
virtues in modern societies. (Hume does not consider natural feelings related to anger,
such as resentment and indignation, as possibly underlying the sense of justice.) See
Hume, *Enquiries* (II), p. 255, on the "ethics of Homer," and cf. "Of the Authenticity
of the Poems of Ossian," *Works*, vol. 4, pp. 417-18. The natural virtues that Hume
emphasizes, however, are presented as not contingent on changing social systems. Hume
does briefly point out that anger and hatred, in moderate degree, are still spontaneously

rather acquiesces in the judgments of the ordinary moral sense in this respect. The greater part of his analysis focuses on the more complicated topic of the artificial virtues, where standards of judgment are more independent of natural motives, and where the work of moral philosophy accordingly has larger scope. Benevolence, gratitude, and compassion, although undeniably virtues, represent only one side of moral life; the important problems arise only when they are juxtaposed to the realm of artifice.

Hume's political philosophy in a sense begins with the postulation of the concept of artificial virtue, under which heading he places justice and other moral qualities associated with the realm of the public and the political.[48] Besides the spontaneous moral impulses, he says, "there are some virtues, that produce pleasure and approbation by means of an artifice or contrivance, which arises from the circumstances and necessity of mankind" (T. 477). The precise nature of such artifices or contrivances constitutes the central issue of political philosophy. Hume investigates them on several different levels: the ends they achieve and the standards by which they are justified, the motivational basis in human psychology and experience that makes their realization possible, and a largely conjectural account of their "origins" and historical development. I follow Hume's analysis of these problems with regard to the artificial virtues in general, although it is the paradigmatic case of justice to which I resort for illustrations; later I consider more closely the two most important of these virtues, justice and allegiance, examining their specific content and the nature of the political institutions through which they are realized.

There are, according to Hume, five categories of artificial virtues, all of them "mere human contrivances for the interest of society" (T. 577): justice, allegiance, the laws of nations, chastity and modesty, and good manners. What these categories have in common is that each prescribes a practice or contains a number of rules of conduct ordinarily regarded as obligatory on people in relevant situations. Actions in accordance with these rules meet with moral approbation

---

approved, and that the absence of them in a character is generally regarded as "imbecillity" (T. 605).

[48] The doctrine of artificial virtue is an original element in Hume's moral theory, representing his principal divergence from Hutcheson's moral sense theory. D. D. Raphael detects affinities to Hobbes; see his "Hume's Critique of Ethical Rationalism," in *Hume and the Enlightenment*, ed. William B. Todd (Edinburgh: Edinburgh University Press, 1974), p. 16. Some commentators on Hume have sought to minimize the distinction between the two kinds of virtue; for a rebuttal of this view and an analysis of artificial virtue, see Charles E. Cottle, "Justice as Artificial Virtue in Hume's *Treatise*," *Journal of the History of Ideas* 40 (1979): 457-66.

and are called "right" actions, and the disposition to obey the rules constitutes virtue as an attribute of character in individuals, who are accordingly adjudged to be just, loyal, chaste, or polite. Of the five categories, the first three are clearly political (and consist to a large extent of legal rules), whereas the other two are not—or at least are less obviously so.

Justice is the artificial virtue on which Hume concentrates most in both the *Treatise* and the second *Enquiry*. Under this rubric he discusses principally the rules regarding the distribution of goods or property in society, rules that provide substance for the general imperatives to give each his due and to abstain from what belongs to another; he also includes the rule of fidelity, or promise-keeping, and in one place he adds the duties of integrity and veracity, or truthtelling.[49] Hume's justice thus includes, in its acknowledgment of property rights and the obligation of promises, much of what was traditionally held to constitute the laws of nature, and he occasionally so characterizes his rules of justice.[50] In promise-keeping and truth-telling, moreover, Hume deals with duties that in the history of ethics have frequently been advanced as examples of deontological or rational moral obligations and that, along with the issue of rights, have been held to pose difficulties for utilitarian theories.[51] These philosophical traditions offer perspectives from which one may examine Hume's argument that these duties arise from "contrivance" or "artifice," an argument that refers them to the political realm of human "invention" in the area of common needs and public life.[52]

[49] Hume, *Enquiries* (II), p. 204.

[50] *Treatise*, pp. 484, 526, 533, 543, and 567. See Duncan Forbes, *Hume's Philosophical Politics* (Cambridge: Cambridge University Press, 1975), chap. 1, for an acceptance of Hume's claim to belong to the (empirical) tradition of modern natural law.

[51] D. D. Raphael, "Hume and Adam Smith on Justice and Utility," *Proceedings of the Aristotelian Society* N.S. 73 (1972-1973): 87-103.

[52] Jonathan Harrison, in his detailed commentary on *Treatise* III.ii, suggests that Hume's account of justice misses an important part of what is ordinarily meant by this concept: since the virtue of justice is assumed to consist in obedience to a scheme of rules, one cannot raise questions about the justice (or equity, or fairness) *of* the rules or, in the case of rules of property, about distributive justice. (Harrison also notes that Hume omits discussion of retributive justice and proper procedures associated with the punishment of offenders.) One can, of course, raise questions about the *utility* (the consequences for the happiness of society) of different possible rules of justice and their actual or expected outcomes. See *Hume's Theory of Justice* (Oxford: Clarendon Press, 1981), pp. 28, 39, 43. Harrison holds that Hume's "theory of justice" in reality addresses the (important but distinct) social virtue of abiding by rules. This view accords with the interpretation presented here, except that Harrison unaccountably uses "justice" to cover all Hume's artificial virtues; pp. 42-43, 55, and passim.

Under allegiance Hume discusses the more narrowly civic virtues: the duty to obey the laws, to support the legitimate authority of government, and, by extension, to fulfill the positive obligations of citizenship, such as they may be in different regimes. Hume neglects this last aspect of the virtue of allegiance, since the governments he usually envisions and discusses are not founded on an ideal of civic participation; but any such duties (e.g. to vote) would be artificial in Hume's sense and would fall under this rubric. Under the heading of allegiance Hume examines the ends of government, the historical origins and development of governments and the various forms they may take, and the criteria of the legitimacy of particular governments, on which the duties of allegiance in actual cases depend. These matters are treated in sections on allegiance and "political society" that follow the sections on justice in the *Treatise* and *Enquiry* as well as in several important essays, where Hume attempts to present to a wider audience doctrines that for the most part are set forth in the *Treatise*.[53] In other essays and in his *History of England* Hume attends to the institutional forms that government has taken in England and elsewhere, along with consideration of their particular merits and demerits and the nature of their historical development.[54]

The other three categories of artificial virtue are of less concern in this study. As laws of nations Hume denotes the rules that are applicable, and the moral obligations and virtues that arise, in time of war and generally in international relations, a topic on which he touches only briefly.[55] Under modesty and chastity Hume refers to all the moral rules regarding the relations of the sexes, including the approved patterns of marital and familial relationships. This is a topic to which Hume adverts frequently in scattered passages, exploring such topics as the prohibition of incest, the status of homosexuality in ancient Greece, the rule of monogamy, and the double standard of conduct for the two sexes, as well as more frivolous aspects of sexual conventions in modern polite society.[56] It is important to have moral rules

[53] The most important new dimension in the essays is Hume's concern with theories of legitimacy as matters of party ideology and controversy.

[54] See Forbes, *Hume's Philosophical Politics*, esp. Part 2, for Hume's views on the British constitution in relation to the particular constitutional controversies of the period.

[55] Hume, *Treatise* III.ii.11; cf. also *Enquiries* (II), p. 187. For rather substantial discussions, see Mackie, *Hume's Moral Theory*, pp. 113-18; and Harrison, *Hume's Theory of Justice*, pp. 229-41.

[56] Hume, *Treatise* III.ii.12; "A Dialogue," in *Enquiries*, pp. 324-43; and the essay "Of Polygamy and Divorces." On incest see Hume, letter of 10 January 1743, to Francis Hutcheson, *Letters*, vol. 1, p. 48. By chastity Hume usually denotes rules respecting

of this sort in mind as we examine what Hume means by "artificial virtue," of which these (even the most fundamental rule against incest) are alleged to be examples. The same holds true for the final category, good manners, by which Hume denotes all the rules of etiquette and civility that facilitate social intercourse and "conversation." These virtues, which are largely equivalent to the "qualities immediately agreeable to others" of the *Enquiry*, however obligatory they may be, are not always regarded as "moral" requirements in quite the same way as, for example, the rule of fidelity, although Hume's system challenges the moral philosopher to specify the nature of the difference (beyond the degree of blame in the case of infringement) between them.

The rules of chastity and good manners are beyond the scope of this study, primarily because they are not political virtues in as clear a sense as justice and allegiance are. It should be noted, however, that Hume, regarding them as artifices (like justice) erected to meet social requirements, is interested in the manner in which they have varied, historically and under different political regimes, according to a society's (or a ruling group's) opinion of its ends and needs. Both manners and sexual mores differ significantly, he points out, in a courtly monarchy like France and a commercial republic like Holland, or in either of these and a small military republic of ancient times. These observations provide an illustration of the manner in which moral judgments may differ in different times and places in the case of the artificial virtues, although the fact that (in Hume's view) all societies acknowledge some rules falling under each of these five headings implies underlying moral uniformity beneath apparent diversity. The prominent place that Hume gives to good manners, and the importance he (like others of his age) attaches to them, despite their obvious artificiality, emphasizes the absence of any pejorative connotation in his use of this concept: artifices are of the essence of orderly social life, whose general value Hume never doubts—a fact that clearly reveals the limits of his skepticism with respect to moral life.[57]

---

sexual relations, whereas modesty refers to associated conventions respecting demeanor (especially for women), which Hume assumes provide a necessary support for chastity, given the natural force of contrary inclinations. See Annette Baier, "Good Men's Women: Hume on Chastity and Trust," *Hume Studies* 5 (1979): 1-19; in addition to analyzing Hume's theory of chastity, Baier raises the important question whether a moral artifice, although it must be *useful* or beneficial to all concerned, need be *equally* useful to all—to which Hume's answer is evidently negative. This seems especially clear in the case of property, given the particular rules Hume defends.

[57] Hume defends in particular the "refined" manners of modern civilization, associated as they are with "luxury," over the "rude" manners of simpler societies, ancient or

What then are the common characteristics of the "artificial" virtues, and how do they differ from the natural virtues? The first and main point is that these virtues depend on the existence of publicly acknowledged systems of rules: virtue as an attribute of personal character is in these cases a disposition or determination to govern one's conduct according to ethical rules (or in some cases, laws), and right actions are actions that conform to the rules. The fact that these virtues are necessarily realized through rules is closely related to their quality of being public institutions or practices:[58] they are conceivable only as being mutually understood and accepted by a number of people, and they achieve their ends only insofar as their observance is uniform throughout a society, or at least among a large proportion of its members. The virtue and the value of benevolence are manifested in every act—even isolated acts—motivated by natural and spontaneous feelings of benevolence. The virtue of justice, however, does not correspond to any specific feeling; it is manifested rather through acting according to certain rules, along with—in order to be fully worthy of approbation—a sense of obligation, or a conscious determination to obey the rules as the motive of the action. What it means to be just, or to make an obligatory promise, is in fact defined by a set of rules: the rules Hume has in mind are therefore examples of rules that may be said to be "constitutive" of the practices (property rights, promising, allegiance, chastity, politeness) in question.[59]

---

modern; see esp. "Of Money" and "Of Refinement in the Arts." Hume's preferences among modern manners and virtues, moreover, have led some to discern aristocratic rather than bourgeois affinities; see David Miller, *Social Justice* (Oxford: Clarendon Press, 1976), pp. 175-77; and for a fuller discussion, his *Philosophy and Ideology in Hume's Political Thought* (Oxford: Clarendon Press, 1981), chap. 6. A. J. Beitzinger, "Hume's Aristocratic Preference," *Review of Politics* 28 (1966): 154-71, connects Hume's alleged aristocratic affinity to his advocacy of the reasonings of the "wise" over the "vulgar."

[58] Hume's artificial virtues involve "practices" in the sense in which this term has been used influentially by John Rawls, "Two Concepts of Rules," *Philosophical Review* 64 (1955): 3-32.

[59] Ibid. Rawls derives the obligation of promises from this concept of rules: to engage in the practice is to undertake an obligation; to question the obligation is to display ignorance of the practice. Such an analysis would work for most of Hume's artificial virtues, although he justifies their obligatory quality by reference to the utility of the practices. Cf. also Henry David Aiken, "An Interpretation of Hume's Theory of the Place of Reason in Ethics and Politics," *Ethics* 90 (1979): pp. 66-80, on the relation of moral reasons and justifications to social practices and linguistic conventions. Note that dilemmas may arise from conflicts between two different rule-determined obligations (e.g. between the rule of truth-telling and the rules of politeness) as well as between a rule-determined virtue and a natural one. Hume, like Rawls, compares the case of games with that of the artificial virtues of justice and allegiance; *Enquiries* (II), pp. 210-11.

Hume emphasizes the necessity of general rules, whether they be deliberately framed or the products of unplanned evolution, for the regulation of conduct whenever people come together for collective activities or simply mingle "promiscuously": "They cannot even pass each other on the road without rules."[60] Part of the utility of the artificial virtues (especially the rules of good manners[61]) derives, like that of some traffic rules, simply from the coordination of conduct that is achieved through mutual observance of rules, irrespective of their content. But even the rules of the road, Hume says, are "chiefly founded on mutual ease and convenience," and he suggests that the specific contents of the rules constituting the artificial virtues are usually determined by their supposed usefulness in furthering our purposes. The evident beneficial effects of such rules, and the necessity of their general observance, explain the fact that strong feelings of approval and disapproval surround their observance or infringement.

Another feature of the artificial virtues is that the rules and obligations associated with them must be precise as well as general, a fact that has to do with the nature of the ends they are intended to achieve. Many of our spontaneous judgments of virtue and vice, Hume points out, being derived from our feelings, are a matter of degree, even though they must be enunciated in a general and impartial form. Our judgments regarding the matters covered by the artificial virtues, however, must be exact as well as impartial: " 'tis certain, that rights, and obligations, and property, admit of no such insensible gradation, but that a man either has a full and perfect property, or none at all; and is either entirely oblig'd to perform any action, or lies under no manner of obligation" (T. 529). The artificial virtues involve obligations that are often specifiable in a way that the obligation of compassion, for example, and other natural virtues, is not; some of them are even defined as matters of legal as well as moral obligation, where the necessity of clear and precise rules is obvious.

The clarity, precision, and general scope of the rules determinative of this kind of moral virtue, finally, suggest a degree of removal from the spontaneous impulses of human nature: the rules, and systems of rules, are the artifices whose presence renders the virtues of justice, allegiance, and so forth artificial virtues. Acting in accordance with rules is not natural in the way that acting benevolently is; it is not ordinarily motivated by immediate and spontaneous natural feelings—although it may become habitual, and thus draw on what Hume has

[60] Hume, *Enquiries* (II), p. 210.

[61] Ibid., p. 262. The forms by which a valid promise or marriage is concluded, which are stipulated by subsidiary rules, are arbitrary, like much in etiquette, though they must be precisely observed.

argued is an influential and (in a different sense) natural human attribute. Such rules must therefore be, or must have been, contrived, either deliberately and with forethought or gradually, in the course of history; they must have been either invented or simply discovered by chance or experience to be desirable and retained and enforced for this reason.[62] People lead much of their lives, and acknowledge one whose class of moral values that prescribe the conduct of life, according to rules, which at best are only indirectly supported by the "original qualities" of human nature. The realm of artifice is thus contingent and problematic in the context of Hume's theory of human nature.

The other main characteristic of the artificial virtues is that, unlike the natural ones, they are subject to justification entirely in terms of utility, or their conduciveness to the happiness and indeed the very existence of society. Their beneficial tendency, Hume says, is "the *sole* cause of our approbation" of them (T. 578), and in the *Enquiry* he argues that "the necessity of justice to the support of society" is the "sole foundation" of that—and by implication, of the other artificial virtues.[63]

It is again necessary to distinguish two different kinds of inquiry that Hume conducts in his moral theory, the elucidation of ethical standards and the psychological account of the motivation of an agent in making a moral judgment or acting morally. In his discussion of justice and the other artificial virtues, Hume frequently refers to the "interest of society" that they are evidently designed to promote. Often, especially in the *Treatise*, a close reading reveals that Hume is speaking of motives: he argues that people's view of "interest" and utility must have had something to do with the "origin" of the rules of justice, and that it figures in people's judgments in accordance with the rules. This question of motivation in the case of the artificial virtues is a complex one, and I take it up in the next section. Here, in saying that utility is the sole "foundation" of these virtues, I refer to the ethical point, made more clearly in the *Enquiry*, that whatever their motives or sources in human nature, the general good of society is the standard or end in terms of which the institutions or practices of justice, government, and so on are to be evaluated. In this sense utility may be said to be a "cause of approbation" of justice insofar as we reflect on

---

[62] On balance, Hume more often suggests that rules or laws evolve or arise gradually from cumulative social experience rather than being the decrees of a sovereign will or legislative authority; hence in his treatment of government he stresses executive and judicial but not legislative functions. His theory of artificial virtue, however, is formally indeterminate on this matter. Cf. Friedrich A. Hayek, *Law, Legislation, and Liberty*, vol. 1: *Rules and Order* (Chicago: University of Chicago Press, 1973), p. 74 and passim.

[63] Hume, *Enquiries* (II), pp. 203-204.

it and give a considered opinion, in abstraction from specific cases and personal interest. When Hume says that "reflections on the beneficial consequences of this virtue [justice] are the *sole* foundation of its merit,"[64] he must be understood to be making an ethical claim about justification and not a psychological point about motivation. This distinction pertains to the important fact that standards of justification are distinct from motives in the case of the artificial virtues, just as acting according to rules does not correspond to a spontaneous impulse of human nature. The rules or artifices under consideration here are contrived to achieve certain purposes, or to meet certain needs, and they are therefore subject to evaluation and criticism in a utilitarian fashion, in terms of their adequacy in attaining their ends.

The artificial virtues are accordingly never immune from criticism, as the natural virtues, being immediate expressions of natural feelings, are: the concept of artificiality connotes susceptibility of deliberate change, regardless of whether or not the rules that are in effect are the product of deliberate contrivance or of historical accident and evolution. The role of reasoning or ethical deliberation is accordingly of great importance in the case of these virtues. The realm of artifice is the realm of political choice, or of collective moral self-determination, potentially or actually; the existence of a moral standard against which moral rules and political institutions may be measured, furthermore, indicates a role for the philosopher, who may offer either justifications or criticisms of existing rules and clarify their relation to our ends. The extent to which Hume assumed this educative role with respect to the politics and morals of his time is beyond the focus of the present study, although I shall sketch his generally conservative approach to such a role in the next chapter. The point to be made here is the way in which the structure of Hume's moral theory makes criticism possible with respect to the artificial virtues, which, although they are related to real human needs, are not direct and unalterable expressions of human nature.

Although utility is the proper standard of judgment in the cases of justice and allegiance, Hume emphasizes that the beneficial consequences in question are the product of the maintenance of general systems of rules and not of specific acts falling under them.[65] This

---

[64] Ibid., p. 183.

[65] Hume does not specify his ethical doctrine in such a way that we can determine whether, in modern terms, he is an act- or a rule-utilitarian. He certainly emphasizes rules and argues that the benefits of the artificial virtues are derived only from common observance of entire systems of rules. But typical act-utilitarian defenses of moral rules, where much importance is attached to the development of firm habits of obedience,

point brings out most strikingly the discrepancy between artificial and natural virtue. Every act of benevolence or gratitude, taken in isolation, tends to produce its good effect immediately and is so approved, without consideration of long-range consequences or questions of the coordination of the actions of numerous people. Acts of justice, in contrast, cannot occur in isolation but are instances of a system of general and impartial rules; moreover, "a single act of justice, consider'd in itself, may often be contrary to the public good; and 'tis only the concurrence of mankind, in a general scheme or system of action, which is advantageous" (T. 579). Although every benevolent or compassionate act is virtuous and yields good, whether or not these virtues are generally observed, a virtue like justice depends on the "concurrence" of a large number of people in the same rules. Since an artificial virtue yields beneficial consequences only on this condition, it is not merely self-interest that dictates that one "embrace that virtue" "only upon the supposition, that others are to imitate [one's] example" (T. 498). To tell the truth, to make and keep a promise, or to abstain from another's property in circumstances where no one else is prepared to do so (or where others define these duties by different rules) would border on absurdity and would produce no general good. Since in Hume's view all these virtues are oriented toward the ends of mutual advantage and the preservation of society, they are efficacious and meaningful only as general schemes.

The other important point that emerges here is the tension within a system of artificial virtue between the value of the system as a whole and the utility of individual examples of it. This disparity may be seen in light of the potential conflict between a natural virtue like compassion and the rules of justice as applied to specific cases: "if we examine all the questions, that come before any tribunal of justice, we shall find, that, considering each case apart, it wou'd as often be an instance of humanity to decide contrary to the laws of justice as conformable to them" (T. 579). One's moral sense is often offended in particular cases by the demands of justice (or any other artificial virtue), which can be justified only by appealing to the consequences of upholding the system as a whole. It is, moreover, not only our "humanity" but also our cool view of utility that sometimes seems to militate against inflexible application of rules. The restoration of a

---

seems consistent with Hume's moral psychology and philosophy of human nature as a whole. Cf. Mackie, *Hume's Moral Theory*, pp. 91-92, who distinguishes the justification of a practice (as in Hume) from that of a rule, and Harrison, *Hume's Theory of Justice*, pp. 66-73, for "cumulative-effect utilitarianism."

fortune, required by law, from a meritorious person to a miser is, taken as a single act, "contrary to *public interest*" (T. 497). A more comprehensive view of utility, however, takes account of the cumulative effects of large numbers of acts dictated by uniform rules and the related social values of peace and order, the products of rules, over a long period of time. Hume argues that this larger view dictates that the system of stable rules be maintained intact:

> But however single acts of justice may be contrary, either to public or private interest, 'tis certain, that the whole plan or scheme is highly conducive, or indeed absolutely requisite, both to the support of society, and the well-being of every individual. 'Tis impossible to separate the good from the ill. Property must be stable, and must be fix'd by general rules. Tho' in one instance the public be a sufferer, this momentary ill is amply compensated by the steady prosecution of the rule, and by the peace and order, which it establishes in society. (T. 497)

More needs to be said concerning some of the problems raised by this reasoning, including Hume's claim that observance of the rules of the artificial virtues must be inflexible, and the nature of the social order that results. The argument as presented so far, however, defines the terms of a significant kind of moral tension that arises commonly in social life, and it indicates the direction of Hume's resolution.

The artificial virtues as Hume presents them are matters of public concern and, in various degrees, public enforcement. They constitute a system of social arrangements and public morality that are distinct from, and may not always be consistent with, the natural virtues, which are practiced more typically in more intimate contexts.[66] The distinction between them has to do with the distinction between the

---

[66] It may be questioned whether promise-keeping and truth-telling are exclusively public or social virtues; it might seem that with respect to these there could be justice between two isolated private individuals or between friends. Hume's account is more persuasive if we think of his "fidelity" and "veracity" as referring to public acts—to formal contracts and public testimony. In these cases promise-keeping and truth-telling are assimilable to the observance of property rights and to other artifices, and the argument for inflexible rules, based on the utility of order and predictability of social relations, is compelling. In this interpretation one avoids the question of whether secret "death-bed" promises and so forth are obligatory when utility is opposed. Insofar as the theory of artificial virtue pertains only to the public realm, Hume's insistence on uniform application of the rules might not hold for secret transactions, which are outside the public realm. The duty to fulfill secret promises would then be an ethical issue that Hume does not raise, although he does assert that a secretly incurred debt must be repaid (T. 480-81).

spheres of public and private life, and everyone, to the extent that one is involved in both spheres, is liable to be confronted with the type of dilemma described here, namely, that arising from the distinction between rules and acts. It is the public scope of the artificial virtues, where the concept "public" includes all members of a society indifferently and connotes their future as well as their present welfare, that necessitates the impartiality and the inflexibility of the rules through which they are realized. The public interest cannot be estimated from the consequences of any particular action, since the most important public values are achieved through the regular operation of a general system as such: these values include above all peace, including the absence of continual disputes about the merits of particular cases, and more generally social order, in the sense of the kind of rational or predictable conduct of affairs that permits individuals realistically to make plans and entertain expectations about the future.[67] Hume does not discuss in detail the nature of the good or goods at which the artificial virtues aim: in terms of the formal structure of his theory (as with any utilitarian theory) the good or end could vary and with it the specific content of the moral rules. Hume takes it for granted, however, that in any society a certain degree of peace and order, or regularity, is both necessary and desirable; and whatever the exact nature of the property arrangements, government, sexual mores, and so on prescribed by the artificial virtues, public order will always be one of the ends they achieve. The utility of the order and stability that arise from the steady application of rules (apart from their content) is therefore an important element in the justification of the artificial virtues and a reason why the preservation of the integrity of the system overrides considerations of utility in every particular case. The actual rules that constitute any particular system of justice will have their particular utilities as well, and they can be assessed in terms of their success in achieving a society's more particular goals.[68] But whatever the specific ends envisioned in the rules, all the artificial virtues con-

[67] Hume ranks "peace and security" as the first ingredient of public happiness; "Of Parties in General," *Works*, vol. 3, p. 127. He mentions disappointment of expectations—important in view of his emphasis on settled habits and rules—in *Enquiries* (II), p. 310. Miller emphasizes the security inherent in the stable possession of claim-rights, the conferral of which he takes to be the function of Hume's rules of justice; *Social Justice*, p. 71.

[68] Some of the specific rules in Hume's artificial virtues may be arbitrary; see note 61 above. He regards other rules as widespread because of their correspondence to certain propensities of the imagination (a feature that carries with it a special kind of convenience). For criticisms of Hume for not applying the standard of utility to specific rules as rigorously as he does to the general necessity of having rules, see John Plamenatz,

tribute to this general end of social order; and it is the priority of this end above the others that dictates that the rules must be observed rigorously rather than treated as guidelines to be overruled when the special circumstances of a case indicate that utility might better be advanced by making an exception.

The final characteristic of the artificial virtues, in contrast to the natural ones, is their contingency and variability, features that follow from the previous point that they are "contrivances" designed with a view to utility. All the artificial virtues are contingent on the existence of society and its fundamental requirements, and they vary in specific content with different societies' conceptions both of desirable ends and of the appropriate means for attaining these ends. Here it is helpful to distinguish between two levels of generality in Hume's analysis: between his treatment of the conditions, ends, and characteristics of systems of artificial virtue as such, and his closer but necessarily less complete discussion of the actual contents of the rules that make up particular cases of such systems.

At the level of particular content one finds a great deal of apparent variation and change: a summary view of different countries and of history brings to light an extensive array of diverse systems of property, forms of government, and manners and mores. This diversity has, since the beginnings of political speculation, led philosophers of a skeptical orientation to regard such institutions as "conventional" rather than "natural," and Hume's argument concerning their "arti-ficial" character represents a continuation of this line of thought.[69] The additional fact that the artificial virtues exhibit change, or have a history, appears further to support Hume's position that they are to be conceived as in some sense invented to serve human purposes. Hume doubts that whole systems of artificial virtue were ever consciously devised or "contrived" *de novo*, as means to specified ends, although such a possibility is not ruled out. No society can exist without some version of the artificial virtues, and we lack adequate evidence con-cerning states of human existence (if any) prior to the emergence of "societies" governed by rules of this sort; accounts of origins and foundings must be largely conjectural and deductive, as are Hume's own. Changes of a more partial and gradual sort, however, may be

---

Man and Society (London: Longmans, 1963), vol. 1, pp. 309-10, and *The English Utilitarians*, pp. 29-30. Cf. also Frederick G. Whelan, "Property as Artifice: Hume and Blackstone," in *Property: Nomos* xxii, ed. J. Roland Pennock and John W. Chapman (New York: New York University Press, 1980), pp. 111-13; and Miller, *Philosophy and Ideology*, pp. 67-76.

[69] See esp. Hume, "A Dialogue."

readily observed: if whole systems of justice or allegiance are rarely discarded and replaced, specific rules and details are constantly subject to modification, much of it deliberate, the consequence of argument roughly of a utilitarian form, however it may be couched in the idiom of a particular time and place, and mediated by forces of habit and imagination. The realm of choice that constitutes the essence of politics pertains to this potential variability of the rules, arising from their artificiality, by means of which society strives to define and attain its ends.

At the more general level of analysis, however, Hume discovers that certain constant features underlie the apparent diversity and flux of the artificial virtues. Their common mode of justification is of course one such feature, as is the necessity that they operate through uniform rules, which in Hume's view corresponds to the universal social requirement of stability and order: in these respects artificial virtues everywhere are similar. Hume also suggests that any society will require some set of rules corresponding to each of his categories of artificial virtues and will accordingly develop institutions and a supportive sense of obligation regarding property, fidelity, authority, sexual relations, and the conduct of diplomacy and war. The common needs of all societies produce artifices and artificial virtues that have a family resemblance everywhere. The differences and even contradictions among the various systems may usually be resolved to a common set of human values, which different societies pursue in differing degrees and by diverse means.[70]

Although the artificial virtues are functionally and formally similar everywhere, their very existence is nevertheless contingent on certain specifiable circumstances. Since these conditions for the most part are always satisfied, Hume's point is mainly a logical one; the delineation of such limiting conditions, however, serves to clarify further the function and mode of justification of these virtues.

Hume's principal point is that the artificial virtues are necessary for the very possibility of sustained social life, along with the less explicit corollary that certain more "civilized" systems of rules facilitate the development of social life on an increasingly orderly and prosperous basis. In his largely conjectural accounts of the "origins" of justice Hume envisions a gradual transition from primitive, small-scale forms

---

[70] See Hume, *Enquiries* (II), p. 202: "How great soever the variety of municipal laws, it must be confessed, that their chief out-lines pretty regularly concur; because the purposes to which they tend, are everywhere exactly similar. In like manner, all houses have a roof and walls, windows and chimneys, although diversified in their shape, figure, and materials."

of collective life, familial or tribal, in which the natural virtues hold sway exclusively, to increasingly large-scale "social" collectivities. Hume does not specify the scale that collective life must attain before it constitutes a "society" in need of rules and artifices; he implies that this is the case with any group extensive enough, or for any other reason characterized by such impersonality, that personal loyalties and attachments do not suffice to ensure order. As this may be a matter of degree, so the evolution of artifices from more natural, familial institutions may be gradual.

The artificial virtues are as necessary to human life as is society itself, to the mere existence of which (in the first instance) they are a means; and in discussing them Hume generally assumes that, excepting a few isolated primitive communities, people are always in need of "society" and in fact are found to live in society. A man by himself is weak and necessitous; his abilities are unimpressive because unspecialized; and he is subject to misfortune. "By society all his infirmities are compensated; and tho' in that situation his wants multiply every moment upon him, yet his abilities are still more augmented, and leave him in every respect more satisfied and happy, than 'tis possible for him, in his savage and solitary condition, ever to become. . . . By the conjunction of forces, our power is augmented: By the partition of employments, our ability encreases: And by mutual succour we are less expos'd to fortune and accidents" (T. 485). All the advantages of society thus enter into a full justification of the artificial virtues, whose function is to regulate conduct in conditions of life where uncontrolled spontaneous impulses would lead to discord and chaos. Of the three benefits Hume lists here, it is the second, unattainable in small groups, that most decidedly requires and advances large-scale social organization, as he makes clear in his economic essays. The division of labor, as Hume's "partition of employments" was successfully renamed by Adam Smith,[71] moreover, is the source of the occupational differences and inequalities of wealth that create the need for ever more complex definition and regulation of rights, duties, and liabilities that constitute much of "justice" in modern societies. The prosperity that Hume ascribes to the property system of modern European states constitutes, as a desirable end, a special reason for approving of those particular

---

[71] Adam Smith, *The Wealth of Nations*, ed. Edwin Cannan (New York: Modern Library, 1937), p. 3. Smith ascribes the division of labor to a "propensity to truck, barter, and exchange," which he suspects is an "original quality" of human nature. The practice of bartering and exchanging, however, would seem to involve what Hume calls justice, since it presupposes some conception of property, and would therefore be artificial in his theory.

rules of justice, which establish private property and contractual economic freedom. More generally, however, stability with respect to
property and all the other matters regulated by the artificial virtues is
a necessary condition of society as such, any form of which would to
some degree offer the advantages enumerated above.

If the rationale of the artificial virtues is bound up with the advantages accruing from social life, it follows that these virtues would not
exist outside their appropriate social context. To people unfamiliar
with society, they would be inconceivable; for someone suddenly removed from society, they would lose their quality of being virtues,
since they would no longer have any tendency to achieve their end;
for a Robinson Crusoe they would be impossible as well as nonob-
ligatory, since one cannot conceivably be just, loyal, or chaste in isolation from other people. The artificial virtues, therefore, are contingent on the same circumstances that necessitate and permit the
establishment of society, which Hume analyzes as the "concurrence
of certain *qualities* of the human mind with the *situation* of external
objects" (T. 494). Human conventions such as justice serve as a "remedy to some inconveniences" (T. 494) that arise when these circumstances constitute a mean, as they normally do, between conceivable
extreme states of affairs.[72]

The qualities of human nature that Hume invokes are *"selfishness
and limited generosity"*: people are largely motivated by the prospect
of personal pleasure, qualified mainly by the natural impulse of benevolence, extending with sympathy to restricted circles. If human
nature were different in either respect, neither the artificial virtues nor
rule-governed society would be necessary, in one case, or possible, in
the other. The "philosophical fiction" of the golden age (T. 493-94)
describes a situation in which people are characterized by complete
altruism or "extensive benevolence" (a passion whose existence Hume
denies). In such a situation, the "use of justice" would "be suspended
. . . nor would the divisions and barriers of property and obligation
have ever been thought of." Some such situation actually prevails in
families, and among friends, where affection abolishes distinctions of
"mine and thine" (T. 495); were human nature other than it is, "the
whole human race would form only one family; where all would lie
in common, and be used freely, without regard to property." Such a
fiction, Hume points out, is attractive, and "during the ardour of new
enthusiasms, when every principle is inflamed into extravagance, the

[72] See D. Clayton Hubin, "The Scope of Justice," *Philosophy and Public Affairs* 9
(1979): 3-24.

community of goods has frequently been attempted."[73] The failure of experimental attempts to do without rules of justice in groups too large to be united by personal affection, however, suggests that hopes for any fundamental alteration in human nature are futile; these failures confirm the view that such rules are adapted to the features and requirements of human nature as it is. Artificial justice compensates for the incapacity of merely limited or partial benevolence, however forceful this may be, to produce harmony in society as it does among intimates.

Hume does not discuss at equal length the opposite possibility, corresponding to the "philosophical fiction" of the (Hobbesian) state of nature, conceived as the condition people would be in were human nature characterized exclusively by avarice, ambition, cruelty, and selfishness (T. 493).[74] I shall discuss in the following section Hume's explanation of the sources and motives in human nature that make possible the artificial virtues; it is apparent that the absence of any such sources would constitute a limiting condition of social life and morality at the other extreme.

The other aspect of the circumstances of justice to which Hume calls attention is the scarcity of external goods in relation to human needs and desires. Hume's assertion in the passage quoted above that, in society, our "wants multiply every moment," implies—plausibly— that *relative* scarcity is a constant feature of human life; and it is on this concept that his account depends. The two contrary philosophical fictions may be brought to bear on this point as well. In a "golden age" in which nature supplied a "profuse *abundance*" of all the conveniences that anyone could desire, there would be no need for justice in the sense of rules for the distribution of property, and hence no society structured by such rules, although there might be some form of common life (T. 494).[75] Hume argues that such a situation prevails in modern Europe with respect to air, water, and the open sea, which exist in such quantity that there is no need for rules regarding ownership with respect to them or hence any possible injustice in their use.[76]

---

[73] Hume, *Enquiries* (II), p. 185-86.

[74] Ibid., p. 189n.

[75] Ibid., pp. 183-84. Hume says that there would be "conversation, mirth, and friendship," as well as the exercise of the natural virtues. It is clear enough why abundance would obviate the need for rules of property and for government to enforce such rules; it is less clear that fidelity would cease to be a virtue in this situation, and rules of modesty and good manners would surely still have a place.

[76] Ibid., p. 184. In other countries, where the distribution of population and resources differs, one finds rules of property for water but not for land.

The case opposite to this would be that of extreme scarcity of the necessities of life, to the point where nothing can "preserve the greater number from perishing, and the whole from extreme misery." Hume offers as examples a shipwreck, or the dissolution of a besieged city in wartime: in such cases, he argues, "the strict laws of justice are suspended, in such a pressing emergence, and give place to the stronger motives of necessity and self-preservation." This passage seems to make the factual point that in such situations the rules of justice would in all probability not continue to be observed. It is clear from the context, however, that Hume means to assert in addition that the rules would no longer be obligatory—that justice would no longer exist as a virtue, since it would no longer tend to accomplish any desirable end (although the natural virtues—"humanity"—would retain their moral status): "The use and tendency of [justice] is to procure happiness and security, by preserving order in society: but where the society is ready to perish from extreme necessity, no greater evil can be dreaded from violence and injustice; and every man may now provide for himself by all the means which prudence can dictate, or humanity permit."[77] A comment Hume makes regarding justice in the largely hypothetical presocial state applies to such circumstances of social disintegration as well: it is not "that it was allowable, in such a state, to violate the property of others" but rather that, there being "no such thing as property," there consequently could be "no such thing as justice or injustice" (T. 501). One can readily conceive how in extreme cases of social dissolution the usual rules regarding promises, obedience to authority, manners, and chastity might all be relaxed or waived under the force of necessity, their quality of being moral duties no longer obtaining.[78]

Hume offers two other examples of situations in which the rules of justice are rightly regarded as suspended. A man who falls into the "society of ruffians" and is wholly at their mercy is obliged only by the "dictates of self-preservation": whereas the criminal band itself is presumably united by rules of justice of a sort, the captive, not partaking of their society, neither shares in nor is bound by that virtue. Again, during war between civilized nations, the rules of war (an aspect of the law of nations) supersede the temporarily suspended rules of justice between them. Moreover, if a civilized nation were at war with "barbarians, who observed no rules even of war, the former must also

[77] Ibid., p. 186.

[78] For criticism of this point see Jonathan Harrison, "Utilitarianism, Universalization, and our Duty to Be Just," *Proceedings of the Aristotelian Society* 53 (1952-1953): 110-12.

suspend their observance of them, where they no longer serve to any purpose."[79] In all these cases, the ordinary rules of artificial virtue lose their obligatory force or undergo modification in accordance with circumstance. Contingency such as this, closely allied to the utilitarian standard of justification, is a central attribute of their artificial status.

Hume's briefly stated doctrine regarding equality, which he adds in the *Enquiry*, is the final premise defining the scope and applicability of the artificial virtues. Hume raises the hypothetical case of a species of creatures living in proximity with us that, though "rational," were of "such inferior strength, both of body and mind, that they were incapable of all resistance, and could never, upon the highest provocation, make us feel the effects of their resentment"; and he argues that such creatures could possess no "right of property" against us, nor would we "lie under any restraint of justice with regard to them." The reason for this is that "our intercourse with them could not be called society, which supposes a degree of equality; but absolute command on the one side, and servile obedience on the other."[80] The artificial virtues have reference to the needs of social life, and they serve to regulate the affairs of members of society, a doctrine that raises the prior questions of the meaning of "society" and of potential eligibility for membership in it. Hume's imprecise utilitarianism avoids formulaic details that became explicit in later versions, among them the proviso that every member of society is to be counted equally in the calculus of pleasures and pains. The utility that Hume invokes as justification for the artificial virtues, however, also seems to presuppose a basic egalitarianism: every member of society has an equal right to be considered when the "happiness of society" is being estimated. This in turn raises the fundamental question of the basis of this equality, or of equal membership, a problem on which Hume touches only in the brief *Enquiry* passage under consideration.

The raising of this question is presented as simply another logical exercise designed to demonstrate the limited scope and hence the artificiality of the artificial virtues, although it serves to raise some important substantive issues. Hume's hypothetical case corresponds to the relation of humans to animals, and an understanding of why there is (in the usual view) no justice between us and them, as there is benevolence and compassion, sheds light on the essential distinction between the two kinds of virtue. In many countries, Hume says, women

[79] Hume, *Enquiries* (II), pp. 187-88. This point is in accordance with opinions prevailing at the time in international law.

[80] Ibid., p. 190.

are "reduced" to a similar (slavish) position; he does not mention the case of children, who in some respects seem to fit his example but who surely participate in justice, at least to the extent of having certain rights.[81] That the problem is not academic, however, is especially evident in Hume's reference to the Europeans' treatment of the American Indians: our superiority, he says, "tempted us to imagine ourselves on the same footing with regard to them [as to animals] and made us throw off all restraints of justice, and even of humanity, in our treatment of them." Here apparently, even among human beings, great differences of culture and physical force precluded "society" of the sort that involves a mutual system of morality.[82]

What is the basis of the fundamental equality that for Hume is a necessary condition for participation in common systems of artificial virtue? Is there a standard that would be inclusive of all human beings that might be counterposed to historical claims, and conduct based on claims, of radical inequality? In the first place it is clear that Hume rejects any distinctively human quality of "rationality" as constituting the crucial distinction: reason has no such elevated status in Hume's view of the mind, and the ability to reason in itself does not even set people decisively apart from animals.[83] The hypothetical inferior creatures with whom Hume says we would rightly have no relations of justice have two characteristics. They are weaker than we are in both body and mind, and therefore "incapable of all resistance" and at our mercy, a consideration that suggests that Hume adheres to the Hobbesian position that the relevant equality constitutive of claims of moral and political rights is equality of the natural instinct and capacity for self-preservation. This interpretation is borne out elsewhere, in Hume's acquiescence in the plausibility of consent, given the fact of the roughly equal condition of human beings in this respect, as the conjectural

[81] A. D. Woozley, "Hume on Justice," *Philosophical Studies* 33 (1978): 91-93. Annette Baier argues that Hume has women especially in mind in this passage, and she offers a complex, Hegelian reading of Hume's remarks here on resentment and related matters; "Hume on Resentment," *Hume Studies* 6 (1980): 133-41.

[82] Hume, *Enquiries* (II), p. 191. Cf. also Hume's tentative comments regarding his suspicion that there may be natural differences in ability among the races; he does not indicate whether he believes Negroes are disqualified for membership in society and thus fittingly enslaved. Hume evinces skepticism regarding an exceptional report of a talented Jamaican Negro, in keeping with his methodological principles, which are discussed and criticized above, chapter III, section 1. Hume, "Of National Characters," *Works*, vol. 3, p. 252 and note.

[83] Hume's hypothetical inferior creatures are "rational," a feature that does not differentiate animals from humans except in degree, as Hume argues in the *Treatise* I.iii.16 and *Enquiries* (I), sec. 9.

original basis for the establishment of authority.[84] The second feature of the inferior creatures, however, is more interesting in light of Hume's science of human nature: they are incapable of making us "feel the effects of their resentment" at our failure to bring them under our rules of justice. In Hume's psychology we feel the resentment of another through sympathy, and we sympathize with other beings only when we apprehend such similarity between them and ourselves that we infer vividly the reality of a recognizable affective state from external signs. This sympathetic capability is a matter of degree. We sympathize even with animals at the level of physical pain, which explains our impulsive benevolence and pity toward them. An inability to sympathize with a more refined mental state such as resentment, however, would indicate a lack of similarity at this higher level of our emotional and moral constitution. Equality in this interpretation is thus founded on psychic similarity and the possibility of communication of passions, an equality stemming from a common human nature although having to do with moral sensibility rather than with a capacity for physical self-defense.[85]

Did the Indians, by these criteria, constitute another species "intermingled with men," justifiably excluded from just dealings? Hume's language (the Europeans were "tempted to imagine" themselves superior) conveys a note of criticism, but he makes no general normative claim here of equal rights for all human beings in some fundamental respect. His allusion to the historical event is rather designed to illustrate the contingency that is one of the defining features of the artificiality of certain virtues: a conception of moral equality, like the environmental circumstance of moderate scarcity and the dispositional circumstance of limited generosity, is a condition and a limitation of

[84] "When we consider how nearly equal all men are in their bodily force, and even in their mental powers and faculties, till cultivated by education; we must necessarily allow, that nothing but their own consent could, at first, associate them together, and subject them to any authority." Hume, "Of the Original Contract," *Works*, vol. 3, pp. 444-45. Cf. also "The right of self-preservation is unalienable in every individual"; "Of Public Credit," *Works*, vol. 3, p. 372. Hume thus appears to share what Leo Strauss has argued is a fundamental assumption of modern political philosophy, although his allusions to it are brief. Hume's theory, however, is not explicitly one of individual rights, although some such notion (a right to equal consideration) is latent in utilitarianism.

[85] Cf. Joseph Cropsey, *Polity and Economy* (The Hague: Martinus Nijhoff, 1957), p. 19, for a similar argument about Adam Smith's notion of equality. Cf. also Thomas Jefferson, letters of 10 August 1787, to Peter Carr, and 25 February 1809, to Henri Gregoire, in *The Portable Thomas Jefferson*, ed. Merrill D. Peterson (Harmondsworth: Penguin, 1975), pp. 424-25, 517; and Adrienne Koch, *The Philosophy of Thomas Jefferson* (New York: Columbia University Press, 1943), pp. 116, 143.

artificial virtue. Elsewhere, however, Hume argues that the extensive natural and culturally determined differences among people exist along with the common possession of a capacity to acknowledge moral distinctions.[86] In what appears to be the most relevant respect for a normative moral theory—the possession of a moral sense—all human beings count equally in Hume's philosophy.[87]

These, then, are the principal characteristics of the artificial in contrast to the natural moral virtues: their realization through concurrence in rules, the priority of rules to particular cases, the utilitarian mode of justification, and their variability and contingency with respect to various psychological and environmental circumstances. I have also mentioned the general end of social order that all the artificial virtues advance: the clarification of this end and of the instrumental relation of the rules to it, together with similar clarification of the more particular ends served by specific rules, constitutes the ethical task posed by the acknowledgment of these virtues; in both the *Treatise* and the *Enquiry* Hume offers the outlines of a defense for what he takes to be the ordinarily accepted rules of justice and allegiance.

The greater part of his analysis of the virtues, however, concerns their sources in human nature, and this problem will provide the framework for the remainder of this chapter. Part of the meaning of the term "artificial" as applied to such virtues as justice has to do with the lack of immediate correspondence between the kind of conduct and moral judgment they demand and the spontaneous impulses of human nature: one does not follow a rule as impulsively as one exercises one of the instinctual passions. It might be suspected that those virtues that rest on instinctual passions would be stronger than the artificial ones; certainly one can envision tension. Yet systems of artificial virtue are successful in regulating moral life, and the stability of society depends on their capacity to restrain natural impulses. The

---

[86] Hume, *Enquiries* (II), p. 170. In this Hume follows Hutcheson, who is said to have "democratized" the moral sense (which in Shaftesbury's version was an elitist principle); see William Robert Scott, *Francis Hutcheson* (New York: Augustus M. Kelley, 1966), p. 186. Hume's frequent distinction between the "wise" and the "vulgar" refers to the use of the reasoning faculty and not to moral capacity.

[87] This underlying equal moral capacity qualifies individuals for participation in a system of virtue and social rules. These rules may permit or establish various forms of conventional inequality (with regard to property, authority, civil and marital rights, etc.) within a particular society. It is with respect to the common sense of obligation that all members of society are equal. In *Enquiries* (II), pp. 193-95, Hume reviews arguments against an (enforced) equal distribution of goods; but in "Of Commerce," *Works*, vol. 3, pp. 296-97, he points to the moral and political advantages of a rough equality of wealth among citizens.

question of how justice and other artificial virtues can exist at all thus becomes an important problem for Hume, one that presents a challenge for his previous discoveries regarding human nature. In the case of the distinctively political virtues such as justice and allegiance, moreover, this is the central problem of political psychology, involving the stability of regimes and the elementary fact of acknowledged obligation. Since the motivation of the artificial virtues is most problematic when they conflict with natural virtues, as in the opposition of justice and benevolence, I shall consider this paradigmatic case in more detail before proceeding in the following section to Hume's account of the sources of artificial virtue.

The latent tension and occasional overt conflict between the natural and the artificial virtues pertain to a distinction between motives immediately operative in particular circumstances and the requirement that certain categories of conduct conform to general and inflexible standards. The utility of the artificial virtues arises from the steady application of rules, indeed, of whole systems of interrelated rules. Their application in any specific instance may have undesirable consequences, and it may well strike the ordinary moral sense as unfair and objectionable. This kind of case not only presents a complication for the justification of the moral rules; it may also pose a genuine practical moral dilemma, insofar as it is a natural moral virtue that is opposed to the imposition of the artificial rule in the particular case. The examples Hume offers usually concern justice, which requires the allocation of property and the observance of other rights in accordance with impartial and general social rules (laws) rather than with what are felt to be the merits of the particular case or our feelings toward the persons involved (T. 447, 532). The crucial point is that the feelings at variance with the demands of justice may be moral feelings—passions constitutive of one whole dimension of the moral sense, motives ordinarily approved as virtuous. Benevolence, compassion, and friendship are indisputably moral values, arising forcefully from "natural motives," but they do not take cognizance of rules and conventions serving long-range social interests. Hume's classification of the types of moral virtue has the merit of indicating the importance of this fundamental type of conflict between the natural and the artificial. In this framework it appears that the most profound and tenacious opposition in human nature to justice and allegiance conceived as general systems of legal obligation stems not from selfishness but from an alternative set of moral demands.[88]

---

[88] Hume in some respects is associated with a tradition that understands justice and

The moral conflict between natural and artificial virtue corresponds to certain psychological and sociological facts on which Hume touches in his account of the passions. The natural virtues, as we have seen, are certain of Hume's direct (or instinctual) passions regarded in a certain light, and as such they are immediately aroused in us in the presence of their appropriate objects; their intensity varies according to the vivacity of the occasioning perception, which in turn depends largely on its contiguity, or its familiarity, to the feeling agent (T. 535). For this reason the natural virtues are associated in Hume's theory with an account of the strength of the affective ties that bind together small groups in contrast to the more extensive and impersonal social unit. Familial affection and loyalty are among the natural virtues, creating special feelings and moral duties within the circle of relations; friendship (and its variants, such as collegiality) is another intrinsically restricted virtue, whereas the others (benevolence, pity, gratitude) are more lively and efficacious to the degree that those who are the objects of these feelings are known to us or are present to our senses or in our imagination.[89]

An important fact about moral experience in this sphere is that our estimation of virtue and duty follows the natural course of our feelings and quite properly varies with their strength and direction. This is especially clear in the case of the family: "A man naturally loves his children better than his nephews, his nephews better than his cousins, his cousins better than strangers, where every thing else is equal. Hence arise our common measures of duty, in preferring the one to the other. Our sense of duty always follows the common and natural course of our passions" (T. 483-84). Hume's account of the gradual growth of a larger society, with the rules of justice it requires, portrays people as emerging from a primitive situation of familial or clannish social organization in which the natural affections are an adequate basis for moral life (T. 486-87).[90] Natural impulses also constitute the moral

---

government as the realization of a higher form of individual self-interest, and that usually assumes that the principal obstacle to justice is therefore narrow self-interest, taking the form of an unrestricted will to domination or acquisition. Stewart, *Moral and Political Philosophy of Hume*, pp. 108-109 and passim, misses what is distinctive in Hume's philosophy by assimilating him too closely to this tradition. Cf. also Miller, *Social Justice*, p. 171.

[89] Morton Grodzins argues that family loyalties are normally stronger than civic duty even in modern society; *The Loyal and the Disloyal* (Chicago: University of Chicago Press, 1956), p. 44. Sissela Bok explores conflicts between fidelity to clients and peers— the "tribal emotions" of "defending one's own"—and the larger society's rule of veracity; *Lying* (New York: Random House, 1978), chap. 11.

[90] There is a difficulty in Hume's theory in that the family itself, portrayed as the

and psychological basis for other forms of restricted collective life—
for groups of friends, for parties and factions, and for patriotism.[91]
Limited circles such as these form the social environment for the greater
part of an ordinary person's life, and the exercise of the natural virtues
is the fitting standard by which a person's conduct is evaluated in such
contexts:

> We perceive, that the generosity of men is very limited, and that it
> seldom extends beyond their friends and family, or, at most, beyond
> their native country. Being thus acquainted with the nature of man,
> we expect not any impossibilities from him; but confine our view
> to that narrow circle, in which any person moves, in order to form
> a judgment of his moral character. When the natural tendency of
> his passions leads him to be serviceable and useful within this sphere,
> we approve of his character. (T. 602)

The conclusions Hume draws from this theory of "limited generosity," which he opposes to facile assumptions of selfishness as the
sole determinant of behavior and judgment (T. 486), however, are
ambivalent. Occasionally he argues optimistically that natural benevolence, restricted as it is to particular objects, forms part of what
appears to be a plan of natural social harmony: the general good is
more appreciably advanced through each individual's consultation of
the good of his own circles than if his generosity were dissipated on
general objects.[92] In the *Treatise*, however, the "partiality" and "unequal affection" characteristic of the natural virtues are shown to be
potentially at odds with the demand for impartiality and regularity
inherent in artificial rules: spontaneous generosity, approved by the
uncultivated moral sense, "instead of fitting men for large societies,
is almost as contrary to them, as the most narrow selfishness" (T.
487).

The natural dispositions of human nature—including limited selfishness and confined generosity—are thus an inadequate basis for
social life, and the remedy, Hume argues, lies in artifice, or in the
establishment and enforcement of a second dimension of moral virtue,
in which rules counteract impulse and create more general obligations
and patterns of conduct. This realm of artifice corresponds to a wider,

---

setting for the natural virtues and held together by them, would appear to be defined
by the artificial (and variable) rules of "chastity" and thus conceptually dependent on
some form of larger social order.

[91] Hume, *Enquiries* (II), pp. 224, 225n.

[92] Ibid., pp. 225n., 229n. This is said to be "wisely ordained by nature"—a suggestion
of providential design or an "invisible hand" that Hume does not explain.

more impersonal, and more public form of collective life. This form of life and its morality are superimposed on, but do not efface, the private and familial forms of life with their more spontaneous sense of virtue, which are psychologically more fundamental and more natural, less variable and contingent. The dichotomy that Hume posits between artificial and natural virtue precludes his looking to the family as a model for larger social organization or appealing, in the manner of Burke, to the veneration of ancestors or to other natural, familial sentiments as a support for political institutions. It is rather the fact that these two distinct kinds of virtue with their correlative forms of life ordinarily coexist that renders cases of conflict between them likely, conflict that may be viewed from the point of view either of ethics or of sociology. Since Hume's perspective on this issue is developed in the pursuit of moral philosophy, it is not surprising that the ethical problem is uppermost in his writing; but the direct link between artificial virtue and large-scale political life means that the social referents of the two kinds of virtue are a matter of continual if often implicit concern.

Hume's two types of virtues prescribe two kinds of potential moral obligations, felt and acknowledged as such, between which important conflicts of a generic sort arise: claims of personal gratitude or special loyalties, compassion for the unfortunate or the victimized perhaps above all, may offer grounds for a violation of property, the breaking of a promise, or an infraction of the law, even where the property, promise, and law in question are recognized to be legitimate institutions. Dilemmas such as these present Hume's moral philosophy with the problem of priority: what principle is to determine such cases, and what is its basis? Hume does not state this problem in so direct a manner, but an implication in all his discussions of the artificial virtues is that they must take precedence over the natural virtues in cases of direct conflict. This normative position follows from empirical arguments regarding the necessity of social order to the preservation of human life, and the necessity of the artificial virtues to this end, which has the status of an overriding value in Hume's philosophy. The artificial virtues are contrivances in some sense chosen or acquiesced in as devices corrective of people's natural impulses—in practice, at any rate, even if the contrary sentiments persist—with a view toward the attainment of this most general and other more specific social ends.[93]

---

[93] The artificial virtues "correct" the feelings that underlie the natural virtues just as critical reasoning can correct impulsive belief by applying philosophical rules of inference. But in the moral sphere the correction is only at the level of practice: the natural feeling (e.g. pity) may persist even when one applies a rule (e.g. a rule of justice) that

To acknowledge the artificial virtues as such, and to admit to their necessity and beneficiality, is at the same time to justify their priority, since it is of their essence to subordinate natural impulses and particular judgments to general rules.

Hume conveys various general impressions of the moral stature of human nature. Occasionally he speaks of humanity's "general corruption" as necessitating rigorous regulation by laws,[94] and this attitude plays a role in Hume's thinking on government, where his advocacy of constitutional restraints and checks and a government of law stems from his opinion that the safest assumption in politics is that *"every man must be supposed a knave."*[95] More often, however, Hume's view is balanced: in reality people are motivated by a mixture of egoism and limited benevolence, together with the other passions, mediated by habit and occasional vagaries of the imagination; and the natural virtues are presented as an appropriate and satisfactory guide, by and large, for the usual course of private life. It is nevertheless the purpose of the artificial virtues, and the institutions through which they are realized, to impose restraints and controls on impulse and feeling arising from particular circumstances and narrow views and to modify judgment and conduct where necessary in accordance with general social requirements. Social life requires the submission of impulse to rules, the subordination of some of the spontaneous features of human nature to artifice. Hume accepts this necessity with equanimity, only rarely protesting against the "tyranny" of social rules over natural impulses;[96] he displays no inclination, such as one finds among some of his contemporaries as well as among later radicals and romantics, to exalt personal feeling and an intuitive sense of justice over established laws with their inevitable occasional inequities.[97] Rules

---

does not take cognizance of particular hardships; and the pity continues to be a natural virtue, though one whose exercise must be suppressed in this situation.

[94] Hume, *Enquiries* (i), pp. 44-45n.

[95] Hume, "Of the Independency of Parliament," *Works*, vol. 3, pp. 117-18.

[96] A rare example of unbridled naturalism is Hume's defense of clerical concubinage as a means of circumventing the Medieval Church's rule of celibacy: "This commerce was really a kind of inferior marriage . . . and may be regarded by the candid as an appeal from the tyranny of civil and ecclesiastical institutions, to the more virtuous and more unerring laws of nature." *History of England*, chap. 11, vol. 1, p. 413. This passage is plainly inconsistent with Hume's moral theory. The natural virtues are not *more* virtuous than those established by artifice; and in any case all rules regarding "chastity," including those surrounding acceptable forms of concubinage, would be artificial, their virtue dependent on social opinion and custom rather than on simple inclination.

[97] A striking contemporaneous portrayal of this kind of conflict is found in Diderot's

of justice, and all such public standards, are subject to criticism and amendment, by formal or informal processes; but whatever their content, these virtues are useful only if they are observed on a regular basis. They constitute a body of morality inescapably different from that determined by natural feeling and never entirely coincident with the dictates of the heart.

Hume's general doctrine of the priority of the artificial over the natural virtues provides the moral basis for the political theory of legalism and constitutionalism that he propounds in his political essays. Common, statutory, and constitutional laws are specific political varieties of rules constituting artifices in his sense of the term; the feeling of moral obligation that normally attends them is an aspect of the acknowledged virtues of justice and allegiance shared by the members of a civil society. Hume's preference for a government of laws, not of men, follows from his recognition of the dependence of society on artifice rather than on feeling;[98] the corollary of this is the claim that laws must supersede private judgment in matters of social interest.

The general claim of priority, however, does not entirely solve the ethical problem that he has identified in the conflict of two opposing sorts of moral claims on an individual in a particular instance. The remaining difficulty is that Hume argues not only for the general observance of rules such as those of justice over particular impulse but also that the application of such rules must be absolutely uniform and inflexible—"either by spite or favour" (T. 502)—if they are to achieve their purpose. This is most strikingly expressed in his metaphorical contrast between the two kinds of virtue:

> The happiness and prosperity of mankind, arising from the social virtue of benevolence and its subdivisions, may be compared to a wall, built by many hands, which still rises by each stone that is heaped upon it, and receives increase proportional to the diligence and care of each workman. The same happiness, raised by the social virtue of justice and its subdivisions, may be compared to the building of a vault, where each individual stone would, of itself, fall to the ground; nor is the whole fabric supported but by the mutual assistance and combination of its corresponding parts.[99]

Hume likewise compares the working of justice with the rowing of a boat by a crew: benefit is derived only from a coordinated scheme, in

---

Entretien d'un Père avec ses Enfants (1772), in Denis Diderot, *Oeuvres Philosophiques,* ed. Paul Vernière (Paris: Garnier, 1964), pp. 430-36.

[98] Hume, "Of Civil Liberty," *Works,* vol. 3, p. 161.

[99] Hume, *Enquiries* (II) p. 305.

which all those involved must concur in the same rules without exception (T. 490).[100]

The apparently misleading feature of these comparisons is their implication that every single act of justice is necessary for general advantage to be derived from a system of justice, a point that if true would justify completely inflexible rules rather than ones that are merely generally observed. In fact it seems that infrequent violations of an artificial moral rule (assuming they do not become precedents) would not detract from its general benefits in the way that a single flaw in a vault may cause the collapse of the whole structure. Reflections of this sort of course intensify the kind of moral dilemma that I have been considering: the claims of benevolence over justice may be especially strong in a case of hardship if one has reason to believe that a single infraction (a secret one, for example) would not be likely to endanger the general practice of observance. The difficulty lies in formulating rules or guidelines to govern exceptions to the rules and in the extent to which such a principle could be made public.[101] Hume, it scarcely need be added, does not consider the possibility of establishing a discretionary authority above the rules: neither the adequate knowledge nor the right motives requisite to such an ideal governor can reasonably be expected.[102]

Whether or not Hume believes that application of the artificial rules of morality must be rigorously uniform in order to be efficacious, he evidently does not believe that any principle for exceptions can be stated, let alone publicly acknowledged. His reasons for insisting on inflexibility have to do with his account of the nature of the motivations by which systems of artifice can exist at all: depending as they do, in the final analysis, on habit, their efficacy depends on commitment that is likely to be attained only through their elevation to a higher status than that held by any natural virtues.[103] Such an elevation, as we shall see, like the virtues themselves, is artificial; and the sense of natural

[100] See the following section and note 117 below.

[101] Cf. Harrison, "Utilitarianism"; and Miller, *Social Justice*, p. 165.

[102] Cf. Hume, *Enquiries* (ii), pp. 304-305, on Cyrus—that is, a Platonic prince, ruling on the basis of disinterested wisdom.

[103] G. E. Moore, *Principia Ethica* (Cambridge: Cambridge University Press, 1971), p. 162, offers an argument for the inflexible observance of moral rules that seems Humean in spirit. We should never break a generally useful rule (such as promise-keeping) because we can never *know* that we have before us a case where the infringement would have better consequences than the observance; the probability that we are in error in so supposing is greater, in light of experience, than the probability that the rule is beneficial.

virtue, along with natural feelings from which it arises, is far from being eradicated as human beings are socialized.

4. Artificial Virtue and Human Nature

The potential tension between justice and benevolence raises in a striking form the problem of the motivation or sources of artificial virtue in human nature. This is not problematic for the natural virtues, which correspond to natural motives; but how can judgment and conduct in accordance with artifices and rules be accounted for? Above all, how can virtue of this kind be sufficiently strong to override natural impulse in cases of direct conflict? This is, more generally, the question of the basis in human nature of the sense of obligation and the obedience to general rules of conduct on which social and political order depend, and to it Hume brings the distinctive discoveries of his science of human nature. His approach combines ethical (as earlier he combined epistemological) issues with psychological and behavioral ones, inasmuch as he takes the sense of moral obligation that accompanies ordinary belief in the virtues of justice, allegiance, and so forth to be the central fact in need of explanation.

Hume characterizes human beings as being motivated as a rule by two basic impulses, usually labeled selfishness and limited or "confin'd generosity" (T. 519). Selfishness or egoism, referring to people's motivation according to the desire or aversion they experience at the prospect of their own pleasure or pain, seems opposed to many of the requirements imposed by justice and the other artificial virtues, which are justified in Hume's ethics by their furtherance of the general good. Generosity, on the other hand, is as a natural feeling too variable and partial: each instance of it is a distinct impression aroused in us by a "particular individual event" and not subordinated to general principles, although fairly constant patterns of response may be observed in the appropriate circumstances (T. 531). Justice among other things demands equal and impartial treatment, according to rule, of friends, strangers, and (one's personal) enemies alike; there is, however, no such passion as general or "extensive" benevolence corresponding to the general orientation of justice—no "love of mankind, merely as such" (T. 481)—and indeed, if there were, the very need for artificial rules would disappear (T. 495). Hume therefore concludes that the laws of justice, though universal to human society—and in this sense perfectly "natural" to human beings (T. 484)—"can never be deriv'd from nature, nor be the immediate offspring of any natural motive or inclination" (T. 532).

On the other hand, Hume maintains that it is reasonable and necessary to inquire into the motives of virtue: "No action can be requir'd of us as our duty, unless there be implanted in human nature some actuating passion or motive, capable of producing the action" (T. 518); genuine moral duties must be possible of fulfillment, human nature being what it is.[104] If in the case of the artificial virtues there is no natural or immediate motive, then there must be another sort—perhaps one could call it an artificial motive—adequate to their exercise. The concept of artifice, for Hume, connotes not irreconcilable opposition to the principles of human nature but rather a construction upon them. Although artifices function to restrain the (violent) passions, they are nevertheless the products of human contrivance and hence at the service of human nature: "All they can pretend to, is, to give a new direction to those natural passions, and teach us that we can better satisfy our appetites in an oblique and artificial manner, than by their headlong and impetuous motion" (T. 521; cf. 526). Artifices have as their end the satisfaction of our desires, or rather some of them—the calm and long-range ones—at the expense of others, and their realization and efficacy must be derived, mediately or indirectly, from natural propensities. The artificial virtues could not exist if they were wholly at odds with our nature, and Hume does not envision, in the manner of Rousseau, a thorough denaturing or moral transformation of people as the precondition and the cost of social or civil life. Just as it does not obliterate and replace natural virtue, so artificial virtue must be supported, though "obliquely," by motives available in human nature as Hume has previously delineated it.

In Book III, Part 2, "Of justice and injustice," Hume takes up the problem of motives right away ("*What reason or motive*" does a person have to repay a debt in accordance with an explicit promise?), and the first answer that comes to mind is a "regard to justice, and abhorrence of villainy," that is, a "sense of duty and obligation" (T. 479). Similarly, Hume says that he can discern no "inclination" or motive to keep promises, "distinct from a sense of their obligation" (T. 519). This answer, he adds, seems satisfactory only for "man in his civiliz'd state, and when train'd up according to a certain discipline and education" (T. 479). A sense of duty is indeed the reason that is ordinarily given for their just conduct by people living in a society that adheres to certain norms of justice; yet as a matter of reasoning

---

[104] This point is discussed extensively in Rachel M. Kydd, *Reason and Conduct in Hume's Treatise* (New York: Russell and Russell, 1964). See also R. David Broiles, *The Moral Philosophy of David Hume* (The Hague: Martinus Nijhoff, 1964).

this appears to be circular: a feeling of obligation constitutes, in the mind of an agent, the virtuous quality of the rules that dictate the obligation. Hume therefore quickly surveys other possible motives, finding them all inadequate: a "concern for our private interest or reputation" does not always coincide with justice; a *"regard to publick interest"* is "too remote and too sublime"; the "love of mankind" does not exist as a distinct passion but is mediated in various degrees by special qualities of persons and by variable sympathy; and private benevolence is clearly too limited in scope (T. 480-82).

Hume accordingly returns to the first answer, that given by common opinion: the usual motive for observing the laws of equity is "the very equity and merit of that observance" (T. 483). It is characteristic of the artificial virtues that a sense of duty, or a conscious regard for virtue as such, constitutes the usual efficient cause of their perform- ance, and so the origin of this sense of duty in turn becomes a central concern of Hume's theory. We already have an intimation of the answer to which Hume finds his way: the "discipline and education" of people living together in a civilized social state is the instrument by which the sense of duty is generated, or by which artificial content is provided for the natural moral sense in accordance with the general needs of society. This solution, however, is not the most conspicuous theme in Hume's treatment of the basis of artificial virtue, and we must examine the role of two other principles, sympathy and self- interest, to which he devotes a large amount of attention before coming to the role of education; it is only in light of the inadequacy of these other possible sources of justice that the place of the latter factor in Hume's theory may be established.

The principle of sympathy has attracted the attention of many com- mentators on Hume's ethics who have seen it as playing the crucial motivational role in a manner apparently consistent with Hume's el- evation of the passions over reason; this is a topic, however, that is not always treated with precision. Throughout the lengthy second part of Book III of the *Treatise* Hume discusses the origins of justice and government principally in terms of enlightened self-interest, an alter- native that I consider below. In Part 3, however, he revitalizes the doctrine of sympathy that he had put forward in Book II and applies it to the problem of the source of the artificial virtues, reasoning as follows: the artificial virtues are "contrivances for the interest of so- ciety," that is, means to an end; however, "the means to an end can only be agreeable, where the end is agreeable"; and, "as the good of society, where our own interest is not concern'd, or that of our friends, pleases only by sympathy: It follows, that sympathy is the source of the esteem, which we pay to all the artificial virtues" (T. 577). Hume, however, immediately dilutes this argument, suggesting that sympathy enters into all our feelings and judgments concerning virtue, the natural as well as the artificial, insofar as they all bear a relation to the good of the larger society, any "extensive concern" for which can arise in us only through sympathy. This is the doctrine that Hume carries over into the second *Enquiry*: "sympathy," used there synonymously with "humanity," is simply alleged to be an original principle in human nature by means of which "everything, which contributes to the happiness of society, recommends itself directly to our approbation and good will" and which "accounts, in great part, for the origin of morality."[105]

One who reads these passages in the light of the more detailed psychology of the *Treatise* may well suspect Hume of evading the problem of motivation. The "more public affection" that sympathy becomes in the more popular work is not obviously distinguishable, as a passion, from the "love of mankind" or "extensive benevolence" that Hume explicitly denies in the *Treatise*. The notion of sympathy itself, moreover, loses its precision, becoming in some passages almost identical with the faculty of moral approbation whose operation, in the problematic cases where the artificial virtues must supersede the natural, it is ostensibly being invoked to clarify. Some commentators have offered a reading of Hume's moral theory that is more correctly applied to that of Adam Smith, in which "to sympathize with" means "to approve of" a given motive of action.[106] Hume's doctrine, however, differs from Smith's in an important respect: sympathy as it enters into moral judgment is not a sharing in another agent's motive but rather a capacity to envision and share in the happiness of the beneficiaries of certain actions or classes of actions, which are then approved, together with the motives of the agents who perform them, following reflection on the means-end relation between the motive and

---

[105] Hume, *Enquiries* (II), p. 219 and note, and passim.

[106] Adam Smith, *The Theory of Moral Sentiments* (Indianapolis: Liberty Classics, 1969) III.1, p. 203: "We either approve or disapprove of the conduct of another man, according as we feel that, when we bring his case home to ourselves, we either can or cannot entirely sympathize with the sentiments and motives which directed it." The only suggestion of sympathy with motives in Hume occurs in the *Treatise*, p. 604. Smith's theory also makes frequent reference to a "sympathetic" or "reasonable" or "impartial spectator." Such a concept is sometimes ascribed to Hume on the strength of his single allusion to a "judicious spectator" (T. 581); see, for example, Richard B. Brandt, *Ethical Theory* (Englewood Cliffs, N.J.: Prentice-Hall, 1959), p. 173. See also D. D. Raphael, "The Impartial Spectator," *Proceedings of the British Academy* 58 (1972): 340.

the felicitous outcome. Although sympathy in Hume's later work may occasionally appear to be equivalent to the moral sense, it is invoked primarily in connection with the utilitarian aspect of his theory, as a way of explaining why the utilitarian standard in fact has the intuitive appeal that it does. A consideration of the connection between sympathy and utility will reveal the role that sympathy legitimately can play in Hume's theory, but it will at the same time show that it cannot in general provide a sufficient motive to underlie the artificial virtues.

Utility as we have seen is the sole principle or criterion of the artificial virtues for Hume and, by and large, in ordinary opinion. To grasp the utility of an institution or practice such as justice requires reflection on the ends it is intended to serve—in general, the happiness of society; the apprehension of an instrumental relation such as this is a matter of reasoning, in Hume's sense, about matters of fact. To acknowledge the relation, however, is not necessarily to approve of the institution or the practice; the further question arises, why does utility please us? The function of sympathy in the second Enquiry is to provide an answer to this ultimate question facing the utilitarian. Sympathy here is an alleged disposition in human nature to share in the happiness of others in a very general way, in a moment of calm and disinterested reflection, as the immediate prelude to a feeling of approval toward whatever is conducive to that happiness. Hume argues that an imaginative view of the happiness of others, however remote from us in time or space, arouses sympathetic pleasure in us, when there is no personal interest or proximate object to distract our attention and our feelings; otherwise utilitarian arguments would not hold the attraction for us that they do.

This argument is plausible in one sense, namely, as a description of the process of reflective approval or justification of an artificial (utility-grounded) virtue. It is not plausible, however, as an account of the source of actual judgments in particular circumstances, in accordance with artificial moral standards, or of actions in accordance with artificial virtues in the face of conflicting incentives. The process of reasoned justification needs to be distinguished from the practical problem of motivation and conduct. Hume occasionally says that our sense of approbation in the case of the artificial virtues arises from "reflecting" on their "tendencies" over the long run (T. 577-78);[107] it is clearly in connection with such a "reflective" state that Hume discerns the operation of the generalized sympathy of the Enquiry, and so in these passages he should be understood to be describing the

[107] See also Hume, Enquiries (II), p. 201.

mental processes of one who is engaged in justifying the virtuous status of justice rather than the state of mind of someone caught up in an actual conflict of interest or a dilemma in which justice is opposed by instinctive benevolence. The state of reflective approval is a matter of experience: the task of ethical justification can be undertaken only in a state of comparative philosophical detachment, in which personal concerns and proximate circumstances are neutralized or ignored. A reflective state such as this involves the maximum of reasoning of which we are capable and the entire domination of the calm over the violent passions; it is therefore a state not likely to be sustained in the ordinary course of life, given Hume's general understanding of human nature. The ratiocination required in the clarification of the utility of the artificial virtues, moreover, is often a complex matter, not readily retrievable on short notice; a full, reasoned defense of justice on every occasion on which one is obliged to be just could not be relied on as an effective component of motivation. The postulation of a detached state of mind, finally, does not meet the crucial practical problem, which concerns precisely the situation in which more spontaneous feelings, especially those having both the force of instinct and the moral stature of natural virtues, make their presence felt in the mind, interfering with the adherence to rules and general practices. The generalized sympathy of the *Enquiry* thus may be said to play a necessary role in ethical justification, conceived in Hume's characteristic manner as a psychological process describable in naturalistic terms.[108] This process, however, cannot be accepted as a plausible account of the strength of the artificial virtues in the regulation of our feelings and conduct in the usual course of life.

Can sympathy in Hume's more technical usage, then, be regarded as a potential source of support for the artificial virtues? The answer to this question must be in the negative, and the difficulties are apparent in a close reading of what Hume says about sympathy in connection with justice. Sympathy in the *Treatise* is a communicative mechanism by which (any) passion manifested in one person may be apprehended and thence actually shared by another. It is, like the principles of association, a basic faculty or disposition of the imagination; it operates in close relation with those principles in that a sympathetic response is asserted to vary in force and vivacity with the degrees of resemblance and contiguity (proximity) between the individuals momentarily joined by this form of communication. This variability of

---

[108] Cf. "A sympathy *with public interest is the source of the* moral approbation"— as opposed to the motive, attending justice (T. 499-500).

sympathy implies a correspondence between it and the natural virtues, which also vary in force (and prescribe unequal duties) depending on the nearness of their objects. It is therefore not clear how sympathy, as Hume portrays it, could be the motive for bringing our particular judgments into accordance with general rules, especially when the application of rules does violence to feeling. In Hume's exemplary case of the disposition of an estate, it seems likely that sympathy with the feelings of the needy and deserving claimant would have the effect of reinforcing our natural impulses of benevolence and pity toward him, at the expense of the rightful (miserly) heir. More important, the sympathetic feelings aroused in favor of a present sufferer of misfortune would most likely be far more lively than our generalized and vague sense of the happiness of all the anonymous future beneficiaries of a system of laws; the good that we envisage as the result of a particular act of generosity is both more vivid and more certain than the general benefits of strict justice. The future happiness of society is a comparatively remote and intangible object, and sympathy with it, in Hume's psychology, could be a factor in motivation only when nothing immediate obtrudes. The artificial virtues become problematic, however, precisely in cases where immediate objects engage our feelings, and here the effect of sympathy would be to intensify the inclination to violate a rule whose felicitous consequences are distant.

Hume acknowledges these points in considering objections to his system: "We sympathize more with persons contiguous to us, than with persons remote from us: With our acquaintance, than with strangers: With our countrymen, than with foreigners. But notwithstanding this variation of our sympathy, we give the same approbation to the same moral qualities in *China* as in *England*. They appear equally virtuous, and recommend themselves equally to the esteem of a judicious spectator. The sympathy varies without a variation in our esteem" (T. 581). People are quite often in fact capable of impartial judgments despite the real variation in sympathy, to which (alone) they evidently cannot be attributed. All explicit moral judgments, even those regarding the natural virtues, must be disinterested; the formulation of a moral judgment that may be communicated to others, moreover, requires some degree of reflective effort in order to "render our sentiments more public and social."[109] But although all moral language must be general, judgments in accordance with the artificial virtues, which refer to publicly acknowledged rules, demand a doubly "*steady* and *general* [point] of view" (T. 581-82). Since sympathy alone

[109] Hume, *Enquiries* (II), p. 229.

seems inadequate to this requirement, Hume at this point calls on another psychological disposition, that of the imagination to follow "general rules," to "correct" the operation of sympathetic feelings, which often fail to fall in line with the general perspective required by morality, and to explain how adherence to general standards is possible (T. 585).

The applicability and the efficacy of this principle in connection with sympathy, however, remain in doubt. It is, we recall, through a natural generalizing propensity, together with the cumulative force of habit, that the mind attains its unshakable belief in the regularity of causes and the identity of objects; and it is through a capacity to formulate "general rules" that it derives factual inferences from particular bits of evidence. General rules are the products, and extensions, of the repeated experience that in Hume's account generates the tenacious mental force of custom or habit. This complex of mental dispositions, so prominent in Hume's philosophy as a whole, seems a promising source for a solution to the present problem. Efficacious moral rules are possible ultimately because there is in human nature a capability of grasping and habitually following rules; and the special functions of learning and habit in the sphere of moral sentiment and moral artifice do indeed, as we shall see below, constitute Hume's most satisfactory means of accounting for the artificial sense of duty that people give as their reason for being just. It is not clear, however, just how the generalizing faculty comes to be linked to the sympathetic capacity so as to overcome the natural variability of feelings. Hume indeed, in an earlier passage, seems to reject any natural correspondence between the inconstant rule-following propensity of the imagination and the strictly rule-determined judgments and conduct associated with artificial virtue (T. 531). Hume's general denial that any natural motive, or the "immediate offspring of any natural motive" (T. 532), can serve as the basis for artificial virtue applies in this case: even the general rule-following tendency of the imagination, that is, is not *naturally* regular enough to provide a motivational basis for justice, whose inflexibility beyond the limits of our natural dispositions is central to its artificiality. Sympathy must be corrected and generalized, but this is not, as Hume occasionally implies, a spontaneous process; it requires the additional impact of training and education. Despite its important role throughout his moral psychology, therefore, sympathy is not the factor on which Hume must ultimately rely in his account of justice and government.

The second alternative that Hume explores is the possibility that rational or enlightened self-interest on the part of individuals might provide the motive for acceptance and adherence to the rules of justice and the other artificial virtues. The view that the general interest of society might (for the most part) be advanced through the uncoerced "harmony" of all the separate private interests was to become a widely accepted tenet of later utilitarianism and of certain branches of classical liberalism; and it is a thesis that Hume seems to adopt throughout much of the *Treatise*, applying it to the problem of the "source" in individuals of the artifices that he argues are necessary to the general good.[110] The unplanned order to which this (broadly economic) theory mainly points arises from the operation of markets, in which individuals are free to pursue their interests by voluntarily exchanging their assets and entering into contractual relations. The theory also holds that the institution of the market itself, with its rules and conception of justice, is likewise agreed to by each individual out of consideration for his own interest. This argument from self-interest does have some plausibility in light of Hume's theory as a whole, although he does not explicitly relate justice to a market model. I shall argue in particular that it provides a plausible account of the reasoning and motivation that might characterize individuals in another sort of reflective state— that preceding the hypothetical original "convention" by which the artificial virtues (and government) are established. But it is not satisfactory as a general explanation of the regularity or of the sense of duty with which people habitually observe moral rules. Above all, it does not provide an answer for the problematic cases, where the obligations imposed by the artificial virtues conflict directly with private interests and natural sentiments.

Hume's most pronounced reliance on the motive of self-interest is found in his treatment of the "origin of justice and property" (T. III.ii.2). The account given here is somewhat ambiguous for present purposes precisely because it deals with "origins": Hume offers an abstract and conjectural account of the process by which individuals in a presocial condition would have come to acknowledge the need for rules of justice (especially for stability of property) and accordingly

---

[110] Some such view is most characteristic of Mandeville, of the five authors on the "science of man" whom Hume acknowledges in the *Treatise*; Mandeville stands in conspicuous contrast to Shaftesbury and Hutcheson. But compare note 153 below. Hume's recently discovered manuscript alterations in Book III of the *Treatise* tend to accentuate the assumption of egoism or rational self-interest that informs that work's treatment of the artificial virtues, in contrast to the greater altruism or "sympathy" of the *Enquiry* (II). See R. W. Connon, "The Textual and Philosophical Significance of Hume's MS Alterations to *Treatise* III," in *David Hume: Bicentenary Papers*, ed. G. P. Morice (Austin: University of Texas Press, 1977), pp. 186-204.

would have entered into a convention or agreement to establish them; a similarly abstract account of the origin of government follows (T. III.ii.7). These accounts are admittedly hypothetical; Hume recognizes, in the *Treatise* no less than in his *History* and in historically minded essays such as "Of the Original Contract," that actual governments have mostly been founded by war and conquest, and that systems of justice are the products of gradual growth, their origins obscure, and not the outcome of deliberate agreements (cf. T. 540-41).

Hume's account of origins is therefore a mental experiment of the sort conducted by political philosophers who have envisaged the establishment of civil society by contract in an initial state of nature. Clearly part of Hume's intention in offering his own version of this scheme is to emphasize the distinction between his "convention" of mutual self-interest, with its utilitarian justification and suggestion of gradualism, and the more legalistic notion of a "contract," with its implication that obligation is derived from a formal promise.[111] This difference aside, however, Hume's position in these sections bears a strong generic similarity to those of Locke and the continental jurists of the period: he provides a deductive account of the manner in which artifices might have been established by the consent of individuals, given certain assumptions about human nature and the initial position that are much simpler than the views to which he adheres throughout most of his philosophy. The rational egoist whom Hume here portrays acknowledging the necessity of the rules of justice is unrealistic in terms of Hume's own enumeration of human beings' usual imaginative and emotional attributes.[112] Moreover, the incentives that might induce someone initially to agree to the establishment of a system of rules would not, in all likelihood, be the same factors that would be

---

[111] Besides the different implications for a theory of obligation, Hume's version of the original "convention" differs from Locke's founding "compact" in that it establishes all the artificial virtues and not simply "allegiance." Hume's well-known critique of contractualism follows from this: allegiance cannot be derived from promising, since all the artificial virtues, including fidelity, are on the same plane, none prior to the others. If justice (promise-keeping) *were* a natural virtue, or enjoined by natural law, then it would be reasonable to derive civil obligations from it (T. 542-43). Cf. Jeffrie G. Murphy, "Hume and Kant on the Social Contract," *Philosophical Studies* 33 (1978): 68-72.

[112] In this very section of the *Treatise* Hume explicitly rejects the descriptive validity of the postulate of "selfishness" or egoism: "tho' it be rare to meet with one, who loves any single person better than himself; yet 'tis as rare to meet with one, in whom all the kind affections, taken together, do not over-balance all the selfish" (T. 487).

present as motivational influences in every particular case in which an individual is called on to obey those rules.

The conjectural "savage condition" of people living in isolation from one another, or in isolated family groups each held together by "limited generosity," would suffer, Hume says, from numerous disadvantages. The most rudimentary of these, obvious even to an uncultivated mind, would be the extreme instability of material goods in the absence of any generally accepted rules of possession. The means of alleviating this situation, moreover, would occur to the slightest reflection: "nothing can be more simple and obvious" (T. 493) than the institution of some basic rule or rules of property (whatever the details of their content) whose general observance would bring (at least) the undisputed good of security. A technical difficulty in this account is that the individuals involved would not only have to see the desirability of *some* scheme of rules but would also have to concur (simultaneously) in the *same* rule(s), which seems more difficult to imagine. Hume argues that the utility of three basic rules of justice (stability of possession, transference of property by consent, and the obligation of promises) is sufficiently obvious that these would be likely to emerge as the substance of an original convention or agreement, by which they are established as obligatory.[113] (These rules would necessarily have to be articulated further, in subrules, and could be modified by subsequent agreements.)[114] Supposing everyone (or a large number of people) to engage in this line of reasoning, Hume argues that each

[113] The rule of promise-keeping as first conceived pertains to future or reciprocal transfers of goods (or services); once established, this convention is soon found to be useful in facilitating cooperative endeavors of many kinds.

[114] Many commentators have emphasized the prominence of property in Hume's theory of justice, noting that his three rules (perhaps rephrased as private property, market exchange, and the sanctity of contracts) correspond to the conception of justice alleged to be typical of the commercial society emerging in Britain (and most conspicuously in Scotland) in Hume's day. Although there is undoubtedly truth in this observation, I for the most part treat Hume's theory at a higher level of abstraction. The analysis of the artificial virtues is persuasive irrespective of the exact content of the rules (which Hume in any case acknowledges are historically variable). See C. B. Macpherson, "The Economic Penetration of Political Theory: Some Hypotheses," *Journal of the History of Ideas* 39 (1978): 101-18, for the view that Hume's political theory is founded in an economic outlook. Macpherson's further suggestion that Hume is among "those who held most strongly that society was necessarily contentious and hence exploitative" (p. 111) suffers especially from a shortage of evidence and a failure to consider the larger context of certain statements. For a response see David Miller, "Hume and Possessive Individualism," *History of Political Thought* 1 (1980): 261-78; Miller, however, here and in his books, agrees that Hume is properly regarded (in part) as an ideologist of his society.

individual's perception that his own interest in security coincides with an identical interest on the part of others will suffice to effect the necessary agreement:

> It is only a general sense of common interest; which sense all the members of the society express to one another, and which induces them to regulate their conduct by certain rules. I observe, that it will be for my interest to leave another in the possession of his goods, *provided* he will act in the same manner with regard to me. He is sensible of a like interest in the regulation of his conduct. When this common sense of interest is mutually express'd, and is known to both, it produces a suitable resolution and behaviour. (T. 490)

The belief that a system of rules will serve to advance a person's own interests motivates that person to agree to their adoption; the "common interest" is simply in the mutuality of private interests, mutually expressed and acknowledged; no sympathetic sharing of feeling or concern for the welfare of others is supposed. Assuming here that self-interest is the sole actuating force (apart from the instinctual passions in their restricted sphere), Hume argues that only self-interest is "capable of controlling the interested affection . . . by an alteration of its direction," when reflection reveals "that the passion is much better satisfy'd by its restraint, than by its liberty" (T. 492). An only slightly enlarged view of private interest leads to the conclusion that all of one's ends have a higher likelihood of being realized if everyone submitted to the restraint of rules that, although prohibiting certain immediate gratifications of impulse, ensure greater satisfaction in the long run. Thus, Hume says, we "cannot better consult" our own interests than to agree to such restraints (T. 489) if others do likewise; everyone, similarly motivated, concurs, and the conventions of social life are established.[115]

There are three difficulties with this account, however, if it is read

---

[115] That Hume's rules of justice are the product of rational self-interested choice is the argument of David Gauthier, "David Hume: Contractarian," *Philosophical Review* 88 (1979): 3-38. Since Hume's justice is not a dominant, stable, and therefore automatic convention, like rowing a boat, its establishment requires explicit agreement; it is "contractual" in that appeal is made to "mutual expected utility" or the (apparent) prospective well-being of each person, rather than that of society as a whole, as the basis of the agreement. This seems correct as an interpretation of Hume's account of the "origins" of justice and hence as a way of justifying it. But in practice the operation of the rules does *not* always maximize each person's private interest, even though each may be better off than if there were no rules. Hence motivation to be just is problematic: "interested obligation" is insufficient.

as a description of the manner in which people are motivated to abide by the prescriptions of artificial virtue rather than as a simplified, deductive model showing how, under certain conditions, the conventions might have originated. These pertain to the inconsistency of such an emphasis on self-interest in the light of Hume's science of human nature as a whole; to a logical problem in the argument as it stands; and to the failure of this account to take into consideration the sense of duty that surrounds such rules as matters of moral virtue. I shall also consider two additional factors—the concern for reputation and the role of coercive sanctions—that Hume calls on to strengthen the argument from interest. The conclusion will nevertheless be that this approach, like the appeal to sympathy, is inadequate as a complete explanation of the facts of artificial moral life.

We have sufficiently examined Hume's psychology to be suspicious of reliance on rational or enlightened egoism, such as is resorted to in these passages, as inconsistent with some of his own most characteristic discoveries concerning human nature. It is not so much the egoism that is questionable, since Hume does hold that egoistic desire is a commonly influential, although not the exclusive, motive of human action. Doubts arise, however, about the "rationality" in this model, understood as the ability routinely and decisively to repress proximate in favor of remote objects of desire, or to maintain the supremacy of the calm over the violent passions to the degree required to sustain a system whose benefits are general and largely intangible. The difficulty does not concern the neutral, reflective state in which people can readily be conceived as deciding in the abstract that rules of justice would be a useful thing (in comparison with an absence of any rules); rather, it concerns the probable motivation of individuals in actual circumstances, in which they are called on to be just in opposition to immediate feelings and at least in apparent opposition to immediate and partial interests.

"Men often act knowingly against their interest" (T. 418), says Hume in discussing the force of violent passions, and any passion, when aroused in particular circumstances, can distract a person from the "view of the greatest possible good." Even if we ignore the possible influence of selfless, instinctual passions (such as benevolence and anger) and confine our attention to self-interested motives, it does not seem likely that a person with the imagination and passions that Hume describes could be counted on consistently to pursue the sort of long-range interest involved in adherence to a system of rules. Desire is aroused by the precedent idea of a pleasurable object; the capacity of an idea to affect our passions or volition (or indeed to produce our belief in its probable existence, especially if this requires an inference to the future) varies with its force and vivacity. Any factor that can excite the imagination is capable of stimulating the passions and the will, which are thus susceptible to all the vagaries of the former (T. 424) and especially to its tendency to be more strongly influenced by that which is present or contiguous, or by that of which it has a distinct conception, or by that to which it is accustomed, over that which is remote or out of the ordinary. Only sustained reasoning and a steady calmness of temperament can overcome the natural vivacity and attractiveness of the close-at-hand, and although these qualities are of course to be found in various degrees in different people, they are not ones that Hume usually regards as frequently encountered or especially strong. Experience confirms that people—"unjust and violent as men commonly are"—will naturally choose immediate advantage over justice, when (as is likely) they have a clearer idea of the former (T. 426). "Accordingly we find in common life, that men are principally concern'd about those objects, which are not much remov'd either in space or time, enjoying the present, and leaving what is afar off to the care of chance and fortune. Talk to a man of his condition thirty years hence, and he will not regard you. Speak of what is to happen tomorrow, and he will lend you his attention" (T. 428-29). The difficulty, according to Hume's psychology, of rendering a distant, imaginative interest efficacious as a present motive leads him in the second *Enquiry* to repudiate explicitly efforts to derive morality from the "self-love" hypothesis.[116]

It is, however, real people in "common life," confronted frequently by such opposition between their "real," present interests and the distant, "imaginary" ones promised by observance of the artificial virtues, who are required to be just and law-abiding. Doubts regarding the efficacy of reasoned self-interest appear openly when Hume discusses the origin of government, in a section where its function is portrayed as principally that of enforcing the rules of justice. Men are, Hume repeats, "in a great measure, govern'd by interest"; and furthermore the "interest, which all men have in the upholding of society, and the observation of the rules of justice," is both great and evident. But if this is the case, why do we find in experience such a constant tendency to disorder and the violation of rules; or, why does a coercive agency appear to be universally necessary to ensure justice on a wide scale, so as to accomplish its ends? The answer is that "men are mightily govern'd by the imagination" (T. 534), an observation that

[116] Hume, *Enquiries* (II), p. 217.

leads directly to a view of human behavior that is incompatible with the previous claim that the motive of self-interest along with the "palpable" advantages of justice are sufficient to explain its existence. "This is the reason why men so often act in contradiction to their known interest; and in particular why they prefer any trivial advantage, that is present, to the maintenance of order in society, which so much depends on the observance of justice. The consequences of every breach of equity seem to lie very remote, and are not able to counterballance any immediate advantage, that may be reap'd from it" (T. 535). Hume's solution to the problem in this section is the establishment of government, founded on rules of allegiance, for the purpose of guaranteeing the observance of justice. This solution also has difficulties, since allegiance is an artificial, rule-based virtue of the same order as justice, and it might be thought to involve similar problematic issues of motivation. In the case of government, however, Hume in his treatment of origins quickly abandons the abstract model of interest and deliberate choice and turns to a historical picture of war and evolution that does not suffer from the problems that accompany the thesis of rational self-interest, on which he relies more exclusively in the case of the origins of justice.

The thesis of self-interest seems to fail in the first place, then, on a psychological ground internal to Hume's science of human nature. Reason, or simply the ability to engage systematically in Hume's restricted conception of correct reasoning, is not to be counted on. Even if it were true that the artificial virtues are actually and always in the long-range interest of every individual, the usual features of the human mind would indicate that (whatever may be the case concerning hypothetical or reflective agreement) the actual realization of such interest is unlikely.

The second objection concerns a logical rather than a psychological problem, one that has beset the theory of justice as a convention of self-interest ever since Glaucon first expounded it in Plato's *Republic*. Hitherto we have accepted Hume's premise that the rules of justice and allegiance are in the interest of each person taken separately, questioning only whether people as they are could be counted on to act with an eye to such a remote and nonvivid object. Doubts, however, may be cast on this premise, as Hume knows. It may indeed be true that a rationally self-interested individual would acknowledge that general observance of the artificial virtues would be to his own advantage (and to that of others), that is, that a general adherence to justice would provide him with security of possessions and expectations and increase the probability that any of his private goals will be attained. (Surely a person is likely to be better off than if there were no such rules.) More precisely, however, it seems that it would be advantageous if the rules of justice were obeyed by and large, and especially by others; but it is not at all clear that anyone has an interest in their uniform and inflexible observance or that a person would be better off by obeying them on every occasion. Only under special conditions would someone perceive a personal interest in abiding by rules whose general observance one acknowledges to be beneficial, to whose establishment one would agree, and to the upholding of which one would exhort others.

Hume occasionally speaks as though a sufficient condition for the congruence of every private interest with the common interest were always met by the very nature of justice: this would be the case if the benefits of a system of justice would be lost unless observance were complete and constant. Hume (fallaciously) compares the mutual "convention" by which self-interested men are said to agree on rules of justice with the case of two men who row a boat, a project that they pursue "for common interest, without any promise or contract" and that requires that each participant do his part without shirking.[117] But systems of justice, unlike rowing a boat, involve large numbers of people, and they remain generally advantageous even if single individuals violate the rules, so long as most people observe them. Furthermore, in a large society, in contrast to the case in which only two participants must cooperate, a single individual is not likely to be constantly in view of the other participants in the system, and it is a matter of experience that a person will occasionally be in situations not only in which his personal interest seems to lie in a violation of a rule but also in which it is likely that such a violation can be committed undetected. This (egoistic) logic is apparent in positive cooperative enterprises as well as in the problem of obedience to rules:

> Two neighbours may agree to drain a meadow, which they possess in common; because 'tis easy for them to know each others mind; and each must perceive, that the immediate consequence of his failing in his part, is the abandoning the whole project. But 'tis very difficult, and indeed impossible, that a thousand persons shou'd agree in any such action; it being difficult for them to concert so

---

[117] Ibid., p. 306; also *Treatise*, p. 490. This image is similar to that of the vault in contrast to the wall, as representing justice in contrast to benevolence. Boat-rowing, in addition, involves only a tacit coordination of efforts, whereas justice—although the desirability of *some* scheme may be immediately obvious—requires agreement on *specific* rules, which need to be spelled out. See note 115 above.

complicated a design, and still more difficult for them to execute it; while each seeks a pretext to free himself of the trouble and expence, and wou'd lay the whole burden on others. (T. 538)

It is therefore not the case that "every individual person must find himself a gainer, on ballancing the account; since, without justice, society must immediately dissolve" (T. 497). Society would dissolve only if large numbers of people broke the rules; and an individual may sometimes lose, rather than gain, by acting justly. Hume himself briefly acknowledges this problem, in relation to justice, in his brief reference to the "sensible knave," who sees that "an act of iniquity or infidelity will make a considerable addition to his fortune, without causing any considerable breach in the social union" and who will therefore take advantage (when he can) of exceptions to the rule that "honesty is the best policy." He offers no answer to this reasoning other than an appeal to moral feelings.[118]

It is apparent that in a society of rational egoists, each reasoning according to this pattern, the artificial virtues—although they would be acknowledged to be such—could not be realized, and the motive of self-interest offers no remedy. The logic of the situation is that of the "collective goods" problem in economic theory. The goods achieved by the implementation of a system of artificial virtues, of which peace and social order are the most characteristic, are public and indivisible— goods that, if they are provided at all, will be enjoyed by everyone indifferently, regardless of whether or not one makes any personal contribution to their realization. Seeing this, the rational individuals of this model would have no incentive to observe the prescriptions of the artificial virtues as a matter of course, and especially if in particular circumstances there were any personal cost in so doing, though they would admit to the desirability of general compliance with the pre- scriptions. This logic is often applied to the difficulties encountered in generating positive efforts or contributions from the potential bene- ficiaries of some scheme or project;[119] but it applies equally to the case

[118] Hume, *Enquiries* (II), pp. 282-83. See also note 31 above. Miller, *Philosophy and Ideology*, p. 81, accepts Hume's (improbable) claim that every individual gains from the inflexible observance of justice, and he therefore holds that government is necessitated only by imperfect rationality.

[119] Mancur Olson, Jr., *The Logic of Collective Action* (New York: Schocken, 1965), provides the best-known discussion. Olson argues that collective action to provide public goods becomes more difficult the larger the group, both because each individual's share of the good is smaller and because mutual surveillance and the imposition of penalties on would-be free riders is more difficult (or costly). The need for rules of justice arises, for Hume, in a large society.

where the potential good is simply the order that would result from regulations of conduct, and where the contribution required is mere obedience to rules or abstention from certain actions. Even enlightened self-interest in its pure form, then, is inadequate as a general motive for artificial virtue. At most it can explain only how in a reflective or disinterested moment each individual in a group of individuals might agree in principle that justice would be to their common advantage, and this is all that Hume can be taken to have shown in his account of the "origin" of this virtue.[120]

There are, however, two further factors that may modify the situation of the hypothetical egoist and that may accordingly influence the egoist's motivation. The concern for one's reputation or the esteem of others (a source of pleasure and pride) has been emphasized by some commentators on Hume and stressed as a sociable motive by the classic utilitarians.[121] Hume has no hesitation in granting that a reasonable pride is a valuable buttress to virtue and that sensitivity to others' opinions of us is a natural proclivity: "By our continual and earnest pursuit of a character, a name, a reputation in the world, we bring our own deportment and conduct frequently in review and consider how they appear in the eyes of those who approach and regard us."[122] Nor is a good reputation simply a source of pride: it may also be a prerequisite for taking part in and enjoying the benefits of the cooperative schemes that are made possible by the artificial virtues, since the participants in such schemes will avoid dealings with anyone who is generally known to be, or is suspected of being, dishonest or a shirker of obligations.[123]

The difficulty with reliance on this motive is that it is efficacious only in the case of public actions, or actions that the agent believes will be observed and commented upon. It is therefore a motive likely to be significant in maintaining the virtue of "good-manners," the conduct required by which takes place entirely under the eyes of others; and it no doubt plays a role in the supererogatory manifestations of

[120] Hume contributes, in these sections, to the "radical individualist" model that later became prominent in political economy and democratic theory. Hume is not always scrupulous in distinguishing his use of this *model* from adequate explanations of actual social phenomena. See J. Roland Pennock, *Democratic Political Theory* (Princeton: Princeton University Press, 1979), pp. 170-79.

[121] See T. H. Green, "Introduction" to Hume, *Works*, vol. 2, pp. 57-58, 67, 70. Bentham, *Morals and Legislation*, p. 238, argues that concern for reputation is a motive that is likely to coincide with utility.

[122] Hume, *Enquiries* (II), p. 276; also p. 265. See also "Of the Dignity or Meanness of Human Nature," *Works*, vol. 3, pp. 155-56.

[123] Baier, "Good Men's Women," p. 3-4.

allegiance, such as the quest for office and other public endeavors in support of the state. But it would not be a satisfactory answer to the objection of a Glaucon to the requirements of justice, where infractions can often be committed in secret, or in impersonal social contexts where one's reputation is not at stake. The very term reputation, of course, implies the possibility that the reality of virtue may be absent.

The factor of reputation thus seems simply to alter the terms of the egoist calculus in some instances without providing a convincing solution for the hard cases. Hume does offer one further elaboration of this theme: "This constant habit of surveying ourselves, as it were in reflection, keeps alive all the sentiments of right and wrong, and begets, in noble natures, a certain reverence for themselves as well as others, which is the surest guardian of every virtue."[124] Reverence for oneself (or self-respect) is evidently not a character trait that readily lends itself to analysis in the terms of the rational self-interest model. Hume suggests that it arises from the concern for reputation, but it is felt as an independent motive only when the esteem of others is no longer deliberately sought as a pleasurable object—when this kind of sensibility becomes so habitual as to influence conduct in situations when one's reputation is not actually vulnerable. This doctrine, which conforms to Hume's general psychology, may well illuminate one of the sources of the sense of duty that people ordinarily invoke in explaining virtuous conduct. The only difficulty with it is Hume's own reservation that such reverence, being restricted to "noble natures," cannot be counted on as a usual motive.

Aside from this detail, the element of reputation would modify the rudimentary dictates of self-interest only in certain limited types of social contexts. In particular, it would be efficacious in small groups, where everyone's conduct and probity are subject to scrutiny: it would provide an added incentive to the oarsman to contribute his fair share. But artificial rules are necessary precisely for the preservation of societies that are too extensive to be regulated by face-to-face incentives and impulses; impersonality is not only one of the attributes of artificial systems of rules but also a normal social condition of their necessity. If increasing impersonality of social relations implies a decreasing scope of mutual personal esteem, then the "love of fame" can serve only in a limited way as a motive to justice.

The second and more important factor that may be introduced into the rational-choice model is government, conceived as an agency whose

---

[124] Hume, *Enquiries* (II), p. 276. This is close to Adam Smith's position that people have the capacity to assume the perspective of an impartial spectator toward themselves.

function is to increase the probability that obedience to the rules will more often appear to be in the interest of each self-interested individual, mainly through the imposition of coercive sanctions, or the attachment of rewards and punishments to the prescribed and proscribed conduct. The role of government may be understood both as correcting people's natural tendency to mistake their interest by preferring the near to the remote, and as alleviating the logical difficulty that arises when individuals are assumed to be motivated solely by rational self-interest. A coordinating and coercive agency such as a government makes it likely that there will be general observance of the rules, so a given individual need not fear that his observance will be pointless or that he will be a dupe or "cully of [his] integrity" (T. 535); at the same time, by the threat of punishment for violations it gives him a special and tangible incentive to obey.[125] It is of course true that such an agency will be successful in effecting voluntary obedience to the rules of justice only to the degree that its potential sanctions are credible, and perhaps only so long as individuals believe that the benefits of justice are actually being provided.[126] Seen from this perspective government is a factor of the same order as concern for reputation— an additional circumstance taken into account by rational egoists; hence its efficacy in upholding a system of justice would not extend to violations that could profitably be committed entirely in secret, or to cases in which the egoist has no reason to believe that sanctions will be exercised. Governmental enforcement of the laws is costly, and indeed the costs might be prohibitive if everyone were disposed to

[125] Among others, Michael Taylor, *Anarchy and Cooperation* (London: John Wiley and Sons, 1976), pp. 118-28, presents this—basically Hobbesian—interpretation of Hume's theory of the state. Resort to coercive authority is said to be necessary because Humean justice is *not* (contrary to what Hume seems to say) a true convention but rather a public good, hence unstable, given rational self-interest. True conventions solve coordination problems, not prisoners' dilemmas, and therefore compliance with them (as well as initial agreement to them) occurs spontaneously. Taylor maintains that this distinction accords with Hume's own characterization of a convention as "only a general sense of common interest; which . . . [when] mutually express'd . . . produces a suitable resolution *and behaviour*" (T. 490, emphasis added). It also accords with modern technical usage, as in David K. Lewis, *Convention: A Philosophical Study* (Cambridge: Harvard University Press, 1969). For an argument that Hume is correct in supposing that justice would be established as a true convention, see Mackie, *Hume's Moral Theory*, p. 88.

[126] A system of coercive sanctions, altering the circumstances and scope of the alternatives among which an individual chooses, brings *voluntary* acquiescence according to Hume's concept of the "liberty" of action; in another sense it acts as a causal or determining factor, producing regular and predictable effects. Hume, *Enquiries* (I), pp. 97-98.

violate the rules whenever it seemed possible to do so with impunity; actual governments need to deal only with a limited criminal element, and they depend on most people's voluntary obedience to the laws, through the internalization of a sense of duty. Despite these limitations, however, there is no doubt that government fulfilling this function on a regular basis is a realistic (if costly) solution to the problem, the only possible solution, perhaps, if (as Hume assumes in these sections) self-interest were indeed the principal attribute of human nature.[127]

There remains the difficulty of conceiving how government itself is possible and can be effective under present assumptions. This problem is twofold: how can self-interested individuals, who would not observe the rules of justice alone, be expected to establish and support a government whose task is to compel them to be just? Further, how can the governors, who must also be assumed to be self-interested, be expected to confine themselves to their proper function in exercising the means of coercion? Hume takes up these issues in his section on the "origin" of government; his proposed solutions need to be considered because although Hume subsequently develops a more historical, evolutionary account of the actual origin and growth of states, he adheres to the maxim that in evaluating forms of government it is always prudent to assume that people *are* largely motivated by selfishness (even though this is not strictly true) and to take precautions accordingly.

An established government is sustained through conduct on the part of the citizens in accordance with the artificial virtue of allegiance, which prescribes (at least) loyalty to authority and obedience to law. The rules of allegiance are of the same type as those of justice, and if the citizens of a state are assumed to be motivated entirely by self-interest, we face the same difficulty of understanding how individuals would choose to abide by them. In the usual situation in which a government exists and commands a set of sanctions, this problem is of course diminished: the government enforces the rules of allegiance (thereby effecting its own perpetuation) in the same way and at the same time that it ensures observance of justice, which in this scheme is its principal purpose. The problem then is one of conceiving how

---

[127] Walter Berns, *For Capital Punishment* (New York: Basic Books, 1979), pp. 83-86, argues that "liberal legislators," having abandoned religion and traditional moral teachings and having encouraged the pursuit of self-interest, have been compelled to rely on punishment (deterrence) to secure obedience to law. On pp. 141-42, however, Berns acknowledges that liberal states have also relied on moral education, provided by private institutions.

the government could have originated, along with the contrivance of mechanisms to prevent abuses of power.

Hume proposes solutions to both these difficulties by invoking a distinction, which we have noted before, between the capabilities of human nature in a state of comparative reflectiveness and its inclinations when directly confronted by objects in which it is interested. The doctrine of people's "incapability" of preferring remote to contiguous objects refers only to the latter situation; when reflecting (that is, reasoning calmly) on objects, whether near or remote, one always "resolve[s] to prefer the greater good," even if in the event the intervention of closer and more vivid objects of desire hinders one's adherence to the original resolution. Further reflection on experiences of this sort, moreover, makes us aware of such weaknesses in our nature and leads us to make second-order resolutions to seek out and take corrective measures (T. 536-37). In particular, people must discover some "expedient" by which they "lay themselves under the necessity of observing the laws of justice": under the guidance of reflective foresight, they must deliberately establish some institution or mechanism that on future occasions will confront them with a certain "necessity," a direct and strong incentive, to repress the inclination of the moment and obey the rules whose generally beneficial effects they acknowledge. Since we are unable to change our nature, we must "change our circumstances and situation, and render the observance of the laws of justice our nearest interest" (T. 537). It is rational and plausible that people, who can recognize their "infirmities" (and the self-defeating logic of their collective situation) but lack the capacity to correct them directly, should choose or vote to lay themselves under restraints—even unpleasantly coercive restraints—that they know will bind them for the future. Such a choice is a psychological possibility precisely because of the limitations of the imagination that necessitate it: the unpleasantness of the restraints in operation is a "remote" object at the moment of the choice to establish the machinery of restraint, which is thus, in respect to the course of action involved, a "reflective" moment.[128]

In Hume's account of "origins" people deliberately alter the circumstances of their future choices by the institution of government as a regulative and potentially coercive agency. More precisely, they el-

---

[128] Olson, *Collective Action*, p. 86. That people do make such choices is noted by students of the manner in which collective goods are attained through compulsory organizations. People also vote to enact laws that punish actions to which they realize they themselves may be tempted; this is perfectly rational and not hypocritical. Cf. John Rawls, *A Theory of Justice* (Cambridge: Harvard University Press, 1971), p. 249.

evate certain individuals into special positions—civil magistracies—by virtue of which they are empowered to adjudicate and enforce the rules of justice.[129] The problem of the restraint of the governors is solved by a similar manipulation of circumstances: the offices and powers of government must be so arranged that the magistrates, kings, or rulers "have no interest, or but a remote one, in any act of injustice" but have an "immediate interest in every execution of justice" (T. 537). The history of Cromwell suggests that the prospect of power creates temptations to crime that are "in general irresistible to human nature"[130] and bears out the general thesis that "those, whom we chuse for rulers, do not immediately become of a superior nature to the rest of mankind, upon account of their superior power and authority" (T. 552). For this reason the artifice embodying the virtue of allegiance must contain subsidiary rules limiting the exercise of the power it establishes and channeling it in the proper directions.[131]

Hume does not tell us in his philosophical works exactly how this may be done effectively, although in his political essays he enters into the complicated practical problem of the most satisfactory constitutional design, showing himself to be a supporter of the English form of mixed government that many contemporary political scientists believed represented the best solution. The general point is that insofar as he entertains the hypothesis that self-interest is the motive to be counted on in understanding how the artificial virtues come to be

[129] Neither fear, nor resentment of the few by the many, is a motive in the establishment of government in this abstract account. Nor is any violence or coercion contemplated; it is a matter of rational individual choice, in keeping with the assumptions of the model, that takes account of the fact that rationality is limited by impulse. For Hume's dismissal of fear as the motive to be counted on, see "Of the First Principles of Government," *Works*, vol. 3, p. 111.

[130] Hume, *History of England*, chap. 57, vol. 5, p. 289.

[131] There is a significant ambiguity in the *Treatise* passage quoted above. Hume says that magistrates are persons who, "being satisfied with their present condition, and with their part in society, have an immediate interest in every execution of justice." If "present condition" is taken to refer to the previous social position of the persons elevated to magistracies, then Hume appears to be recommending that government be in the hands of members of a social class that has a special interest in the preservation of order and the existing rules of property. If, however, it is taken to mean their "present condition" *as* magistrates, then Hume appears to envision the convergence of private and public interest as coming about as a result of constitutional design, together with ambition on the part of some to seek the rewards of public offices, circumscribed as these are by contrived checks on power. The latter interpretation, which I find more plausible, is supported by Hume's further statement that people must (deliberately) "*render* the observance of justice the immediate interest of some particular persons" (T. 537, emphasis added).

realized, Hume is led by the logic of the argument first, to an acknowledgment of the necessity of government to fulfill an executive function with respect to the rules of justice; and second, to advocacy of a government internally contrived to ensure that the putatively self-interested governors are restricted to their appointed function. In all this Hume clearly belongs to a conspicuous tradition of Anglo-American political thought that extends from Hobbes to *The Federalist* and beyond. These positions are also consistent with the general emphasis on "artifice" that is central to Hume's political theory: government conceived in this manner is a kind of secondary artifice erected to effect the operation of the most important of the artificial virtues and to secure its advantages.

This scheme far from exhausts Hume's understanding of the nature and role of government in creating the conditions of moral life, as we shall see, just as self-interest is not the sole or even the most important of the motives that activate individuals as Hume usually describes them. The foregoing account of government is presented, and should be understood, as an abstract model, utilizing simplified assumptions. On the other hand, self-interested desire constitutes one real tendency of human nature, and governments do exercise the coercive, situation-altering role that this model assigns them. Hence this account provides a partial explanation of the manner in which the artificial virtues are established and social life preserved. It is not a complete account, however, nor is it the one that is most consistent with the doctrines of human nature that are most distinctive of Hume's work as a whole, a fact that conspicuously differentiates his political theory from that of Hobbes. Government itself, Hume says in a passage to be considered shortly, rests ultimately on opinion, and especially on that "opinion of right" or habitual sense of moral obligation through which the virtue of allegiance is realized beyond what could be attributed to a government's actual coercive sanctions; and it is to the source of this "opinion" and habitual obedience that we must now look.

The final objection to the thesis that self-interest is the effective motive of the artificial virtues is drawn from experience, and it brings us back to our point of departure—to the "sense of duty" or regard for virtue as such that Hume recognizes as the spontaneous response of most people to queries about their reasons for being just. One difficulty with the argument that individuals observe moral rules because it is in their interest to do so is that it overlooks the quality of virtue and the attendant sense of moral obligation that are features of these rules as they are ordinarily apprehended. The sense of the virtue of justice, or its rightness, is an evaluation that in Hume's moral psychology is constituted by a particular kind of feeling; and this feeling (approbation) needs to be considered as a possible influencing motive of the will in cases where people deliberately conduct themselves in accordance with standards they regard as virtuous.

The air of paradox surrounding the theory of "self-love," Hume says, implies that it violates the safest rules of reasoning regarding the "operations of the human mind." In any case, the claim that interest is the usual motive to virtue is refuted by the evidence of experience, since we in fact approve and undertake actions that we realize are "prejudicial to our particular interest." On those occasions when our personal interest *does* happen to coincide with the requirements of virtue, moreover, we are conscious of the influence of two distinct sentiments or motives in our mind. Further, in the course of our moral life we commonly exhort others to adhere to ethical standards "without endeavoring to convince them, that they reap any advantage from the actions which we recommend to their approbation and applause."[132] All these considerations from the *Enquiry* elaborate the point made succinctly in the *Treatise* that although "*self-interest is the original motive to the* establishment *of justice*," it is neither the source of the "moral approbation" attending justice nor, by implication, the continuing motive for adherence to justice in particular cases following its establishment (T. 499-500). Evidence drawn from actual moral life suggests that the moral sentiments play a role in practical motivation, or that the feeling of approbation itself, apart from desire or aversion and distinct from the operation of sympathy, can be an efficacious factor in the realization of the artificial virtues. This thesis might account for the sense of moral duty in terms of which people often articulate the motives that underlie their upright behavior; and it provides a clue to how artificial virtue can prevail even in those conflicts in which neither sympathy nor self-interest seems to suffice. The investigation of the manner in which "regard to justice" itself (T. 479) can become a regular motive to justice in society leads to the final phase of the present inquiry into the sources of artificial virtue.

Hume's first thought on this matter, as we have seen, is of the "sense of duty and obligation" that most people acknowledge as a sufficient reason for keeping their engagements. Further reflection suggests, however, that this motive characterizes human beings only "in [their] civiliz'd state," when they are "train'd up" in a certain way (T. 479); it is not a natural motive, just as the virtues it sanctions are not natural, and it often manifests itself in opposition to spontaneous impulse.

---

[132] Hume, *Enquiries* (II), pp. 215-16, 299.

Failure to discover any natural motive adequate to account fully for justice, however, leads Hume to the conclusion "that the sense of justice and injustice is not deriv'd from nature, but arises artificially, tho' necessarily from education, and human conventions" (T. 483). A theory of moral education, it emerges, is essential to Hume's doctrine of the artificial virtues and thus to his understanding of political life, although he does not develop such a theory quite as fully as he does the alternative doctrines of sympathy and self-interest.

The significance of education in this connection is consistent with Hume's philosophy as a whole, and it serves as a main channel of continuity between his moral and political theory and his previous psychological conclusions regarding human nature. Hume's exploration of the normal functioning of the imagination, and of the manner in which ideas and beliefs are generated in the mind, leads him to an appreciation of the role of testimony, of the strength of received or customary opinion, and of the force of social communication in the formation of an individual's cognitive assumptions and convictions. From an individualist starting point Hume ends by concluding that "more than one half" of all our beliefs are derived from education, which may be construed as a special variety of experience, achieving its effects through special application of the basic imaginative propensities of association, habit, rule-following, and so forth (T. 116-17). Likewise, in the analysis of passions, Hume passes from the enumeration of the various feelings of which an individual is capable to the social dimension in which most of the passions are manifested. Relying principally on the mechanism of sympathy, but drawing as well on habit and other factors that serve to enliven and direct the course of our perceptions, Hume develops in the sphere of the passions—and thus also in morals—as in that of beliefs a theory of communication by which an individual appears as a member of a community, sharing in its common stock of feelings, values, and concerns. There is hence a parallelism in the development of Hume's views regarding natural sociability—or the psychic capacity for such sociability—in both parts of his analysis of the mind; his conclusions combine into a broad view of human educability, or susceptibility to social influence, that provides the ground for claims regarding the function of education in moral life. In the sphere of morals, it may be added, the tenor of Hume's remarks on education undergoes a subtle but significant change. In Book I of the *Treatise*, while noting the practical inescapability of reliance on testimony Hume warns that education is frequently the source of erroneous beliefs, which are properly subject to the standards of critical reasoning (T. 117). In the sphere of the artificial virtues the principle of utility likewise provides a basis for reasoned criticism of moral conventions; but since this standard is imprecise, and since artificial moral life in any event requires practical acquiescence in uniform conventions, the role of education (and thus of traditional beliefs) appears to be less suspect and even more inescapable. In any event, the "discipline and education" in the passages cited above are topics for which we are prepared, and in examining the role of education in moral and political life we shall at the same time see how some of the important themes of the preceding investigations are integrated into Hume's political theory.

A consideration of education will also clarify one of Hume's best-known comments on the problematic fact of governmental authority: "Nothing appears more surprizing to those, who consider human affairs with a philosophical eye, than the easiness with which the many are governed by the few, and the implicit submission, with which men resign their own sentiments and passions to those of their rulers."[133] The first answer that comes to mind—that they are ruled by force—is not satisfactory: force, Hume contends, is usually (by virtue of sheer numbers) on the side of the governed; and even in those cases in which a ruler such as the sultan of Egypt or the emperor of Rome does appear to control a subject population by means of armed force, the question remains how the ruler retains the support of his mamelukes or praetorian bands. These considerations lead Hume to conclude that "It is therefore, on opinion only that government is founded,"[134] opinion in favor of the system of rule, even if it is confined to members of the ruling group. To any people not actually in revolt or under coercive threats or constraints may be imputed an opinion supportive of authority, even if the opinion is so inarticulate that obedience to authority may be appropriately described as "implicit submission," which Hume suggests is frequently the case. On the other hand, as *The Federalist* authors argue (alluding to Hume), even "the most rational government" must concern itself with fostering, and avoid undermining, the favorable opinion that adds "reverence for the laws" to rational assent.[135]

The argument is elaborated by Hume's further claim that the relevant opinion may be of three kinds. It may be an opinion of interest—of the "general advantage which is reaped from government; together with the persuasion, that the particular government, which is estab-

---

[133] Hume, "Of the First Principles of Government," *Works*, vol. 3, pp. 109ff.

[134] Ibid., p. 110.

[135] *The Federalist*, with an introduction by Edward Mead Earle (New York: Modern Library, n.d.), no. 49 (Hamilton or Madison), p. 329.

lished, is equally advantageous with any other that could easily be settled." This kind of opinion supports government to the same degree that self-interest may be accepted as a viable motive for the artificial virtues. The other two kinds of opinion concern "right." Opinion regarding "right to property," or the rightfulness of the rules of property associated with a given regime, is an indirect source of support to government insofar as property (or economic matters generally) is "of moment in all matters of government."[136] More important, in Hume's view, is opinion regarding the governing authorities' "right to power" as such: people are often "prodigal both of blood and treasure" in expressing their allegiance to a rightful government. These two latter kinds of opinion, being of "right" in contrast to interest, are opinions regarding values and obligations: they are convictions or judgments that a particular system of authority is such that obedience to it constitutes an expression of the virtues of justice and allegiance, and that disobedience would constitute an infringement of a moral obligation.

This doctrine is a reformulation of the point that the rules of justice and allegiance and the other artificial virtues depend in the last resort on a "regard for justice" itself, or an "opinion of right," for their realization. Indeed, the existence of society itself, and not only of governments, depends on common convictions regarding this kind of virtue. It is to discover the sources of this "opinion," or of the "moral incentives" that must complement or even supersede the interests of individuals, that we must look into the potentialities of education.[137]

The artificiality of virtues such as justice and allegiance suggests that they, like the rules and practices through which they are manifested, are the products of convention (or perhaps, as Hume notes some skeptics have held, of invention), thus arising from education and "afterwards encouraged, by the art of politicians, in order to render men tractable." Hume agrees: "precept and education, must so far be owned to have a powerful influence" that it can not only alter the intensity of moral feelings but even occasionally "create, without any natural principle, a new sentiment of this kind."[138] In the

---

[136] Hume criticizes Locke's theory of property rights and their relation to government; "Of the First Principles of Government," *Works*, vol. 3, p. 111; and *Treatise*, pp. 491, 505n. D. D. Raphael argues that Hume's emphasis on rules of property in his treatment of justice reflects a desire to confront Locke; "Hume's Critique of Ethical Rationalism," in *Hume and the Enlightenment*, ed. Todd, p. 18.

[137] Cf. Olson, *Collective Action*, p. 61n.

[138] Hume, *Enquiries* (II), p. 214. Although moral institutions are conventional, however, Hume's argument here is that they must ultimately draw on the basic (and real)

Enquiry education is viewed as forwarding and enlarging the spontaneous tendency of all people to sympathize with the happiness of others and thus to approve of whatever conduces to this end. In the *Treatise*, similarly, after arguing that sympathy is the source of the moral approbation attending justice, Hume goes on to assert that the natural "progress of the sentiments" must be "forwarded by the artifice of politicians, who ... have endeavour'd to produce an esteem for justice, and an abhorrence of injustice" (T. 500). In both works Hume, acknowledging that sympathy alone and unguided is insufficient as a source of motivation for the artificial virtues, calls on education as the means by which the natural tendencies of sympathy may be harnessed and put at the service of the social necessity of judgments in accordance with rules.

The association of education with sympathy is Hume's first suggestion concerning the method by which education achieves its effects. The generalized sympathetic capacity of the *Enquiry* needs to be disciplined in such a way that it tends to be activated by the prospect of collective well-being that is the objective of the specific moral rules of a given society. Education seen in this perspective must render habitual the reasoning that proceeds from the rule to the intended beneficial consequences so that a vivid conception of the end-state, and the ensuing feeling of approval, will be each individual's ready mental response to any instance of rule-application. Each particular system of justice or allegiance, embracing both ends and means that differ in details from those that characterize other systems, will require a supportive educational program designed to direct the approbatory feelings naturally aroused through sympathy toward its own distinctive goals, and thence toward the rules that it ordains as means to those goals.

The problem posed in the *Treatise* is somewhat different, corresponding to the treatment of sympathy there as a variable mechanism for enlivening passions. Here the function of education is to regularize, as much as possible, sentiments generated sympathetically, mainly through the strengthening of the natural (though inconsistent) rule-following propensity of the imagination, which must be harnessed in the service of the rules of conduct prescribed by artificial virtue. This propensity is the imagination's tendency to conceive of conditions and sequences as extending beyond our actual impressions of them, a

---

moral sentiment that finds utility "pleasing." This passage therefore contains a criticism of those dogmatic moral skeptics (Mandeville may be intended) who denied the reality of genuine morality or moral motives.

psychic function with close affinities to the even more important principle of custom; as Hume applies it in his analyses of both the understanding and the passions the rule-following propensity is in continual tension with the equally prominent principle of the differential impact on the mind of vivid and faint perceptions, near and remote objects. In Hume's theory of moral judgment such a rule-following or generalizing capacity is requisite to the reasoning from cases to rules and from rules to distant ends that forms part of the reflective justification of the artificial virtues. More important for motivation is the possibility that this capacity may be brought to bear on the moral sense directly so that feelings of approbation come to be attached habitually to the artificial virtues, and to the rules of conduct and character traits they prescribe, with sufficient tenacity to overcome the influence of more immediate objects. Our feelings, including our sympathetic and our moral feelings, are naturally in a constant state of "fluctuation" and "contradictions," corresponding to our continual change of circumstances. Morality, however, especially in the case of the artificial virtues, requires a "more *stable* judgment of things" (T. 581). The regularity demanded in a common moral life, and especially in the public enunciation of our judgments, forces us to learn to control the spontaneous impulses of our feelings and "correct" the natural variability of sympathy, the principal determinant of our feelings toward other people (T. 603). In the case of the rules of chastity in particular, Hume notes, where legal enforcement is impracticable and temptations to transgress the rules are forceful, moral education makes special use of the imagination's propensity to follow general rules, extending them beyond the point apparently required by utility (T. 572-73).

We learn to live both in our physical and in our social environment by developing expectations, sometimes so strong as to be indubitable, regarding regularities of causes and objects; we conceive the world as displaying order of this sort by virtue of the generalizing ability of the imagination activated under the influence of repeated experience. Likewise in the moral world, through the exercise of the same faculties, we must achieve a similar regularity of mental processes—a regularity of evaluative rather than cognitive judgment, or a regularity of feeling and volition toward certain kinds of objects. The mind through natural propensities confers order and stability on moral as on other kinds of experience, bringing rules and coherence to the discontinuities of its perceptions, and overcoming its own contrary disposition to fasten on the particular, the vivid, the "miraculous." From this perspective a moral education, in which we learn what sorts of moral judgments are appropriate in given circumstances, provides the repeated experience necessary for moral rules to be internalized and fixed in the imagination as a guide for the natural moral or approbatory sentiment, just as our uniform experience of physical regularities generates the strong habits of expectation that govern the feeling constitutive of causal belief. The disciplining of our social feelings and control of their manifestations are largely the product of social intercourse and communication. Conceived broadly as education, such discipline can be formal or informal; the important thing is that individuals be confronted with a moral environment stable enough in its advocacy of and adherence to the artificial virtues that they absorb its standards, which accordingly take a place among the other perception-governing principles of the imagination.[139]

Moral experience can never, perhaps, be so uniform and vivid as to yield habits of artificial virtue strong enough always to overcome contrary impulses—let alone as strong as the basic habit of belief in the regularity of nature. Hume does not envision the complete superseding of the natural by the artificial virtues; natural feelings, moral and otherwise, persist in potential opposition to social rules. This tension is one of the inherent antiutopian features of Hume's political theory, along with his epistemological objections to theories of perfectibility. Education will have performed its function if unruly feelings can be successfully suppressed, although not obliterated, when they conflict with moral rules, to the degree necessary for the preservation of acceptable social order; and Hume believes this is generally the case, although he recognizes that "the *heart* does not always take part with those general notions" (T. 603).

In another passage Hume connects the learning process associated with artificial virtues with the learned conventions of speech: "Experience soon teaches us this method of correcting our sentiments, or at least, of correcting our language, where the sentiments are more stubborn and inalterable. . . . Such corrections are common with regard to all the senses; and indeed, 'twere impossible we cou'd ever make use of language, or communicate our sentiments to one another, did we not correct the momentary appearance of things, and overlook our present situation" (T. 582). Hume's observations on language, and on the relations between words and perceptions, are few, but the suggestion here seems promising: psychological tendencies such as custom and rule-following apply to words as well as to ideas and

---

[139] Cf. Bernard Williams, *Morality: An Introduction to Ethics* (New York: Harper and Row, 1972), p. 6, on the internalization of moral rules.

passions; and systems of artificial virtue are by their very nature, as Hume also notes, marked off by a specialized and consistent moral vocabulary, itself conventional and a common social possession, the correct use of which is learned by individuals as members of a particular society.[140] The implication here that acquiescence in the rules of artificial virtue is not infrequently restricted to the level of speech is testimony to the difficulty of modifying human nature in the direction required by social life. Although the correction of language (and so of express judgments) is certainly one of the ends that education must accomplish, however, Hume holds more fundamentally that sympathy and feeling can themselves be guided to the proper general objects, through habituation and education, sufficiently to effect a reasonably constant observance of rules.

Hume suggests that education can, in addition to directing feeling, perform a role of clarification with regard to the utilitarian basis of the artificial virtues, an enterprise to which can be attributed some further impact on motivation. The artificial virtues are contrived to serve social purposes, and they are justified, on reflection, in terms of their utility in achieving these ends. The reflective state Hume sometimes invokes, it is true, cannot plausibly be expected to accompany every instance in which a moral judgment is made or an action undertaken in accordance with a moral duty.[141] Nevertheless, the reasoning process that grasps both the nature of the social ends and the instrumental relation of the rules to those ends, however perfunctory it may be in most cases, cannot be dismissed entirely as an influencing factor on the will; and to the extent that the role of reasoning may be enlarged in everyday moral life, there is further scope for the influence of education. This argument, furthermore, may be radically extended within the utilitarian structure of Hume's analysis to the point where beliefs about what is good, and the classification of objects that the individual members of a society regard as desirable, are the products of a common education.

Two cognitive problems, regarding ends and means, present potential obstacles to a person's grasp of the rationale of the rules constituting the artificial virtues. Some apprehension of the meaning or

---

[140] A common interpretation is that the meaning of words for Hume must be entirely private, precluding communication; see Antony Flew, *Hume's Philosophy of Belief* (London: Routledge and Kegan Paul, 1961), p. 39. But Hume says in passing that languages are established by convention: *Treatise*, p. 490; *Enquiries* (II), p. 306. See Pall S. Árdal, "Convention and Value," in *David Hume: Bicentenary Papers*, ed. Morice, pp. 51-68.

[141] Hume, *Enquiries* (II), p. 203.

purpose of the constraints and duties that one is called on to acknowledge, however, would appear to be a necessary concomitant of a sense
of duty in effecting right practice. Some conception of the structure
of the artifice in question is one of the features that distinguish a sense
of artificial duty from the natural impulses of the moral sense, and
some form and degree of education must therefore be supposed as the
source of the relevant ideas, arranged in a coherent and convincing
manner.

It is of course possible that the relation between artificial virtue and
social benefits might be so obvious that the learning process is spontaneous and passive (as is the process by which everyone learns to
expect the future to resemble the past) and that no special institutions
are required for this purpose. Hume sometimes speaks as though this
were the case, as with respect to the practice of promising, and he
accordingly suggests that acquiescence in the scheme is spontaneous
(T. 522). This account, however, is too facile, and indeed it contradicts
an earlier observation. The end made possible by all the artificial
virtues (especially justice) is the very possibility of social life on an
extensive and orderly basis. The advantages of social over savage life,
however, are not fruits to be enjoyed immediately in their fullness but
rather the products of indefinite growth and the increasing refinement
that a stable society permits; they are, moreover, advantages the recognition of whose source in a rule-governed society is a matter of
sophisticated analysis. People in "their wild uncultivated state" would
not be "sensible of these advantages" (T. 486); and the intellectual
problem would appear to be as great within an ongoing society as it
would be in Hume's conjectural presocial situation. The artifices of
moral life are complex, obscure, and generally taken for granted.
Within society, however, there can be a solution to this problem in
education, whereby the outlines of a reasoned understanding of social
rules and benefits can be communicated and rendered habitual as an
element of thought and belief. This educative process begins with the
training that children undergo by the authority of their parents (T.
486), although moral convictions increase in tenacity as they seem to
the agent to be corroborated by experience over and above testimony
and precept. The socialization process that Hume sketchily portrays
includes the direct instillation of patterns of behavior, or the formation
of character by what is today called conditioning. At least part of the
process, however, is cognitive: society requires that its members be in
some degree "sensible" of the nature of the ends whose attainment it
permits, and such awareness is perpetuated in each generation by
education.

If we turn from the general end of peace and order, achieved by systems of moral rules in all societies, to the more specific content of the rules adopted by different societies, the function of education becomes more precise and more indispensable. Part of the meaning of the "artificiality" of such virtues as justice and chastity is the variability and alterability that these rules, like forms of government, display. Rules are accompanied by a sense of moral obligation insofar as they are generally approved, and since the means to an end are approved insofar as they are understood to be serviceable, each system of artificial virtue must be accompanied by a program of education designed to acquaint people with an understanding of the putative usefulness of these particular rules.

Hume was aware of contentions about the *mere* conventionality—in the sense of arbitrariness or "relativism"—of all manners, morals, and institutions. He explores this theme, traditionally associated with philosophical skepticism, most vividly in a short, dramatic comparison between the morals of the ancient Greeks and those of the moderns, the French in particular. After recounting a number of shocking practices (homosexuality, suicide, infant-exposure, tyrannicide, and the like) acceptable among the ancients, and noting that various modern practices would have seemed equally distasteful to them, Hume's friend in the "Dialogue" concludes that "fashion, vogue, custom, and law [are] the chief foundation of all moral determinations."[142] Hume agrees that there is great diversity among the moral beliefs of different peoples; but he contends that if one traces matters "a little higher" and examines first principles, one can perceive underlying similarities. Not only would the ancients and moderns agree on a wide range of virtues (including natural virtues, natural abilities, and "fidelity" and "truth" from Hume's category of "justice"), but furthermore all the practices condemned by the modern moral sensibility can be explained either as understandable responses to special circumstances or as designed to achieve ends of which we would approve by means different from those we would choose. Hume concludes that "the principles upon which men reason in morals are always the same; though the conclusions which they draw are often very different."[143] There are no moral beliefs or social institutions so bizarre that they do not display a similar structure of validation in terms of utility and that they cannot be seen to depend on certain "original principles" or "primary sentiments,"

[142] Hume, "A Dialogue," in *Enquiries*, p. 333.
[143] Ibid., pp. 335-36.

that is, those that respond to a prospect of general happiness and approve of social rules that are believed to conduce to this end.

It nevertheless remains true that on any view short of the most general, disparities in moral beliefs among societies are often more conspicuous than uniformities. It is distinctive systems of artificial virtue that principally set one society off from others and confer on it its special identity. The general end of the preservation of society and secondary ends such as the stability of property and the provision of defense may all be served well enough (in the eyes of those who live under them) by a great variety of different rules, indeed by rules and institutions that are sometimes directly contrary to ones that contribute to the same goals in other systems. This may be the consequence of the "peculiar circumstances" in which a given society finds itself or of different conclusions of collective reasoning, a circumstance that is not surprising in light of the complexity of causal relations and the diversity of historical experience. Above all, it is custom more often than deliberate choice that no doubt determines the specific content of most of the rules a society acknowledges and through which a largely implicit confidence in their utility is conveyed from one generation to another. The stability of any actual system of artificial virtue depends on sufficient motivation in the members of a society to approve and adhere to its particular rules rather than to any number of potential alternatives that might plausibly be held to accomplish the same ends. To the extent that this motivation arises from a conviction that certain particular rules are as good as (or better than) available alternatives in achieving their purposes, individuals must acquire such a belief, and their education must provide them with the reasons and evidence on which their belief is based.

All this is not to claim that artificial virtue depends on each individual's having a full understanding of the often complex justification of which acceptable moral rules are in principle susceptible; this capacity is reserved to the philosophically minded or the reflective, who Hume believes constitute a minority in any society. Nor is it to say that belief in the efficacy of moral rules must be uncritical: criticism and proposals for reform, which emanate from failures to find satisfactory justifications for this or that practice, are likewise the province of those who reflect at greater than usual length on them. It is, generally speaking, these reflective ones who serve as society's educators (and critics), making the understanding of the artifices and the mode of their justification accessible, at least in outline, to all. A rough grasp at least of the "interest of society" and of the means by which it is served, if joined to sympathetic feelings, can be construed as an effective element in moral motivation—though certainly not in itself a sufficient one.

With respect to "reflection" on interest and utility as this may figure as a component of motivation, it is reasonable to suppose that education may help to compensate for the peculiar "weakness" of the imagination—its propensity to be unduly affected by the near over the remote—that, as we have seen, constitutes one of the obstacles to the thesis that a large view of interest supports the artificial virtues. This is a cognitive problem, a matter of faulty reasoning, to which some are more subject than others; mental processes in Hume's account, however, are responsive to training and guidance, and there is reason to hope that through appropriate training the proportion of "calm" to "violent" passions, and with it the capacity for reasoning, may be increased among the members of a society. Such calmness or moderation is conducive to virtue in the realm of artificial social life, since the determination of duty depends on the studied "ascertaining" of "true interests" and the full circumstances of "public utility." The discerning of true rather than apparent interests is often difficult: Hume cites widely held but fallacious judgments on alms-giving to beggars, tyrannicide, liberality in princes, and luxury as examples of moral beliefs that arise from the confinement of attention to the more vivid proximate rather than long-range effects of the practices. The preferable rules of artificial virtue are those that pertain to distant consequences and that frequently stand opposed to the conclusions of a more restricted reasoning, as well as to natural impulse.[144]

The "sounder reasoning" required in cases such as these is the outcome of long experience, suitably reflected on by those so inclined. Education compiles and promulgates the more important conclusions of sound reasoning, broadening the common understanding of social and moral institutions. In view of the typical frailty of the human understanding, it is not likely that its improvement through any scheme of education can be expected to attain a state of perfection. There is no doubt, however, that Hume conceives his philosophical role as consisting in part in the effort to eradicate some of the more common misconceptions standing in the way of a calm view of social utility, and thus to remove one source of antagonism to the most salutary rules of morals and politics. How far he regards this enterprise as likely to be effective is doubtful. The story of Aristides and the Athenians, in which Hume sees "nothing so extraordinary," suggests

---

[144] Hume, *Enquiries* (II), pp. 180-81; Hume rejects alms-giving, tyrannicide, and liberality, and endorses luxury.

that it is only through the use of eloquence, and through the with-holding of certain information, that the dispassionate philosopher is able to guide the people to justice (their true interest) and persuade them to abstain from immediate advantage. Optimism is encouraged by this story only in the fact that the people acknowledge the authority and submit to the guidance of the philosopher (or educator) (T. 425-26).[145]

This story, with its suggestion that people embrace justice only in general terms, when apparent proximate interests to the contrary are not permitted to obtrude, reveals the limits to the effects that may be expected of education conceived as a process of clarification of the general ends at which the artificial virtues aim. The revelation of true interest will not always suffice to bring individuals' conduct into accordance with rules, unless through an arousal of moral feelings strong enough to overcome personal desires they can be brought to redirect their volition toward general objects. This observation brings us to a final consideration of the place of education in the theory of the artificial virtues, in which it is seen not simply as a corrective adjunct to the forces of sympathy and self-interest but as a force that works directly on the moral sense itself.

The "sense of duty" or "regard for justice" itself that upright citizens claim to feel may, in Hume's psychology, be thought of as a kind of artificial motive corresponding to and providing the normal practical basis for the artificial virtues. Just as these virtues are necessarily the product of artifice, manifested through adherence to rules contrived to meet society's needs, so the motives that typically permit their realization are also the effect of artifice. Just as governmental institutions, in one of their functions, constitute a kind of secondary artifice ensuring observance of the rules of justice, so the institutions of education may be regarded as another kind of secondary artifice—more diffuse and not always so formal, visible, or coercive—whose function is to mold the natural moral sense in such a way that its spontaneous responses and judgments are in accordance with the standards of the society in question.

Education, Hume says, is an important source of (artificial) moral distinctions, but it achieves its effects by working on more fundamental qualities of human nature. Sympathy and interest (both natural principles) can serve as sources of moral action when they are modified

---

[145] The story is from Plutarch's life of Aristides. The optimism encouraged by its outcome is limited by the fact that the Athenian people had, on a previous occasion, ostracized Aristides; one citizen voted for the ostracism because he was tired of hearing Aristides continually called "the Just."

in certain ways by education; but education in the sense of discipline and training in a regular moral environment may also be conceived, consistently with Hume's science of human nature, to attain its end more directly, through habituation of the natural faculty of approbation in the forms of conduct and evaluation considered by a society to be right. Habit is the principal element in Hume's account of mental life; and the maxim that "custom is the great guide of human life" finds here an application of equal centrality in Hume's moral theory as it receives in his theory of the understanding. Patterns of feeling and judgment wrought by artifice on the natural disposition of the mind to form habits of response are in the final analysis the surest foundation of the artificial virtues.

Some such view as this seems to underlie Hume's distinction between interest and morality as two separate foundations for the artificial virtues (T. 499-500, 523, 533). Hume argues that people have first of all an "obligation of interest" (a "natural" or prudential obligation) to obey the rules of justice upon observing "that 'tis impossible to live in society without restraining themselves by certain rules." An acknowledgment of interest, however, neither wholly accounts for observance of the rules nor fully explains the special feeling of *moral* obligation that accompanies them. Thus, Hume says, "afterwards a sentiment of morals concurs with interest, and becomes a new obligation upon mankind"; this is that sense of duty with respect to the moral rules on which such rules ordinarily depend. What is its source? "*Public interest, education,* and *the artifices of politicians,* have the same effect in both cases" (T. 523): these are the factors that both assist in teaching people their real interest (and its usual congruence with the general interest) and then accomplish the transformation of the sense of interest into the sense of moral duty. "The sense of morality in the observance of [the artificial] rules," Hume says elsewhere, though it tends to develop naturally (or spontaneously) with practice, is "augmented by a new *artifice,* and . . . the public instructions of politicians, and the private education of parents, contribute to the giving us a sense of honour and duty in the strict regulation of our actions with regard to the properties of others" (T. 533-34). This account makes clear the twofold structure of artifice that Hume sees in the realization of a virtue such as justice; it also identifies the formation of an autonomous sense of duty oriented toward artificial rules as a function of education. The sense of moral obligation, though it may follow an awareness of interest, is a distinct motive, just as the peculiar sentiment of approbation is distinguishable from other feelings in Hume's enumeration of passions. It is, or becomes, moreover, a stronger motive than interest, insofar as it actuates judgment and conduct in accordance with rules beyond the point that personal interest would dictate, and even in instances where personal desire is contrary. The development through education of this type of artificial or socialized moral sense establishes the "moral basis" necessary to the preservation of any regime, whether this term refers to government in a narrow sense (in which case allegiance is the virtue required) or to any system of artificial rules whose collective observance promotes the common good, though not always immediate private goods.[146] By this process virtues of a special order are brought into existence: artificial contrivances are invested with the quality of virtue or moral value and come habitually to be associated with feelings of approbation and duty in the minds of people, in whom there are thus generated motives adequate to right conduct.

As we should expect from Hume's view of human nature, habit and custom provide the principal dynamic in terms of which this training of the moral faculty is to be understood.[147] Although necessities and interests are found to stand behind every system of justice, it is nonetheless

> the influence of education and acquired habits, by which we are so accustomed to blame injustice, that we are not, in every instance, conscious of any immediate reflection on the pernicious consequences of it. ... What we have very frequently performed from certain motives, we are apt likewise to continue mechanically, without recalling, on every occasion, the reflections, which first determined us. The convenience, or rather necessity, which leads to justice is so universal, and everywhere points so much to the same rules, that the habit takes place in all societies; and it is not without some scrutiny, that we are able to ascertain its true origin.[148]

In his recognition of habituation in virtue as a central element in a practical science of morals and politics, Hume joins a venerable tradition of moral philosophy. Habit as a supplement to reason in the promotion of practical virtue has a prominent place in the classical

[146] Cf. Edward C. Banfield, *The Moral Basis of a Backward Society* (New York: The Free Press, 1958), esp. chap. 5, which describes the consequences of the absence of such an artificial moral basis.

[147] Cf. Friedrich Nietzsche, *On the Genealogy of Morals*, trans. Walter Kaufmann and R. J. Hollingdale (New York: Vintage, 1969), First Essay, sec. 1, on English [sic] psychologists and habit.

[148] Hume, *Enquiries* (II), p. 203.

doctrines of ethics that Hume admired;[149] the skeptical tradition in particular, with its doubts regarding cognitive claims and reasoning powers in general, not only carries this emphasis on the habitual or customary quality of moral life even further but frequently acquiesces in its propriety for practical purposes.[150] This theme likewise appears in modern literature, not only in the studies devoted explicitly to education and socialization but also in analytic treatments of obligatory institutions and rules of the sort that are clearly "artifices" in Hume's sense of the term. Rawls, for example, points to the function of training in connection with the "practice conception" of rules: children are initiated into a moral practice (learn "what it means to say 'I promise' ") by learning that obligatoriness is part of the concept of the rules defining the practice.[151] Flathman points to a motivational state brought about by training or education, intermediate between fully conscious "action" and merely conditioned "behavior," as the usual basis for adherence to rules, in particular those definitive of political obligation.[152] The conception of the respective functions of habit and reason in moral life in Hume's writings is similar: moral obligations are justifiable by a process of reasoning; the reasons are disseminated and arouse conviction as an aspect of education, and they may be sought out and reexamined in moments of doubt. In practice, however, agents observe moral rules more as a result of the training they have received, and its direct association of moral feeling with the rules, than because they are in command of convincing reasons for their actions. Education hence lays the moral foundations of a society in two ways: it extends as far as practicable the component of reason in moral judgments from the sphere of philosophical reflection to that of general awareness, in the process rendering a certain kind of reasoning itself a matter of custom; and it supplements the cognitive element with the direct habituation of the moral sentiments so that people confront the artificial rules and obligations of their society with the evaluative and volitional responses appropriate to moral virtue.

[149] See Aristotle, *Nicomachean Ethics*, trans. H. Rackham (New York: G. P. Putnam's Sons, 1934), esp. II.i and x.ix.6-13.

[150] See above, chapter I, notes 17 and 27, on the ancient skeptics' frequent acceptance of custom as their rule of life in practical affairs over and above their acknowledgment of its normal force in molding beliefs and practices.

[151] Rawls, "Two Concepts of Rules," p. 17.

[152] Richard E. Flathman, *Political Obligation* (New York: Atheneum, 1972), pp. 73-74. Cf. Gilbert Ryle on competence in the application of rules, developed through "training," an aspect of "knowing how" as opposed to "knowing that"; *The Concept of Mind* (New York: Barnes and Noble, 1949), p. 42.

This analysis of the artificial virtues in Hume's political theory leads, then, to the conclusion that moral education necessarily plays a role in the motivation of this kind of virtue if the envisioned practices and institutions are to be realized. Hume himself is brought to this conclusion, and although he does not develop a detailed theory of education, his psychology clearly contains suitable materials for such an enterprise. I conclude this discussion with mention of the practical means by which Hume suggests the educative function in society typically proceeds.

In speaking of the need for the "original motive" of self-interest to be transformed into a sense of moral duty, Hume alludes to the "artifice of politicians" as one of the means by which an "esteem for justice" is produced (T. 500). Politicians "talk of *honourable* or *dishonourable*, *praiseworthy* or *blameable*," thereby upholding through public speech the standards of virtue accepted in their country. Hume then immediately passes to the role of private education and the training that takes place in the context of the family, the arena in which each individual first learns the advantages of cooperation. Parents undertake to train their children in the valuation of the artificial institutions that maintain society as a whole, even though the rules thus inculcated prescribe impartial conduct and relations with which familial loyalties themselves may conflict (T. 500-501). In envisioning the family as an educative agency for the artificial virtues, Hume assumes that natural virtue is properly subordinated to the artificial, and that the family is integrated into the larger society; one can imagine societies in which the relation between the two spheres of life and the two kinds of virtue is more antagonistic and unstable than Hume here portrays it as being. Hume implies that it is largely the parents' sense of their children's interest that motivates them to instill a firm sense of justice in them; parents grasp that family members must learn to adapt to the general standards and requirements of society. Whatever the place of interest in the parents' motives, however, it is through habituation that the characters of children are formed to such a degree that appropriate moral responses occur with nearly as much regularity and conviction as the belief that the future will resemble the past: "By this means the sentiments of honour may take root in their tender minds, and acquire such firmness and solidity, that they may fall little short of those principles, which are the most essential to our natures, and the most deeply radicated in our internal constitution" (T. 501). A sentiment of honor is the sense of self-respect associated with the impulse to act justly out of a regard for justice itself; and the rooting of this special sentiment in the psychic constitution of a member of society provides the requisite artificial motive to social virtue.

Elsewhere Hume suggests a fuller meaning for the "artifice of politicians" that he mentions in the *Treatise* as a means by which a public sense of moral obligation is promoted.[153] Politicians or statesmen as part of their governing function contrive and perpetute a general system of education in virtue; indeed, the laws and public institutions of a society, which are administered, debated, and from time to time reformed by politicians, constitute as a whole an ongoing scheme of public education in artificial virtue. Hume's political science places substantial emphasis on the formative effects of political institutions and forms of government on the character of a people. More generally, any extensive public artifice, such as a government or a system of property, will tend through the training of the imagination and sensibilities of the people who live under it to elicit the kinds of habitual responses and conduct that are favorable to its operation. Hume occasionally speaks as though the educative function of the laws should be a conscious concern of the statesmen who are engaged in their formulation; he even evokes the classical image of the legislator-founder, who bequeaths to posterity a system of laws so designed as to be stable and self-perpetuating.[154] The legislator (in hand with the philosopher) engages in the critical enterprise with respect to the laws to which the artificial virtues, being grounded in utility and social needs, are always potentially subject. Reflective legislators, however, will also understand the importance of their role as educators, recognizing that the most solid foundation of government and justice lies in the formation of the people's moral sense, that "general virtue and good morals in a state . . . can never arise from the most refined precepts of philosophy, or even the severest injunctions of religion; but must proceed entirely

---

[153] This term suggests Mandeville, in whose view politicians must contrive ways of directing purely egoistic motives (vices) into publicly beneficial channels. See Bernard Mandeville, *The Fable of the Bees*, ed. F. B. Kaye (Oxford: Clarendon Press, 1957), vol. 1, pp. 51, 116, and passim. This doctrine is criticized in the *Treatise*, p. 500; for Hume statesmen work with a natural moral capacity, a moral sense. Cf. James Moore, "The Social Background of Hume's Science of Human Nature," in *McGill Hume Studies*, ed. David Fate Norton, Nicholas Capaldi, and Wade L. Robison (San Diego: Austin Hill, 1979), esp. p. 32.

[154] Hume, "Of Parties in General," *Works*, vol. 3, p. 127. See Forbes, *Hume's Philosophical Politics*, pp. 224-26, for Hume's emphasis on the impact of forms of government on character and social life; see also pp. 316ff. on Hume's invocation of the legislator, one of his few borrowings from the classical-Machiavellian tradition of political discourse.

from the virtuous education of youth, the effect of wise laws and institutions."[155]

I conclude this chapter with a few observations on the general view of society to which Hume is brought by this line of analysis. Society is held together by and depends on what Hume calls artifices, practices constituted by general and impartial rules that are effective because they have the obligatory force of moral virtues in the minds of the members of society. There is a sense in which these artificial institutions are not "natural" to the mind, and indeed on occasion they conflict with natural impulse and natural virtue. On the other hand, they are not as a rule, and not exclusively, maintained by the existence of coercive sanctions operating on self-interested motives but are able to draw support from a variety of other features of human nature as well. Society, though based on artifice, is "natural" in that it is the normal condition of human life, and people see this perfectly well; and their nature, although its immediate propensities are not always consistent with the requirements of social artifice, provides the materials that are readily molded into a social character. This process, together with the moral discipline that accomplishes it and the features of the public virtues and political institutions that are its outcome, is the central study of the moral part of Hume's science of human nature.

I have dwelt on the twofold structure of Hume's moral theory, with its central distinction between the natural and the artificial virtues. An emphasis on the dichotomous aspect of the theory is illuminating, since the special characteristics of systems of artificial moral rules determine the central problems of political philosophy. It would be misleading, however, to concentrate entirely on the contrasts and tension between artificial and natural, the requirements of social life opposed by the promptings of impulse. In discovering the motivational sources for the artificial virtues we find that Hume's psychological doctrines offer the means by which this gap may be at least partially bridged. Although artificial virtue is realized through the offices of supportive artifices, the formal and informal institutions of government and education, it is not the product simply of authoritative direction or manipulation of resistent individuals; rather, these institutions work on certain constitutive elements of human nature, which render the human character a malleable and potentially social one. In his moral theory as earlier in his studies of belief and of the passions, Hume's account of the mind carries him from his initial methodological individualism to a broad view of the social and political deter-

[155] Hume, "Of Parties in General," *Works*, vol. 3, p. 127.

minants of experience. In morals as in the two other areas the most important category for describing mental operations and experience turns out to be habit or custom, in this case the process by which people learn through practice the demands of collective life and assimilate the appropriate patterns of conduct and of judgment. Because the capacity to be affected by customary experience and practice, and to develop corresponding habits, is a natural attribute of the mind, the dichotomy between nature and artifice is less marked than might appear in an abstract analysis of the two kinds of virtue. The moral rules that make social life possible are indeed artifices, but the process of habituation by which each person learns their meaning and their moral status draws on the most basic natural propensity of the individual's mental constitution.[156] Through usage artificial virtue becomes "natural" in effect, as natural as the inductive reasoning regarding causes and effects in which regular patterns of experience permit us to engage with complete confidence. The sphere of habits forms what may be called people's second nature, and for Hume as for the ancient moralists it is in this sphere that the underpinnings of ethics and politics are located.

I have noted above, in the testimonial sources of belief and in the sympathetic contagion of passions, two of the ways in which Hume acknowledges the force of social communication in generating a person's experience. A common set of moral beliefs and institutions above all, however, is the defining feature of a particular society, and the common sharing in conceptions of virtue and obligation represents the principal tie between the minds of individuals and the society to which they belong. Individuals partake of a "national character," which is the link that constitutes succeeding generations as a single society;[157] and it is fundamental moral and political convictions that principally constitute such a collective character—the common sense of right on which artificial virtue is founded.

[156] Cf. Sheldon S. Wolin, "Hume and Conservatism," *American Political Science Review* 48 (1954): 1007.
[157] Hume, "Of National Characters," *Works*, vol. 3, pp. 248-49.

CHAPTER V

Skepticism and Politics

1. The Scientific Enterprise in Perspective

The task of this final chapter is to examine more fully the relations between Hume's epistemological and psychological doctrines and his political philosophy. The central problem concerns the implications of his skeptical philosophy of mind for political theory, a topic that has general significance insofar as Humean skepticism (and his manner of moving beyond it) represents a perennial philosophical conviction, with affinities to doctrines advanced repeatedly in the history of western thought. We have already observed several fundamental tensions or ambivalences in Hume's philosophy, including those between the skeptical critique of reason and the scientific enterprise, between skeptical criticism grounded in perpetual doubt and the complementary naturalism, and between the social necessity of reasoned artifice and the more fundamental nature comprising feeling and instinct. Hume's practical embrace of science, naturalism, and social artifice, in alliance with a mitigated form of skepticism, constitutes the philosophical and moral basis of the cautious and moderate constitutionalism that he advocates in his political writings, the consistency and defensibility of which are the principal issues in his political thought.

At the end of the last chapter we considered the importance of education, and the potential role of the philosopher as educator, in supporting social order and the morality of artifice. I now turn to the question of how Hume himself, a skeptical philosopher, approaches this task and to a consideration of the substance of his practical teaching. The political meaning of a philosophy of skepticism would appear to reside in the nature of the practical rule of life (in the terminology of ancient skepticism) that a skeptic like Hume adopts, and in some form he advocates publicly, in the aftermath of his skeptical doubts and despite his admitted inability to provide a full, rational validation of his beliefs. Hume of course went on, after his epistemological analysis, to pursue ethics, political philosophy, and history, all of these involving definite cognitive and moral commitments. In this he resembles others in the skeptical tradition who have frequently emphasized the need for rules of life in addition to the capacity for theoretical suspension of judgment, and who have sought to enunciate the rules that seemed to be most in accordance with their doubts regarding knowledge and reason. The skeptic like other people must live and therefore continues to be faced with the practical issues of belief, judgment, private virtue, and public rules of right conduct, notwithstanding his repudiation of dogmatic contentions. Hume calls himself a skeptic and advocates mitigated skepticism as a way of life; but unlike some of the famous skeptics of the past, he does not confine himself to raising doubts perpetually (like Pyrrho) or to reporting on the vagaries of his own imagination and feelings (like Montaigne). He clearly has positive doctrines to advance, doctrines both scientific and moral; and his concern with questions of style and presentation show him to have been interested in being widely heard and correctly understood. Like the other prominent philosophers of the Enlightenment, Hume assumes the role of a teacher of the public, frequently expressing his settled conviction that the reception of his doctrines would bring about a change for the better in the beliefs and in the way of thinking of his contemporaries, with correspondingly favorable consequences in practice. The doubts that he raises with respect to the potentialities of reason thus do not extend to doubt that he has discovered something of importance, or to doubts regarding the propriety and the benefits to be hoped for in the publicizing of his discoveries. Whatever doubts he may have entertained on these scores, at any rate, are effectively subordinated to the pursuit of a vocation as a public philosopher and, later, that of philosophical historian, in both of which roles he addresses himself prominently to political issues.

We must therefore consider more closely the positive and practical teaching in Hume's philosophy, looking into its relation to his skepticism, and inquire into the grounds of his evident conviction of the salutary qualities of his teaching. I argue in what follows that Hume's political doctrines are consistent with (although not strictly implied by) his theory of the understanding. Hume's political science, with its affinities to liberal theory and its conservative practical bearing, that is, follows from his analysis of knowledge and reason—from his skepticism and his ensuing adoption of a naturalistic solution to his doubts. This feature lends unity to the whole of his philosophy and strengthens its various parts; it also suggests that the political doctrines should be interpreted in light of the preceding account of human nature, in accordance with Hume's presentation. In this section I briefly review Hume's main philosophical doctrines and their relation to his science of human nature, arguing that Hume's scientific enterprise itself has a political significance in its educative intentions. In the following sections, I consider Hume's more specifically political teachings.

Hume's study of the human understanding leads him to the conclusion that the bounds of possible knowledge are narrower than was generally supposed by prevailing philosophic opinion, and his aim is to define the nature of these limits so that extravagant claims might be rejected and inquiries confined to the proper sphere. Hume concerns himself principally with the problematic area of our supposed knowledge of "matters of fact and existence," questioning the logical validity or ground of certainty with regard to any possible knowledge in this sphere beyond the immediate, private, and transient existence of our perceptions themselves. All knowledge of matters of fact beyond this depends on two great assumptions. All claims that we apprehend real objects that exist independently of ourselves assume that our sense impressions accurately represent such objects; all knowledge of things beyond what is immediately present to us—such as knowledge of the past and future, and of relations held to be generally true—assumes the validity of inductive inference, which in turn presupposes the uniformity of nature. The assumptions of objectivity and uniformity, however, themselves pertain to matters of fact. If their truth may be assumed, then one may, through careful attention to the evidence of experience and through adherence to strict rules of inference, engage in reasoning concerning matters of fact. In this respect Hume only urges methodological caution, grounded in an awareness that all knowledge based on experience (and especially predictions of the future) can only be probable, and a consequent openness to the possibility that any factual claim is subject to falsification or modification in light of further evidence. These modest admonitions, which follow equally from philosophical empiricism and from the reliance of common sense on experience, are at variance with the rationalist or doctrinaire impulse, common in politics in Hume's as well as in more recent times; and the exposure and dissipation of some of the dangerous effects of this impulse emerge as practical intentions in much of Hume's political and historical writing.

Further reflection reveals, however, that the two basic assumptions cannot themselves be validated by experience, the reliability of which they must be invoked to substantiate; nor is there, within Hume's perceptualist premises, any other means of confirming their truth. They are and remain, it appears, matters of belief, and the tenacity with which they are ordinarily held suggests to Hume that his further investigations into human nature might appropriately center on the capacity for belief and related psychological phenomena. In the meantime, however, the apparent lack of logical justification for these two "natural" beliefs occasions the skepticism that Hume presents as the inescapable conclusion of reflection on the understanding.

Hume's skepticism takes two different forms, which he most clearly distinguishes in his first *Enquiry* as Pyrrhonist (or "extreme") and Academic (or "mitigated"). Extreme skepticism consists in total doubt and suspension of judgment regarding all possible knowledge. With respect to Hume's own analysis, it involves doubting the fundamental assumptions regarding the external world and causality and hence all possible assurance about matters of fact beyond the immediate experience of a flow of impressions in our minds; it also involves doubts regarding the rational basis of moral judgments, although Hume argues this point more briefly and with greater equanimity, since he holds that morality, originating in sentiment and convention, is not seriously threatened by the critique of reason. The Pyrrhonist rehearses the famous skeptical arguments of the *Treatise*—arguments that are "indeed difficult, if not impossible, to refute," thereby throwing all reasoning into "a momentary amazement and confusion."[1] In the *Enquiry* the possibility of such extreme doubt is played down as mere intellectual amusement, although in the *Treatise* it is presented as a matter of serious philosophical interest, even if it can be pursued only in this study. In both works, however, Hume points decisively to the manner in which the practical concerns of life lead philosophers, like other people, to adopt principles whose validity they cannot prove as working assumptions for the reasonings in which they cannot avoid engaging—or better, to admit that their "natural" conviction of the truth of these principles is in fact stronger than any doubts they may theoretically entertain, and to accept this natural disposition as the appropriate rule of reasoning. By a parallel naturalistic transition in his moral philosophy Hume is likewise led to accept for practical purposes the moral (and political) values that he finds to be deeply seated in himself and in others—though they too, like the cognitive beliefs, have their ultimate basis in feeling rather than in reason. Underlying both these movements away from skepticism, moreover, is an identical impulse—the fundamental disposition of the mind to seek order. The natural belief in the order or regularity of nature is what permits reasoning about and hence some degree of control over our environment, whereas the sentiment of reflective approval that attends the artificial virtues arises from a conviction of the value of the social order that they create. This pattern that emerges from the resolution

---

[1] Hume, *Enquiries* (I), pp. 159-60.

of his skepticism constitutes the unity of Hume's philosophy as a whole and determines the fundamental content of his practical doctrines.

The amount of attention Hume devotes to his skeptical analyses shows that he takes them seriously, and his conclusions set the terms and define the epistemological basis for all his subsequent work. Like the ancient skeptics, however, Hume recognizes that a practical "rule of life" is needed to complement his philosophic suspension of all belief. Hume characterizes the resulting position as "mitigated skepticism," an outlook that he asserts ought to be preserved "in all the incidents of life" (T. 270). This form of skepticism involves the provisional acceptance of the two basic assumptions, thus permitting careful inquiries into matters of fact leading to probabilistic conclusions founded on the evidence of experience. Such acceptance is not difficult: it is largely a matter of yielding to a natural disposition of the mind or of admitting, for practical purposes, a tentative "diffidence" regarding "philosophical doubts" in addition to the doubts themselves, a state of mind that Hume suggests is the most truly skeptical (T. 273). Mitigated skepticism is later (evidently) consistent with Hume's similar yielding to the promptings of the moral sentiments. These, like the various propensities of the imagination, are accepted subject to certain philosophical refinements, or a discipline that in crucial instances subordinates impulse to rules. Hume's ensuing political philosophy accordingly involves both moral commitments derived from this qualified acceptance of natural sentiment and findings from his empirical science of human nature and society—and is thus the most fully developed outcome of the program of mitigated skepticism.

In admitting the premises of objectivity and uniform causation the philosopher in search of knowledge of fact applies them rigorously and regularly: unlike the "vulgar" the philosopher rejects all temptations to characterize certain phenomena—complex or unfamiliar happenings—as matters of mystery, miracle, special providence, or even of chance (except as a special form of indeterminate causation). Much about the world may remain uncertain—that is, available experience may not provide adequate grounds for conclusions of a very high order of probability on many matters; but if one sets out to engage in inferential reasoning about matters of fact at all, Hume argues, one ought to do so consistently, not arbitrarily invoking different principles to explain what may somehow appear to be different sorts of things. The adoption of simple and uniform principles for the explanation of factual relations in Hume's mitigated skepticism is in the final analysis susceptible only of a pragmatic justification: what

Hume calls the "philosophical" as opposed to the "vulgar" outlook in arriving at convictions about the world simply leads in the end to more useful or preferable consequences, just as moderate skepticism surpasses the Pyrrhonian in its personal and social benefits or the "durable good" that results from it.[2] The inadmissibility of exceptions to a single standard of causality is also grounded, it may be added, in Hume's epistemological premises, since his theory of perceptions construes all occurrences as of the same order, with no basis for fundamental distinctions between opposing kinds of experience.

Inquiries consistent with mitigated skepticism must also be conducted with an awareness of their logical and evidential status and a recognition of the bounds beyond which claims would be unjustifiable. The skeptic's provisional acceptance of the supposition of the uniformity of nature permits reasoning from past experience to general cases and to the future. But this minimal basis for inductive reasoning decidedly does not provide any understanding of the intrinsic nature of objects or of causal relations beyond the observation of resemblances and sequences among one's perceptions. Hence in all his investigations the skeptic must resolutely abstain from any claims of insight into the essential nature of things, from any imputation of objective existence or of causality except in terms of specific evidence, and from stating conclusions as more highly probable than there are experiential grounds for: "A wise man, therefore, proportions his belief to the evidence."[3] The skeptic believes because he finds that he cannot live without some beliefs, and perhaps because he finds that belief is satisfying in itself, that curiosity, of which science and inquiry are born, is a natural inclination that overcomes the total doubt attainable only in the most rigorous moments of thought. Consequently he adopts well-defined cognitive principles as a practical rule of life, a rule of right reasoning that will serve as the foundation for his investigations into matters of fact and the beliefs about the world on the basis of which he will act.

The adoption of this rule (with subordinate rules of evidence and inference) is a self-conscious and guarded process. Periodic revivals of Pyrrhonist doubt have the salutary effect of reminding the inquirer that all positive doctrines rest on certain nonjustifiable beliefs, and that all particular convictions draw their strength merely from the natural force of various psychological propensities. These reflections

[2] Ibid., p. 159. This judgment is fully intelligible only in light of Hume's subsequently developed moral theory.

[3] Ibid., p. 110.

serve to warn us of the most characteristic sources of error in human reasoning: the inconstancy with which the ordinary understanding adheres to the epistemological premises that make any inductive reasoning possible, and especially the tendency of the natural inclination to belief to succumb to illusions of insight into the identity of certain kinds of objects and into the nature of connections among things, issuing in conclusions that overstep what is indicated by the evidence. Extreme and mitigated skepticism are hence closely linked in Hume's philosophy, despite his apparent discarding of the former as he proceeds with his study of human nature and affairs; the Pyrrhonist doubts, though in the background, continue to provide the ultimate ground of the caution and tentativeness that Hume holds to be the appropriate state of mind for all philosophical endeavor.

Hume's skeptical crisis is thus resolved through a recognition of the manner in which belief overcomes doubt sufficiently for the purposes of life. His naturalistic acquiescence in this state of affairs—his acceptance of the normal and most forceful dispositions of the mind as the most appropriate guide for reasoning and judging—constitutes the positive side of his skeptical teaching. On this foundation Hume adopts the stance of the "experimental" scientist and resumes his projected investigation of human nature and morals. Hume's later work, although it contains occasional allusions to the value of skepticism, or at any rate of "scrupulous hesitation" (T. 107) in reasoning, is replete with apparently confident assertions of fact and generalizations, adding up to a full-scale psychological and social science. In this there is no contradiction, as some of his critics have thought. On the contrary, an affinity between skepticism and empirical or experimental scientific investigation has been a recurrent theme in philosophy ever since the ancient Pyrrhonists themselves. The early modern empiricists, notably Bacon and Locke, were eager to grant that the human mind lacks many of the forms of direct insight into things claimed by other philosophical traditions, seeing in this concession an opportunity to sharpen the focus of useful or applied science. The heightened epistemological self-consciousness that Hume proposes, in which first principles appear as "mere" beliefs or constructive hypotheses rather than as certain "knowledge," represents a continuation of this aspect of his predecessors' work.

The compatibility of (mitigated) skepticism and modern science, furthermore, is frequently attested, often together with an acknowledgment of the ultimately pragmatic justification of the fundamental tenets of the latter. The Humean notion of cause as a "law" expressing some uniform sequence or relation, it is said, simply proves in practice to be a more useful conceptual tool than do alternative notions.[4] Modern science, moreover, is content to acknowledge the force of Hume's claim that we lack rational insight into either the necessity or the nature of the causal relation and to accept his contention that a scientific explanation must be framed in terms of probability, always open to potential challenge in light of new evidence.[5] The scientist makes inquiries on the assumption of the uniformity of nature, but the contents of this nature in terms of the characteristics of objects and particular causal processes, like the truth of any particular inductive generalization, are questions that remain ever open to the revelations of future experience.

In his insistence that any general claim about matters of fact, in the absence of insight into the essential connections among things, must be continually validated in experience, Hume's proposals and warnings on scientific method resemble what has received the name of positivism. But although positivist science may appear to be a rationalistic enterprise of an ambitious sort, aiming to achieve comprehensive knowledge of the world, its methods rest squarely on the premises and analysis of Hume's skepticism. Its data are the discrete facts of sense perception, connected only by the observed resemblances and sequences that are provisionally generalized and projected, pending the test of future experience. In principle, as in Hume's imagination, anything can cause anything; we never attain any genuine comprehension of the properties or connections among things or any decisive "explanation" of a cause and effect relation beyond observed patterns of correlation or uniform sequence. In this sense it may be said that modern science is fundamentally Humean, or skeptical in Hume's "mitigated" sense, acknowledging the limitations on possible claims of knowledge that are imposed by an awareness of the grounds of all reasoning.[6]

---

[4] Lewis White Beck, " 'Was—Must Be' and 'Is—Ought' in Hume," *Philosophical Studies* 26 (1974): 221, 225. Ascriptions of both causality and moral predicates are justified pragmatically for Hume. Cf. William James, *Pragmatism* (New York: Longmans, Green, 1907), p. 180.

[5] On the relation of Hume's "inductive fallibilism" to modern scientific philosophy, see D. C. Stove, "The Nature of Hume's Skepticism," in *McGill Hume Studies*, ed. David Fate Norton, Nicholas Capaldi, and Wade L. Robison (San Diego: Austin Hill, 1979), pp. 203-25; and "Why Should Probability Be the Guide of Life?" in *Hume: A Re-evaluation*, ed. Donald W. Livingston and James T. King (New York: Fordham University Press, 1976), p. 58. Cf. also Arnold Brecht, *Political Theory* (Princeton: Princeton University Press, 1959), p. 80, also pp. 168ff. on skepticism and modern science.

[6] See David Fate Norton, "History and Philosophy in Hume's Thought," in *David

In this spirit, then, and motivated in the first instance by his natural speculative curiosity, Hume pursues in systematic and positive fashion his science of human nature, propounding, however provisionally, certain doctrines and conclusions. The subject matter that almost exclusively interests him is that which he designates "moral subjects"— the questions of human thought, behavior, and values that constitute a continuous science of psychology, morals, and politics. His initial doctrine of the understanding not only exemplifies Hume's scientific project in its descriptive, psychological approach to issues such as belief; it also establishes, in the rules of right reasoning that it lays down, the logical and methodological basis for the project as a whole. The scientific observer regards the phenomena of human conduct and judgment as objects united by relations of resemblance, proximity, and sequence, with the objective being to discern the various uniformities, and especially the causal relations, that experience (or experiments) reveals among them; the observer necessarily assumes the regularity of this (human) as of all other parts of nature and of the moral and social as well as of the physical world. On this basis Hume's investigations proceed, as we have seen, from the study of the individual mind to that of social life and history, where moral rules and practices and political institutions figure prominently among the objects of his analysis.

The assumptions and ambitions apparent in this project seem to suggest substantial confidence in the powers of reason and the potential intelligibility of the world in the face of scientific investigation. Such confidence is characteristic more of Hume's earlier than of his later writings, in which he admits doubts that the world of politics, for example, will ever yield many truths of any high order of probability to the method of "experiment" or observation. Hume's standards for the identification of a causal relation, demanding as they do frequent observation of similar cases, not only dictate caution in method and claims but also generate doubts whether anything approaching satisfactory knowledge of such complex and variegated fields as history

Hume: Philosophical Historian, ed. David Fate Norton and Richard H. Popkin (Indianapolis: Bobbs-Merrill, 1965), pp. xxxvii-xxxviii, for the claim that a recognition of this connection between skepticism and science was common in Britain when Hume wrote the _Treatise._ The main difference between modern science and Humean positivism is the former's recognition of the crucial role of models, hypotheses, paradigms, and so forth in the determination of problems for investigation and the development of theories to be tested. An observer does not simply collect facts or receive perceptions but rather seeks something of which he has an idea, and what counts as a relevant fact is in a sense predetermined by the questions he brings to the data.

and government can be attained in practice. Hume's own conclusions with respect to the effects of different political institutions are in the end fairly general and tentative, although sufficient for him to defend clear preferences among them, as we shall see. His narrative account of the development of the English constitution (which appears to have been a unique historical achievement), emphasizing the consolidation of the claims of Parliament in the seventeenth century, calls attention to the decisive importance of the adventitious factor of religious enthusiasm, which, being in Hume's view a fundamentally "unaccountable" phenomenon, vitiates any conclusive scientific understanding of this most important event.[7]

Reasoning about matters of fact has the capability, in Hume's account of volition, of guiding action, which may be called reasonable action to the extent that it is undertaken with as full and as accurate a view of objects and consequences as it is possible to attain. The probable knowledge that scientific investigation is likely to yield about social and political matters may thus be serviceable as a basis for practical choice and action. Although purely philosophical inclinations may have initially motivated Hume's investigations, the fact that he continued his moral and political studies for a lifetime suggests that he was persuaded of their usefulness to the nonphilosophical part of society, just as his efforts to publicize his philosophy were related to his conviction of the beneficial effects of the moderate skepticism in which it culminates. Part of the usefulness of Hume's teachings, perhaps, lies precisely in their negative aspect: excessive credulity is encountered more frequently than indecision, overconfident and unwarranted claims of certainty more so than lack of positive belief. Hume's skeptical science has the task, in the face of these circumstances, of disputing unsubstantiated claims, reducing beliefs to their appropriate degree of probability, and disseminating an element of its own skeptical self-consciousness into popular argument, as well as of contributing its own modest but more accurate discoveries of facts and causes. Above all, this skeptical science disputes claims of direct insight into the nature of the connections among things—both im-

[7] Hume's History of England underscores the importance, in the Parliamentary victory, of the alliance between Parliament and the Puritan party, that is, a party of the sort that Hume calls "unaccountable" in "Of Parties in General," Works, vol. 3, p. 130. This term should be taken in a scientific sense: religious fanaticism obeys no discernible laws by which it can be comprehended, so far as Hume can see. Likewise in a famous passage Hume declares the matters embraced by religion to be "a riddle, an aenigma, an inexplicable mystery"; "The Natural History of Religion," Works, vol. 4, p. 363.

putations of causality made, as they too often are, on the basis of some fanciful analogy or the claim of a cognitive grasp of the intrinsic links or influences among objects or events, and convictions regarding immutable "fitnesses" of things, or absolute values, independent of the needs of human nature and society that are reflected in our feelings and customs.

People act on their beliefs, and most people are not naturally either skeptics or cautious reasoners. The natural capacity or propensity to acquire beliefs, mediated in the usual course of things by habit, occupies the central place in Hume's account of the mind. Any positive knowledge that Hume's science could ever presume to offer, consisting of cautiously probable statements about the conjunctions of perceived objects, must often, it would seem, appear pale and insubstantial in comparison with the potential force of feelings and those convictions to which feeling contributes its full strength. Hume's pursuit of science in the face of such acknowledged obstacles reflects his commitment to an ideal of reasonableness or moderation in thought and action and to the public promulgation of this ideal through his more popular writings. To the speculative is thus added the political philosopher, who through that very science aims to influence the quality and direction of public affairs.

2. NATURALISM, CONSERVATISM, AND PHILOSOPHIC DETACHMENT

As the student of human nature, pursuing the factual investigations from which no values can in a strictly logical sense be derived, Hume appears in some respects to be a precursor of the modern behavioral sciences. This, however, is only one aspect of his social philosophy. Although he certainly wishes to clarify and utilize the new "experimental method" in relation to moral topics, it is evident that Hume is principally concerned with ethical questions for which the empirical science of human nature, although it provides necessary illumination, cannot in itself provide answers.

In taking the virtues, particularly justice, as the culminating focus of his system, Hume raises and offers guidance on questions concerning the proper conduct of life that lie beyond the bounds of the positivist science that he practices and that he believes provides the evidence regarding human nature and political life in light of which the philosopher must arrive at practical decisions and moral commitments. In his account of the virtues Hume advances the outlines of a (qualifiedly) utilitarian ethics in addition to a psychological analysis of moral judgment; and in his political philosophy he expresses views on the characteristics of desirable regimes in addition to his various studies of the relations among observed political phenomena. The normative dimension in Hume's moral and political philosophy emerges out of inquiries conducted on the basis of his skeptical analysis of the human understanding, which not only dictates the scientific form of his work but also, through the manner of his resolution of the skeptical crisis, indicates the naturalistic form of his skeptical rules of life and practical teachings. Hume's moral choices as well as his scientific commitments represent positive alternatives to pure skeptical doubt; the former are no more (or less) grounded in reason than are the latter, but they are equally important in life and in the philosopher's attention.

Hume's study of human nature in the aftermath of his resolution of the skeptical crisis falls into two parts. The analysis of the passions is suggested by the main conclusions of the initial study of the understanding, which emphasize the role of sentiment and other non-rational mental processes in thought; Book II of the *Treatise* thus continues and enlarges the investigation of the human mind that had begun with epistemological questions. The most important psychological discoveries from this stage of his philosophy are then carried over into the second broad area of research, that concerning morals and politics, thereby giving unity to the whole of the science of human nature.

The central theme of Hume's study, one that he enunciates most explicitly at the close of Book I of the *Treatise*, comes to be his concentration on those psychological attributes of human nature that appear to compensate for the inaccessibility of logical certainty in our thought and beliefs, both in our apprehension of matters of fact and in the sphere of values. Sentiment consequently emerges as one of the central categories of Hume's philosophy—one that includes the special feelings constitutive both of the belief that is accorded to certain ideas and of the judgments of value that underlie moral distinctions, and the feelings that provide the necessary affective element in volition. Other important factors include custom, and the closely related inertial tendency of the imagination to follow "general rules," and certain habitual patterns of association, which both in reasoning and in moral judgment are the source of the regularities with which we apprehend the world and conduct ourselves in it. Continuity between Hume's epistemology and his moral philosophy resides descriptively in his reliance on the same imaginative and affective features of human nature to explain uniformities of belief and judgment, both cognitive and evaluative; normatively, continuity is established through his qualified acquiescence in these natural facts, arising from his approval of the order to which they conduce as a fundamental desideratum of human life.

The naturalism that Hume adopts following his skeptical crisis concerns the discovery—which must in part be characterized as a deliberate act of choice—of appropriate guides for living, a skeptic's "rule of life," in some of the normal features of human nature as the philosopher comes to understand their operation. This transition in Hume's philosophy to the normative plane represents indeed a kind of derivation of "ought" from "is"—the sort of derivation of which Hume calls into question only the logical cogency, not the propriety as a considered act of philosophical choice. In deciding to place reliance on custom as the guide of life, for example, or on the principle of utility as the appropriate (as well as the actual) standard of certain values, Hume does not commit the rationalistic fallacy of claiming he is in possession of truths logically grounded and validated; rather, he deliberately acquiesces for practical purposes in what he takes to be his (and other people's) most basic and trustworthy feelings and mental dispositions.

This naturalistic solution to the skeptic's problem of living, like the psychological categories in which Hume seeks an explanation of human nature, may be seen in the two main parts of his philosophy. His adoption of the principle of uniformity in the field of scientific logic is paralleled by his qualified adoption of the principle of utility in the field of morals and politics. Both these standards, though firmly grounded in natural dispositions of the mind, are developed through philosophical analysis: the propensities of habit-based "natural belief" are elaborated into rules of inductive inference to be rigorously applied, whereas the general inclination to approve of others' happiness is assessed in light of the potential tension between the artificial virtues, with their special features, and the natural ones. Whatever their refinements, however, these standards are developed from, and approved as, fundamental tendencies in human nature as it is, conceived as being well suited, by and large, for the proper purposes of human life. Hume's philosophy is thus in the end characterized by a basic, nondiscordant dualism: skeptical doubt remains as a theoretical possibility, pursued to the highest degree only in the study, coupled with an acceptance of certain naturalistic standards for thinking and judging. The lessons of mitigated skepticism—caution and diffidence in reasoning and a critical stance toward all nonevident contentions—continue to inform the practical conduct of the wise person even while he accepts both his own nature and (at least provisionally) the moral values countenanced by sentiment and convention, convinced that reason alone is not capable of supplying good grounds for any alternative.

Naturalism so characterized exhibits a certain quality of passivity and may justifiably be suspected of having conservative implications for practice, the exact nature of which requires some consideration. As a scientist Hume seeks to maintain a potentially critical distance both from the psychological dispositions and from the artifices and institutions of the moral world that he subjects to analysis and clarification. On the other hand, his awareness of the limitations of any such analysis, and more important his fundamental conviction that analytical reason is incapable of providing definitive guidance in life, sets limits to the enterprise of criticism and may sometimes even appear to vitiate it altogether. Philosophical naturalism of Hume's type in other words may be charged with threatening to degenerate into thoroughgoing acquiescence in the immediately given, whereas his continuing capacity for skeptical doubt, although it renders such acquiescence tentative, serves to accentuate the weakness of any potentially critical faculty. This is a charge to which I shall turn after noting one qualification with which Hume's critics would surely agree.

The translation of Hume's epistemological position into practical conservatism is a process that refers mainly to the moral and political part of his philosophy. An analogous transition in his doctrine of the understanding is conceivable, and intimations of the form it might take may be glimpsed in the thought of such fideistic skeptics as Montaigne: it would dictate the acceptance not only of the circumscribed and rigorously applied natural belief in the uniformity of nature but of all the common forms of belief that appear to be tenacious and functional in ordinary life, including ones of the sort that Hume always regards as merely superstitious, both groundless and useless. Hume's practical position with respect to the proper conduct of the understanding is consistently that of science, involving strict adherence to empirical evidence and carefully drawn rules of inference. In this field, therefore, Hume stands out as a philosophical radical. The import of his inquiries is to challenge received beliefs of all kinds—most notably such abstract (and intuitively attractive) political doctrines or myths as that of the original contract and the prevalent arguments for both revealed and natural religion, all of which he finds wanting in terms of his conception of our possible knowledge of *"matter[s] of fact and existence."*[8] Hume's attitude regarding the applications of science often

---

[8] The best-known expression of this radicalism on the theoretical plane is the recommendation that any work not containing *"abstract reasoning concerning quantity*

resembles that of some of his Enlightenment contemporaries, who saw in the new epistemological theory of sensations and ideas a tool for the destruction of harmful prejudices in matters of belief.

It was of course Hume's skeptical and apparently destructive writings on religion that offended the conservative-minded in his day (Dr. Johnson being a good example) and that seemed inconsistent in light of his alleged political "Toryism." Many traditional religious beliefs and practices, being so apparently at odds with the scientific outlook, he labels superstitions—and, moreover, regards as dangerous to the social order through their unaccountable effects on their adherents. More refined forms of belief, such as those that Hume confronts in his *Dialogues Concerning Natural Religion*, receive the verdict of insufficiently probable, according to standards of scientific evidence, to warrant the belief of a reasonable person.

The question arises, however, in light of Hume's skeptical philosophy as a whole, why the basic elements of religious faith—the existence of God, the world as a purposive creation, the experiences of sin and grace, hope of an afterlife—may not be accepted as (at least) a kind of salutary fiction or artifice of the imagination? After all, the widespread appeal of such beliefs suggests that (like the belief in the regularity of nature) they correspond to a deepseated propensity of human nature, of the sort that Hume is prepared to accept as his guide in other respects;[9] and they may likewise be regarded as having a certain cognitive and moral utility. Causality, it must be remembered, is in the end an imaginative fiction for Hume (a word that of course is not equivalent to falsehood), and thus the logical structure of scientific reasoning is itself a mental artifice. Instead, however, Hume chooses to treat religion as a set of claims about "matters of fact" (a religious "hypothesis"[10]) and finds it wanting in the terms set by his science.

Hume does not raise this question directly in his writings, but his likely answer can be adumbrated. Hume believes that he can persuade people to accept and adhere to scientific reasoning, and to moral

---

or number" or "*experimental reasoning concerning matter of fact*" be committed to the flames as "nothing but sophistry and illusion." Hume, *Enquiries* (I), p. 165. Cf. also Hume's claims of "singularity and novelty" and his argument that such "bold attempts" are valuable in encouraging people to "shake off the yoke of authority"; *An Abstract of a Treatise of Human Nature*, ed. J. M. Keynes and P. Sraffa (Cambridge: Cambridge University Press, 1938), pp. 3-4.

[9] Cf. Hume, *Dialogues*, p. 154. Cleanthes argues that the religious conviction regarding design is one of the "plain instincts of nature." Philo and Demea generally agree that religion is an expression of wide and deep feeling.

[10] Ibid., p. 216.

practices such as justice, *as* artifices, on the ground that they are useful for human purposes. Recognition of their artificial status does not especially weaken them or undermine the convictions that attend them. Religious faith, by contrast, is presumably incompatible with its acknowledgment as a fiction or artifice. Artifices are either human contrivances (like government) or expressions of human nature, refined by the discipline of reason (like rules of inference). Religion can be interpreted along these lines, but not by its genuine adherents; and it can be promoted on this basis only as an exoteric doctrine, one that is regarded as useful for ordinary people but needless for the knowledgeable, who understand its true nature. Hume's frequent distinction between the "wise" and the "vulgar" does not lead him (as a similar distinction led other Enlightenment philosophers) to adopt this attitude toward religion. His disinclination to do so stems partly from his confidence that standards of right reasoning can be widely disseminated (reducing the gap between wise and vulgar) and partly no doubt from his rejection of the view that religion is necessary and beneficial even for ordinary people, in the way that causal reasoning and justice are necessary for all.[11] Hume's failure to embrace religious faith as he embraces the latter two artifices must therefore be seen as a deliberate choice in the face of his skepticism and not as a position that is necessitated by his philosophy.

Hume's views on religion, then, are the most conspicuous case of the potentially radical uses of his philosophy—its capacity to challenge received beliefs as insufficiently supported by evidence and hence to be discarded or reassessed. On a longer view, it is true, Hume's science of human nature reveals that the hoped-for discarding of beliefs discredited by philosophical standards of knowledge would not be so easy as some thought. Credulity, custom, receptivity to testimony, and the sympathetic communication of passions are among the strongest features of human nature. The same faculties and processes are the source of beneficial as well as of harmful patterns of thought and conduct, and superstition partakes of the same imaginative factors that produce all belief, including the philosopher's particular conviction that the most advantageous rules of reasoning are scientific ones. Considerations such as these give pause to Hume's critical enterprise, but he never ceases to advocate his mitigated skepticism and scientific

---

[11] Hume, *Enquiries* (II), pp. 198-99, where superstitions are distinguished from justice by the criterion of utility, even though rules of religious rituals and rules of property are equally artificial and "magical" in their effects—that is, certain performances or verbal formulas, carefully executed, are held to effect a real alteration of the spiritual or legal state of affairs.

outlook as the proper attitude, certainly for philosophers and usually, in some degree, for everyone.[12] A charge of undue passivity in the field of cognition and right reasoning would therefore appear to be unfounded.

It is with respect to morals that Hume's naturalism takes on a more distinctly conservative aspect. Hume accepts what he takes to be the most fundamental and universal values generated by the normal moral sentiments, just as he accepts his propensity to believe in the necessity of causes even though he can see no basis in his perceptions for this belief. (Indeed, and in marked contrast to his generally skeptical reputation, Hume may properly be seen on the whole—like Hutcheson—as upholding the validity of ordinary moral distinctions at a time when these were under attack by some thinkers.[13]) Hume also sees in the principle of utility, as he previously had in the principle of the uniformity of nature, the underlying criterion of the normal dispositions of judgment and belief. He does not, however, specify the principle of utility, refining it into a precise formula or critical standard of judgment, in a way analogous to that in which he attempts to specify certain detailed rules of inductive logic corresponding to his concept of causality as a philosophical relation. The principle of utility remains, for Hume, a general way of affirming that all judgments of value are related in some way to human needs and human happiness, but it is never rendered precise enough to serve as the basis for radical criticism of ordinary moral judgments and practices. Furthermore, utility, conceived as the general and long-range interest of society, proves inadequate as a way of characterizing the tendency of the natural virtues and the sorts of actions generally approved in accordance with them, nor does the principle provide decisive guidance in resolving conflicts (involving conflicts of indisputably moral feelings) between natural and artificial virtue. Hume's own doctrine that natural feelings must occasionally, in the greater interest of social stability, yield to artifice lacks the decisiveness with which he attempts to oppose scientific

[12] Cf. the ambiguous conclusion of Hume, *Enquiries* (i), sec. 11. The interlocutor (evidently not speaking for Hume, although he has the final word) defends a policy of toleration of "every principle of philosophy," including those that challenge ordinary religious beliefs, on the ground that philosophical doctrines are politically harmless; but he suggests that "good citizens and politicians" will refrain from disabusing the people of religious "prejudices" that have beneficial moral effects. There is tension between this view (if it is Hume's) and his more usual and direct claims that skepticism is generally beneficial and that morals do not depend on religious sanctions.

[13] David Fate Norton, *David Hume—Common-Sense Moralist, Sceptical Metaphysician* (Princeton: Princeton University Press, 1982), esp. chaps. 1 and 3; the antimoralists included Mandeville and, more remotely, Hobbes.

reasoning to superstition; it does not pretend to overcome the tension involved in the conflict nor to deny the propriety and (in most circumstances) the value of the natural moral feelings.

Hume moreover does not exhibit enthusiasm for developing precise criteria by which to evaluate specific artifices. The utility of the artificial virtues has to do in part with the stable social order they promote through their formal quality of prescribing rules of conduct and in part with their effect of substantively contributing to happiness in more specific ways. This latter criterion, however, remains indefinite: the actual contents of moral and political artifices such as justice vary from one society to another, as do the conceptions of happiness that they are supposed to further, as Hume recognizes. Although he expresses certain preferences regarding forms of government and property, upholding those of modern Europe and of Britain in particular, he maintains a degree of relativism in this matter that is grounded in his conviction of the lack of any rational basis for moral distinctions. Human nature and feeling directly manifest an array of largely invariable natural virtues, which Hume accepts as such. Historical experience on the other hand provides extensive evidence of moral artifices of somewhat different kinds and their effects. Among these the philosopher may discover certain broad uniformities (as Hume believes he does in some respects, such as in the keeping of promises), and he may attempt to point out the distinctive merits or demerits of alternative practices when differences appear. But Hume's moral and political philosophy displays in general no such radicalism as one finds in some of his strictures on the understanding and right reasoning. He evidently has, and sometimes declares, his own preferences (which happen for the most part to be in accordance with values widely shared among educated people of his time); but his recommendations in moral affairs are for the most part expressed in such a manner as to leave little doubt concerning their provisional status as preferences or inclinations: few are stated without qualification, and it is with diffidence that Hume ever advances beyond the level of moral analysis to the defense or advocacy of particular institutions. One finds no such general and firm espousal of a particular set of values analogous to his consistent advocacy of the skeptical and scientific viewpoint in matters of philosophy.

Hume's naturalism in the moral part of his philosophy, therefore, being untempered by as well-defined a critical standard as he adopts for the purposes of reasoning, might appear to imply a cautious and unassertive approach to practice; such an outcome, moreover, might seem paradoxical in contrast with the occasional iconoclastic forays of his purely analytical exercises. There is one important qualification to this interpretation, which I shall explore more fully below: philosophical investigation reveals that one great segment of morality pertains to artifices, which are recognized to be contingent and variable according to historical circumstance and hence in some degree susceptible of deliberate criticism and, on occasion, of conscious change. Artificial virtue thus in important respects stands in the same relation to natural moral impulses as Hume's previously elaborated philosophical reason, likewise governed by inflexible (logical) rules, stands to the natural impulses of association and belief. This parallel is significantly weakened by the fact just mentioned, namely, that Hume lacks any such precise criteria for proper moral artifices as he has for proper reasoning. Such criticism in the political realm as Hume's philosophy is capable of, however, derives from its acknowledgment of the artificiality of certain areas of morality, including especially those relating to political institutions. I shall return to this point after a closer consideration of the charge that Hume's skepticism leads to undue passivity in practice, in consequence of his naturalistic acquiescence in the given, especially with regard to received social values.

Accusations that Hume's skepticism leads to an uncritical and complacent conservatism in politics were made notably by later liberal critics—by writers who inherited some of the optimism regarding reason and progress characteristic of the Enlightenment *philosophes*, from whom Hume in important respects stands apart, as well as a commitment to utilitarianism as the doctrinaire and reforming program that it became after Hume. John Stuart Mill, for example, who regarded Hume as "the profoundest negative thinker upon record," comes to the following conclusion: "This absolute skepticism in speculation very naturally brought him around to Toryism in practice; for if no faith can be had in the operations of human intellect, and one side of every question is about as likely as another to be true, a man will commonly be inclined to prefer that order of things which, being no more wrong than any other, he has hitherto found compatible with his private comforts."[14] Leslie Stephen, in a similar vein, argues that a "cynical conservatism" is the political expression of a "heretical scepticism" for which history must be "a meaningless collection of facts"; and he charges that Hume "evidently inclines to the side of authority as the most favourable to that stagnation which is the natural

[14] John Stuart Mill, "Bentham," in *Essays on Ethics, Religion, and Society*, ed. J. M. Robson, vol. 10 of the *Collected Works of John Stuart Mill* (Toronto and London: University of Toronto Press and Routledge and Kegan Paul, 1969), p. 80.

ideal of a sceptic."[15] Verdicts such as these rest on a perception in Hume's teaching of a practical tendency that is correctly associated with the ancient Pyrrhonist variety of skepticism, whose rule of life, in accordance with a characteristic misology and political pessimism,[16] dictated passive acquiescence and outward conformity to the customs of one's society. This practical orientation served as a complement to sustained subjective indifference and suspense of judgment, all as a means toward the Pyrrhonist's personal goal of peace of mind.[17]

Can something of this passivity be detected in Hume's teachings? The practical bearing of his philosophy is derived mainly from his naturalism, which dictates acquiescence in those propensities of human nature that most satisfactorily compensate for the inadequacies of reason. This position, carried to an extreme, might prescribe the provisional acceptance, for practical purposes, of any belief, judgment, or custom to which the agent feels inclined or in which the social environment encourages concurrence: one perception would be as good as another, and the philosopher would be deprived of any means of distinguishing salutary beliefs from mistaken ones. Occasionally Hume appears to adopt the thoroughly behavioralist perspective that could serve as the preliminary to this position, arguing that all beliefs and feelings are merely the "necessary result of placing the mind" in certain circumstances. From this point of view the philosopher's role of offering justification or criticism of beliefs might seem to be negated, as Hume immediately suggests.[18] In fact, however, Hume does proceed with his researches, exploring the nature of belief in scientific detail and, moreover, propounding standards of philosophical right reasoning within whose bounds he determines to indulge his curiosity. Probable knowledge in the service of reasonable conduct, and not Pyrrhonist ataraxy, becomes the goal of his thought. Nor are the received moral values and institutions of his environment simply accepted, in the Pyrrhonist fashion, uncritically: social artifices, like reasoning, are subjected to scrutiny, their relation to the primary features of human nature elucidated, consequences considered, and alternatives explored.

---

[15] Leslie Stephen, *History of English Thought in the Eighteenth Century* (New York: Harcourt, Brace, and World, 1962), vol. 2, p. 157.

[16] "Pyrrhonism began in republican Elis, when Greek liberty was passing away." Norman Maccoll, *The Greek Sceptics from Pyrrho to Sextus* (London: Macmillan, 1869), p. 98.

[17] Such a practical doctrine would in most circumstances appear to be conservative in effect, although not in a principled fashion. It would not so much defend the *status quo* as resolve to live in conformity with its standards.

[18] Hume, *Enquiries* (I), p. 46.

Analysis and not mere feeling is the basis of Hume's conservatism, even if analysis of moral life reveals, among other things, the importance of feeling.[19]

In his acceptance of a scientific criterion of probability in reasoning Hume inclines, as he himself says, more to the Academic than to the Pyrrhonist strain in skepticism.[20] If Pyrrhonism conduces to an unprincipled conservatism of indifference and passivity, Academic skepticism has a different practical import. Its very spirit of investigation, which Hume exemplifies, precludes the fatalistic passivity of the Pyrrhonists even if it is acknowledged, as in Hume's case, that the philosophic or inquiring spirit is at bottom simply a peculiar kind of inclination. The practical conservatism or moderation of Academic skeptics, in contrast, is derived from the caution prescribed by their methodological guidelines for right reasoning, from their insistence on close adherence to experience, and from their distrust, on epistemological grounds, of any claims or predictions (and ensuing practical programs) regarding the future that are not based on meticulous observation of the past. Such a skeptic may (like Descartes) resolve to follow the customary rules and opinions of society while engaged in the philosophical and potentially critical enterprise of seeking justification for his beliefs, until he reaches definite conclusions of his own.[21] Hume does not enunciate such a principle explicitly, although some such presumption in favor of received opinions and institutions, especially with respect to the habit-supported artificial moral virtues, appears to be latent in his approach to criticism. The skeptic, moreover, doubts that his reflection will eventually yield certainties in accordance with which he can subsequently conduct himself. The probable reasoning pursued by the Academic skeptic may clarify moral problems and judgments, but it can never itself provide "distinctions of virtue and vice": with regard to the determinative issues of value and choice the philosopher like other people recognizes that he must be guided

[19] Cf. Dr. Johnson's remark that Hume was a "Tory by chance." Victor G. Wexler, *David Hume and the History of England* (Philadelphia: American Philosophical Society, 1979), p. 22. Hume's and Johnson's very different types of conservatism—the latter's characterized by religion, nostalgia, reverence for authority, and a strong belief in the necessity of subordination—are sketched in Ernest Campbell Mossner, *The Forgotten Hume: Le Bon David* (New York: Columbia University Press, 1943), chap. 8.

[20] Hume, *Enquiries* (I), sec. 12.

[21] Cf. René Descartes, "Discourse on the Method of Rightly Conducting the Reason," in *The Philosophical Works of Descartes*, trans. Elizabeth S. Haldane and G.R.T. Ross (Cambridge: Cambridge University Press, 1970), vol. 1, p. 95. Hume comments favorably on Descartes's method; *Enquiries* (I), p. 150.

by his feelings. His judgments are inescapably the provisional expressions of his own nature, mediated by habit and social custom, and not the definitive expression of certain qualities and relations in things.

Considerations such as these do not lead Hume, however, to the conclusion, as Stephen says, that the social world is entirely "undecipherable": he recognizes both scientific knowledge and moral virtue, even if claims are frequently advanced in both areas with inappropriate degrees of assurance. Hume's conservative inclination arises indeed from his skepticism—not, however, from a perverse spirit of paradox but from a cogent philosophical position, together with the diffidence in reasoning that it prescribes and the naturalism that he adopts as his practical guide and as the apparent condition of any reasoning and morality at all. A conservative orientation so grounded can be viewed as "cynical" only by one for whom skepticism itself is a kind of "heresy," that is, by one who adheres to convictions regarding the powers of reason for which Hume could find no good grounds.

The later liberal critics of what they regarded as Hume's excessive passivity and conservatism appear to have been disturbed above all by his skepticism, in which they discerned an outlook at variance with their own earnest commitment to progress and whose affinities to science and hence to possible scientific reformism they overlooked. They may also have been inclined to assimilate Hume's political philosophy to that of Burke and to the kind of traditionalist conservatism that emerged around the turn of the nineteenth century. In chapter III I suggested some respects in which Hume's science of human nature, with its emphasis on sentiment and custom, provided materials that were developed by later conservative writers; and on this level a definite line of continuity exists between Humean skepticism and Burke's social theory, notwithstanding the latter's less analytic approach. Criticisms of Hume of the kind just mentioned call for a consideration of his views on government and his reluctance to lay down precise and universalistic criteria for legitimate government apart from established usage, a position that is in some respects comparable to the Burkean doctrine of prescriptive right.

Government for Hume, like systems of property and the other institutions sanctioned by the artificial virtues, is as we have seen a contrivance of an "inventive species" to further our interests and avoid the inconveniences that attend its absence. The duty of allegiance to government is consequently an artificial moral duty—though it is in part derived from what Hume calls the "natural obligation" that people have to safeguard their basic interests—and is justified in general on utilitarian grounds.[22] The duty of allegiance must be developed through education and habit into a genuine moral duty, felt as such through an enlargement of the moral sentiments, since although the existence of government and its rules is on the whole in the interest of everyone (as compared with their absence), it is not always in the immediate interest of each person to obey and to make a contribution to them on each separate occasion. The general necessity and justification of government (usually conceived in terms of executive and judicial functions) and of attendant obligations are thus clear in Hume's theory, falling under the general approval and indeed priority that he accords to artifice and artificial virtue.

On the question of the proper form of government, however, or the criteria of legitimacy of particular governments, Hume's theory is less precise; indeed it is quite conservative in its import, in the common sense of tending to support existing, or traditional, institutions. As is usual with utilitarian theories, questions of form and origins are subordinate to the question of ends. The important issue is whether or not the operations of a government (or any social institution) tend to advance the general welfare as well or better than plausible alternatives and seem to be arranged to encourage the expectation that they will continue to do so. Given the difficulties, on strict Humean scientific grounds, of estimating the potential performance of untried alternatives, and of calculating the costs of implementing a new system of government, this orientation has evidently conservative practical implications, indicating the desirability of preserving whatever seems to be of value in what exists and otherwise of cautious and incremental reformism of the sort that I consider more fully below.

Beyond this, however, Hume is sometimes interpreted as holding that the particular form or composition of government is a matter of indifference, or at least that the superiority of one government to another is usually negligible in comparison with the preferability of some stable government to none and especially when one considers the dangers of sedition or the "endless confusion" that would accompany the practice of continually choosing among potential governments (T. 555). In light of this consideration, it has been suggested, Hume resorts to the psychological factor of salience as a rational way of choosing among alternative indifferent conventions, which in the case of government normally means acquiescence in the established (or long-established) form of government. Resort to salience can itself

22 Cf. Hume, "Of Passive Obedience," *Works*, vol. 3, p. 461.

be justified on utilitarian grounds as a means of avoiding fruitless disputes. Hume, in other words, "supposes that the utility of upholding established practice [with respect to government] takes precedence over the utility of the practice itself."[23]

This interpretation summarizes a doctrine regarding the "objects of allegiance" (T. III.ii.10) that is somewhat more elaborate than the account might suggest, and it overlooks Hume's definite preference, to be discussed in the final section of this chapter, for the rule of law and a constitutional regime of a fairly definite type. The conclusion that for Hume there is usually a decisive ground for upholding established forms and usage, however, is correct. As in the case of justice the necessity of stable rules of property outweighs the apparent desirability of particular distributions of goods, so the need for stability in government calls for agreement on certain general rules determining title to rule, or the distribution of authority, in addition to the general agreement on the need for government itself. With political authority as with property, furthermore, the initially attractive idea that its distribution should be in accordance with personal merit, or be adjustable in light of present social circumstances, is inconsistent with the larger requirements of stability and certainty of title. Hume therefore advances five rules (long possession, present possession, conquest, succession, and positive law) that are both widely followed in practice and, in his view, provide reasonable foundations of authority—always assuming, of course, that the governments thus established have in practice "an evident tendency to the public good" (T. 561). In these rules, Hume grants, factors of the imagination are important, though for the most part these factors "concur" with considerations of public utility or interest (T. 559, 562), just as the specific rules of property he endorses (apart from transference by consent) are likewise psychologically grounded. Imagination is not a principle that is normally opposed to utility in Hume's philosophy of human nature, however, since the facility with which the ordinary imagination can grasp the rules of government and justice contributes significantly to the development of the sense of duty and habits of obedience on which these artifices depend.

Hume's first rule of government—long possession—is the one that receives the most notice as a normative principle throughout his writ-

---

[23] David Gauthier, "David Hume: Contractarian," *Philosophical Review* 88 (1979): 35.

ings.[24] In spite of Hume's usual avoidance of the overly intransigent (in his view) language of rights, this rule bears a close resemblance to the idea of prescriptive right: rights generally, and the rights of governmental authority in particular, are generated by usage and tradition, a process that corresponds to the psychological fact (in both Hume's and Burke's views of human nature) that sentiments grounded in habit or custom are most forcefully determinative of people's actual conceptions of right, in keeping with people's normal preference for order and continuity in social relations. Hence Hume observes that "antiquity always begets the opinion of right [to power]," which is one of the three valid foundations or "original principles of government"; this factor, he suggests, must be balanced against considerations of property rights and the public interest (when these fail to coincide) in determining the legitimacy of government.[25] In a more explicitly normative vein Hume asserts, following a review of partisan opinions on the matter, that "the true rule of government is the present established practice of the age." The criterion of "established practice" in this context stands opposed to appeals to "the rights of mankind" or "liberty" in the abstract, whereas that of "present practice" is directed against those who would have recourse (in an inescapably arbitrary fashion) to an "ancient constitution."[26] This principle likewise governs the judgments Hume expresses in his *History*.[27]

Several points may be made concerning this doctrine that long usage or established practice is usually the best rule for determining the rightfulness of particular governments. This principle, first, does not prescribe any particular form of government, a question on which even at this level Hume appears to be indifferent. In speaking of "long possession" Hume may be thinking mainly of dynastic titles to the crown in monarchical or mixed governments, a perspective that tends to assimilate political to property rights in keeping with his parallel

---

[24] As a rule of property, possession carries weight only in the unusual case in which clear title cannot be established on the basis of a previous exchange. It is the *first* rule of government, however, since titles to authority (except in the cases of venal offices, dynastic marriages, and cessions of territory by treaty) are not usually the objects of deliberate exchange.

[25] Hume, "Of the First Principles of Government," *Works*, vol. 3, pp. 110-11.

[26] Hume, "Of the Coalition of Parties," *Works*, vol. 3, pp. 468, 465, 467.

[27] Thus Hume defends both Elizabeth (revered by the Whigs), not because her government was liberal but despite the fact that it was arbitrary, and Charles I (the Whigs' villain) on the ground that they both abided by established constitutional practices; *History of England*, Appendix 3, vol. 4, pp. 344-45; and Note T to chap. 59, vol. 5, p. 553. Cf. Wexler, *Hume and the History of England*, pp. 32-33, on the consistency of this work.

treatment of the artifices of government and justice. The rules Hume adopts, however, pertain to the justification of all public authority (not only that of the executive), and they are, as he points out, compatible with virtually any form of government—"from the monarchy of France to the freest democracy of some Swiss Cantons."[28] Hume does occasionally express a strong preference for legal and constitutional government, which he regards as best calculated to achieve the proper ends of all government. The legitimacy even of a constitutional regime, however, is grounded in usage and effectiveness, not in its mode of origin or conformity to an abstract model.

In his willingness to accept "democracy" or a democratic component in a mixed government like that of Britain, but only if legitimated by tradition and consistent with the ends of government, Hume is not far removed from the common opinions of his age. Even the Whigs, who sought to establish the contractual basis of government, appealed to an "original contract" and thus to history, and not to the present will of the people, as Hume observes; and although he praises the same present "system of liberty" that they defend, he emphasizes that any such well-formed government is likely to be a "complicated fabric," the product of long historical development and deriving its authority principally from long usage.[29] Hume grants that the consent of the governed, when present, would constitute one sound foundation of authority, and of course he holds that the artifice of government is in general a convention on whose desirability people would reflectively agree; but he rejects the contention that explicit consent to a particular government (much less to every law) is a necessary condition of its legitimacy. Hume, unlike later conservatives, was not faced with the radical democratic claim that the popular will ought to determine every exercise of public authority; but (like Burke afterwards) he does draw attention to a paradox in this sort of argument—the fact that most ordinary people would themselves deny its truth, and that they are rather inclined to acknowledge established practice and utility as conferring right on governments.[30] On such matters, Hume adds, "the opinions of men . . . carry with them a peculiar authority, and are, in a great measure, infallible" (T. 546; cf. 552).

[28] Hume, letter of [29 March 1764] to Catherine Macaulay, in *New Letters of David Hume*, ed. Raymond Klibansky and Ernest C. Mossner (Oxford: Clarendon Press, 1954), p. 81.

[29] Hume, *History of England*, chap. 23, vol. 2, pp. 513-14.

[30] Hume, "Of the Original Contract," *Works*, vol. 3, pp. 450, 445-47. Hume does not invoke the familiar common lawyers' argument that long usage implies consent; cf. Sir William Blackstone, *Commentaries on the Laws of England* 1.74.

Hume's attitude to revolution and revolutionary regimes may likewise be mentioned in this connection. Notwithstanding his rejection of a right of revolution as a deduction from the contractarian theory of government, Hume is perfectly willing to grant, on the ground of "public interest," that resistance to authority may be justified "in cases of grievous tyranny and oppression" (T. 552-54, 565). Here as in the more usual case where tradition generates allegiance, common practice provides norms that it is pointless to challenge in the name of an abstract theory (such as that of "passive obedience"). Hume does not attempt, however, to specify the conditions in which the overthrow of an existing government is called for, and he criticizes "casuists" whose "chief study" and emphasis concern exceptions to the usual rule of political obedience.[31] Hume's attitude to revolutionary changes in the history of the English government, furthermore, is ambivalent. In his narrative of the Wars of the Roses Hume surveys a number of arguments on behalf of the House of Lancaster that might have been advanced by an adherent of Henry VI, whose grandfather had illegally usurped the throne: appeal is made to the general consent that attended that revolution, to the "tyranny" of the preceding regime, and to the "public interest." The strongest argument, however, seems to be that although the Lancastrian title was at first invalid, it has "acquired solidity by time" ("the only principle which ultimately gives authority to government") and by virtue of beneficial rule over the course of three reigns.[32] Similarly—and with greater practical import—Hume suggests that although the legitimacy of the accession of William III in 1688 may have been doubtful, the ensuing regime fifty years later (when he writes) has acquired a claim on the allegiance of its subjects in consequence of good government, the passage of time, and general acquiescence (T. 566). As a psychological matter legitimacy is then conferred retrospectively on the Revolution and its consequences; but whether Hume on his principles could or would have justified the departure from legality and custom when it occurred is not made clear.[33]

Hume's principal rule for assessing the legitimacy of particular governments is thus another case in his philosophy of a derivation of an "ought"—a criterion of political right—from the "is" of normal prac-

[31] Hume, "Of Passive Obedience," Works, vol. 3, p. 462.

[32] Hume, History of England, chap. 21, vol. 2, pp. 426-29. The arguments of the Yorkists, who on strict legal grounds seek to restore a long-defunct regime, seem in Hume's presentation to be less persuasive.

[33] Hume's argument in "Of the Protestant Succession" is the same prudential one that is expressed in the Treatise: the existing regime is now legitimate, whatever one may think of its origins.

tice, just as his more general ethical criterion of utility, to which the rules concerning the specific "objects of allegiance" are subordinate, is likewise derived from a fundamental fact, a disposition of human nature. Hume's rules of government are political expressions of his general maxim that custom is the guide of life, a maxim that has normative as well as descriptive force in all the branches of Hume's philosophy. Such derivations are naturalistic, in that moral and political norms (as earlier the norms of right reasoning) are discovered and adopted from the usual course of our feelings, including those, such as political sentiments, that are normally guided by habit and convention. Naturalism is a somewhat awkward term to apply to Hume's political philosophy, since government and allegiance pertain to the realm of the artificial as distinguished from the realm of natural virtue and spontaneous feeling in his moral philosophy. Artifices such as government, however, rest in the final analysis on the moral sentiments, on people's "opinion of right," which are themselves expressions of human nature, even if indirect and mediated by social custom.

Hume's doctrine of prescription with respect to government is thus grounded in his psychological study of human nature and his analysis of the artificial dimension of moral life. The criterion of utility or public interest remains paramount; appeal is made to the rule of established practice to decide among comparatively indifferent alternatives, and it is justified by reference to Hume's findings concerning the important role of custom and habitual moral sentiments in upholding any complex and obligatory moral artifice, for which neither immediate feeling nor immediate interest is likely to provide adequate support. Hume's theory consequently provides reasons for adherence to a rule of prescriptive right in certain areas. He does not defend such rights, however, as something independent of utility; nor does he defend them, as Burke sometimes does, as being in conformity with a natural moral order. Hume's approach here may be connected with the fact that he does not emphasize reverence for the past or the ancestral, as Burke does, as an actual and desirable emotion of great force in social life; he is not a romantic traditionalist.[34] Hume's dichotomy between the natural and the artificial, moreover, rules out

---

[34] Hume says that objects imagined as existing in the future are generally more vivid than those in the past: our imagination has a natural tendency to proceed forward in time, in keeping with Hume's account of reasonableness in action (T. 430-32). On the other hand he argues that, of objects distant from us in time (and therefore difficult to imagine clearly), those in the remote past are more likely to arouse esteem: "Hence we imagine our ancestors to be, in a manner, mounted above us" (T. 437). Thus Hume's psychology offers materials for explaining sentimental traditionalism, but he does not develop this theme. See Wexler, *Hume and the History of England*, pp. 48-57.

appeal to rights of descent and the associated sentiments that are appropriate within the family as a pattern for political institutions. Hume's acceptance of established practice as an appropriate foundation for particular "objects of allegiance" is rather connected with his philosophical empiricism and thus to his scientific commitments, as well as to the skepticism that forms the background to this entire enterprise. Just as experience is authoritative with regard to all possible knowledge of matters of fact, so experience in the form of history and tradition—the accumulated manifestations of human nature in the relevant respects—is authoritative as a source of moral and political values. Just as mental habits unify experience into orderly cognitive patterns, rendering it a reasonable guide to the future, so also does social custom, embodying collective convictions of right, underlie the artificial rules and other continuities that constitute order in our social experience. Hume's is therefore a conservative outlook that, though it leads to definite recommendations on moral and political questions, is firmly grounded in his philosophical skepticism; but Humean skepticism, far from being aimless or opportunistic, is quite consistent with reasoned positions on practical matters.

Despite the extreme skepticism of the study, then, Hume has well-developed doctrines that belie charges of an uncritical and complacent acquiescence in the *status quo*. He teaches rules of right reasoning that govern a properly delimited science, together with certain conclusions about matters of fact, arrived at through scientific investigations, that are of clear practical import. The negative corollary of his positive science—the limitations by which he shows proper reasoning is circumscribed—also has a practical lesson in the moderate skepticism that he urges as a salutary attitude in all our affairs and conclusions. In the field of morals he enunciates the principle of utility as the standard that in large degree underlies ordinary judgments of virtue and vice, and he applies his science to the project of clarifying the complicated factual issues on which much ethical and political argument depends. Although Hume accepts human nature, with its given features, as the only possible source of values and standards, he retains a philosophical position of detachment that permits him to assume a role as educator vis-à-vis the public that is potentially, and is sometimes in practice, critical. Scientific reasoning offers a basis from which he challenges received beliefs and opinions, including political opinions, that he regards as detrimental in their effect; and if his principle of utility does not afford him so clear-cut an ethical standard with which to challenge received moral values and moral feelings, the application of his science to moral and political controversies constitutes a substantial philosophical contribution to matters of practice. Finally, in the defense of artifice and the social values of order and security associated with the artificial virtues, Hume adopts a distinctive political attitude, which manifests itself in his essays as an advocacy of moderation, constitutionalism, and the rule of law. Hume's political outlook is in important respects conservative, but it is not so much the indifferent passivity born of Pyrrhonist doubt as it is the outcome of a sustained analysis of human nature and moral life, together with the expression of well-defined preferences and a sustained skeptical distrust of rationalistic or visionary efforts to transcend the limitations of concrete experience.[35]

Hume's critical and educative enterprise demands a degree of detachment from the affairs of current political life—a vantage point from which he can observe and comment, taking an active interest without being involved in the partisanship that characterizes politicians. Hume deliberately adopts such a position with respect to public life as an aspect of his decision to persist in his philosophical researches following his skeptical crisis. The key moment in the resolution of this crisis comes when Hume leaves his study to seek the company of others in "the common affairs of life," finding there in the strength of the ordinary beliefs and feelings of human nature the clue to his further studies. At this moment Hume is tempted to forsake philosophy for some form of the active life (T. 269);[36] instead, however, he eventually returns to his study, preferring philosophy to business, though refreshed and invigorated by his contact with friends and affairs. Hume chooses the life of philosophy determined to stay in touch with the "ordinary affairs of life" and to make them the object of his study, acknowledging that nature is in the final analysis stronger than reason. He adheres to his now-mitigated skepticism confident that it is the most appropriate attitude for practical purposes, taking as his motto the precept that "In all the incidents of life we ought still to preserve our scepticism" (T. 270). His investigations from this point are motivated by distinct feelings, to which, in light of his new appreciation of human nature, he pays his respects: these include not only his natural curiosity and the pleasures of mental activity, and his desire for fame, but also an "ambition" of "contributing to the instruction of man-

[35] Frederick M. Watkins, "Introduction" to David Hume, *Theory of Politics* (Edinburgh: Nelson, 1951), pp. vii-viii. Hume is said to be a "conservative rationalist" inasmuch as he looks to reason (or science), properly limited, to solve problems.

[36] See Ernest Campbell Mossner, *The Life of David Hume* (Austin: University of Texas Press, 1954), chaps. 6, 7, for the biographical circumstances of Hume's commitment to philosophy.

kind" (T. 271). Hume finds within himself, that is, an inclination not only to persist in his philosophic inquiries but also to make his views known, in the conviction that his skepticism might be, in some form, a useful doctrine to be offered to the public.[37]

The role of educator that Hume assumes mediates between the study and life, between the speculative possibility of questioning all opinions and the world of belief and activity in which the strongest propensities of human nature most often are manifested. Nevertheless Hume, in adopting the philosophical way of life, detaches himself in some degree from the active sphere of life, including the political. On several occasions later in his life Hume accepted public employments, though never without misgivings;[38] he grants that people are sociable and active as well as reasoning beings, and he suggests in general that "nature has pointed out a mixed kind of life as most suitable to the human race."[39] For himself, however, Hume embraces the philosophic way of life while acknowledging that the sustained reasoning and skepticism proper to the philosopher are neither natural nor to be expected—or wished for—in the majority of people. In this position of reflective detachment Hume retains his capacity to doubt, but he occupies himself principally with his study of human nature and society and his analysis of the ordinary beliefs of those who are not so prone to doubt as he is. From his diverse speculations he formulates both a general attitude and a number of specific conclusions that he regards as potentially beneficial and practically capable of having an impact when communicated to wider audiences.

Most generally Hume seeks to promulgate his mitigated skepticism, including his restrictive standards of proper reasoning, among people of action, thereby injecting a salutary note of caution and reserve into their proceedings. He expresses this view of his enterprise, for example, à propos of his *History*, a work that he intended to contribute to the moderating of partisan zeal in English political life: "I only propose

---

[37] For Hume's comments on the advantages to both parties of philosophers' remaining in contact with the nonphilosophical world of letters and society, see "Of Essay Writing," *Works*, vol. 4, pp. 367-70, and his remarks at the very end of Book I of the *Treatise*. Hume's stance may be considered in light of the classical distinction between the contemplative and the active life.

[38] See, for example, Hume, letter of 12 December 1761, to the Earl of Shelburne, and his letter of 13 September 1763, to Adam Smith, in *The Letters of David Hume*, ed. J.Y.T. Greig (Oxford: Clarendon Press, 1932), vol. 1, pp. 347-48, 395. Hume's most noteworthy public endeavor was as secretary to the British embassy in Paris. See Mossner, *Life*, chaps. 30-34.

[39] Hume, *Enquiries* (I), p. 9: "Be a philosopher; but, amidst all your philosophy, be still a man."

my Doubts, where I am so unhappy as not to receive the same Conviction with the rest of Mankind."[40] The incessant proposing of doubts about matters of practical concern not only advances science; it also conduces to greater moderation and prudence in conduct and public affairs, redounding to the general advantage. The "mind of man," Hume says, can no more rest perpetually in the narrow circle of familiar objects than it can sustain a Pyrrhonist suspension of all belief; it will adopt some larger intellectual commitment as a guide, and Hume sees the choice as one between the forms of credulity that he calls superstition and his own skeptical philosophy:

> We ought only to deliberate concerning the choice of our guide, and ought to prefer that which is safest and most agreeable. And in this respect I make bold to recommend philosophy, and shall not scruple to give it the preference to superstition of every kind or denomination. For as superstition arises naturally and easily from the popular opinions of mankind, it seizes more strongly on the mind, and is often able to disturb us in the conduct of our lives and actions. Philosophy on the contrary, if just, can present us only with mild and moderate sentiments. (T. 271-72)

This passage expresses most clearly Hume's conviction that there is a lesson in his skepticism that is susceptible of being translated into a practical and public program, apart from the personal inclinations that underlie this orientation on his own part—his preferences for a "safe" guide in life, for an absence of disturbance, and for "mild and moderate" sentiments, calm passions rather than violent ones.

These preferences signify a generally conservative outlook that complements Hume's efforts to suspend judgment and the caution and diffidence in reasoning that are characteristic of skeptics in their attitude of detachment. Such conservatism, however, is to be distinguished from a partisan position: the term conservatism, referring to a programmatic political doctrine or ideology, is anachronistic when applied to Hume; it may also be misleading, given his belief that a position of detachment from partisan political controversies is the appropriate one for a philosopher. Hume's proudest claim is to be impartial, a term he uses as nearly equivalent to philosophical;[41] and the lack of congruence between his views and the "official" doctrines of the actual political parties of his day—Whig and Tory, Court and

[40] Hume, letter of 3 September 1757, to Andrew Millar, *Letters*, vol. 1, p. 265.

[41] Hume's claim of "Moderation and Impartiality in my Method of handling POLITICAL SUBJECTS" first appears, as a kind of manifesto, in the Preface to the first edition of his Essays; *Works*, vol 3, p. 41. The claim is frequently repeated.

Country—bears out his claim to have taken a balanced and nondoc-
trinaire view of all controversial issues.[42] His sole overriding allegiance,
rather, is to philosophy and careful reasoning; and even here his work
was done in comparative isolation and not in the context of such a
party as was constituted, for example, by the Encyclopedists and other
less skeptical *philosophes* in France in the same period.[43] Hume's
impartiality on disputed and complex questions is the product of his
determination to adhere to philosophy, with its commitment both to
engage in scientific reasoning and to acknowledge the limitations on
all such reasoning:

> It belongs, therefore, to a philosopher alone, who is of neither party,
> to put all the circumstances in the scale, and to assign to each of
> them its proper poise and influence. Such a one will readily, at first,
> acknowledge that all political questions are infinitely complicated,
> and that there scarcely ever occurs, in any deliberation, a choice,
> which is either purely good, or purely ill. Consequences, mixed and
> varied, may be foreseen to flow from every measure: And many
> consequences, unforeseen, do always, in fact, result from every one.
> Hesitation, and reserve, and suspense, are, therefore the only
> sentiments he brings to this essay or trial.[44]

Scientific and skeptical impartiality on complicated questions means
nonpartisanship, for the philosopher, in practice. Hume as a political
scientist devoted much attention to the origins of political parties and
to the function of parties in the British constitution, regarding them
as a natural and largely beneficial phenomenon in a free government.

[42] The clearest examples of Hume's efforts to consider both sides of disputed matters
are his juxtaposition of the essays "Of the Original Contract" and "Of Passive Obedience," in which he criticizes versions of the "official" Whig and (pre-1745) Tory
doctrines; and the essay "Of Superstition and Enthusiasm," where the respective virtues
and (especially) vices of two opposite types of religious sentiment are examined. Hume's
impartiality in these two cases consists in rather severe criticisms of both sides of
prevalent disputes; impartiality with respect to popular opinions in these cases, that is,
means partiality toward his own standards of right reasoning and philosophy. Cf. also
E. C. Mossner, "Was Hume a Tory Historian? Facts and Reconsiderations," *Journal
of the History of Ideas* 2 (1941): 225-36; and Duncan Forbes, *Hume's Philosophical
Politics* (Cambridge: Cambridge University Press, 1975), esp. chaps. 5, 6, for Hume's
opinions on issues dividing the court and country parties of his day.

[43] Hume was well received by the *philosophes* in Paris in the 1760s; see his letter of
December 1763, to the Rev. Hugh Blair, *Letters*, vol. 1, p. 419. Diderot's anecdote of
Hume's discomfiture in the face of dogmatic atheism at Baron d'Holbach's exemplifies
the differences between Hume's skepticism and the assurance of the *philosophes*. Mossner, *Life*, p. 483.

[44] Hume, "Of the Protestant Succession," *Works*, vol. 3, pp. 474-75.

His intention in his essays on parties and the prevailing party ideologies was to moderate partisan zeal by calling attention to plausible elements in the competing doctrines, and thus to confine partisan conflict to forms that were compatible with the survival of the constitutional regime as a whole.[45] Philosophers as such, however, remain above parties—an aspect of their detachment from active life and politics in general.

The skepticism apparent in the passage just quoted, which pertains to the debate over the merits of the Hanoverian succession, reveals the practical outcome of the diffidence that Hume cultivates. Those who embrace the active life must choose their positions and defend them in the daily contention of political struggle, and the philosopher as scientist of human nature is interested in their motivation and choices: people of "mild tempers, who love peace and order" tend to incline to the monarchical part and the Court Party in a mixed constitution, whereas people "of bold and generous spirits," loving liberty, are attracted to republican ideals and the Country opposition.[46] The philosopher, however, who sees the usefulness of the existence of both such parties in sustaining a mixed government, abstains from partisan commitments. He might support the weaker side in order to redress a perceived imbalance, as Hume claimed to be doing in writing a "Tory" history of the early Stuarts, to counterbalance the Whig orthodoxy. More characteristically, however, the philosopher is found in an attitude of perpetual "hesitation" that precludes clear-cut allegiances as well as active involvement in politics. The writing of history, more generally, with its careful attention to empirical complexity, is a useful enterprise in the skeptic's larger campaign to dispel dogmatic ideologies and promote political moderation.[47] The skeptic's contribution is principally that of an educator, indirect, and yielding its benefits over a period of time that is lengthier than that encompassed by the usual projects of politicians. In this spirit Hume pursues his studies and proposes his doubts, pointing out both the cogent and the fallacious elements in the reasoning of all parties, tempering their claims, reducing distinctions to matters of degree and probability, and

[45] Hume, "Of the Coalition of Parties," Works, vol. 3, pp. 464-70, on the advantages of limited partisanship. Cf. Isaac Kramnick, Bolingbroke and His Circle (Cambridge: Harvard University Press, 1968), pp. 119ff. Hume states that his goal is to "encourage moderate opinions, to find the proper medium in all disputes," p. 464; elsewhere, too, he speaks of "promoting moderation"; "That Politics May Be Reduced to a Science," Works, vol. 3, p. 107.

[46] Hume, "Of the Parties of Great Britain," Works, vol. 3, pp. 133-34.

[47] See Wexler, Hume and the History of England, generally and esp. pp. 97-98.

generally ending by supporting a position of compromise or mediation.[48]

This attitude of detachment is in effect conservative in its very caution and hesitancy and insofar as its skeptical standards of admissible reasoning tend to engender a comprehensive distrust of projects of the sort that constitute political radicalism. Such projects typically involve causal reasoning too extravagant for the complex data of social life to sustain, and they frequently entertain expectations of a future that will transcend, or differ utterly from, the past experience of humanity; and on either count they fail to meet the criteria of "reasonableness" set by Hume's philosophy. Hume's position does not, however, consist in a defense of a particular set of political principles, as did later varieties of conservatism. All political principles and arguments, rather, are equally subject to philosophical criticism and to persistent skeptical doubts. This, at any rate, is the practical meaning of Hume's choice of a philosophical and skeptical way of life, and it is the thrust of much of his writing on political topics. The question of the extent to which this attitude of diffidence and "lesson of moderation in all our political controversies,"[49] which is the immediate practical offshoot of his epistemological skepticism, is developed into a more substantive conservative position is the topic of the following sections.

Hume the political philosopher is therefore above all a teacher of skepticism, in the conviction that this doctrine will in itself have beneficial effects on the affairs of the world, although he strongly doubts that many people will follow him far, either in his "abstruse" reasonings or in his manner of life. In the discipline of his study he seeks to overcome the numerous flights of fancy that, although pardonable in children and poets, are "so signal a weakness" in a philosopher (T. 224-25); and he hopes that his example will temper the beliefs of ordinary people (and their leaders), who stand for the most part between these extremes. "And though a philosopher may live remote from business, the genius of philosophy, if carefully cultivated by several, must gradually diffuse itself throughout the whole society, and bestow a similar correctness [of reasoning] on every art and calling."[50] He hopes that his investigations of the "secret Springs & Principles" of human nature may conduce to the improvement of morals in the

---

[48] Geoffrey Marshall, "David Hume and Political Scepticism," *Philosophical Quarterly* 4 (1954): 247-57; Shirley Robin Letwin, *The Pursuit of Certainty* (Cambridge: Cambridge University Press, 1965), p. 76.

[49] Hume, "Whether the British Government Inclines More to Absolute Monarchy, or to a Republic," *Works*, vol. 3, p. 126.

[50] Hume, *Enquiries* (I), p. 10.

same way that the science of anatomy is of service to a painter;[51] and he argues that the popular teachings that effectively guide people's beliefs and actions depend on a foundation provided by the "accurate and abstruse" philosophy of the sort that he pursues.[52] Above all, Hume appeals to the common sense of ordinary people, upholding in general the normal propensities of belief and sentiment while cultivating the doubt and detachment on the basis of which he can critically examine the grounds and the consequences of particular beliefs, as Kant clearly saw.[53] The common sense of human nature is the only available guide, but its soundness depends on an admixture of skepticism that tempers its tendency to credulity and its pretensions to insight and teaches it its due limitations.

3. ARTIFICE, ORDER, AND POLITICAL MODERATION

Hume's philosophical detachment is nonpolitical insofar as it involves the sort of impartiality and doubt that preclude the active choices and partisan commitments of everyday politics. Hume's vocation indicates a political role in a more diffuse way, however, to the extent that philosophers engage in teaching certain of their conclusions to the public, and in particular to the politically oriented members of it. The profession of public man of letters provides Hume with an intermediate position between his study and the active affairs of life, the latter of which he acknowledges to be the proper sphere for most people.

That he took up this profession, rather than remaining entirely involved with his "abstruse" studies, has been attributed to various motives. Some of Hume's critics have suspected that, like the ancient sophists (themselves skeptics of a sort and teachers of a political theory of artifice), he was mainly concerned with the pecuniary rewards of his popular works. It is apparent, however, that his writings, predictably controversial, were by no means calculated to achieve maximal popularity or to flatter the public of his time and its favorite opinions. Hume himself admits to a love of fame as a motive of his

[51] Hume, letter of 17 September 1739, to Francis Hutcheson, *Letters*, vol. 1, pp. 32-33. The same image is used in *Enquiries* (I), p. 10.

[52] Hume, *Enquiries* (I), pp. 5-10.

[53] Immanuel Kant, *Prolegomena to any Future Metaphysics*, ed. Lewis White Beck (Indianapolis: Bobbs-Merrill, 1950), p. 7: "I should think that Hume might fairly have laid as much claim to common sense as Beattie and, in addition, to a critical reason ... which keeps common sense in check and prevents it from speculating, or, if speculations are under discussion, restrains the desire to decide. ...." Hume indeed does lay claim to common sense; *Enquiries* (II), p. 170.

writing, a point that has been regarded as disreputable by critics who have seen his skeptical teachings as mere paradoxes. I have argued, by contrast, not only that Hume's skeptical analyses represent genuine philosophical conclusions but also that they are publicized in the conviction of their salutary practical effects; their notoriety was incidental and probably inadvertent. The fame Hume aspired to, judging from the philosophical traditions to which he alludes in the Introduction to his *Treatise*, is of a higher order and depends on the ability of his teachings to persuade and influence the thought and action of others in the long run. Thus Hume's love of fame is related to another of his stated motives, his desire to contribute to the instruction of humanity. This ambition arises from his conviction that he has sound views to teach, or that his science of human nature will be "superior in utility" to other doctrines (T. xxiii). The teaching of sound views is a moral and indeed a political enterprise, one that confronts the political affairs of its age, although always maintaining (in Hume's case) a certain distance and reserve.

The most general aspect of Hume's teaching pertains to his endeavor to inject "a small tincture of Pyrrhonism" and hesitation into the deliberations of public persons, who, in his view, along with "the greater part of mankind," are "naturally apt to be affirmative and dogmatical in their opinions," and who "throw themselves precipitately into the principles, to which they are inclined."[54] The care and diffidence in reasoning that Hume advocates are practically sound in their tendency to promote tolerance, reduce partisan zeal, and encourage a moderate and circumspect conduct of affairs.

In addition to this general attitude Hume propounds a distinctive set of positive teachings, the conclusions of his scientific investigation of human nature and of morals. Though connected to his skepticism and thus to his general posture of hesitancy, these conclusions amount to a distinctive political doctrine that Hume advances as containing probable truths concerning moral and political institutions, assessed in light of his commitment to utility and consequently to the artifices through which the happiness of human society is promoted. In his political science as in other parts of his philosophy, notwithstanding his attention to the logical distinction between fact and value, Hume engages in the characteristic skeptical enterprise of selecting a set of practical guidelines for the appropriate conduct of life, which in the final analysis is an ethical enterprise and a matter for comprehensive philosophical reflection and choice. The outcome is a conservative

---

[54] Hume, *Enquiries* (I), p. 161.

doctrine, complementing his persisting skeptical diffidence, whose main themes are order, the desirability of legal and constitutional government, and advocacy of moderation and caution with respect to political action and change.

The central element in Hume's political philosophy, as we have seen, is his analysis of the artificial virtues, including their justification as values, their sources in human nature, and their problematic relation to natural feelings. It is the artificial virtues, Hume contends, that make orderly social life possible at any level more extensive than the family, and he leaves no doubt, in his apparently exceptionless ascription of priority to the artificial over the natural virtues in cases of conflict, that he regards the benefits derived from society so conceived to be paramount ones. Hume's defense of artificial virtue can be construed as having the logical form of a hypothetical imperative: his science reveals both the advantages of society and the necessity of certain kinds of rules for the subsistence of society, yielding the practical conclusion that these rules should be observed to the extent that their consequences are sought. Hume makes clear, however, not only in his ethical writings but also in his general expressions of preference for philosophical and political moderation over fanaticism, and for the calm over the violent passions as a reasonable standard of conduct, that he values the order and stability that follow from artifice as appropriate moral ends and as the guiding consideration of political deliberations. Accordingly his objective analysis of artificial virtue is presented in close conjunction both with an ethical teaching upholding the propriety and priority of this type of virtue and with political recommendations in favor of the rule of law, constitutionalism, and moderation that are closely associated with it.

Hume's analysis of the artificial virtues appears to have some of the features of a rationalistic theory of politics. His discussions of justice and allegiance in the *Treatise* and second *Enquiry* are couched in abstract terms, in which certain typical features are alleged to characterize all systems of property and government. These features, moreover, are rational ones in various senses. The principal formal characteristic of the artifical virtues is that they prescribe conduct and judgments in accordance with sets of rules that must be applied uniformly to all cases falling under them. The rules regarded systematically, furthermore, are analyzed as being the (possible) products of instrumental rationality, that is, as means adapted to achieving the general interests of society—the basic interest of all the members of society in orderly procedures and in a predictable social environment in which to pursue their private ends, as well as various substantive public goals. Since Hume also contends that the rules are for the most part in the long-range interest of each individual as well as of the society collectively (or would reasonably be viewed prospectively as such), they appear to be rules that might have been designed, and would in principle be accepted as obligatory, by enlightened individuals in a calm moment of reflection. An "assimilation of politics to engineering," a science by which we deliberately contrive means—and frequently invent novel means—to satisfy our desires, might even seem to follow from this conception of artifice. Such a rationalistic scheme as this, however, might appear to be at variance with Hume's modest estimate of human reason and to set him apart from later conservatives, with their distrust both of abstractions and of any suggestion of a rational will in politics.[55]

Hume does not suggest, however, that artificial rules are or ought to be in practice defined and accepted in so deliberate and rational a manner as this. He exhibits an awareness, both in the more historical passages in the *Treatise* and to a greater degree in his more popular writings, that actual systems of justice and government are the largely unforeseen outcomes in most cases of long, gradual, and irregular processes of historical growth; that explicit and rational consent on the part of individual subjects has rarely if ever constituted either the origin or the basis of legitimacy of political regimes; and that the utilitarian rationale of social artifices is in most instances implicit and incapable of being articulated by those who nevertheless acknowledge them as involving moral obligations. On all these issues Hume's findings as a moral and political scientist confirm the skeptical conclusions of his study of the mind: custom and imagination, and not reason, are the guides of human life, moral as well as cognitive. Even the artificial virtues, which are in some degree variable and hence putatively the objects of conscious choice and in which the philosopher can discern a formal structure and criterion of justification, depend for general compliance on nonrational, principally habitual, propensities of human nature, just as the specific forms they take in different societies appear to be more the product of local custom and fortuitous evolution than of reasoned choice. These observations might appear

---

[55] Michael Oakeshott, *Rationalism in Politics* (New York: Basic Books, 1962), p. 4 and passim. Hume occasionally speaks as an "engineer" with respect to constitutional design; but one can advocate experimental reform of artificial structures on the basis of experience and utility, and with due regard for the importance of custom, without being guilty of rationalist hubris. See also F. A. Hayek, *Law, Legislation and Liberty*, vol. 1: *Rules and Order* (Chicago: University of Chicago Press, 1973), p. 29, on Hume as an exponent of "critical" but not "constructivist" rationalism.

to be mere addenda to a fundamentally rationalist theory of politics were they not so much in accordance with the skepticism and the psychological doctrines that form the core of Hume's understanding of human nature. The emphasis on custom, not only as a psychological and historical fact but as, in the end, the most appropriate guide in life, constitutes the central element of continuity in Hume's philosophy as a whole, uniting his theories of the mind and of morals in a comprehensive theoretical and practical doctrine. The abstract models of political artifices that Hume develops are the exercises of a scientist attempting to generalize and clarify the data of observation. They must be set, however, in the context both of his theory of human nature and of his skepticism; and it is the attitudes characteristic of his continuing (mitigated) skepticism that yield his practical orientation to politics.

Moral rules and political institutions, Hume says, are the universal products of a naturally "inventive species" (T. 484) endowed with a certain mental constitution and faced with certain needs. Their strength is derived from natural dispositions, most generally from the natural sociability that is manifested in sympathy and in the mind's susceptibility to the influence of testimony and education. The moral force of the social virtues depends in the end, as Hume emphasizes in the *Enquiry*, on a generalized benevolence that interests each individual to some degree in the well-being of others, at least in reflective moments when more intense passions, such as those aroused by proximate personal interests, do not predominate. The artificial virtues, once inculcated in individuals and realized as social institutions, serve to bring natural impulses under control, subjecting them to general rules, and giving specific contents to the sociable and benevolent inclinations of the members of a particular society. They must be "invented," but at the same time they also must draw on natural propensities and capacities; and if they are to be efficacious they must become so much matters of habitual belief and judgment that they constitute a "second nature" in their adherents. The artificial virtues are perfectly "natural" in one of the common senses of that word: they are characteristic of human societies everywhere, even though they are a matter of education and not so spontaneous a manifestation of human nature as, for example, the sentiments that determine the natural virtues.

The question then arises whether Hume's naturalistic disposition to look favorably on the normal and apparently unavoidable tendencies of human nature extends to this sphere, leading him to accept the artificial virtues as the appropriate standard for social life in a fashion analogous to that by which he accepts the natural belief in the uniformity of nature as the basis for reasoning. The affirmative answer that must be given to this question is the foundation of Hume's normative political philosophy in the same way that his approval of certain innate propensities of the imagination is the foundation of his normative standards of right reasoning. His general defense of artifice and his prescription that the artificial virtues take precedence over natural feelings are consequences of his explicit preference for the order established by rules as an essential ingredient of social happiness. Hume arrives at his acceptance of artificial virtue in his moral philosophy by a line of thought similar to that which is apparent in the resolution of his skeptical crisis. His study of human nature reveals the existence of a variety of affections, including moral or approbatory feelings, just as it reveals a variety of imaginative phenomena determining forms of thought and belief. Skeptical doubts may be applied equally to all the judgments arising from these sources: the philosopher can see no basis in reason for criteria of "right" in the moral world any more than for "necessity" in our reasoning about matters of fact. Nevertheless, the moderate skeptic seeks rules of life in both areas, holding his extreme doubts in abeyance; and in both cases his procedure is the same: he distinguishes certain fundamental or normal propensities, whose effects he has reason to believe are salutary, and accepts them provisionally as his guide. In this way Hume arrives at his cautious rules of inductive reasoning as well as an acceptance of the validity of both the natural and the artificial virtues.

Such acquiescence is naturalistic: normative standards are generated by, or adopted from, the features of human nature; "is" yields "ought," although without any claim of rational demonstration. In neither case, however, is the acquiescence entirely passive. Hume selects, on pragmatic grounds, certain of the potentialities of the imagination as the basis of his rules for correct reasoning, whereas in the sphere of morals he deliberately ranks the artificial above the natural virtues, having clarified the operations and sources of both and identified the ethical standard of the former in the principle of utility. Hume places social artifice over instinct in moral life just as he defends a certain type of reasoning (a logical artifice) over the uncontrolled sway of belief and fancy in the understanding. In both cases, however, the philosophical standards remain skeptical and somewhat tenuous. They are not "proven" but are simply grounded in the philosopher's conviction that they are the "safest" or most advantageous guides in practice, and that they are on the whole most conducive to the ends that most people, upon reflection, acknowledge as desirable. In defending these standards, moreover, the philosopher does not repudiate or transcend human nature, since his standards are only refinements of certain given instincts of belief and feeling. He continues to recognize the strength of all the nonrational dispositions and the necessity of drawing on them in the "invention" and maintenance of a cautious and orderly way of life based on skepticism and artifice.

In Hume's choice of practical principles the underlying impulse is that preference for order and moderation of which we have already found evidence. His philosophical rules of reasoning are more desirable than other tendencies of the imagination because they promise to afford the cognitive agent a wider and more stable grasp of objects, to render the world of ideas more uniform, and to lead to less precipitate and therefore more "reasonable" judgments and actions. The priority of the artificial virtues is related in a comparable way to a preference for a social environment characterized by stable objects, uniform sequences, and a future that resembles the past, one that is thus predictable, if only according to the restricted criteria of observation and probability. The inflexibility with which Hume contends a scientific or otherwise prudent reasoner must adhere to carefully drawn rules of inductive inference is paralleled by the inflexibility that he argues should attend application of the rules of the artificial virtues. To yield to immediate feeling, or to seek an exception to the rules in favor of impulse, is like understanding the world with resort to invocations of miracles. Cognitive and moral order is secured by rules, which in both cases are constitutive of the stability and uniformity that satisfy what Hume regards as the predominant inclination of our nature. It is this emphasis on rules and order that constitutes the most fundamental element of conservatism in Hume's political thought.[56]

To delineate and to defend the workings of the realm of artifice is in itself a critical enterprise, involving a repudiation of other conceivable guides for living, ranging from uninhibited natural feeling to divine revelation. Beyond this, Hume's political philosophy prompts more precise critical investigations of the artificial virtues and corresponding social institutions, a project that encourages in practice a cautious and experimental reformism in the context of a general adherence to moderate government. Hume endorses the commonly adjudged "virtuous" quality of justice and allegiance through a series of reflections analogous to his naturalistic resolution of skepticism. His tendency to approve the commonly approved extends to the artificial virtues, however, only in a general sense: justice, chastity, good man-

[56] Cf. Christopher J. Berry, *Hume, Hegel and Human Nature* (The Hague: Martinus Nijhoff, 1982), p. 79.

ners, and so forth, appear after all to be regarded as virtues universally—broadly similar everywhere, inseparable from human society,
and evidently functional in sustaining it. Any more detailed inquiry,
however, quickly reveals that actual systems of artificial virtue differ
considerably in their specific features, so much so sometimes that only
philosophical analysis can perceive their fundamental resemblance.
The diversity of actual rules is important evidence of their artificiality,
of the fact that they are not spontaneous but are in some sense invented
to meet experienced needs and to achieve the particular versions of
happiness adhered to in different societies. Variation implies change-
ableness, a feature of artifice that is confirmed by the study of history,
and that in turn gives practical import to criticisms and ensuing proposals for reform in morals and politics. Recognizing this, the political
science pursued by the Humean philosopher is capable of playing a
critical and even a prescriptive role.

Analysis of moral and political institutions aims first at the clarification of their operation and consequences through "experimental"
observation and conclusions regarding causal relations. Accepting the
consequentialist ethic commonly applied to the artificial virtues, and
assuming that their ends can be specified, Hume's political science
explores the degree of success with which the means are adapted to
the ends. It exposes shortcomings and proposes remedies for apparent
dysfunctions and inefficiencies, and in this way it contributes to the
overall soundness of a system of artifice. The artificial portion of moral
life, being an elaborate set of purposive contrivances, lends itself particularly well to the sort of empirical, causal reasoning in which the
skeptical philosopher meticulously engages. Indeed, what Hume regards as admissible as reasoning about matters of fact is eminently
suited to the analysis and criticism of artifices as he conceives them:
as functional contrivances their validity is always subject to the test
of future experience, corresponding to the logical status of the causal
inferences with which they are associated; social artifice and Humean
"fallibilist" inductivism go together. The application of such reasoning
to ethics and politics is undoubtedly the central practical concern of
Hume's philosophy, the mission of the "wise" in contrast to the credulous "vulgar," and the condition of the calmness and moderation
that he values.[57]

The scope of legitimate criticism permitted by Hume's skepticism

---

[57] See Norman Kemp Smith, The Philosophy of David Hume (London: Macmillan,
1949), pp. 539-40, for the view that reason as a complement to custom is Hume's final
choice as a guide in life. See note 5 to this chapter on Hume's "inductive fallibilism."

and by his moral naturalism, however, is restricted, and opposition to programmatic or radical proposals is as conspicuous a part of his political philosophy as is its claim to doubt and to examine received opinions of every kind. Several reasons may be offered for this orientation beyond the general attitude of caution and diffidence that Hume regards as the appropriate one for a skeptic to take with respect to any positive doctrines.

There are in the first place the special difficulties attending reasoning, in accordance with Hume's standards, in the sphere of morals. These difficulties arise both from the great complexity of objects and causal relations in this area and from the frequent impossibility of repeating observations or of designing controlled experiments. The artificial virtues are required to supplement the natural ones precisely because of the scope and complexity of the problems facing an extensive society, of coordinating the conduct of many people to their general advantage over lengthy periods of time. It is thus to be expected that the rules and institutions they ordain will be complicated—the more so, Hume suggests, as the way of life of the society is the more "refined" and differentiated and as a society retains a rich heritage of mores and institutions from its past. The very need for inflexible rules, sustained by customary obedience, arises from the fact that the benefits derived from them are in many cases too remote, too general, or too much taken for granted for most people to apprehend fully, let alone be constantly aware of, their manner of accomplishing their purpose. Philosophers through their sustained investigations are in a better position than the average person to grasp the utility of a particular rule, but they will be reluctant ever to claim to have achieved a complete understanding of so multifaceted an object as a system of moral artifices. Any potential positive reform that may be "invented" or envisioned for the improvement of the rules would have to be put forward with circumspection and with acknowledgment of the impossibility of predicting completely even its proximate consequences for the system as a whole. In morals and politics as elsewhere, probable knowledge regarding matters of fact can be derived only from experience. Philosophers therefore reflect on experience, and they may encourage experimentation to the end of enlarging experience. But the difficulties of maintaining scientific control over the objects of one's experiments in the field of morals and politics must reduce the scope of projects of this sort and of the claims and proposals one is prepared to make with an eye to practice. To embark on courses of action of which one must admit that many of the consequences are, on the basis of past experience, unpredictable, would be at variance with Hume's standard of reasonable conduct.

Although the complexity of the subject matter is a contingent difficulty facing the skeptical critic of morals, the second ground of caution is more deeply rooted. When the ends of the artificial virtues are stipulated, the scientist can apply careful reasoning to the question of their instrumental efficacy. But may the ends be regarded as given? Hume's principle of utility identifies the happiness of society as the end; this, however, is a concept that Hume invokes, in his moral theory, in very general and imprecise terms. Actual systems of artificial virtue differ from one another in part because the goal of happiness may be conceived and specified in different ways. Hume does not claim that there is any single valid set of criteria for human happiness, although he suggests that certain broad conditions such as the survival of society and a minimal level of peace and orderliness will form part of any society's ends. The principle of utility is, however, a formal one, indicating the structure of justificatory arguments for certain kinds of practices. It contains, in Hume's version, little substantive content— and this simply that which Hume takes to embrace the common ends of all societies, hence a standard that experience might vitiate. Analysis and clarification of ends are a significant part of the philosopher's business, and when ends have been specified, his science may then issue in recommendations for their realization. Criticism of actual moral rules or political institutions, however, can be advanced only if there is prior general agreement on the nature of the desired ends— a state of affairs of which the existence (and the ascertainment) is unlikely in practice. Criticism and proposals with respect to "ultimate ends"—things "desirable on [their] own account"—there may certainly be, but it is here precisely that Hume denies that there are any distinctions given by reason, and that his naturalism accordingly manifests itself. "Ultimate ends" are things in "immediate accord or agreement with human sentiment and affection,"[58] beyond which Hume admits that he cannot arouse any conviction.

A final ground for a cautionary approach to criticism arises from Hume's analysis of the sources in human nature of the strength of artificial virtues. Although these institutions and practices may be thought of as contrivances, and although they may be reflectively justified by reference to distant consequences, they would have little stability if they did not draw on fundamental, nonrational psychic tendencies in human nature. Hume's investigation concludes that habit

[58] Hume, *Enquiries* (II), p. 293.

or custom, both mental and behavioral, is the feature on which they depend: it is our habitual propensity to embrace general rules that allows artificial moral rules to become firmly fixed in our imagination, and it is habits of judgment and action instilled through education that create a likelihood of compliance with these rules when sympathy or interest might incline us otherwise. Custom is therefore the source of moral order in society, just as it is the foundation of the basic belief in the orderliness of nature in our cognitive life. Custom in moral affairs, moreover, just as in the understanding, is the product of repetition and of uniform experience; habits cannot be modified or created at will, and certainly not endowed with the strength and dependability of well-established ones. The influence of custom in moral and political life is a matter of fact, discovered by science; but as one of the facts relevant to a practical decision it must be taken into account if a course of action is to be reasonable. Consequently the benefits that a Humean philosopher may expect from a proposed alteration in a particular moral or political artifice must be balanced against the disadvantage arising from the weakening of the general force of habit attached to the system of artifices as a whole. This calculation, like many others pertaining to morals, is practically difficult—a reason, as always, for diffidence on the part of the skeptic; but the centrality of custom in Hume's philosophy may normally be expected to render this consideration a weighty one.

The relation between theories of knowledge and of politics is not likely to be one of strict entailment. The active element of judgment and volition in political choice depends, from the point of view of Hume's analysis, on affective or temperamental factors; perhaps, a skeptic might speculate—"diffident of his philosophical doubts"— theories of knowledge themselves may be similarly derivative. Nevertheless there is a certain coherence in the association of different assessments of the capacities of the mind and of reason with different political orientations, and Hume, who combines political theory with extensive epistemological inquiries, serves as a case in point.[59] I have suggested several respects in which skepticism is conducive to a politics of caution and dependence on custom that is conservative in effect, if not in a doctrinaire fashion. Likewise certain important types of political radicalism involve cognitive claims, theoretical or practical, that

---

[59] Cf. Sheldon Wolin, *Politics and Vision* (London: George Allen and Unwin, 1961), p. 297. Wolin suggests that the distinction between liberal and radical ideas has to do with a lesser or greater estimation of the powers of the mind, contrasting Locke with English radicals and the British empiricists in general with eighteenth-century French rationalist radicals.

would appear inadmissible to a skeptic, since they presuppose a view of the mind in which truths of various kinds are taken to be more readily accessible than they appear to be to a philosopher of skeptical outlook. It is thus not surprising that Hume opposes radical or doctrinaire claims of all kinds, exercising his philosophical vocation of disseminating a "tincture" of healthy doubt and attempting to moderate the zealous and intractable conflicts that arise from presumptuous and dogmatic claims.

Political opinions and movements sharing a basis in dogma and intellectual assurance manifested themselves in diverse forms in Hume's lifetime, and his attitude was always one of suspicion and doubt. In the earlier part of his career radicalism in Britain appeared in the form of militant Jacobitism, culminating in what seemed at the time a serious armed challenge to the established regime. Hume regarded rebellious Jacobitism, like other doctrines of extreme partisanship, as founded on a "speculative system of principles" together with an unphilosophical unwillingness to consider empirical evidence bearing on its claims.[60] While paradoxically maintaining the divine right of hereditary monarchic authority and the illegitimacy of resistance Jacobitism refused allegiance to the established Hanoverian succession. Hume's two best-known attacks on partisan ideologies are believed to have been composed around the time of the Rebellion (1745), with the evident intention of contributing to a reconciliation of parties as well as to the defense of the established regime on the sober basis of utility.[61] The fact that the regime of which Hume was a largely contented subject was based on revolutionary (that is, contractarian) principles meant that the conservative bearing of his philosophy manifested itself first in arguments against the claims of a reactionary or counterrevolutionary form of radicalism. He endeavored to balance these, however, with arguments against the more doctrinaire elements in the prevailing Whig orthodoxy, attempting to reduce discussion of liberty, the contractual basis of government, and the right of resistance (in all of which he saw some value) to the common and flexible ground of utility, their validity weighed in light of circumstances. "The conclusion shows

[60] Hume, *History of England*, Note N to chap. 39, vol. 4, p. 536. Dogmatic opinions on key historical events, as well as speculative doctrines, serve as "touchstones of party-men" (e.g. Whigs, Jacobites, and Irish Catholics) for Hume. His historical research in each case casts doubt on their reading of the facts.

[61] See Mossner, *Life*, pp. 179-80, on the composition of "Of the Original Contract" and "Of Passive Obedience." A third essay directed to the same purpose is "Of the Protestant Succession," published in 1752.

me a Whig, but a very sceptical one" was his own assessment of where he stood, a writer not entirely trusted by either party.[62]

The types of radical political thought that were later to contribute to the revolutionary movements in France and elsewhere were just beginning to come into prominence in the latter part of Hume's life, and his reactions to them, which it is possible to glimpse in his correspondence, display the questioning doubts and withholding of assent that one would expect.[63] Perhaps most illuminating is Hume's politely skeptical exchange with Turgot on the latter's theory of progress and human perfectibility.[64] Hume's own study of history reveals certain patterns of development but also a good many fortuitous and hence ungeneralizable factors. He does not discern sufficient uniformity to postulate a clear-cut stadial pattern of progress in the past, as did Ferguson and Smith as well as Turgot; far less does he claim to apprehend any general laws of history or causal agency of progress whose operation might with any probability be projected into the future. Change without the assurance of progress, the imperfections of human nature (including defects of reason above all), and the value of civilization conceived as artifices maintained through adherence to law and custom—these are the lessons of Hume's study of history.[65] Hume's propensity to doubt thus extended from matters of religion (miracles), where he met with applause from his French *philosophe* friends, to the radical political conclusions that some of them drew from their confidence in reason and the progress of social science.

Neither Hume's version of the principle of utility nor his psychology lent itself to the purposes of English reformers, such as Priestley and Bentham, who preferred to trace their intellectual genealogy back to Locke by way of Hartley.[66] His response to the American Revolution,

[62] Hume, letter of 9 February 1748, to Henry Home, *Letters*, vol. 1, p. 111.

[63] There are difficulties in relying on Hume's increasingly rancorous later correspondence in the study of his political philosophy. In particular, his stated opinions regarding Wilkes and the serious issues raised in the Wilkes affair are too obviously colored by his reactions to the anti-Scottish manifestations connected with that movement.

[64] Hume, letter of 16 June 1768, to Turgot, *Letters*, vol. 2, p. 180. Turgot's letter of 3 July 1768, to Hume may be found in *Letters of Eminent Persons Addressed to David Hume*, ed. John Hill Burton (Edinburgh: William Blackwood, 1849), pp. 163-64. Anticipations of a future "perfected" state of humanity cannot be grounded in inferences from past experience in a manner consistent with Hume's logic; they cannot, therefore, be the basis of action in accordance with his standard of reasonableness.

[65] E. C. Mossner, "An Apology for David Hume, Historian," *Publications of the Modern Language Association* 56 (1941): 667-69, provides a good summary.

[66] Elie Halevy, *The Growth of Philosophic Radicalism* (Boston: Beacon Press, 1966), p. 11.

which in some form he did foresee, was comparable to Burke's: an understanding of its roots in British political traditions and in the tensions of imperial administration is coupled with an expedient willingness to accept and make the best of the probable outcome. He did not see America, with Turgot, as "the hope of the human race" or, with Diderot, as "an asylum against fanaticism and tyranny."[67] Also suggestive is Hume's lack of appreciation of Rousseau—both his unfavorable opinion of his writings and the temperamental difference between them that underlies it.[68]

In this perspective it is ironic that an uncharacteristic speculation of Hume's was apparently influential in shaping the thought of James Madison and consequently in some degree the outcome of the American Revolution. In one of his essays Hume indulges in abstract republicanism, designing (in the manner of Harrington) a "perfect commonwealth." Here he asserts, contrary to common opinion and to the authority of Montesquieu, and (more important) contrary to experience, that republican government is perfectly possible in an "extensive country," even sketching the well-known arguments that Madison was to develop in *Federalist* no. 10: "In a large government, which is modelled with masterly skill, there is compass and room enough to refine the democracy, from the lower people, who may be admitted into the first elections or first concoction of the commonwealth, to the higher magistrates, who direct all the movements. At the same time, the parts are so distant and remote, that it is very difficult, either by intrigue, prejudice, or passion, to hurry them into any measures against the public interest."[69] The irony is that Hume offers this highly untypical essay as a speculative exercise, almost a *jeu d'esprit*, and he begins it with the disclaimer that to "try experiments merely upon the credit of supposed argument and philosophy, can never be the part of a wise magistrate, who will bear a reverence to what carries the marks of age." He does, however, allow (in apparent seriousness) that un-

---

[67] Turgot and Diderot, as quoted by Peter Gay, *The Enlightenment: An Interpretation*, vol. 2: *The Science of Freedom* (New York: Knopf, 1969), pp. 556-57. For Hume's clearest statement of his opinions on policies toward the colonies, see his letter of 26 October 1775, to William Strahan, *Letters*, vol. 2, pp. 300-301.

[68] Hume regarded Rousseau's works as "extravagant," excelling in "eloquence" rather than in substance. See his letter of 22 January 1763, to the Comtesse de Boufflers, *Letters*, vol. 1, pp. 373-74. He therefore admired the *Nouvelle Heloise* and found Rousseau's own opinion that the *Contrat Social* was his most important work "preposterous." Letter of 25 March 1766, to the Rev. Hugh Blair, *Letters*, vol. 2, p. 28.

[69] Hume, "Idea of a Perfect Commonwealth," *Works*, vol. 3, p. 492. Hume says that Harrington's plan is more plausible than those of Plato and More in that it does not "suppose any great reformation in the manners of mankind"—as do the more extreme forms of political radicalism.

usual circumstances might someday permit an effort to realize these ideas "in some distant part of the world." Hume's empiricism of course permits and indeed encourages cautious experimentation, with political institutions as in other matters, within limits that are difficult to specify. The confidence that the *Federalist* authors and other American revolutionaries expressed in philosophy or science as a guide to fashioning new governments, however, often seems to have exceeded these limits.[70]

Some of the even more radical doctrines that began to gain adherents in the second half of the eighteenth century—democratic republicanism, formulaic utilitarianism, and prophetic historicism—all have in common some form of the rationalist presumption against which Hume's skepticism consistently sets itself: a claim of direct intellectual insight into the nature of things, either an alleged matter of fact such as the immanent laws of historical development or distinctions of virtue and vice, right and wrong, that are at variance with common opinion and sentiment. Such claims posit forms of knowledge and certainty that are not grounded in experience, just as the practical radicalism they inspire represents an attempt to transcend the experience of the past in action. Hume, to be sure, sees legitimate roles for such "philosophical fictions" as the utopian "*golden age*" or the antiutopian "*state of nature*" (T. 493-94)—both as "poetic" entertainments and as heuristic devices in philosophical argument, serving for example in Hume's own theory to illuminate the limiting conditions or "circumstances" of justice. One must remember, however, that poets are "liars by profession" (T. 121) and withhold credence from their fantasies, however pleasurable and forceful in the imagination they may be.[71] Philosophers must attempt to distinguish reasonable belief, apportioned according to appropriate evidence, from imaginative fictions, just as they draw a distinction for practical purposes between reasonable beliefs and Pyrrhonist doubt. They must remember that "a rule, which, in speculation, may seem most advantageous to society, may yet be found, in practice, totally pernicious and destructive"[72]—a warning that is itself grounded in experience. Hume's skepticism thus precludes

[70] Douglas Adair, " 'That Politics May be Reduced to a Science': David Hume, James Madison, and the Tenth *Federalist*," *Huntington Library Quarterly* 20 (1957): 345-49. Madison also drew on Hume's analysis of factionalism in "Of Parties in General"; see Adair, pp. 355-56.

[71] Thus Hume joins the list of political philosophers, which includes Plato and Hobbes, who have set themselves against the pernicious influence of poets in political life.

[72] Hume, *Enquiries* (II), p. 193. Hume refers to "fanatics" who demand a distribution of authority and property in accordance with personal merit or virtue and to egalitarian "levellers."

the intellectual assent necessary to practical utopianism of any sort, which in his eyes either confuses appealing fantasies with reasoned convictions about probable matters of fact or turns to the former rather than the latter as its guide for action. Political radicalism in particular, expecting or demanding as it does an unprecedented change in the course of nature (including human nature) as it has previously been experienced, cannot be reconciled with Hume's standards, either of logic or of reasonableness.

It should be reaffirmed that the connection between an epistemological doctrine such as Hume's and a practical political orientation is not a strictly determined one. Skeptical doctrine, for Hume as well as for the ancients, includes not only a capacity for suspension of judgment arising from criticisms of reason but also a practical "rule of life" to serve as a guide for living in lieu of certainty, or pending the eventual discovery of some possible means of knowledge. The skeptic's choice of this guide is a matter of self-conscious and tentative acceptance of some inclination that seems to be more probable or more trustworthy than the alternatives. This dualism between intellectual doubts and the practical rule in itself involves a recognition that the relation between speculation and practice is not one of logical implication. That Hume's skepticism is opposed to political radicalism in practice, therefore, ought not to be interpreted as an inescapable outcome, for example, of his perceptualism or his analysis of causality. His political philosophy must, rather, be understood in the context of his philosophy as a whole, including his peculiar manner of resolution of his doubts and the particular preferences that he expresses, directly or indirectly, in the course of selecting what he regards as "reasonable" guides both for reasoning and for action and morals.

Here we return to the controlling influence of Hume's fundamental preference for order and stability as pragmatic criteria—preferences that extend to politics and moral life as well as to the determination of correct forms of reasoning and acceptable belief. People do generally tend to believe, in contrast to the hopes of visionaries, that the future will resemble the past, by and large, and they usually act accordingly. Philosophers, Hume says, ought to assume rigorously the truth of the principle of the uniformity of nature, apportioning belief to evidence by careful inference from past experience in accordance with it, a rule of reasoning that leads to systematic criticism of belief in "miracles," whether allegedly accomplished or expected in the future and whether religious or political.

This rule is not the only conceivable alternative. A skeptic such as Hume could consistently choose, for example, to acquiesce in the beliefs of his community, refraining from criticism on the ground that everything is ultimately uncertain, in the manner of the legendary Pyrrho himself. On the other hand, denying the logical necessity of the future's resemblance to the past, he might conceivably contemplate with equanimity predictions of a future unlike anything hitherto experienced. Claims of this sort with respect to the moral and political world are evidently involved in certain types of radicalism and may perhaps be interpreted, in their widespread appeal, as corresponding to some basic propensity of human nature. Or he might, moved perhaps by extreme discontent with past and present circumstances, repudiate experience altogether as a plausibly useful guide for the future, turning to some indeterminate alternative without regard for considerations of inductive logic. Or he might discover the solution to the problems of both knowledge and conduct, as many skeptics have, in religious faith. Instead of any of these alternatives Hume chooses to base his beliefs on the principle of uniformity, asserting the appropriateness of past experience as a guide for expectations of the future in the moral as in the physical world. This choice, he says, is a "safe" or "diffident" one. It reflects an uneasiness of the imagination (which he takes to be a general feature of human nature) in the face of deviations from accustomed patterns or discontinuities in habitual associations. It is also a choice, Hume suggests, that in practical terms is most likely to put us in control of events, able to further our ends through comparatively accurate predictions of effects and consequences. It is therefore a choice consistent with (or determinative of) what he calls reasonable conduct.

Hume's rigorous adherence to the principle of uniformity thus represents a choice of one rule of "reasonable belief" from among several that appear to be available to a skeptic. He follows this principle, moreover, in a special form that is directly conducive to his specific political attitudes. Past experience, after all, is not at first glance entirely uniform in many important respects, and unexpected events occur; this is why belief in miracles is so common, and it is why the philosopher must be disciplined to assume the existence of "secret causes" for apparently chance events and to withhold pronouncements on the causes of many seemingly adventitious and unique events in history. The past that one might expect the future to resemble apparently includes revolutionary upheavals and important discontinuities (in addition to more regular patterns of change), at least in the moral world. The principle of the uniformity of nature, it has been pointed out, is nonfalsifiable: whatever happens becomes part of our experience, and our formulations of causal laws must be modified accordingly.[73] If the natural world yields evidence for many such laws to sustained scientific observation, thereby seeming to confirm the reliability of the principle in this realm, the same cannot be said so confidently, perhaps, of the human world, where the actions of innumerable voluntary agents combine to produce (frequently) unpredictable configurations of events, and where "accidental correlations" among phenomena are often difficult to identify as such.[74] Reliance on experience, although *usually* "safe," does not always lead to correct conclusions, perhaps especially in politics, a realm of action and voluntarism as well as of rules and custom.[75]

Moreover, the fact that in the moral world people usually and collectively act in accordance with their belief that the future will resemble the past tends, in this sphere, to confirm their expectations. Regularity in the moral world therefore appears to be contingent, one might conclude, on this pattern of conduct; and thus—though the pattern is in a sense "natural" to people—the regularity is not given by a nature that is external to human agents (as the regularity of causal sequences in the physical world seems to be) and is consequently not inescapable. People could conceivably act so as to render the future of their social world unpredictable and chaotic; or they could be urged, by someone who eschews the usual preference for order and continuity, to pursue a visionary future—a future that (though unprecedented) might even be realized through the causal efficacy of the vision and the action themselves.[76]

[73] Cf. Bertrand Russell, *The Problems of Philosophy* (London: Oxford University Press, 1959), chap. 6. See p. 63 for the example of the chicken whose neck is finally wrung by the man who has fed it every day. The fact that surprises occasionally happen, however, does not discredit the principle of reliance on experience, which must yield only to a better principle. Cf. also Hume's own "rational Indian," who would (quite reasonably) doubt reports about the freezing of water; *Enquiries* (I), p. 114n. I am indebted to Professor Kurt Baier for drawing my attention to this matter.

[74] Cf. Barry Stroud, *Hume* (London: Routledge and Kegan Paul, 1977), p. 65, on historical accidents, and p. 255, note 8, on the weak version of the uniformity principle required for inference from past to future.

[75] Humean logic and the practical gradualism he recommends may also be inadequate for coping with cumulative social problems that exhibit exponential expansion; cf. the problem of the 29th day by which environmentalists have dramatized the need for drastic action: Donella H. Meadows et al., *The Limits to Growth* (New York: Signet, 1972), p. 37. Cf. also John Plamenatz, *The English Utilitarians* (Oxford: Basil Blackwell, 1958), pp. 29-30: Hume "did not consider the case of a rapidly changing society, in which men's habits, formed in an earlier age, no longer suit the one in which they live."

[76] Hannah Arendt says that new beginnings, which are the mark of political "action," always have a "character of startling unexpectedness," appearing "in the guise of a miracle"; *The Human Condition* (Chicago: University of Chicago Press, 1958), p. 178.

The philosopher's belief in uniformity therefore does not entail commitment to the assumption that there will be no alterations, even abrupt ones, in political regimes: Hume himself foresaw the probability of the American Revolution in the light of his political science and his study of history. Uniformity and regularity of objects and causal sequences do not imply absence of change but rather only that change itself must be grasped as an element of experience, displaying some form of recognizable order or, in Hume's terms, coherence. It is conceivable that even radical political change might reasonably be expected on the basis of past experience, and even welcomed and advocated; it would seem, however, that a change that is not expected to bear close resemblance to any previous patterns of change could not be an event with respect to which one could hope to discover a "reasonable" course of conduct. We must therefore inquire more closely into the connection between Hume's versions of skepticism and science and the antiradicalism that characterizes his political philosophy.

The answer to this problem would appear to lie in a fundamental and special preference, complementing Hume's general preference for order as a determinant of his practical rule of life, for stability in the institutions and processes of the moral world. Such stability permits the thinking and feeling agent, creature of habit and regular expectations that he is, to be at home in a social environment and to receive the psychic satisfaction that attends the familiar and the customary. In accordance with some such disposition as this, Hume portrays the "reasonable" philosopher as expecting, believing in, and acting in conformity with a future that closely resembles the past with which he is closely acquainted, rather than a more comprehensively viewed past in which—it may be granted—there have been occasional large disruptions and unexpected events. The future to be anticipated—and forwarded by one's own actions and teachings, since moral and political futures depend on human choices and beliefs—is to be an extension of that part of experience that consists of familiar routines and orderly sequences, over which one feels a sense of control based on comparatively satisfactory comprehension, rather than that part that contains "unaccountable" or thus far unexplained events and unusual conjunctions, whose continuation cannot be projected into the future with any foresight of particulars.

When the principle of uniformity is specified in this manner, it becomes more clear how Hume's rule of right reasoning is related to his practical attitude regarding conduct in moral and political affairs. Great transformations in society—not to mention alterations in moral values or national characters—are complex events, therefore unusual or even unique, and thus not readily susceptible of philosophic understanding. Hume's reasonableness calls for cautious action in accordance with philosophical reasoning—belief proportional to evidence. Although a skeptic may acknowledge in general terms the possibility of great events in the future as in the past, it will be only rarely that the skeptic's scientific understanding can encompass a view of revolutionary change in the actual course of experience with sufficient probability to produce credence and to warrant some extraordinary course of action. In general the basic assumption of the orderliness of nature, as Hume extends it to morals and politics, dictates the unlikelihood of such changes and prescribes action oriented toward a future not far divergent from the past with which we are most familiar.

Skepticism therefore does not determine any single type of practical conclusion—as one might expect from a philosophical position that denies, or perpetually questions, the possibility of rational insight into the connections among things. A skeptical philosopher such as Hume, however, has more than epistemological puzzles to offer. It is the preferences and choices that enter into the adoption of practical rules, typically in the aftermath of the skeptical crisis, in conjunction with a continuing opposition to dogmatic claims, that together determine the skeptic's political views.

4. "A Government of Laws" and An Approach to Change

Thus far in this account of the political doctrine that Hume undertakes to teach in the wake of his skepticism I have reviewed the conception of artifice that is central to his political science and recalled the claim of priority—amounting to a normative prescription—for the artificial virtues over the natural ones in instances of conflict between them. I have called attention to the potential role of criticism that Hume's science has the capacity to play with respect to the artifices of the social world, given their contingent status as contrivances susceptible of change, and the instrumental mode of their justification. I have considered several grounds for the caution and diffidence with which Hume feels the task of criticism ought appropriately to be approached, grounds that are related to his previous skeptical and psychological studies. Finally, we have seen how Hume's characteristic opposition to various kinds of political radicalism is based not only on a skeptical rejection of the sorts of intellectual insight from which doctrinaire positions and aspirations to transcend experience typically follow, but also on an underlying preference for order and continuity, both in reasoning and in moral life, as being most in accordance with his own dispositions and with what he believes are the normal propensities of human nature.

Some of these considerations are methodological, as befits the work of a philosopher who comes to political questions from extensive inquiries into the workings of the mind: a skeptic such as Hume, for whom all is theoretically doubtful and all positive claims properly tentative, wishes to be very sure of the steps by which he finds his way to practical conclusions. Many of Hume's philosophical endeavors consist of criticisms of what he regards as inadequately grounded dogmas, and he takes pains to avoid falling into a dogmatic way of speaking himself (cf. T. 273-74). The resulting emphasis on the grounds for caution in reasoning, and the criticisms of transgressions of its proper bounds, may appear a largely negative enterprise. In this concluding section, however, I turn to two doctrines of Hume's political philosophy that offer a more affirmative teaching—doctrines that reflect his view of what would constitute sound opinion in the community at large. These doctrines are Hume's legalism and constitutionalism on the one hand and on the other an approach to political reform that can be labeled conservative utilitarianism. Both of these represent general positions that Hume nowhere presents explicitly, or under these names, but that may be distilled from many passages in his writings on politics. They are fundamental components of his political philosophy, arising from his more abstract treatment of artifice in his moral theory and forming the bridge between this theory and the specific judgments and opinions advanced in his political essays.

Hume's legalism, or preference for a regime in which all (or nearly all) authority is exercised through a regular, public, and evenly administered system of laws, stands out as the most consistent normative element in all his writings on politics.[77] This ideal of "*a government of Laws, not of Men*," Hume says, was regarded in classical political theory as the particular virtue of republican government but has in modern times been largely realized in the "civilized monarchies" of Europe as well. Such legal governments "are found susceptible of order, method, and constancy to a surprising degree"; security of persons and property is assured; industry and the arts accordingly

---

[77] Hume is a major proponent of the "legalism" discussed by Frederick M. Watkins, *The Political Tradition of the West* (Cambridge: Harvard University Press, 1948). Cf. D. D. Raphael, "Hume and Adam Smith on Justice and Utility," *Proceedings of the Aristotelian Society* N.S. 73 (1972-1973): 93.

flourish.[78] The rule of law and personal security and liberty under law appear to be the most important criteria of good government in modern societies.

Hume speculates that governments originated, "in the first ages of the world," with grants of discretionary authority to rulers in whom the people had confidence. The rule of law is a later and refined development, especially as, on a short view at least, the inflexibility of law may be compared unfavorably with the potential advantages of a wise discretion:

> All general laws are attended with inconveniences, when applied to particular cases; and it requires great penetration and experience, both to perceive that these inconveniences are fewer than what result from full discretionary powers in every magistrate; and also to discern what general laws are, upon the whole, attended with fewest inconveniences. This is a matter of so great difficulty, that men may have made some advances, even in the sublime arts of poetry and eloquence . . . before they have arrived at any great refinement in their municipal laws, where frequent trials and diligent observation can alone direct their improvements.[79]

Sometimes, moreover, such as during the Middle Ages, social conditions justify a degree of royal absolutism: "In an age and nation where the power of a turbulent nobility prevailed, and where the King had no settled military force, the only means that could maintain public peace, was the exertion of such prompt and discretionary powers in the crown." The English public (in the case alluded to) acquiesced in this state of affairs until the seventeenth century, when "the tempers of men, more civilized, seemed less to require those violent exertions of prerogative" and a legal regime was established, a development of whose effects Hume fully approves.[80]

In some countries of modern Europe, Hume recognizes, the thesis is still maintained that the rule of an enlightened and unchecked monarch can be both more efficient and more fair than when judges are restrained by "methods, forms, or laws." In opposition to this view Hume argues that the exercise of arbitrary power has an "oppressive and debasing" effect on its subjects, in addition to its usual tendency to degenerate into "negligence or tyranny." This debasement of subjects induces a slavishness that is incompatible with refinement of taste

[78] Hume, "Of Civil Liberty," *Works*, vol. 3, p. 161. Cf. F. A. Hayek, *The Constitution of Liberty* (Chicago: University of Chicago Press, 1960), p. 172.
[79] Hume, "Of the Rise and Progress of the Arts and Sciences," *Works*, vol. 3, p. 178.
[80] Hume, *History of England*, chap. 50, vol. 5, pp. 23-24.

and advances in civilization generally. It is from law, in contrast, that there "arises security: From security curiosity: And from curiosity knowledge."[81] The belief that law is, on balance, inconvenient therefore indicates a cognitive difficulty—of grasping the long-range consequences of social institutions—that arises from features of the mind that are prominent in Hume's psychology. Undue emphasis on the particular inconveniences of a system of law is a manifestation of the normal tendency of the imagination to be influenced by the greater vivacity of the near over the remote, or by immediate impulse rather than calm reflection. Hume's advocacy of the rule of law, with its many beneficial consequences over time, is accordingly connected to his general advocacy of reflection and artifice in social life and to his hopes that his empirical science might guide political preferences by revealing obscure and distant lines of causation.

Constitutionalism may be thought of as the extension of the rule of law to the processes of government itself, involving the reduction of the directive forces of the state, both legislative and executive, to a system of orderly rules of procedure. The precise delineation and allocation of powers in a constitutional regime, moreover, is typically marked by a concern to limit the scope of governmental authority and to ensure by institutional devices that it remain within prescribed bounds. Hume's preference for a constitutional regime in these senses is reflected in his admiration of the mixed form of the British government, in which the respective powers and proper relations among the different parts were generally held to be determined by well-understood and effective constitutional rules.[82] Such clarity of constitutional structure, Hume notes in his historical study of its origins, is both modern and unusual, and even in the English case it is imperfect. "Perhaps the English is the first mixed government where the authority of every part has been very accurately defined; and yet there still remain many very important questions between the two houses, that, by common consent, are buried in a discreet silence."[83] An actual constitution is the product of history rather than a rational scheme, and its precision is ordinarily limited by this fact.

[81] Hume, "Of the Rise and Progress of the Arts and Sciences," *Works*, vol. 3, pp. 178-80. Cf. Hume's remarks on the abolition of the Star Chamber court and the then-novel project of implementing the rule of law in England; *History of England*, chap. 54, vol. 5, pp. 170-71.

[82] See Wolin, *Politics and Vision*, p. 388, on constitutionalism and Hume as a constitutionalist. Hume's clearest doctrines on constitutional design are found in "That Politics May Be Reduced to a Science."

[83] Hume, *History of England*, Note K to chap. 55, vol. 5, pp. 543-44.

The attainment of constitutionalism, desirable as it is in general, is thus a matter of degree for Hume: the contrary ingredient of arbitrariness in the exercise of authority or in the making of public decisions may be great or small, and a recommendation of constitutionalism need not be expressed in absolute terms.[84] Constitutionalism is, moreover, regarded principally as a means to the end of a government of laws and moderation vis-à-vis the subject, just as in Hume's more abstract scheme the virtue of allegiance and the government it makes possible are presented as instrumental to the realization of the primary public virtue, justice. Hume values a constitutional government more as a condition of a legal regime, with its order and security, than because of any intrinsic value in the comparatively broad distribution of political influence, and perhaps popular involvement, that it normally embodies;[85] and, of course, a constitution need not originate historically (although it might) in anything resembling a social contract, a concept that implies a process more rational and deliberate than Hume believes can generally be the case in political life. Therefore, despite his admiration for the British system, Hume looks favorably on the "absolute" monarchies that prevail on the continent: despite their retention of substantial arbitrary authority vested in the prince, they are for the most part "civilized monarchies" that in practice observe the rule of law and provide a level of security and regularity of administration that in his view approach "perfection."[86]

[84] Discretionary authority may be more appropriate in foreign affairs, which are more dependent than domestic politics on "accidents and chances, and the caprices of a few persons" and thus less amenable either to science or rules. Hume, "Of Commerce," *Works*, vol. 3, p. 288.

[85] Hume does not recommend that Members of Parliament receive instructions from their constituents; his conception of representation thus appears to be Burkean; "Of the First Principles of Government," *Works*, vol. 3, pp. 112-13. He also defends "corruption" in the form of Crown patronage and influence in the House of Commons, thus placing constitutional balance over popular government, which he regards as serving the interests of a particular social group; "Of the Independency of Parliament," *Works*, vol. 3, pp. 117-22. On these matters see Kramnick, *Bolingbroke and His Circle*, pp. 122-27, 290.

[86] Hume, "Of Civil Liberty," *Works*, vol. 3, pp. 156-63. In this essay Hume says he started with the intention of defending "civil liberty" against "absolute government" but that as he proceeded, doubts arose, leading him in the end to conclude that "no man in this age was sufficiently qualified" to make such a case, and that "whatever anyone should advance on that head would, in all probability, be refuted by further experience, and rejected by posterity." This confirms his opening comment to the effect that "the world is still too young to fix many general truths in politics." Hume's impartiality here stems from his perception of disadvantages and special circumstances attending both forms of government. The popular regime in England depends on an "extreme" liberty of the press, which contains the seeds of sedition and anarchy; it also

Hume's classification of regimes is similar to that which Montesquieu was developing at the same time in that he sees the most important contrast as that between arbitrary, despotic regimes and moderate, legal ones. The importance of legality and its concomitants of security and prosperity are greater, both as the desirable ends and as observable facts about certain states, than various distinctions, such as "absolute" in contrast to "popular" or "republican," that can be drawn within the category of largely legal governments. Hume himself was at home both in Hanoverian-Whig Britain and in Bourbon France as these countries were governed around the middle of the eighteenth century, seeing minor defects and particular virtues in each. What he mainly saw, however, was their common feature of legality, to which he attributed the possibility of the civilized manner of life, including the life of letters and philosophy, which he valued as the chief end of government. In his defense of a generic type of contemporary European institutions as superior to the most conspicuous historical alternatives—the ancient republics,[87] the theocratic and feudal forms of rule of the Middle Ages, and the newly influential model or image of Asian despotism—Hume emerges as an exponent of the modern legal state at the height of its predemocratic development. Legality and constitutionalism are important conditions of the attainment of the kinds and degrees of general happiness of which modern societies are evidently capable. Hume's arguments on their behalf are thus related to his basic utilitarian criterion for government and social artifices generally; and his comparative indifference toward the precise forms of government to which allegiance is due should be interpreted in this light.

Hume's constitutional preferences lead him to devote some attention to particular forms and devices that might serve as a "remedy against mal-administration" and that he regards as especially indicative of a "gentle" or nonarbitrary government.[88] This interest in the details of rules and procedures, and in the operation of formal structures, is connected with his ambition to develop a scientific approach to the

---

requires limited partisanship, which threatens to deteriorate into partisan fanaticism, and it seems prone to incur ruinous public debts. These endemic problems counterbalance whatever disadvantages there may be in the small remaining element of executive arbitrariness in a monarchy such as France. Hume is also aware of the historical connection between a standing professional army and absolute monarchy and of England's special circumstances in this respect.

[87] Hume's most important conclusions regarding the superiority of modern over ancient states are found in "Of the Populousness of Ancient Nations," *Works*, vol. 3, pp. 381-443.

[88] Hume, "That Politics May Be Reduced to a Science," *Works*, vol. 3, pp. 108, 105.

study of politics; Harrington and Montesquieu, both of whom Hume admired, were similarly both constitutionalists and practitioners of the modern form of political science that attends especially to questions of institutional design.[89] Hume's type of positivist science, seeking as it does to establish correlations and regular sequences among discrete and specifiable objects, is most comfortable in the field of politics handling factors whose formality renders them, like the quantitative data utilized by later social scientists, easily identifiable and somewhat subject to control. Likewise, the practical proposals emanating from such a science tend to take the form of manipulation of rules and institutions, whose behavior is more accurately predictable than is that of more diffuse factors.

It ought to be added, however, that the orientation of Hume's political science to the operations of rules follows his elaboration of a comprehensive moral theory in which the central theme is the nature of the artificial, that is, the rule-governed virtues. In this perspective the legalism and constitutionalism of his political philosophy appear simply as special applications of his conviction regarding the necessity and ethical priority of artifice in moral life as a whole. An analysis more abstract than that found in any of his essays on specific political topics reveals that the two fundamental political virtues of justice and allegiance are necessarily manifested through observance of systems of public rules—indeed it is this very feature that most decisively differentiates them from that sphere of morality that arises directly from natural sentiment. Constitutionalism and a legal regime therefore appear to be implied by Hume's very concepts of justice and allegiance: a wholly arbitrary regime (if such may be imagined) would simply not exemplify these virtues, whereas one that purported to rest on civic virtue in the sense of the sentiments and ethos of its citizens, apart from rules, would appear to violate what Hume takes to be a necessary dichotomy between the realms of the natural and the artificial. A legal constitution is an embodiment of moral artifice as Hume uses the term; as such it is, in a formal sense, the kind of structure necessary for the practice of one whole aspect of moral life.

The virtue of justice implies a regime of authoritive rules governing such elaborate social institutions as property, inheritance, and contract—matters too "complicated and artificial," Hume says, to be determined by our natural feelings. These rules, furthermore, imply the need for a secondary artifice consisting of mechanisms for adjudication: judges and courts with well-defined jurisdictions, "praetors

[89] Wolin, *Politics and Vision*, p. 392.

and chancellors and juries," whose conventionality is even clearer.[90] The greater precision of laws and procedures characteristic of modern systems of legal justice, in contrast to ancient practices, is signaled by the decline of the "noble art" of eloquence in judicial proceedings—a development Hume accepts with equanimity, his admiration for Cicero notwithstanding. It was defects in strict standards of legality that encouraged the cultivation of eloquence among the ancients; and the inappropriateness of the appeals to feeling that are the essence of rhetoric, in applications of justice, is suggested by Hume's very analysis of that virtue.[91] In this fashion Hume's general moral philosophy provides him with indications concerning desirable practices and institutions in public life.

A certain type of conservative political theory stresses the need for authority, in the sense of a strong and active government, in order to restrain the disorderly inclinations of individuals and create the conditions in which people can live as moral beings. Hume does not emphasize strong government as such, but he acknowledges the necessity of authority in a similar vein: social rules must (frequently) supersede impulse, and we practice certain virtues only by accepting the priority and discipline of such rules. The requisite authority for Hume is embodied in *rules* rather than in *rule*, vested in institutions and practices rather than in persons. Rules of all sorts, whether formally authoritative or merely customary, explicit or tacit, are requisite, Hume argues, to govern conduct whenever large numbers of people must coexist in proximity with one another; their obligatoriness and status as rightful or proper are derived ultimately from their necessity or convenience. The artifices determining such rules constitute a kind of order and uniformity in the moral world comparable to that in which we instinctively believe (for the most part) in the case of the natural world. Adherence to artifices renders our social relations continuous and predictable; it creates conditions in which our past experience is a suitable guide for future conduct, confirms our habitual patterns of judgment, and permits a standard of reasonable action with respect to our expectations about the social as well as the physical world. Hume's justification of legalism and constitutionalism, in the final analysis, appeals to this larger argument concerning artifice and order.

The importance of the artificial virtues in Hume's moral philosophy

---

[90] Hume, *Enquiries* (II), p. 202.

[91] Hume, "Of Eloquence," *Works*, vol. 3, pp. 167-68. Oratory survives, Hume observes, in "affairs of state," including Parliamentary deliberations. Cf. *Treatise*, p. xviii, on eloquence and philosophy.

thus needs to be understood in terms of the parallelism between the order they create in the sphere of large-scale social life and the uniformity of nature to which we are by a basic propensity of our minds disposed to assent and on which the philosopher insists through his adoption of a rigorous scientific logic. The legitimacy that Hume ascribes to the artificial virtues in general must be attributed not only to his approval of the social peace and prosperity that he believes they make possible but more broadly to the same naturalistic process by which he approves of the fundamental tendency to believe in the order and coherence of our perceptions. To the instinctual—and, to the philosopher, appropriate—belief that the future will resemble the past corresponds a human impulse to contrive an analogous uniformity of the moral world through artifice and rules. Hume's normative position in both cases is similar, involving an affirmation of the appropriateness of human nature's basic affinity for custom and order. It is this underlying and unifying theme of Hume's philosophy as a whole in which the legalism of his political theory is ultimately grounded. His political science, with its distinctive methods and limitations, reinforces this practical orientation in part because it is developed from the same philosophical premises.

Hume's emphasis on a government of laws and on a constitutional regime contrived so as to ensure the security of the individual has led some to argue that his political philosophy is in essential respects a version of liberalism. The extent to which this claim can be upheld depends of course on the meaning ascribed to this term, which was not available in Hume's time to denote a specific party or program or to stand in clear opposition to a "conservative" alternative. Hume's political views were formed in the period of the Whig supremacy in England and have also been characterized as "philosophic Whiggism"—a not uncritical defense of the established regime conducted in terms other than those usually employed by party ideologues.[92] To support the status quo, especially out of a systematic distrust of the type of speculative efforts by which programmatic reform is inspired, may appear to be the mark of a conservative; to support the post-1688 regime in England, however, meant to subscribe in some degree to the rule of law, a balanced constitution, a government of limited powers standing above a thriving civil society, and the Lockeian notions of contract and revolution as constituting at least one legitimate foundation for political authority. Hume indeed accepts all these prin-

[92] See, generally, Forbes, *Hume's Philosophical Politics*, and Watkins, "Introduction," p. xxi.

ciples—although on the broad basis of their utility, not by reference to a doctrine of natural rights and not as the exclusive standards of justice and rightful government.

In deciding on the most appropriate general characterization of Hume's political theory, we must take account of the paradox that, two generations after the Revolution, when the proponents of what had previously been traditional and legitimist doctrines appeared as disruptive reactionaries, a true conservative would be found, like Burke a few decades later, upholding a regime whose tried and established principles included much that is central to liberalism. The problem of defining Hume's practical political position is therefore better approached if we avoid the Whiggish elements in his essays and *History* and concentrate on the more general structure and values that emerge from his philosophy. At this level, too, Hume has been interpreted as epitomizing certain key aspects of eighteenth-century liberal theory. The abstract quality of his general political theory, and the primacy of the individual (displaying a constant human nature) in his analysis, are elements commonly associated with this tradition of political philosophy. Hume's methodological individualism leads him to a comparison of the human "soul" to a "republic or commonwealth" in which the identity of the latter is constituted, in liberal (and anti-Platonic) fashion, only by its continually changing membership and its similarly changeable laws (T. 261). Hume is frequently read, moreover, as combining this individualism with an emphasis on the competitive pursuit of personal advantage and property as the most salient features of social life.[93] While granting that these themes are occasionally present I have sought to suggest the one-sidedness of this interpretation through a more complete examination of Hume's theory of motivation and of the numerous ways in which his psychology of sentiment, sympathy, and habit leads to a different and more complex understanding of human nature.

More persuasive is the case that Hume's legalism, central as it is to his normative theory, involves a fundamentally liberal perspective. Government conceived of as "artifice," coordinating (when necessary) the actions of independent centers of decision and exercising limited authority through laws, is the liberal's characteristic solution to the problem of guaranteeing individual freedom and security. Hume's theory, in apparently justifying authority in these terms, has been praised as offering the most satisfactory defense ever advanced of the

[93] Stewart, *Moral and Political Philosophy*, pp. 305ff.

"liberal ideal of personal liberty" under law.[94] There is no doubt that a rational system of law and orderly public procedures figure prominently among liberal values, at least when these are conjoined with an emphasis on individual liberty as the paramount end of a legal system. Without the latter, however, it is more accurate to think of legalism as something distinct from and not necessarily allied to liberalism. The key question would appear to be the degree to which liberty, as opposed to other social goods such as order and security, is valued as the end to be attained through political institutions. Liberty, of course, may refer to political liberty, or rights of participation in rule- and decision-making, as well as to civil and economic liberty; and it may, in all these forms, be conceived in terms of a set of fundamental individual rights that establish norms for positive law and impose constraints on the power of government. When the question is posed in this way, Hume's liberalism is not so clear.

Liberty is not an especially prominent theme in Hume's writings, understood either as a protected sphere for individual choice and action or as an attribute of a society, or of political institutions, in which a substantial set of individual rights is secured; the concept scarcely appears in the general political philosophy of the *Treatise*, and as a political value it receives only qualified praise in the *Essays* and *History*. Individual liberty does not fit into Hume's picture of the sphere of life governed by the natural virtues and sympathy, where the emphasis is rather on the spontaneous affective ties that unite people in limited contexts. In the larger artificial or political realm, on the other hand, Hume's concern is with the rules, and the corresponding obligations to obey rules, that are necessary for social order and that impose restrictions on what other philosophers have regarded as the natural liberty of individuals.

A certain minimal, though extremely important, kind of civil liberty—that is, freedom from arbitrary treatment—is conceptually related to the idea of a legal order, and in his defense of artificial virtue and of the need for precise rules Hume certainly (though implicitly) acknowledges the value of liberty in this sense, in which it is synonymous with one important kind of security. Beyond this, however, desirable forms of liberty in social life are those that are compatible with, or permitted by, the institutions supported by the artificial virtues, whose general purpose is to restrain or direct impulse. Economic

[94] F. A. Hayek, "The Legal and Political Philosophy of David Hume," in *Hume: A Collection of Critical Essays*, ed. V. C. Chappell (Garden City: Doubleday, 1966), p. 340, and throughout Hayek's writings on political philosophy.

liberty thus depends on the forms of property and contract established by the rules of justice; political and civil liberties are defined and maintained as an aspect of government, in the general context of allegiance; sexual and other kinds of personal freedom are restricted under the rules of chastity and good manners. Furthermore, Hume is not a theorist of rights in the sense of claims or immunities that individuals are held to enjoy prior to and against society and its authoritative institutions—although as an advocate of inflexible rules Hume can be read as a strong defender of the legal or quasi-legal rights that individuals may acquire under prevailing social rules.[95] In all these respects Hume's political philosophy upholds liberty only under law, or within the confines of the various artifices that are the focus of his analysis; and within this framework his emphasis is not so much on liberty as it is on the order that is the more fundamental and universal product of artifice.

This orientation may be seen not only in Hume's philosophy but also in his style and personal affinities. Hume himself manifests no desire to break out of the social and literary conventions of his time or to flaunt his individuality. He frequently chooses rather to express his views, when they are unorthodox or startling, in the ironic mode that was consistent with established norms of polite letters.[96] His detestation of John Wilkes no doubt arose in part from his antipathy to Wilkes's deliberate posturing (when he found it to be profitable) as a rebel against established authority and as a symbol of abstract liberty, which in Hume's view degenerates into licentiousness when it is not balanced by respect for order.[97] In all this Hume is a classicist rather than a romantic, and he is representative of the Augustan age, whose commitment to civility finds a reflection in his philosophical doctrine.

Hume does frequently praise the forms of civil and political liberty that, as English lawyers and politicians asserted and as Montesquieu confirmed, were the special feature of the laws and the comparatively popular government of England. Hume associates this liberty with such doubtlessly valuable achievements as commercial prosperity and scientific discoveries; this finding, however, is carefully balanced by the observation that the absolute monarchies of Europe, which are characterized by the rule of law but less personal liberty, have their

[95] David Miller treats Hume's as an example of a rights theory of justice; *Social Justice* (Oxford: Clarendon Press, 1976), pp. 157-79.

[96] John Valdimir Price, *The Ironic Hume* (Austin: University of Texas Press, 1965), p. 6. Hume's irony is usually transparent, however, and his self-imposed restraints on expression do not prevent him from making his points.

[97] Cf. Richard Sennett, *The Fall of Public Man* (New York: Vintage, 1978), p. 105.

special virtues, too, such as superior refinement in the arts.[98] More important is Hume's analysis of English liberty itself as a kind of artifice, an historical creation of the peculiar laws and constitution that evolved there. In contrast to many of his contemporaries, Hume does not believe in the alleged "natural liberty" of individuals (and in its presumptive value), a greater part of which was held simply to have been preserved under the laws of England than in other countries. In the absence of stable government, and indeed through most of recorded history, according to Hume, the condition of most people is necessitous, insecure, and subject to numerous forms of personal domination and violence (such as prevailed during the Middle Ages)—a state of affairs not meaningfully characterized as "liberty." Liberty in the civil sense is rather associated with the modern advances of civilization generally, which have been made possible by orderly government. Liberty is properly thought of as a "plan of liberty" in a certain sense— a complex scheme or arrangement of rules and institutions, though not necessarily one that is consciously designed as such; it is not the silence of the laws but rather a condition that has been gradually brought into being by the development of laws of a certain sort.[99] The special liberty enjoyed by British subjects is thus a modern "invention," or more accurately the fortunate and somewhat fragile product of an unusual and of course unplanned pattern of historical development. It is also a benefit properly viewed as secondary to the social order with which it is closely associated: "Liberty is the perfection of civil society; but still authority must be acknowledged essential to its very existence."[100] Hence attachment to liberty—"though a laudable passion"—should be moderate and "subordinate to a reverence for established government."[101]

Liberty of expression, and of the press in particular, is an aspect of civil liberty that was prized by eighteenth-century English Whigs and that has always been regarded as of central importance by liberals. Here too, however, Hume's position is mixed. The Tacitean epigraph to Books I and II of the *Treatise* signals a commitment to freedom of thought and speech that is not surprising for a philosopher, espe-

[98] Hume, "Of the Rise and Progress of the Arts and Sciences," *Works*, vol. 3, pp. 184-85.

[99] Hume, *History of England*, Appendix 3, vol. 4, p. 345n.; "Of the Coalition of Parties," *Works*, vol. 3, p. 470.

[100] Hume, "Of the Origin of Government," *Works*, vol. 3, pp. 116-17.

[101] Hume, *History of England*, chap. 71, vol. 6, pp. 365-66. This passage is notable for Hume's inclusion of Locke's work among the "despicable" and "extreme" partisan writings that have neglected this point.

cially one who, like Hume, is prepared to follow his reasoning to occasionally unpopular conclusions. Freedom of philosophical inquiry, indeed, sometimes appears to be his principal social value; it is closely connected in his mind with the development of civilization generally, and it serves as a criterion by which he assesses political regimes. The flourishing of letters and all the arts, Hume argues, may begin in republics but is commonly perpetuated in moderate monarchies as well, since its main condition is personal security arising from legal order.[102] Hume's favorable judgment of commercial civilization, too, and his lack of attraction to any form of primitivism, including the virtuous and austere republicanism of the "country" party of his time, are grounded in his conviction that economic prosperity is conducive to philosophy and the arts and to the free atmosphere in which they thrive.[103] The main threat to philosophy, on the other hand, is the intolerance born either of religious "fanaticism" or of extreme political partisanship, a judgment that doubtless has a good deal to do with Hume's efforts—for which his philosophy itself provides weapons— to oppose and mitigate these phenomena. Hume's own partisanship on behalf of philosophy, however, does not take the form of a general plea for liberty, much less an assertion of an unqualified personal right of expression. More than once he appeals, in defense of philosophy, to the harmlessness of speculative doctrines (even when erroneous) in contrast to certain religious and political teachings, with their potentiality for social disturbance.[104] He concludes his largely favorable early essay on liberty of the press in England, which he regards as "extreme" and attributes to the mutual jealousy of the parts in a mixed government, with an implicit warning concerning the dangers of excessive factionalism to which abuse of this liberty may lead.[105]

Hume is thus an advocate of liberty, but only insofar as it is em-

[102] Hume, "Of the Rise and Progress of the Arts and Sciences," *Works*, vol. 3, pp. 177-79; "Of Civil Liberty," *Works*, vol. 3, pp. 157-59.

[103] J.G.A. Pocock, "Hume and the American Revolution: The Dying Thoughts of a North Briton," in *McGill Hume Studies*, ed. Norton, Capaldi, and Robison, p. 331. See also Hume, "Of Refinement in the Arts," *Works*, vol. 3, pp. 301-305.

[104] Hume, *Treatise*, p. 272; *Enquiries* (I), p. 147. On the political dangers of fanaticism, see "Of the Coalition of Parties," *Works*, vol. 3, p. 469.

[105] Hume, "Of the Liberty of the Press," *Works*, vol. 3, pp. 94-98. Note that a reference to this liberty as the "common right of mankind" was dropped from the final edition on which Hume worked. Leonard W. Levy, *Freedom of Speech and Press in Early American History: Legacy of Suppression* (New York: Harper, 1963), p. 139, notes that the degree of press freedom that Hume regarded as "extreme" was in fact rather restricted by modern liberal standards. Hume's late letters are full of apprehension of the dangers of sedition latent in liberty of speech and press.

bodied in and prescribed by a system of law and not as an abstract or primary value. The main end of government is the social order that arises from the rules it upholds, a part of the larger order that is of the essence of artificial virtue. Liberty enters Hume's account subsequently, as one possible component of the welfare or happiness that particular sets of artifices are designed to achieve. With these priorities it is perhaps more appropriate to think of Hume's legalism as conservative rather than liberal, even though it shares with liberalism a concern for the security of the individual and of his basic interests. It is a fear of arbitrariness, a sense of the value of order and of obedience to the law, and an impulse to render social relations stable and predictable—all aspects of a legalistic but not necessarily a liberal ethos[106]—that are the most basic motivations behind the centrality of the concept of artifice in Hume's political theory.

One final point may be made regarding the problem of legalism and liberalism. Hume's interest in formal procedures and general rules is indicated by the emphasis on artifice in his moral philosophy as a whole, and the term artifice carries connotations not so much of the liberal doctrine of government as an instrumentality in the service of individual interests and rights as it does of another term, convention, with its suggestions of choice and impermanence. The artificiality of political institutions and values, as of other elements of moral life, is related to the skeptic's denial that moral distinctions, absolute standards of right and wrong, are given by reason, which is in itself an instance of the skeptic's inability to discover grounds for claims of insight into the true nature and relations of things. Artifices are contrivances intended to create a provisional order in society, yet their artificiality implies both potential change and the absence of rational standards that might provide a final and conclusive justification for any one of conceivable patterns of order. Skeptics, adapting their practice to the metaphysic of flux that is reflected in their perceptualism, do not commit themselves irrevocably to a view of things naturally good and bad any more than to a doctrine of things necessary and certain, thus avoiding (according to the ancient skeptics) the perturbations of mind that afflict the dogmatic.[107] It is typically their concern, however, to uphold the order, often seen as fragile, that society has contrived and that custom sustains. Hume, who shares this outlook, stands therefore at a distance from those liberal theories that

[106] Judith N. Shklar, *Legalism* (Cambridge: Harvard University Press, 1964), pp. 8ff.
[107] Cf. Sextus Empiricus, *Outlines of Pyrrhonism*, trans. R. G. Bury (Cambridge: Harvard University Press, 1967) III.278, p. 511.

regard social order either as unproblematic because largely spontaneous (or "natural") or with suspicion as a threat to liberty, as well
as from those that, grounded in a cognitivist ethics, adhere to a single
and immutable standard of political right.

Hume's approval of artifice is derived ultimately from the natural
desire for order that he apprehends in himself and in others; he accordingly defends the validity of artificial virtue in collective life only
through what may appear a tenuous naturalistic alternative to his
skepticism. In an investigation of human nature, however, the skeptic
typically becomes a psychologist, exploring those features of the mind
that appear to compensate in practice for the limitations of reason;
likewise, the scientist of human nature seeks to discover how innate
or habitual propensities of the mind provide the foundations of a stable
moral life in the absence of rational standards of value. Inquiries of
this sort offer a new perspective on artificial virtue, which, though it
lacks the spontaneity of instinct, is nevertheless a universal and fairly
sturdy feature of human society. When Hume the psychologist explains
the tenacity of artificial virtues rather than their formal structure, he
returns to the same phenomena of the mind that dominate his philosophy from the moment he first recognizes the inability of reason
to justify its own premises. Artificial virtues derive their justification
from elemental needs and feelings of human nature and the circum-
stantial requirements of people living together rather than from reason;
they derive their strength in practice from custom, sympathy, the communication of ideas, and other psychological operations whose effects
are so frequently apparent in our experience.

This larger philosophical context of Hume's doctrine of artifice thus
suggests a final qualification of any interpretation of his political theory
as a liberal one. The skepticism that denies any basis in reason for
moral distinctions precludes a doctrinaire or abstract defense of his
political preferences but rather leads him to develop them tentatively
from his observation of natural needs and dispositions; and although
he concludes with advocacy of a formal system of laws and constitutional procedures, his principal concern as a political scientist is with
the nonrational features of human nature that make such legalism a
viable possibility. Thus although Hume's emphasis on the rule of law
and his view of law as contrivance seem liberal, his theory lacks the
common liberal confidence in reason as the source or foundation of
the social order. The principal interest of his theory, rather, lies in the
relation it displays between artifice and skeptical principles and in its
portrayal of the necessarily habitual or customary psychological foundation of even a liberal regime.

The final element of Hume's political teaching to be considered is his approach to the practical problem of reform, or deliberate political change. This question arises in consequence of the admittedly changeable character of artifices, which Hume portrays, in contrast to the natural virtues, as being potentially within the realm of conscious choice and deliberate action. Since the rules and institutions through which artificial virtue is realized are contrivances for the achievement of certain ends, they would seem to be alterable at will—either by the imposition of rulers or activists or by general agreement. Reform might be undertaken in two circumstances: when there is a change in conceptions and preferences regarding social ends, or when changing conditions or new discoveries of empirical science make it plausible to suppose that the ends can more effectively be attained by means of different rules and institutions than those presently existing. The potential scope of political reform would therefore appear to be broad; indeed the entire sphere of artificial moral virtue, including practices and beliefs exceeding the bounds of what is usually regarded as political, might seem in Hume's system to be susceptible of voluntary reformation. It is with respect to political rules, however, more explicit and attended with more formal sanctions as they generally are, that the issue of reform mainly arises.

This subject raises again the question of the proper role of philosophical criticism, since it is preeminently the philosopher whose investigations have the capability of clarifying and perhaps of effecting modifications in the ruling opinions respecting ends and of influencing reasonings, both popular and official, concerning means. Hume's approach to the problem of reform has been intimated in part already in our examination of the grounds for caution that are so conspicuous in his thought regarding the role of philosophical criticism in moral life—caution that stems both from skeptical diffidence about reasoning powers and from his appreciation of the force and the usual trustworthiness of the ordinary manifestations of feeling and custom. The diffidence that Hume praises as the state of mind proper for a philosopher is manifested, as we should expect, in his practical teachings on political reform, but this does not preclude his developing a positive doctrine. Hume's rules of reasoning look both to the past and the future, invoking experience as a guide to efficacious and prudent action. His efforts to moderate the partisan disputes of his time involved criticisms of the ideologies of both parties, partly on the ground that both were based on allegations about the past to the detriment of a reasonable approach to the future.[108] Hume's own positive doctrine regarding political change may be characterized as one of conservative utilitarianism, in which an appropriate degree of skepticism is combined with a commitment to the discovery of reasonable courses of action and change.

Artificial virtues of all kinds are justified in terms of their utility or their efficacy in promoting certain ends, especially the general welfare of the community. Although utility is their formal ethical characteristic, however, a view of utility is not, according to Hume's science of human nature, the usual efficient cause of judgments in accordance with these virtues on the part of moral agents, nor in every case is it the paramount consideration in their original establishment. Knowledge of both the nature of motivation and the historical origins and development of morals, which Hume's science attempts to provide, is important for the aspiring participant in political life in addition to an awareness of the nature and sources of moral distinctions. The question of the most reasonable practical attitude to take toward an existing system of artificial virtue calls for a fuller understanding of morals and human nature than the mere invocation of the principle of utility might suggest.

Utilitarians might proceed with respect to actual institutions in one of two general ways. They might begin by defining what they take to be the proper social ends, then conceive of what seem to be the most effective means to these ends, and then offer up their conclusions, which would comprise both prescription and criticism of existing institutions insofar as they differ. Such an approach requires that the critic have both a clear preliminary idea of desirable ends and a rather full scientific doctrine respecting moral and political affairs, and that both of these be held with a substantial degree of conviction. Alternatively, they might begin empirically, with a thorough study of actual practices and institutions, seeking to grasp what ends they in fact serve, moving gradually to clarification and possibly criticism of these ends, and finally back to a consideration of possible revisions in the practices; utility in this approach is a presumed characteristic of functioning institutions as well as a critical standard of potentially prescriptive force. It is a method resembling the latter one to which Hume adheres in his practical political teaching, a method that corresponds in important respects to the general skeptical provisos that emerge from his

[108] Duncan Forbes, "Hume's Science of Politics," in *David Hume: Bicentenary Papers*, ed. G. P. Morice (Austin: University of Texas Press, 1977), p. 42.

analysis of reason as well as to the naturalism of his practical rule throughout his philosophy. It is a method that is conservative in effect, in its routinized caution, its shunning of abstract or programmatic conceptions, its close adherence to experience, and its conduciveness to a careful, experimental reformism that takes the given rather than an ideal as its provisional standard of value.

Utilitarianism in Britain after Hume was for the most part a radical doctrine, taking as its objective a thorough revision of received morality and law and their replacement by practices and institutions that would more clearly, precisely, and efficiently increase (or even maximize) the general happiness. Notwithstanding the assurance of some of the doctrine's historical proponents, however, questions inevitably arise concerning the proper attitude of a utilitarian toward the "common sense" morality and opinion in which existing institutions are grounded. Several kinds of considerations may tend to moderate the practical radicalism of utilitarianism.

What ground can critics have, in the first place, for the conviction—strong enough to motivate difficult and unpopular endeavors—that the ends they propose are more truly constitutive of the general happiness than those served by the institutions they seek to discard? The adherence of most people to received opinion and practices (assuming this to be the case) indicates their allegiance, albeit inarticulate, to the ends these practices serve; this at any rate seems the reasonable presumption, with the burden falling on the critic to demonstrate otherwise. It does not seem likely that the forcible imposition of new ends and values, if this were possible, would increase happiness—not, at least, in any future that may reasonably be regarded as susceptible of prediction.[109]

In addition to this there is the further consideration, according to Humean psychology, that the perpetuation of established mental and moral patterns brings its own nonnegligible satisfaction. Even more significant, custom is the usual and perhaps in many cases the necessary support of moral life, the only reliable practical guide in light of the fact that people cannot be expected to engage successfully in utilitarian

---

[109] Hume generally adheres, in his practical recommendations, to the spirit of these reflections. Stephen suggests that he violates his own rule of caution, however, in his essay "Of Suicide," where he appears to reject the traditional ban on suicide simply because he cannot himself discover good reasons for it; *English Thought in the Eighteenth Century*, vol. 2, pp. 80-81. It is possible that in Hume's view social rules having a theological basis are to be exempted from the presumption of utility, just as the testimony of religious enthusiasts is to be systematically discounted. Interpretation of this matter, however, should consider that "Of Suicide" (which Hume did not publish) may have been an endeavor to air a problem for philosophical reflection rather than a proposal for the general public or for legislators.

calculations on all occasions of social intercourse and practical choice. All social rules and institutions, whatever their utility, must therefore be supported by custom and in this way be rooted in a tenacious disposition of human nature. There is admittedly the danger that artifices may become purely customary, outliving their utility or even becoming dysfunctional in changing circumstances. Such cases, when they can be identified, are the proper objects of reform, but even in these endeavors the reformer must not lose sight of the general social value of stable customs and the orderly environment that they create.

Adherence to habit may also as a rule be defended, from the perspective of individual or collective decision making, as a rational means of conserving the resources that are expended in obtaining adequate information about the possible alternatives in any question of action. Indeed, it appears doubtful whether the factual knowledge and inferences requisite to reasonable proposals for large-scale reform can ever be accessible, with appropriate standards of evidence and probability, at least to any single observer. Collective and protracted efforts of scientific study seem called for, as well as similarly careful and extended inquiries into social ends; and it seems reasonable to suppose that the most trustworthy conclusions of such inquiries are more likely to be reflected in the general consensus of opinion than in the speculations of individual critics, subject to error and fantasy as any reasoning is.[110] The utility of moral artifices pertains to the welfare of an entire society over a long period of time; what better guide can there be to such utility than the long experience, and the opinions and beliefs generated by the experience, of the same society in the past?

Considerations such as these historically generated a conservative alternative to the radical current within the utilitarian tradition. The main practical doctrine of this conservative reformism concerns a presumption of utility to be accorded to received opinion and well-established institutions, a presumption vulnerable only to the most careful criticism, and rebuttable only on a showing of the superiority in practice of alternatives in the light of cautious and (so far as possible) controlled experimentation.[111] It is this strain in later utilitarianism for which Hume's philosophy, both epistemological and moral, pro-

[110] Cf. Hume's similar argument with respect to aesthetic judgment, "Of the Standard of Taste," *Works*, vol. 3, pp. 278-79.

[111] Cf. Henry Sidgwick, *The Methods of Ethics* (New York: Dover, 1966), pp. 151ff., on the difficulties involved in calculating the utility of practices and institutions, and Book IV, esp. pp. 460-75, for general arguments for a conservative version of utilitarianism, which he states in terms of the presumptive value of "common sense" or "intuitive" morality. Some such teaching is also found, though not systematically, in Burke's approach to reform.

vides the foundation and to which his political teachings are a direct contribution. Social artifices and moral rules are normally the products of "cultural evolution"; their origins and history are distinct from, although through the mediation of habit and education inseparable from the realization of, the utility that the philosopher sees in them.[112] Their very utility, moreover, has concrete meaning only in terms of the needs, desires, and moral sense of a community over time, and therefore it is only with hesitation that the philosopher can make the transition from historical to prescriptive notions of utility.[113] Not only artifices themselves but, equally important from a practical point of view, the artificial moral sense on which they depend are artifacts, products of tradition and experience that are only as strong as they are stable and that, like belief generally, depend on mental customs requiring the confirmation provided by the continuity of ongoing experience. In reasoning about the happiness of society, as about anything involving matters of fact, the only guide is the evidence of the past. Reasonable conduct with respect to moral and political affairs therefore must be grounded in conclusions derived from experience, and thus in Hume's view in an understanding of moral life in which custom is the most tenacious—and inescapable—feature. Although reasoning does not itself yield values, it does reveal that moral values, matters of feeling as they are, are expressions of human nature in the context of social experience, and that common experience, or history, here as in other respects offers a guide in comparison with which no other stands out as more plausible.[114]

This kind of conservatism is not so much a set of specific principles as it is a practical attitude toward the problem of conduct, bearing especially on proposals concerning political organization and practice that would entail departures from traditional or customary patterns. This attitude, consistent with Hume's skepticism and derived in important respects from his larger philosophy, is found in his writings not as a developed doctrine but in the form of maxims advanced in connection with the specific, timely topics of his essays; it is an approach whose validity Hume also finds confirmed in his study of

---

[112] Hayek, "Legal and Political Philosophy of Hume," p. 343; and *Rules and Order*, pp. 12-20, 22, 44, 65, 74. Hayek emphasizes more than Hume does the evolution of social rules, in the sense of their gradual adaptation to circumstances and social selection based on the successful functioning of the most useful rules.

[113] Sheldon S. Wolin, "Hume and Conservatism," *American Political Science Review* 48 (1954): 1007.

[114] Donald W. Livingston, "Time and Value in Hume's Social and Political Philosophy," in *McGill Hume Studies*, ed. Norton, Capaldi, and Robison, pp. 181-86.

history.[115] It is evidently, along with the advocacy of legality and constitutionalism already discussed, an element of what he intends as his popular teaching on politics—a teaching that embodies the most important conclusions of his "abstruse" philosophy and yet one that he regards as both salutary and as potentially influential when conveyed to the community at large.

Human nature displays certain uniformities with respect to elemental mental and moral characteristics: if this were not so, no knowledge of it would be possible, nor any kind of reasonable action—of which the probable outcome can be anticipated—in social affairs. On the assumption that Hume's hope of a science of human nature is in some degree vindicated, however, reasonable conduct in politics as elsewhere involves utilizing the conclusions of observation and experiment—that is, taking experience as a guide and not expecting abrupt alterations in what has been observed to be constant hitherto. Improvements with respect to matters in which experience reveals change and diversity, on the other hand, are thinkable and desirable, although the "accidental" or ungeneralizable quality of most such experience in the past ought to induce circumspection: "Sovereigns must take mankind as they find them, and cannot pretend to introduce any violent change in their principles and ways of thinking. A long course of time, with a variety of accidents and circumstances, are requisite to produce those great revolutions, which so much diversify the face of human affairs."[116] Sovereigns ought nevertheless, Hume says, to strive for all possible improvements consistent with the "common bent of mankind." Reasonable improvements are those whose outcomes can be foreseen, as fully as possible, on the basis of experiential knowledge of causes and effects. They involve projects that can be undertaken with some confidence in probable future states of affairs. Two special considerations, however, arise regarding the problem of improvement in political institutions, one drawn from the study of history, the other from moral psychology, the two disciplines that distill the experience relevant to this problem.

Rules that determine "properties, rights, and obligations" seem in general, Hume says, to have an "evident tendency to the public good"; investigation of their origins, however, shows that they were often "not intended for that purpose by the inventors" (T. 528-29; cf. 672, Hume's addition to 577). Self-love, fanaticism, fashion, and a variety

---

[115] See Hume's favorable comments on the moderation and gradualism of the Reformation in England; *History of England*, chap. 40, vol. 4, p. 115.

[116] Hume, "Of Commerce," *Works*, vol. 3, p. 292.

of other ephemeral motives have played their part in the creation of institutions now valued. Hume's *History of England* provides a detailed account of how one largely satisfactory system of government came into being through a lengthy, complex, and devious process, the outcome of which was accurately foreseen by few or none of those (the Puritans, for example) who played prominent roles in its development. Reflections such as these must give the reformer pause; successful conscious design of institutions, such as is contemplated in a present reform, is not a project for which precedents may readily be found.

Moral reasoning, furthermore, consists of the weighing of "obscure or opposite utilities,"[117] and the complexity and interrelatedness of social institutions make it easy to overlook advantages in the given and to overestimate the benefits to be derived from the new: "There is no abuse so great in civil society, as not to be attended with a variety of beneficial consequences; and in the beginnings of reformation, the loss of these advantages is always felt very sensibly, while the benefit resulting from the change is the slow effect of time."[118] Political actions furthermore have unintended as well as the intended beneficial consequences, a fact that has to do with the normal inability of reason to encompass all the ramifications of a causal chain. That the unintended consequences are so frequently unpleasant stems from the further fact that the proponents of change will have optimistically confined their attention to the proposed improvements as well as from the inevitable (and perhaps overlooked) disruption of habits and disappointment of settled expectations. Recognition of these circumstances need not inhibit reform altogether, but it should encourage modesty of expectations and attention to the interim and tangential effects that appear in the course of the work. This kind of approach ought above all to attend the establishment or reform of political institutions, which are typically so difficult to comprehend adequately and so influential in their impact: "To balance a large state or society, whether monarchical or republican, on general laws, is a work of so great difficulty, that no human genius, however comprehensive, is able, by the mere dint of reason and reflection, to effect it. The judgments of many must unite in this work: Experience must guide their labor: Time must bring it to perfection: And the feeling of inconveniencies must correct the mistakes, which they inevitably fall into, in their first

---

[117] Hume, *Enquiries* (II), p. 286.

[118] Hume, *History of England*, chap. 35, vol. 3, p. 354. The example is the destruction of the monasteries under Henry VIII.

trials and experiments."[119] Hume's own conclusion, with respect to the British constitution, is to "cherish and improve our ancient government as much as possible, without encouraging a passion for . . . dangerous novelties."[120] The more general recommendation to be drawn from these historical observations is one of methodological caution: a presumption of utility in received beliefs that precludes hasty negative judgment on the value of inherited institutions and places the burden of establishing probability of greater advantage on the advocates of reform.

Moral psychology complements history in offering a body of evidence bearing on the question of reasonable approaches to moral improvement and political reform. It is this part of the foundations of Hume's political philosophy that I have emphasized, forming as it does the bridge between epistemology and politics, and it remains only to illustrate the manner in which Hume's practical injunctions draw on the major findings of his study of human nature. The following well-known passage on the desirability of continuity in government ought to be read in the light of what has previously been said concerning the necessarily customary foundation of artificial moral virtues in general and the further grounding of that doctrine in the basic principles of Hume's psychology:

> Did one generation of men go off the stage at once, and another succeed, as is the case with silk-worms and butterflies, the new race, if they had sense enough to choose their government, which surely is never the case with men, might voluntarily, and by general consent, establish their own form of civil polity, without regard to the laws or precedents, which prevailed among their ancestors. But as human society is in perpetual flux, one man every hour going out of the world, another coming into it, it is necessary, in order to preserve stability in government, that the new brood should conform themselves to the established constitution, and nearly follow the path which their fathers, treading in the footsteps of theirs, had marked out to them.[121]

Interpretation of the moral rules of a community in terms of a model of rational choice, however helpful as a philosophical exercise (and

[119] Hume, "Of the Rise and Progress of the Arts and Sciences," *Works*, vol. 3, p. 185. This passage is quoted by Hamilton in the final paper of *The Federalist*. It echoes Montesquieu, *The Spirit of the Laws*, trans. Thomas Nugent (New York: Hafner, 1966), vol. 1, p. 62.

[120] Hume, "Of the First Principles of Government," *Works*, vol. 3, p. 113.

[121] Hume, "Of the Original Contract," *Works*, vol. 3, pp. 452-53.

which Hume himself occasionally pursues as such), is misleading as a guide to practice. Such an analysis neglects the fact that actual moral artifices must be supported by factors such as habit, sympathy, and a moral sense developed through education—factors that are not so readily subject to revision as the formal contents of rules themselves. Recognition of every individual's requisite membership, with respect to artificial virtue, in a continuing moral community leads Hume in the sequel of the passage just quoted to an explicitly conservative prescription: "Some innovations must necessarily have place in every human institution," but violent innovation is always dangerous—"and if history affords examples to the contrary, they are . . . only to be regarded as proofs, that the science of politics affords few rules, which will not admit of some exception, and which may not sometimes be controuled by fortune and accident."[122] Even apart from the difficulty of controlled experimentation in politics, however, and the normal complexity of the data, the politician must remember that the place of custom in moral life is always one of the facts that must be reckoned with:

> It is not with forms of government, as with other artificial contrivances; where an old engine may be rejected, if we can discover another more accurate and commodious, or where trials may safely be made, even though the success be doubtful. An established government has an infinite advantage, by that very circumstance of its being established; the bulk of mankind being governed by authority, not reason, and never attributing authority to any thing that has not the recommendation of antiquity. To tamper, therefore, in this affair, or try experiments merely upon the credit of supposed argument and philosophy, can never be the part of a wise magistrate, who will bear a reverence to what carries the marks of age; and though he may attempt some improvements for the public good, yet will he adjust his innovations, as much as possible, to the ancient fabric, and preserve entire the chief pillars and supports of the constitution.[123]

These passages reveal the extent to which Hume is brought to a studied acquiescence in political institutions that are held to be legitimate by the general moral sense of society, by a line of thought parallel to that which is evident in the naturalistic resolution of skeptical doubts. His political science culminates in advice regarding reasonable standards of political action, just as his philosophy of mind issues in

[122] Ibid.
[123] Hume, "Idea of a Perfect Commonwealth," *Works*, vol. 3, p. 480.

the rules for proper reasoning that make possible that science. These examples of his political teaching, therefore, appearing as they do in brief essays as Whiggish constitutionalism and cautious conservatism, have their principal interest in their relation to a comprehensive philosophy of human nature and morals, and especially to the mitigated skepticism that Hume adopts as the appropriate rule of life.

INDEX

absolutism, 350, 352, 352n, 353, 359
abstract ideas, 43, 53
Academic skepticism, 15, 15n, 16n, 17n, 19, 29, 29n, 297, 314
acquisition, 244n
action(s), 64, 79, 113, 139, 143-44, 166, 303, 337, 358, 364; distinguished from behavior, 289; collective, 266n; as object of moral judgment, 205; people of, 324; political, 346, 346n; public, 267; voluntary, 88, 153, 162, 164-65. *See also* volition
active life, 323-24, 324n, 327, 329; and contemplative life, 324n. *See also* philosophy, relation to politics
Acton, H. B., 128n
Adair, Douglas, 343n
adjudication, *see* judicial function and power
aesthetic(s), 19, 70, 104, 130, 180n, 204n, 367n; sense, 204n
agreeable qualities, 200, 208-210, 218, 225
agreement, *see* convention
Aiken, Henry David, 226n
Alexander, 151
alienation, 152
allegiance, 5-7, 21, 167, 190-92, 218, 220n, 222-26, 229, 234, 242-43, 248, 250, 259n, 264, 268, 270-73, 277-78, 288, 315-16, 320, 331, 335, 352-54, 359; objects of, 317, 321-22
alms-giving, 285, 285n
altruism, 153, 161, 163, 167, 177, 236, 258n
ambition, 92, 149, 149n, 150-51, 237, 272n
ambivalence, emotional, 155
American Revolution, 341-43, 347
analogy, 108-109, 304
ancestors, veneration of, 246, 321, 321n

ancient world, 94; philosophy in, 17, 64, 100, 293; politics in, 93, 204n, 225, 353, 353n, 355. *See also* Athenians; classics; Greece; Rome; skepticism, ancient
anger, 148, 158, 160, 165-66, 170, 181, 221n, 262. *See also* resentment
Anglo-American political thought, 273
animal spirits, 75
animals, 65, 68, 74, 199, 239-41, 240n
anticlericalism, 14
antiutopianism, 280, 343
approbation, approval, *see* feeling(s), moral
arbitrariness, fear of, 362; in government, 318n, 350, 352, 353n, 354; of treatment, freedom from, 358
Árdal, Páll S., 149n, 155n, 169n, 172n, 281n
Arendt, Hannah, 346n
argument, 303; ethical, 198, 203; political, 98, 234, 322
Aristides, 285, 286n
aristocratic values and society, 149, 151, 226n
Aristotle, Aristotelian, 80n, 138, 138n, 207, 289n
artifice(s), 3-8, 11, 24, 27-31, 58, 85n, 191-92, 197, 218, 223, 227-28, 251, 273, 282, 289, 294, 312, 323, 329-30, 341, 360-63; mental, 17, 110, 308, 334; moral, 9, 22, 108, 225, 225n, 235, 307-309; of politicians, 186, 277-78, 287, 290-91; social, 6, 21, 23, 27, 245-48, 286, 292-93, 313, 333, 351, 354-55, 368; systems of, 336
artificial virtue(s), 6-7, 21-31, 22n, 25n, 144-45, 150, 152, 158, 160, 164, 168, 186, 192-93, 196-97, 206, 209, 222, 222n, 225-43, 228n, 251-58, 262-68, 273-81, 284-87, 290-91, 297,

artificial virtue(s) (*cont.*)
311, 314-15, 331-32, 335-38, 354,
358, 362-65, 371; contingency of,
233-41; distinguished from natural
virtues, 27, 181, 192, 208-210, 213,
218-19, 226, 229-33, 242-47, 246n,
250-51, 280, 292, 306, 310, 312,
321, 337, 354; priority to natural virtues, 7, 24, 167, 182, 216, 246-48,
290, 316, 331, 334-35, 348; variability of, 233-34, 336, 364
arts, flourishing of the, 349, 360-61
association (psychological), 8, 41-43,
42n, 43n, 51, 57, 60, 91, 96-117,
102n, 122-23, 126, 129-30, 136, 147-
48, 168-69, 171-73, 181-82, 255,
275, 305, 312; verbal, 126. *See also*
causation; contiguity; resemblance
ataraxy, 29-30, 64, 313
atheism, 326n
Athenians, 285, 286n
atomism, 131, 164n
Augustan age, 359
austerity, 107
authority, 190, 224, 234, 241, 241n,
242n, 270, 276, 312, 319, 349, 355;
discretionary, 249, 350, 352n; distribution of, 191, 317; legislative, 228n;
and liberty, 360; limits on, 351; of
parents, 282; personal, 153; reverence
for, 314n; yoke of, 308n
avarice, 92, 166, 166n, 237
aversion, *see* desire (and aversion)
Ayer, A. J., 6n, 77n, 85n, 194n, 215n

Bacon, Francis, 34-35, 35n, 300
Baier, Annette, 134n, 149n, 175n, 182n,
225n, 240n, 267n
Baier, Kurt, 346n
Banfield, Edward C., 288n
barbarians, 238
Bayle, Pierre, 12n, 62n
beauty, 204
Beck, Lewis White, 53n, 80n, 301n,
329n
Becker, Carl L., 68n
behaviorism, 74, 76
Beitzinger, A. J., 226n
belief(s), 17, 20, 23, 27, 39-40, 43n, 45-
47, 50-59, 63-67, 69-71, 73, 77, 80,
83, 96, 99, 102, 106, 111-17, 120,
122-23, 127-31, 137, 145-46, 159,
161, 168, 170, 170n, 180, 189, 198,
263, 280, 296, 304-307, 312, 356;
natural, 17, 25, 53n, 70-72, 84, 111,
115, 134, 159, 208, 297, 306, 333;
proportional to evidence, 72, 110,
115, 120, 145, 216, 299, 343-44,
348. *See also* credulity; incredulity
benevolence, 141, 148, 158-66, 160n,
169n, 172-73, 205, 208-212, 216-22,
221n, 226, 230, 236, 239, 241, 243-
44, 248-50, 255-56, 262, 333; particular (limited) distinguished from general (extensive), 158, 160, 164, 167,
179, 181, 221, 236-37, 245, 247,
250, 252-53, 265n. *See also* generosity
Bentham, Jeremy; Benthamism, 102n,
164n, 166, 166n, 176n, 212n, 213-15,
215n, 267n, 341
Berkeley, George, 43
Berns, Walter, 270n
Berry, Christopher J., 94n, 335n
Besterman, Theodore, 12n
Blackstone, William, 319n
Blair, Hugh, 93n, 326n, 342n
blame, 173, 200n. *See also* feeling(s),
moral
Bloom, Allan, 24n
boat-rowing, 248, 261n, 265, 265n, 268
Bok, Sissela, 244n
Bongie, Laurence L., 186n
boredom, 180
Boswell, James, 157n
Boufflers, Comtesse de, 342n
Boulton, James T., 116n
bourgeois society and values, 151, 226n
Brandt, Richard B., 253n
Brecht, Arnold, 301n
Brochard, Victor, 86n
Broiles, R. David, 251n
Burke, Edmund, 116n, 125, 125n, 129,
129n, 130n, 131, 154-55, 155n, 246,
315, 318-19, 321, 342, 352n, 357,
367n
Burton, John Hill, 341n
Butler, Joseph, 162n, 164n, 165n
Butler, Ronald J., 71n

Cannan, Edwin, 235n

Capaldi, Nicholas, 6n, 11-12n, 33n, 291n, 301n, 361n, 368n

Carr, Peter, 241n

Cartesianism, 12, 34, 36, 39, 75, 107. *See also* Descartes, René

Cassirer, Ernst, 193n

Catholicism, Irish, 340n; Roman, 14n, 114, 114n. *See also* Church, Medieval

causation, causality, 13, 16-17, 20, 22, 25, 45-63, 49n, 53n, 70-72, 71n, 74, 77, 83-89, 92, 98-99, 101, 104-110, 112, 114, 116, 122, 130, 133, 142, 181-82, 198-99, 201n, 203, 211-15, 257, 297-301, 310, 344; as principle of association, 103-104, 106, 111, 119

caution (intellectual), *see* diffidence

celibacy, 247n

certainty, 44-45, 92, 196, 296, 303, 305, 314, 343; moral, 70; psychological, 70; of title, 317. *See also* knowledge

chance, 55, 87, 101, 116, 298, 345

change, in artifices, 229; political, 29, 347, 364-65, 370; rapid social, 346n. *See also* criticism (philosophic); radicalism, political; reform(ism)

Chapman, John W., 233n

Chappell, V. C., 15n, 42n, 54n, 66n, 80n, 134n, 208n, 358n

character, 88-89, 90n, 91, 121, 144, 149, 175-76, 181, 200, 206, 223, 268; excellence of, 150n, 204, 209, 212n; formation of, 118, 124, 171, 282, 290-91; as object of moral judgment, 202, 205, 212, 245, 279. *See also* national character

charity, 219

Charles I, 109, 318n

chastity, 222, 224-26, 224n, 225n, 238, 245n, 247n, 279, 283, 335, 359. *See also* family; modesty; sexual relations and mores

checks, constitutional, 247, 272n. *See also* constitutionalism

cheerfulness, 209

Cheyne, Dr. George, 63n

children, 328; care (love) of, 21, 141, 158-59, 220-21, 244; education of, 282, 290; participation in justice, 240

China, 184, 256

Christianity, 13-14, 74; ethics of, 149

Church, Medieval, 247n

Cicero, 15n, 16n, 17n, 29n, 64n, 138, 138n, 178n, 204n, 355

citizenship, 224

civic virtue, 149, 154, 220n, 354

civil society, 248, 356, 360; establishment of, 259

civility, 225, 359

civilization, advances in, 351, 360-61; value of, 341

Clarke, Samuel, 162n, 198n

classicism, 359

classics, classical influence, 138, 150n, 151, 204, 212n, 288, 291, 324n, 349

clemency, 219

climate, 183

coercion, 88, 272n, 276, 292; governmental, 263, 269-71, 269n, 273; self-imposed, 271. *See also* enforcement (of rules)

coherence, 56-57, 101, 131-32, 279, 347

collective goods, 266, 271n

collegiality, 244

commercial society and values, 149, 151, 225, 260n, 361

common life and affairs, 63, 65-66, 110, 180, 186, 263, 323

common sense, 11n, 16-17, 22, 22n, 39, 66, 69n, 90, 109, 115, 120-21, 296, 329, 329n, 366, 367n

community, 128, 176, 183, 192, 345, 371-72; of goods, 237; like-mindedness in, 124, 275; moral sense of, 368

comparison (of ideas), 152, 156, 173, 175, 175n

compassion, 148, 162, 167, 172-73, 220-22, 227, 230, 239, 241, 243-44, 246, 246n, 247n, 256

competition, 152, 155, 184n, 357

concubinage, 247n

conflict, political and social, 151-52, 155-56, 178, 340. *See also* artificial virtue(s), distinguished from natural virtues; dilemmas (moral)

conformity, social, 177, 177n

Connon, R. W., 33n, 258n

conquest, 317

conscience, 201. *See also* moral sense

consciousness, 133, 161, 171
consent, 177, 240, 241n, 259; of governed, 319-20; transference of property by, 260. *See also* rational choice
consequences, ethic of, 214, 336, 338; unintended, 370
conservative, conservatism, 29-31, 126n, 130, 149n, 155n, 188, 214, 295, 308, 313n, 314n, 319, 323, 328, 332, 339, 355-57, 362, 367-68; Hume's, 8, 11, 13, 29, 229, 307, 310, 312-16, 322, 325, 330, 335, 340, 365-66, 372-73; rationalism, 323n
constancy, 56, 58, 131-32
constant conjunction, 49-50, 52, 111-12. *See also* causation
constitution, ancient, 318; English (British), 303, 326, 360, 371
constitutionalism, 8-9, 11, 28, 31, 247-48, 272, 272n, 294n, 317, 319, 323, 327, 331, 332n, 349, 351-56, 351n, 369, 373; British, 5, 224n
contagion (psychological), 125, 150, 170-71, 179, 183n, 293
contempt, 155, 172-73, 175
contiguity, 103-105, 114, 130, 154n, 172, 181, 208, 244, 255, 263
contract(s), 132, 231n, 258, 265, 354, 359; freedom of, 235; justice and, 261n; original, 307, 319; sanctity of, 260n
contractarianism (political), 27, 64n, 259, 259n, 307, 319-20, 340, 352, 356
convention(s), 6, 17, 21, 22n, 24-29, 66, 85, 85n, 124n, 175, 191, 193, 196, 218, 236, 243, 261-62, 261n, 265, 269n, 276-77, 297, 316, 319, 362; linguistic, 226n, 280-81, 281n; literary, 359; original, 258-60, 259n; of self-interest, 264. *See also* nature and convention
conventionalism, 66, 197, 219, 283, 355
cooperative enterprises, 260n, 265, 267
coordination, of conduct, 227, 230, 248, 265n, 269, 337, 357; problems, 269n
corporative view of society, 126n
corruption (political), 352n
Cottle, Charles E., 222n
country, 181; love of, 154, 154n; native, 245

Country party, 326-27, 326n, 361
courage, 151, 171, 186, 204, 206, 221n
Court party, 325, 326n, 327
credulity, 62, 70, 72, 110, 116-17, 116n, 120-22, 127, 130, 144, 303, 309, 325, 329. *See also* belief(s)
crime, criminal, 238, 270; political, 272
criticism (philosophic), 23, 28-30, 66, 68, 71, 74, 101, 117, 119, 121, 123, 126, 128, 182, 192, 194, 197, 202, 207-208, 214, 217, 229, 241, 248, 276, 284, 294, 307, 310-14, 322, 328, 336, 338, 345, 349, 364, 367
Cromwell, Oliver, 272
Cropsey, Joseph, 241n
cruelty, 237
Crusoe, Robinson, 236
curiosity, 65, 74, 116, 130, 157, 166, 179, 299, 302, 323, 351
custom (habit), 8-9, 17, 21-31, 43, 53-55, 63, 65, 77, 82, 97, 101, 112-13, 117-31, 119n, 125n, 136, 158, 177, 181-86, 189, 194, 206, 247, 249, 263, 275, 279-80, 283-84, 288-89, 293, 304-306, 309, 315-18, 321, 333, 338-39, 346-47, 356-57, 363-68, 371-72; mental, 43-44, 43n, 52, 109, 119, 129, 157, 257, 287; social, 20, 118, 313, 315, 322, 362
Cyrus, 249n

Day, John, 190n
deference, 155
degeneration, historical, 94
deliberation, *see* reflection
democracy, democratic, as form of government, 319, 342-43; theory, 267n, 319
Democritus, 116n
demography, 107n
Descartes, René, 35, 39, 75-76, 75n, 132, 132n, 314, 314n
descent, pride in, 151, 151n; rights of, 322
design, political, 370; theological, 68, 86n, 109, 216, 216n, 245n, 308n
desire (and aversion), 73, 79, 126, 132, 139-40, 143, 156, 162-66, 165n, 185, 221, 237, 250-51, 262, 271, 274

despotism, 353. *See also* arbitrariness; tyranny

detachment (philosophic), 68, 255, 322-25, 329. *See also* impartiality

determinism, 85, 85n, 88-89. *See also* causation; free will; liberty and necessity

Diderot, Denis, 12n, 16n, 211n, 247-48n, 326n, 342, 342n

diffidence, 11, 28, 30-31, 76, 217, 297, 306, 311, 315, 325, 327-31, 337, 339, 345, 348, 364

dilemmas (moral), 222n, 232, 243, 246, 249, 255. *See also* artificial virtues(s), distinguished from natural virtues; prisoners' dilemma

diplomacy, 234

discipline, martial, 186

discontent, 345

discord, *see* conflict, political and social

discretion, 208; in exercise of authority, 249, 350, 352n

disinterestedness, apparent, 176; of ideal ruler, 249n; in moral judgment, 160, 179, 201-202, 210, 254, 256; in passions, 162, 164. *See also* impartiality

disorder, social, 152, 158, 263. *See also* conflict, political and social

disposition, 205

dissolution, social, 238, 266

distress, relief of, 220-21

diversity, moral, 20-22, 90, 197, 233, 283-84, 336; apparent moral, 225, 234. *See also* uniformity, moral

divine right monarchy, 340

division of labor, 235, 235n

doctrinaire impulse, *see* politics, programmatic

domination, love of, 153, 244n; personal, 360

dominion, 34-35

double standard, sexual, 224

dreams, 75, 101, 103, 115

dueling, 125n

duty, 198, 204-205, 204n, 221, 230, 235, 244, 251, 285, 316; deontological, 223; family, 152; and inclination, 221; political, 224, 244n; sense of, 27, 192, 206, 216, 244, 251-52, 257-58, 268, 270, 273-74, 282, 286-87, 290, 317. *See also* obligation

dynastic titles, 318

Earle, Edward Meade, 276n

economic analysis and theory, 26, 107, 145, 146n, 166, 191n, 235, 258, 260n, 266

economic life, 90, 132, 166; and government, 277

economic virtues, 212n

economy of nature, 91, 91n

education, 25, 35n, 37, 113, 120-28, 122n, 124n, 136, 150, 168, 176, 183-86, 189, 241n, 294, 333; moral, 124, 251-52, 257, 270n, 275-92, 316, 339, 368, 372; private and public, 290-91

educative role, philosopher's, 203, 229, 284, 286, 294-96, 322, 324, 327, 329-30. *See also* criticism (philosophic)

egoism, ethical, 210n; logic of, 265, 268-69; psychological, 27, 135, 138, 147, 149, 151, 161-67, 164n, 166n, 172, 174-77, 186, 247, 250, 258n, 259, 259n, 262, 266-67, 291n. *See also* individualism; self-interest; self-love

Egypt, sultan of, 276

eighteenth century, 86n, 94-95, 138, 343, 357. *See also* Enlightenment

Elizabeth I, 318n

eloquence, 115, 168n, 286, 342n, 350, 355, 355n

emotivism, 201n

empiricism, 4, 7, 10, 12n, 13, 16, 25, 30, 32, 32n, 35, 37, 38n, 45, 49n, 68-69, 74, 96, 110, 135, 194, 217, 296, 300, 322, 343; British, 33, 339n; and conservatism, 31; and natural law, 20n

Encyclopedists, 326

enemies, attitude to, 158, 163, 200-201; treatment of, 250

enforcement (of rules), 231, 245, 269-70, 272, 279

England, 31, 94, 128, 256, 359; government of, 224, 272, 320, 350, 352n, 359; liberty in, 359-60; philosophy in, 35, 95; politics in, 324, 356; psychology in, 288n; Reformation in, 369n;

England (*cont.*)
rule of law in, 351n; social thought in, 31, 339n, 341. *See also* Great Britain
Enlightenment, 12-13, 13n, 14n, 27, 106, 128, 295, 308-309, 312
enterprise, spirit of, 150, 150n
envy, 148, 155-56, 172-73, 175n
epistemology, 8, 10, 12, 15, 20-21, 28, 32-34, 38-39, 44-45, 50, 56, 59, 65, 68, 73-74, 81, 85, 89, 92, 100, 109, 116, 122, 131, 133, 137, 187, 199, 298, 300, 305, 314, 344
equality, 150n, 239-42, 241n, 242n, 343n; of treatment, 250
equity, 219, 252, 264
error(s), 42, 62, 70-71, 96-101, 104-106, 109, 112-15, 121-22, 128, 130, 134, 182, 275, 300, 367
established practice, 316-22, 318n
esteem, *see* love; self-esteem
etiquette, *see* good manners; polite society
eudaimonism, 141
Europe, European, 237, 311; states, 235, 349; treatment of Indians, 240-41
evolution (of social institutions), 194, 227, 229, 235, 264, 270, 332, 368, 368n
exchange, 235n, 258, 260n, 318n
executive function and power, 228n, 273, 316, 319, 351. *See also* enforcement
expectations, 157, 187, 232, 264, 279-80, 347, 355; disappointment of, 232n, 370; self-fulfilling, 346
experience, 13, 28-30, 43, 48-58, 68, 77, 83-87, 90, 95, 98, 111-15, 118-24, 127, 130-31, 135, 140, 168, 170, 172, 185, 193, 201, 217, 228, 257, 275, 279, 285, 293, 296, 314, 322, 337, 342, 346-47, 355, 364, 367, 369; effort to transcend, 18, 23, 218, 323, 328, 343; future, 55, 301, 336; moral, 244, 255, 273-74, 280, 282; reliance on, 346; repudiation of, 345. *See also* history
experimental method, 36-37, 85, 85n, 86n, 90, 190, 194, 207, 259, 300, 302, 304, 336-37, 343

exposure (infant), 107, 283
external world, knowledge of, 15, 38, 45, 55-58, 71, 132, 297. *See also* objects, existence of

fact and value, 80, 80n, 196, 304, 330. *See also* is-ought
factionalism, *see* partisanship
fallibilism, 18, 146, 301n, 336
falsification, 296, 345
fame, love of, 167, 173-75, 268, 323, 329-30. *See also* reputation
family, 151-52, 175, 181, 182n, 191, 208, 220-21, 221n, 224, 235-36, 244, 244n, 246, 260, 290, 322, 331
fanaticism, 5, 14, 63n, 71, 130, 303n, 331, 342, 343n, 353n, 361, 361n, 369
fantasy, 62, 99, 101, 104, 130, 343-44, 367
fashion, 124n, 125, 283, 369
fear, 142, 154-58, 157n, 170, 179, 186, 272n
feeling (sentiment), 17, 28, 51, 54, 69-70, 78, 99, 102, 111, 114, 128, 137, 146, 168-69, 170n, 189, 226, 243, 281, 294, 304-305, 314-15, 357, 364; moral, 19, 19n, 20-22, 26, 72-73, 77-80, 102, 138, 141, 156n, 164, 194, 197-204, 207, 210-11, 211n, 215-17, 221, 227, 243, 248, 266, 274, 277-80, 278n, 286, 288, 297-98, 310-11, 316, 321, 334, 354; political, 321; and rhetoric, 355. *See also* passion(s)
fellow-feeling, 160, 160n, 169n, 179, 219. *See also* benevolence
fellowship, 178
Ferguson, Adam, 183n, 341
feudal rule, 353
fictions, mental, 17, 51, 58, 62, 72, 96, 98-101, 107, 111, 115-16, 131-33, 157, 308-309; philosophical, 236-37, 343
fideism, 14n, 62, 307
fidelity, *see* promises, promise-keeping
final causes, 77n
Flathman, Richard E., 289, 289n
Flew, Antony, 38n, 50n, 136n, 281n
Forbes, Duncan, 20n, 86n, 91n, 94n, 183n, 223n, 224n, 291n, 326n, 356n, 365n

force, rule by, 276. *See also* coercion

foreign affairs, 352n. *See also* international relations

foundings, 233. *See also* legislator-founder

France, the French, 94, 225, 319, 341, 353; Enlightenment in, 13, 326; government of, 353n; morals of, 283; rationalism in, 339n; revolutionary movement in, 341

free riders, 266n

free will, 55, 88. *See also* liberty and necessity

freedom, *see* liberty

friends, friendship, 92, 158, 176, 181, 208, 220, 231n, 236, 237n, 243-45, 250, 252

future, benefits, 146n, 209; constraints, 271; control over, 104-105, 345; expectations regarding, 232, 328, 345, 369; knowledge of, 46, 49-50, 53, 99, 111, 132, 296, 299, 366; moral and political, 346-48; prediction of, 197, 296, 345; resemblance to past, 18, 22, 50, 53, 53n, 71, 77, 84, 86, 92, 106, 111, 130, 136, 182, 197, 282, 290, 322, 335, 344-47, 356; vividness of in imagination, 321n. *See also* uniformity of nature

Gagnebin, Bernard, 93n

games, 226n

Gauthier, David, 261n, 317n

Gay, Peter, 13n, 14n, 86n, 342n

generalization, 108-110, 128, 130, 279

generosity, 92, 159, 208-209, 219-20, 256; confined (limited), 159, 236, 241, 245, 250, 260. *See also* benevolence

Gibbon, Edward, 93n

Gladstone, W. E., 165n

Glaucon, 264, 268

glory, love of, 151

God, existence of, 45, 86n, 308

Godwin, William, 164n

golden age, 236-37, 343

good, goodness, 80, 140-41, 143, 148, 158-59, 190, 196, 200, 204, 211-12, 232, 256, 262, 281; common, 288; general, 245, 250; public, 230, 317, 369. *See also* interest, public

good breeding, 129, 150. *See also* good manners

good manners (etiquette), 191, 209, 218, 222, 225, 227, 227n, 237n, 267, 335, 359. *See also* politeness

goods, distribution of, 223, 242n, 317; instability of, 260; scarcity of, 237. *See also* collective goods; public goods

government, 6-7, 24, 26-27, 160, 224, 228, 228n, 232, 237n, 244n, 247, 264, 266n, 268-73, 272n, 276-77, 292, 303, 309, 315-21, 331, 351, 355, 360, 362; forms of, 233, 270, 283, 291, 311, 316, 318-19; free, 326; historical development of, 5, 7, 332, 370; of laws, 247-49, 352, 356; mixed, 272, 318-19, 327, 351, 361; moderate, 335, 352-53; origins of, 152, 184, 252, 258-59, 263, 350; popular, 184n, 352, 352n, 359; powers of, 272

governors, *see* rulers

gradualism, 346n

gratitude, 21, 220, 222, 230, 244, 246

gravity, 42

Great Britain, British, constitutionalism, 5, 224n; moral philosophy in, 76, 161, 215, 366; government of, 319, 351-53; political tradition, 342, 360; psychology, 42, 75; radicalism, 340; society in, 260n, 311. *See also* England; Scotland

Greece, Greeks, 94, 224, 283, 313n

Green, Thomas H., 32n, 69n, 162n, 164n, 176n, 267n

Gregoire, Henri, 241n

Greig, J.Y.T., 63n, 93n, 219n, 324n

grief, 142, 156-57, 172, 179

Grodzins, Morton, 244n

Gutmann, Amy, 36n

habit, *see* custom

habituation, 176, 278, 281-82, 293; in language, 119; of moral sense, 216, 268, 287-90; of passions, 141, 184-85

Halevy, Elie, 102n, 212n, 341n

Hamilton, Alexander, 276n, 371n

Hamilton, William, 82n

Hanover, House of, 327, 340, 353

happiness, 25n, 30, 141-44, 156, 158,

happiness (*cont.*)
165, 169n, 179, 198, 208-209, 238, 253, 256, 311, 336, 353, 362; as ethical end, 72, 80n, 160, 172, 202, 210, 212-17, 220, 310; general, 284, 316; greatest, 162, 213-14, 366; of mankind, 248; of others, 176, 278; public, 232n; of society, 145, 228, 232, 239, 253-54, 256, 330, 334, 338, 365, 368
hardship, cases of, 249
Harrington, James, 342, 342n, 354
Harrison, Jonathan, 199n, 223n, 224n, 230n, 238n, 249n
Harrison, Wilfrid, 176n, 212n
Hartley, David, 42, 341
hatred, 70, 126, 148, 153-56, 165, 171, 173, 175, 185, 221n. *See also* resentment
Havelock, Eric A., 38n
Hayek, F. A., 31n, 228n, 332n, 350n, 358n, 368n
Hearn, Thomas K., Jr., 186n, 203n
Hedenius, Ingemar, 204n
hedonism, 162-63, 166
Hegel, G.W.F., 9, 240n
Hendel, Charles William, Jr., 69n, 104n, 165n
Henry VI, 320
Henry VIII, 370n
herding principle, 178
heroism, military, 151
Hirschman, Albert O., 166n
historicism, 343
history, 3, 5, 7, 18, 21, 27, 30-31, 36, 86, 94-97, 104, 119, 121, 190, 193-94, 217, 228, 233, 264, 302, 312, 319, 322, 327, 332, 336, 341, 351, 360, 365, 369; European age of, 193; laws of, 341, 343; scientific systems of, 94
Hobbes, Thomas; Hobbesianism, 75-76, 93, 95, 113n, 125, 132, 138, 149, 150n, 152, 157n, 162, 162n, 177, 188, 191n, 222n, 237, 240, 269n, 273, 310n, 343n
d'Holbach, Baron, 326n
Holland, 225
Holy Land, 106
Home, Alexander, 151n
Home, Henry, 341n

Homer, ethics of, 221n
homosexuality, 224, 283
honor, code of, 125n; sense of, 151, 287, 290
hope, 142, 156-57
Horace, 204n
Horne, Thomas A., 177n
Hubin, D. Clayton, 236n
humanism, 204n
humanity, 160, 217, 219-20, 230, 238, 240, 253. *See also* benevolence
humility, 134, 148-52, 155-56, 165, 170, 173, 175n, 179
hunger, 140, 142, 158
Hutcheson, Francis, 19, 35n, 69n, 73, 138, 138n, 141n, 162n, 201n, 204n, 213, 213n, 216n, 219n, 222n, 224n, 242n, 258n, 310n, 329n
Huxley, Thomas H., 36n, 86n

ideas, theory of, 39n, 40, 56n, 75, 96, 147, 308
identity, personal, 37, 41, 41n, 58, 131-36, 134n
ideologies, political, 71, 98, 109, 113, 125, 224n, 325, 327, 340, 356, 364
illusion(s), 46, 62, 75, 99-100, 140, 300
imagination, 17, 22-23, 41, 43, 49-58, 61-63, 71, 74-75, 80, 82, 96-119, 102n, 123, 126-31, 136-40, 146n, 154, 154n, 157, 159, 161, 169, 171, 179, 181-87, 197, 215, 232n, 244, 247, 255, 257, 263, 271, 275, 278, 280, 285, 291, 298, 301, 317, 321n, 339, 345, 351; flights of, 24, 62, 98-101, 130
imitation, 125, 183, 184n
impartiality, Hume's, 325, 325n, 326, 326n, 329, 352n; of morality, 182, 202, 227, 232, 243, 245, 250, 256, 290. *See also* detachment (philosophic); disinterestedness
impersonality, of artificial virtues, 160; of large society, 235, 244, 246, 268
incentives, 166n
incest, 224, 224n, 225
incredulity, 51, 92-93, 115-16, 131. *See also* belief; credulity
Indians, American, 240-41

indifference, 182; and choice among governments, 316

individualism, and autonomy, 176; methodological, 6, 26-27, 29, 36-37, 97, 101, 117-18, 126n, 131-32, 135, 148, 161, 175, 189, 267n, 275, 292, 357; political, 36-37, 118, 135, 177. *See also* egoism; self-interest; self-love; sociability

indoctrination, 127

induction; inductive (causal) inference, 3, 8, 12n, 16, 22, 25, 33, 45-55, 59, 62, 67, 70, 72, 75, 77n, 80, 89-90, 96, 100, 104-108, 114-15, 120, 122, 128, 142-43, 198, 212, 293, 296, 298-99, 334-36; logic of, 22, 50, 72, 105, 110, 114, 117, 194, 246n, 306, 310, 345

industry, 349; as a virtue, 208, 212n

inequality, 155, 172, 235, 240, 242n

inertia (mental), 58, 129, 188

infanticide, 107

inferential reasoning, *see* induction

inflexibility (of artificial virtues), *see* uniformity

inheritance, 354

injury, 175

injustice, 128, 237-38, 266; opinion of, 198

innate ideas, 39, 40n, 45

insight, 5, 14, 18, 44, 48, 62, 83, 85, 89, 94, 100, 107, 110, 118, 125, 133, 198, 207, 299-303, 329, 343, 348, 362

instinct(s), 70-76, 102, 111-12, 117, 137, 146, 159, 163, 180, 206, 217-18, 221, 221n, 255, 294, 334, 356, 363; sociable, 154, 160. *See also* passions, instinctual

institutions, 355; as object of moral judgment, 205, 214; utility of, 254. *See also* political institutions

integrity, 223

intention, 205, 214

interest(s), 25, 25n, 143-47, 154, 162, 166, 228-29, 271, 274, 277, 285-90, 315-16, 332, 339, 362; common, 261, 265; conflict of, 255; economic, 166; opinion of, 276; private (individual), 6, 132, 167, 252, 258, 261-62, 264-65, 269, 272n, 273, 333; public, 231-32, 252, 255, 272n, 287, 317-18, 320-21, 342; of rulers, 272; social, 220, 243, 248, 252, 258, 284, 331; true, 8, 122, 143, 143n, 145, 285-87

international relations, 224

intolerance, 125, 361

introspection, 21, 35-37, 36n, 41, 85, 97, 132, 134, 193, 200

intuition(ism), 44-45, 47, 49n, 51, 53, 217, 217n, 254; moral, 367n; and sense of justice, 247

invisible hand, 245n

irony, 359, 359n

is-ought, 19, 26, 79-80, 80n, 207, 306, 320, 334

Jacobitism, 340, 340n

James II, 109

James, William, 301n

jargon, 126

Jefferson, Thomas, 241n

Joan of Arc, 93

Johnson, Samuel, 308, 314n

joy, 142, 156-57, 172

judgment, moral, 192-93, 197-205, 205n, 208, 211, 213-14, 279, 304, 365

judicial function and power, 228n, 272, 316, 354-55

justice, 5-7, 5n, 9, 21, 24-27, 145, 150, 152, 160, 164, 167-68, 186, 190-92, 195-96, 205, 208-210, 212, 216-26, 219n, 220n, 221n, 223n, 229-31, 231n, 232n, 235-44, 235n, 243n, 248-73, 255n, 259n, 260n, 261n, 265n, 266n, 277-78, 282-83, 286-88, 304, 309, 309n, 317, 319, 331, 335, 343, 352, 354, 359; distributive, 223n; legal, 355; origins of, 154, 228, 234, 252, 258, 261n, 267; retributive, 223n; sense of, 190, 221n, 275, 290; as a system (scheme), 209, 230, 234, 249, 259, 265; three rules of, 260

justification, 7, 10, 19, 30, 50, 55-59, 64-66, 70, 75, 77, 77n, 80, 82, 139, 190, 194, 196, 203-204, 207, 211, 213, 217, 228-29, 232, 234-35, 239, 242-43, 254-55, 284, 297, 313, 338, 362-63

Kant, Immanuel, 4, 9, 204n, 328, 328n
Kaye, F. B., 291n
Kemp, J., 80n
Keynes, J. M., 42n, 157n, 308n
King, James T., 98n, 201n, 301n
Klibansky, Raymond, 319n
knave, sensible, 266
knowledge, 34, 38, 44-48, 65, 196, 296, 300, 304, 343; theories of, 339
Koch, Adrienne, 241n
Kramnick, Isaac, 327n, 352n
Kydd, Rachel M., 143n, 251n

Laird, John, 6n
Lancaster, House of, 320
language, 36, 113n, 119, 126, 167, 181, 184, 280; conventions, 226n, 280, 281n; and customary usage, 113; moral, 197, 201, 201n, 256, 281; ordinary, 141, 166n. See also jargon; meaning
law(s), 231, 246, 248, 350-51, 355; common, 31, 319n; as educative, 291; of history, 341, 343; international, 239n; positive, 317; regulation by, 247; reverence for, 276; rule of, 31, 247-48, 317, 323, 331, 350-52, 351n, 356, 359, 363; scientific, 346; silence of, 360; systems of, 256, 362. See also government of laws; legal; obedience to law
laws of nations, 222, 224, 238
laws of nature, see natural law
legal, 6, 152, 223, 227; systems, 191. See also law(s); legalism
legalism, 8, 28, 31, 145, 248, 319, 331, 349-58, 349n, 362-63, 369
legislation, legislative power, 228n, 351
legislator-founder, 291, 291n
legitimacy (political), 224, 224n, 246, 315-20, 320n, 332, 357
Leroy, André-Louis, 6n
Letwin, Shirley Robin, 74n, 138n, 328n
levellers, 343n
Levy, Leonard W., 361n
Lewis, David K., 269n
liberal(ism), 31, 36n, 132, 135, 145, 151, 166, 177, 258, 270n, 295, 312, 315, 318n, 339n, 357-63; Hume as a, 8, 356-63

liberality, 285, 285n
liberty, 8, 88, 88n, 269n, 318, 327, 358, 361-63; economic, 236, 358-59; English, 359-60; of expression, 360-61; of imagination, 98-99, 103, 130; under law, 350, 358-59, 362; natural, 358, 360; and necessity, 87-89; plan of, 360; political and civil, 340, 352n, 357-60; sexual, 359; system of, 319. See also free will; press, liberty of
licentiousness, 359
lies, liars, 92, 127, 343
Little, A. G., 162n
liveliness (conceptual), 54, 58, 61, 75, 98-99, 106, 108, 111-16, 127, 130, 136, 154, 168-69, 170n, 175, 177, 180-82, 244-56, 263, 271, 278-79, 285, 321n, 351
Livingston, Donald W., 98n, 201n, 301n, 368n
Locke, John, 19, 19n, 32-35, 32n, 34n, 37-41, 40n, 41n, 42n, 44-45, 44n, 45n, 47n, 49n, 53, 56n, 73, 73n, 74-76, 76n, 95-96, 101, 101n, 118, 122, 122n, 124n, 125, 177n, 198n, 259, 259n, 277n, 300, 399n, 341, 356, 360n
logic, see induction; reasoning, right; rules of reasoning
logical positivism, 4, 84n
love (esteem), 70, 148-49, 153-56, 165, 167, 171-73, 175, 177, 179, 181, 184-86, 268; of country, 154; of life, 140-42, 158; of mankind, 154, 250, 252-53
loyalty, to authority, 270; family, 290; personal, 235, 246
Lukes, Steven, 118n
luxury, 225n, 285, 285n

Macaulay, Catherine, 319n
Maccoll, Norman, 313n
McGilvary, E. B., 153n, 163n
Machiavellian tradition, 291n
MacIntyre, A. C., 80n, 208n
Mackie, J. L., 212n, 224n, 230n, 269n
MacNabb, D.G.C., 54n, 214n
Macpherson, C. B., 260n
McRae, Robert, 95n
Madison, James, 276n, 342, 343n

madness, 101, 115

magistracies, *see* offices

magistrates, *see* rulers

magnanimity, 151

malice, 148, 155n, 156, 173

Mandeville, Bernard, 196, 258n, 278, 291n, 310n

manners, 124-25, 181, 183-84, 225, 233, 238, 283; refinement of modern, 225n. *See also* good manners

marital relations, 224

market(s), 258, 260n

marriage, 227n, 247n

Marshall, Geoffrey, 328n

Masters, Roger D., 24n

materialism, 68, 75

mathematics, 16, 44

Meadows, Donella H., 346n

meaning, 113, 113n, 119, 136, 199, 201n, 281n

meekness, 219

membership in society, 239, 240n, 275, 372

memory, 41, 49-50, 58, 97-98, 111, 121, 133-34, 136

Mercer, Philip, 169n

merchants, 166. *See also* commercial society and values; economic life

merit, 252; of particular cases, 232, 243; personal, 151, 317, 343n

Middle Ages, 350, 353, 360

military affairs, 151, 178, 186, 350, 353n; and republics, 225. *See also* war

Mill, John Stuart, 177n, 312, 312n

Millar, Andrew, 325n

Miller, David, 167n, 226n, 232n, 233n, 244n, 249n, 260n, 266n, 359n

Milton, John, 104, 105n

mind, conception of, 38, 59, 131-35, 304, 339-40

miracles, 13-14, 18, 55, 71n, 87, 92-93, 106, 116, 120-21, 130, 279, 298, 335, 341, 344-45; historical and political, 94, 344, 346n

misery, 172. *See also* distress, relief of

moderation, 9, 11, 14, 23, 28, 30-31, 144-45, 219, 285, 304, 314, 323, 325, 325n, 327-28, 331, 335-36, 369n; in government, 145, 335, 352-53. *See also* skepticism, mitigated (moderate)

modern civilization, 283; Hume's preference for, 225n; justice in, 235

modesty, 222, 224, 225n, 237n

monarchy, absolute, 352; civilized, 349, 352; by divine right, 340; enlightened, 350; as form of government, 318-19, 327, 353n, 359, 361; modern European, 151, 225, 349

monasteries, 370n

monogamy, 224

Montaigne, Michel de, 20, 68, 76, 116n, 117n, 295, 307

Montesquieu, 149, 151, 183n, 191n, 342, 353-54, 359, 371n

Moore, G. E., 249n

Moore, James, 6n, 291n

moral sense, 4, 19, 22, 32n, 73, 79, 162n, 178, 201, 201n, 204n, 206, 211n, 214-17, 220-22, 222n, 230, 242-43, 242n, 245, 252, 254, 279, 282, 286, 288, 291, 291n, 368, 372. *See also* feeling, moral

More, Thomas, 342n

Morice, G. P., 145n, 258n, 281n, 365n

Mossner, Ernest C., 70n, 93n, 219n, 314n, 319n, 323n, 324n, 326n, 340n, 341n

motion, 188

motivation, 9, 78, 90, 90n, 136, 141-44, 147-48, 153, 164, 167, 177, 186, 198, 247, 263, 357; economic, 166; moral, 102, 124, 159, 162, 170, 176, 193, 197, 215, 221, 228-29, 243, 249-58, 261-64, 261n, 274, 279, 281, 284-85, 289-90, 365; political, 157, 327

motives, 221, 226, 251; artificial, 254, 286, 291; as object of moral judgment, 202, 205-206, 214; sympathy with, 253, 253n

Murphy, Jeffrie G., 259n

mystery, 298

national character, 125, 183-84, 293, 347

nationalism, 93

natural law, 20, 20n, 25, 86n, 150n, 223, 223n, 247n, 259n

natural religion, 109, 307
natural virtue(s), 21, 150, 152, 159, 164, 206, 216, 220-21, 221n, 227, 235, 237n, 238, 245, 245n, 247, 247n, 255-56, 283, 310-11, 333, 358. *See also* artificial virtue(s), distinguished from natural virtues
naturalism, 8, 24-28, 25n, 32-33, 54, 56, 66-69, 66n, 68n, 72-81, 112, 117, 138, 146, 180, 189, 195, 197, 201n, 206-207, 212, 214-17, 221, 247, 294-97, 300, 305-307, 310-15, 321, 334, 336, 338, 356, 363, 366
naturalistic fallacy, 80
nature, 20-25, 25n, 28, 50, 63-68, 68n, 69n, 71-77, 80-81, 95, 131, 219n, 323, 346; harmony of, 68, 77, 77n, 101, 245, 245n; second, 293, 333. *See also* uniformity of nature
nature, state of, 237, 259, 343
nature and convention (artifice), 20, 24, 27, 233, 293
necessity, necessary connection, 41, 48-49, 51-55, 80, 88-90, 90n, 100, 105, 131, 199, 334. *See also* liberty and necessity
Negroes, 240n
neighbors, 181, 208
Newton, Isaac; Newtonianism, 12-13, 13n, 35n, 42, 43n, 86n, 91, 91n, 101, 188
Nidditch, Peter H., 19n, 34n, 101n, 198n
Nietzsche, Friedrich, 288n
nihilism, 196
nobility, 350
noble natures, 268
nomos-physis, 20, 24
normative doctrines (Hume's), 7-8, 18, 22, 24, 28, 68-69, 72, 74, 76, 78-79, 81, 110, 123, 142, 144, 159, 194-96, 202-203, 207-208, 242, 246, 305-306, 317, 321, 334, 348-49, 356-57
Norton, David Fate, 12n, 15n, 22n, 33n, 42n, 69n, 71n, 291n, 301n, 302n, 310n, 361n, 368n
nostalgia, 314n
novelty, 130, 157
Noxon, James, 16n, 35n, 77n, 83n, 98n, 110n

Oakeshott, Michael, 332n
obedience, to authority, 192, 238, 276, 316, 320; habits of, 317; to moral rules, 250, 260, 265, 267, 269, 271, 337, 358; to law, 190, 224, 263, 270, 362; passive, 320
objects, existence of, 16-17, 25, 41, 45-46, 55-59, 56n, 71, 84, 98, 100, 111, 131, 136, 257, 296, 298. *See also* external world, knowledge of
obligations(s), 28, 152, 154, 192, 198, 213, 222, 226n, 227, 236, 238, 245-46, 267, 277, 358; of interest (natural), 261n, 287, 315; legal, 243; political, 190, 243, 259, 259n, 289, 332; sense of, 226, 234, 242n, 248, 250-52, 273, 283, 291. *See also* duty
office(s), political, 268, 272, 272n
Olson, Mancur, Jr., 266n, 271n, 277n
opinion, 45-46, 66, 90, 105, 120, 123-28, 133, 136, 171, 183, 202, 207, 252, 254, 275, 342-43, 367; government rests on, 273, 276; of interest, 276; of mankind, 212; political, 127, 319, 322, 340; public, 175; of right, 273, 277, 318, 321; ruling, 364; sound, 349. *See also* ordinary people, opinions of
order, 4, 6-7, 18, 23-24, 31, 53, 151, 185, 197, 279, 297, 306, 318, 322, 331, 334-35, 338, 344, 347-48, 352, 358-63; cognitive, 58, 107, 110, 322, 335; moral and social, 8, 28, 145, 158, 216, 225, 231-35, 231n, 238, 242, 246, 250, 264-67, 280, 283, 311, 322, 327, 335, 339, 355-56, 360-63; as a public good, 266-67; rejection of, 346; unplanned, 258. *See also* uniformity
ordinary people, opinions of, 64-66, 76, 105-107, 110, 114-17, 129-30, 211, 251, 309, 319, 328
Ossian, poems of, 93, 93n
ostracism, 286n
Ovid, 104, 105n

paganism, 151
pain, *see* pleasure (and pain)
Palmer, R. R., 14n

paradox, 61, 64, 66, 82, 131, 138, 274, 311, 315, 319, 330, 340, 357

Paris, 324n, 326n

Parliament (English), 125n, 303, 303n, 352n, 355n

participation, in artificial virtues, 240, 242n; political, 224, 358

parties, 5, 178, 245, 303n, 325-27, 340-41, 356, 364; from principle, 125

partisanship, 29, 122, 125, 178, 178n, 245, 318, 323-30, 340, 343n, 360n, 361, 364; limited, 327n, 353n

Pascal, Blaise, 61n, 166, 179

passion(s), 40n, 54, 73-76, 102, 104, 118, 132, 135-65, 137n, 168, 170-71, 175, 179-88, 197-98, 221, 275, 305; calm distinguished from violent, 8, 25, 139, 141-47, 163, 185, 200-201, 251, 255, 262, 285, 325, 331; direct, 148, 156-58, 157n, 165, 220; indirect, 148, 154, 156, 164-65; instinctual, 140-42, 148, 156, 158-65, 181, 221n, 242, 244, 262; predominant, 186; reason subordinate to, 69, 78-81, 138, 149n, 252. See also feeling

Passmore, John, 13n, 18n, 98n, 145n

past, discontinuities in, 345; idealization of, 98; and ideologies, 364; knowledge of, 46, 50, 53, 111, 296; reverence for, 321

patriotism, 154, 180, 183n, 245

peace, 350, 356; as a public good, 266; as a value, 151, 231-32, 232n, 283, 338

Pears, David, 39n

peasants, 65, 71

Penelhum, Terence, 6n, 15n, 33n, 71n, 134n

Pennock, J. Roland, 233n, 267n

perceptualism, 10, 16n, 26-27, 38-41, 38n, 39n, 44, 58-59, 68, 84, 136, 296, 299, 344, 362

perfectibility (human), 280, 341

pessimism, political, 313

Peterson, Merrill D., 241n

philanthropy, 220n

philosophes, 14n, 312, 326, 326n, 341

philosophy, relation to politics, 229, 286, 291, 304, 323-24, 327-28, 364. See also educative role, philosopher's

physics, 75, 84, 88, 90-92, 102, 188

physiology, 75-76

pity, see compassion

Plamenatz, John, 212n, 232n, 346n

Plato, Platonic, 15n, 38n, 93, 101, 264, 342n, 343n, 357; ruler, 249n

pleasure (and pain), 79, 139, 142, 148-50, 153-59, 162-67, 165n, 170, 172, 175-79, 184, 200, 212-13, 236, 239, 250, 267; mental, 100, 115-16, 166, 179, 323. See also happiness

Plutarch, 286n

Pocock, J.G.A., 31n, 361n

poetry, poets, 100, 104-105, 115, 328, 343, 343n, 350

polite society, 129, 150, 224; letters, 359

politeness, 209, 226, 226n. See also good manners

political choice, 23, 191, 229, 234, 316, 339

political economy, 166, 267n

political institutions, 18, 85, 167, 190, 192, 195, 203, 222, 224, 246, 286, 292, 302-303, 312, 330, 333, 336, 338, 343, 358, 362, 369-70; as educative, 291

political regimes, 195, 288, 305, 332, 340, 347, 353, 361

political science, empirical, 195; Hume's, 83, 95, 97, 102, 137, 147, 291, 295, 330, 336, 347, 354, 356, 363; modern, 10-11, 354. See also science

politicians, see artifices of politicians; rulers

politics, programmatic, 11, 23, 108, 215, 312, 325, 337, 356, 366

polytheism, 71n

poor, the, 155, 173

Popkin, Richard H., 12n, 14n, 15n, 62n, 66n, 302n

population, 107

positivism, 7, 10, 84, 84n, 301n, 302n, 304, 354

possession (of authority), long, 317-18; present, 317

poverty, see poor

power, the powerful, 34, 174; abuses of, 271; psychology of, 152-56, 167, 171-72, 186; right to, 277; temptations of, 272 practice (social), 9, 30, 222, 226, 226n, 230n, 255, 277, 289, 292, 338, 355, 365; justice as a, 27, 249; utility of, 254, 367n

pragmatism, 38n, 77n, 105, 298, 300, 301n, 334

praise, 173-74, 200n, 204. *See also* feeling, moral

predictability (in social life), 231n, 232, 331, 335, 354-55, 362

prediction(s), 314, 337, 345. *See also* future, prediction of

preeminence, desire for, 152

prejudice(s), 37, 42, 108-109, 128, 308, 310n; national, 93, 129

prescription, *see* right, prescriptive

press, liberty of the, 352n, 360-61, 361n

prestigious goods, 152

Price, John V., 70n, 129n, 219n, 359n

Price, Kingsley Blake, 204n

pride, 134-35, 148-55, 149n, 150n, 164-65, 170, 173-76, 175n, 181, 184, 209, 267

Priestley, Joseph, 341

primitive society, 234-35, 244, 260, 282

primitivism, 361

prisoners' dilemma, 269n

private, ambition, 149; consciousness, 132, 211; judgment, 248; life, 246-47; and public, 30, 38, 136, 231-32. *See also* interest, private; property, private

probability, 44-47, 50, 83, 85, 87, 106, 108, 111, 121, 140, 157, 299, 301, 303, 314, 335, 344. *See also* knowledge

profit (motive), 166, 166n

progress, 312, 315, 341

promises, promise-keeping, 208, 223, 225-26, 226n, 227n, 230, 231n, 234, 237n, 238, 246, 249n, 251, 259, 259n, 260, 260n, 265, 282-83, 289, 311; secret, 231n

proofs, 47, 55, 85

propaganda, 127

property, 6, 19, 102n, 135, 151-52, 208, 223, 225n, 227, 230-39, 235n, 237n, 242n, 243, 246, 260n, 272n, 277, 284, 309n, 311, 317, 318n, 354, 359; and liberalism, 357; origin of, 258, 260; private, 236, 260n; right to, 277; systems of, 191, 235, 291, 315, 331

prosperity (economic), 107, 234-35, 353, 356, 361; and liberty, 359

Protagoras, 38n

providentialism, 68, 69n, 101, 216n, 245n, 298

proximity, *see* contiguity

prudence, 30-31, 208, 212n, 238, 287, 320n, 325

psychology, 8, 33, 38, 41, 44, 52, 59, 65, 70, 73-76, 86, 95-97, 100-105, 108, 110, 112, 114, 116-17, 119, 125-26, 128, 130, 133-34, 145, 161, 163, 167-68, 172-73, 178-79, 187, 206, 241, 253, 262, 290, 318, 363; British, 42, 75; modern, 137; moral, 19, 97, 135, 148, 157n, 159, 161, 190, 194, 197, 200, 202, 215, 228, 230n, 257, 274, 371; political, 243

public, 6, 223, 231-32, 231n, 246, 249, 267, 323, 330, 349; affairs, 325; debt, 353n; dedication to, 149, 154; flattery of the, 329; goods, 266, 266n, 269n; meanings of words, 136; philosophy, 295. *See also* good, public; interest, public; private, and public

public spirit, 92, 154, 220n. *See also* civic virtue

punishment, 90, 223n, 269, 270n; desire of (to enemies), 158

Puritans, 303n, 370

Pyrrho of Elis, 15n, 66, 295, 345

Pyrrhonism, 15-16, 17n, 19, 20, 28-30, 61-62, 71-72, 82-83, 195, 297, 299-300, 313-14, 313n, 323, 325, 330, 343

Pythagorean theorem, 47

Quinton, Anthony, 31n

races, differences among, 240n

radicalism, counterrevolutionary, 340; English, 339n; philosophic, 307, 307n, 309; political, 14, 102n, 218, 247, 311, 328, 337, 339-45, 339n, 342n, 348, 366. *See also* politics, programmatic

Rameau's Nephew, 211n

rank, social, 149, 151, 154, 176, 186, 186n

Raphael, D. D., 222n, 223n, 253n, 277n, 349n

rational, rationality, 68, 99-100, 137-39, 146-47, 146n, 166, 203, 207, 217, 240, 262, 271, 271n; rational faculty, 133, 138; rational Indian, 346n; instrumental, 331; social, 232, 358. See also reason

rational choice, 6, 26, 177, 261n, 268, 272n, 276, 316, 332, 371. See also individualism, methodological; self-interest

rational conduct, 17, 145, 202, 367. See also reasonableness, of conduct

rationalism, 13, 16-17, 19-20, 22, 25, 29, 34, 45, 58, 74, 81, 128, 301; critical and constructivist, 332n; French, 339n; fallacy of, 306; in morals and politics, 8, 13, 19, 23, 138, 162n, 196, 198n, 223, 296, 323, 331-33, 343. See also reason

Rawls, John, 226n, 271n, 289, 289n

Raymond, Marcel, 93n

reaction (political), 340, 357

reason, reasoning, 14-15, 19, 21, 61-62, 72-74, 78-81, 97, 121, 128, 139-40, 145, 161, 182, 240, 302, 305, 308, 312-15, 327, 332, 336, 339, 363-66; and correction of belief, 246n; limits of, 8, 20, 28, 30, 40, 50, 55-58, 65, 68, 82, 86, 138, 146, 193, 196, 207, 264, 295, 306, 323, 326, 338, 341, 344, 363; in morals, 194, 197-203, 211, 213, 217, 229, 254-55, 258, 278, 281, 285, 289, 297, 337, 362, 370; in volition, 139-43, 263, 303. See also passion(s), reason subordinate to

reasonable person, 7, 32, 55, 72, 115n, 139, 143-46, 146n, 308. See also rational conduct; reasonableness; wise person

reasonableness, of beliefs, 110, 117, 196; of conduct, 18, 139, 142-46, 185, 202, 303-304, 313, 321n, 328, 335, 338-39, 341n, 344-48, 355, 368-69

reasoning, right, 11, 22, 24, 29, 97, 104-105, 109-110, 122, 130, 144, 182, 195, 208, 299, 302, 309-311, 314, 321-24, 334, 347

Rebellion of 1745, 340

reciprocity, 160, 260n

reflection (in moral life), 192, 229, 254-55, 258, 260-62, 267-68, 271, 279, 281, 284-85, 332-33, 351. See also reason, in morals

reform(ism), 213-14, 284, 312, 315, 332n, 335-37, 349, 364, 366-67, 370-71; conservative, 367; English, 341; incremental, 316; modern, 11

Reformation, 369n

regularity, see causation; future, resemblance to past; uniformity

Reid, Thomas, 32n, 69n, 82, 82n, 83, 91n, 138, 138n

relations, blood, 181. See also family

relativism, 66, 311; ethical, 20, 211, 217, 283

religion, 3, 5, 13-14, 14n, 20, 45, 61, 71-72, 87, 93, 106, 114, 121, 125, 157n, 270n, 303, 303n, 307, 308, 308n, 309, 309n, 310n, 326n, 341, 345, 361, 366n; and conservatism, 314n; and morality, 107, 107n, 291; Roman, 29n. See also Catholicism; Christianity; fanaticism; fideism; God; miracles; natural religion; polytheism; revelation; ritual; superstition

remorse, 155n

Renaissance, 204n

representation, 352n

republican(ism), 342-43, 349, 353, 361; ideals, 327; virtue, 149

republics, 225, 361; ancient, 353

reputation, 134, 173, 175-76, 252, 267-69, 267n

resemblance, 57-58, 103-104, 106, 108, 110, 114, 120, 130, 169-70, 181, 183, 255; imperfect, 106-109. See also analogy

resentment, 141, 158, 160, 163-64, 171, 175n, 221n, 239, 240n, 241, 272n

resistance (political), 320, 340

respectability, 176. See also reputation

restlessness, 129

revelation, 13-14, 61, 335

revenge, 92, 158, 163, 173, 221n

revolution, revolutionary politics, 94, 320, 345, 348, 356; in France, 341; principles, 340. See also American Revolution; Revolution of 1688

Revolution of 1688, 320, 356-57

rewards, 90, 269; heavenly, 106

rhetoric, 355. See also eloquence

riches, the rich, 151, 151n, 154, 171-74, 179, 186. *See also* property; wealth
right, rightness, 80, 190, 204, 211-12, 215-16, 220, 223, 226, 273, 334, 363; common sense of, 293; of government, 318, 320; and wrong, distinction between, 199, 268, 343
right(s), 223, 227, 232n, 235, 240, 241n, 243, 317, 358-59, 359n, 362; to equal consideration, 239, 241n; equality of, 241; of expression, 361; inequality of, 242n; of mankind, 318; natural, 357; opinion of, 277; prescriptive, 315, 318, 321; property, 223, 226, 231n, 277n, 318; of revolution, 320, 340; of self-preservation, 241n
ritual, 113, 114n, 309n
Robertson, John M., 76n, 178n
Robinson, J. A., 54n
Robison, Wade L., 12n, 33n, 291n, 301n, 361n, 368n
Robson, J. M., 312n
romantic(s), 247, 321, 359
Rome, Roman institutions, 29n, 94; emperor, 276
Rorty, Amelie, 149n
Rousseau, Jean-Jacques, 24, 24n, 93n, 152, 191n, 251, 342, 342n
rule of life (skeptical), 17, 20, 26, 29, 104, 289n, 294, 298-99, 305-306, 313, 334, 344, 347
rule-following, 25, 109, 129, 223n, 242, 275, 278-80
rulers, 270, 272-73, 272n, 276, 291, 291n, 327, 350, 364; ideal, 249, 249n
rules, and acts, 232; of artifices, 11, 22, 30, 73, 102n, 160, 182, 191-92, 194, 196, 198, 205-209, 213, 222-35, 232n, 242-45, 249n, 255, 257, 266, 280, 280n, 283, 289, 292, 331-32, 338, 346, 353, 358, 368-69; constitutive, 226, 226n; of cooperative schemes, 249; general, 108, 128, 185-86, 247, 256-57; and impulses, 298, 333, 355; of the market, 258; and order, 6-7, 23-24, 30, 108, 227, 233, 279, 311, 334-35, 362; of reasoning, 8, 22, 72, 109-110, 115, 120, 274, 297, 309, 312, 335, 364; systems of,

229-32, 229n, 242n, 243, 261; traffic, 227. *See also* obedience to rules
rumor, 129n
Russell, Bertrand, 346n
Ryle, Gilbert, 289n

Sabine, G. H., 36n, 126n
salience, 316
Salkever, Stephen G., 196n
savage condition, *see* primitive society
scarcity, 152, 237-38; moderate, 241; relative to desires, 237
Schlick, Moritz, 194n
scholasticism, 34
science, 17-18, 18n, 21-28, 30, 34, 62, 69, 82-87, 90-94, 97, 104, 106, 108, 110, 147, 195, 203, 213, 294, 304, 307, 322; economy of, 92, 96, 154, 210; and liberty, 359; modern, 84n, 86n, 301; natural, 84-85, 87, 89, 92; and skepticism, 300-301, 302n; social, 48, 55, 84-86, 89, 91-92, 94, 341. *See also* political science
Scotland, Hume and, 31, 129, 341n; political thought in, 178; society in, 260n
Scott, William Robert, 242n
secret, promises, 231n; violations of rules, 249, 265, 268-69
secularism, 25n, 68
security, 232n, 238, 260, 264, 322, 351-52, 357-58; of persons and property, 349-50, 356, 361-62
sedition, 178, 316, 352n, 361n
self, idea of, 38, 45, 98, 131-35, 149, 164n, 165, 167, 169, 171, 174, 176. *See also* identity, personal
self-control, 145-46, 185. *See also* moderation
self-esteem (respect), 151, 175, 268, 290
self-interest, 27, 146-47, 150, 155, 160, 178, 230, 244n, 252, 257-77, 269n, 290, 292; mutual, 259, 261; pursuit of, 270n; of rulers, 272-73. *See also* self-love
self-love (selfishness), 22n, 153, 153n, 162, 166-67, 201, 236-37, 243, 245, 250, 259n, 263, 270, 274, 369. *See also* egoism; self-interest

self-preservation, 238, 240; right of, 241n
selfishness, *see* egoism; self-love
Sennett, Richard, 359n
sentiment, *see* feeling; moral sense
seventeenth century, 162n, 303, 350
Sextus Empiricus, 15n, 17n, 29n, 362n
sexual relations and mores, 191, 224-25, 225n, 232, 234; freedom, 359
Shaftesbury, 12n, 19, 76, 76n, 101, 138, 162n, 177-78, 178n, 180, 204, 242n, 258n
Shelburne, Earl of, 324n
Shklar, Judith N., 362n
Sidgwick, Henry, 194n, 204n, 217n, 367n
skepticism, ancient, 17, 20, 63-64, 294, 298, 344, 362; crisis of, 32, 55, 60-63, 66, 82, 112, 147, 161, 195, 300, 305-306, 323, 334; mitigated (moderate), 9, 11, 13, 15-18, 23, 28-29, 32, 39, 56, 59, 64-68, 81-83, 114, 117, 144-46, 189, 195, 206, 217, 294-303, 306, 309, 322-24, 333-34, 373; moral, 19-20, 22, 22n, 196, 198. *See also* Academic skepticism; Pyrrhonism
slavery, slavishness, 240, 240n, 350
Smith, Adam, 116n, 125, 125n, 150n, 155, 155n, 177n, 183n, 191n, 235, 235n, 241n, 253, 253n, 268n, 324n, 341
Smith, Norman Kemp, 41n, 42n, 66n, 69, 69n, 83n, 102, 127n, 138n, 141n, 148n, 165n, 170n, 336n
sociability, social influence, 26-27, 97, 117-22, 125, 129, 131, 134-35, 138, 148, 150, 154, 160-61, 170-71, 176-83, 187, 189, 267, 275, 292, 324, 333. *See also* individualism, methodological
socialization, 125, 250, 282, 288-89. *See also* character, formation of; education; sociability
Socrates, 35
solitude, 178, 180; philosopher's, 63, 81
sophists, 20, 28, 38n, 329
soul, 107, 132-33; compared to a republic, 357
sovereignty, 228n
Sparta, 93

spectator, impartial, 177n, 253n, 256, 268n
speech, public, 290. *See also* language
Sraffa, P., 42n, 157n, 308n
stability, moral and political, 243, 317, 331, 344, 347; of possessions, 260
standard (criterion), logical, 114; moral, 102, 159, 200, 202, 205, 207-213, 215, 217, 221, 228, 276, 322. *See also* normative doctrines (Hume's); utility
Star Chamber Court, 351n
state, 191, 191n, 268, 351; attachment of citizens to, 154; historical development of, 270; liberal, 270n; modern European, 235, 353; theory of, 269n. *See also* government
statesmen, *see* rulers
Stephen, Leslie, 36n, 164n, 194n, 216n, 312, 313n, 315, 366n
Stevenson, Charles L., 201n
Stewart, John, 70n
Stewart, John B., 6n, 191n, 244n, 357n
stock-jobbing, 151n
Stove, D. C., 11-12n, 301n
Strabo, 124
Strahan, William, 109n, 342n
Strauss, Leo, 241n
Stroud, Barry, 6n, 39n, 346n
Stuart period, 125n, 327
subjectivism, moral, 211, 215, 217
subordination, 314n. *See also* rank, social
substance, 41, 56n, 100; immaterial, 132
succession (to rule), 317
suicide, 283, 366n
superstition, 12, 14, 62, 70-71, 114, 157n, 211, 307-309, 309n, 311, 325
Swiss Cantons, 319
symbolism, 114
sympathy, 25-26, 121, 125, 135, 148, 148n, 150, 152, 154-56, 160-61, 167-84, 169n, 170n, 187, 189, 198, 236, 241, 252-57, 255n, 258n, 274-75, 278, 281, 284, 286, 293, 309, 333, 339, 357-58, 363, 372

Tacitus, 360
talents, 204, 206, 218, 283

392 — Index

refinement of, 350
taxation, 125n
Taylor, A. E., 36n, 93n
Taylor, Michael, 269n
teleology, 68, 68n, 77
temperance, 208
testimony, 14, 26, 37, 90, 92-93, 97,
119-29, 135-36, 168, 187, 275, 282,
293, 309, 333, 366n; public, 231n
Thales, 35
theologians, 138
thrift, 210n, 212n
time, idea of, 43, 57
Tocqueville, Alexis de, 177n
Todd, William B., 222n, 277n
tolerance, toleration, 12, 310n, 330
Tory, Toryism, 4, 308, 312, 314n, 325,
326n, 327
tradition, 21, 31, 37, 124, 318-20, 322,
368
traditionalism, 125, 315-16, 321, 321n,
357
tragedy, 180n
tranquillity, 209
transference (of property) by consent,
260, 317
tribal, life, 235
trust (in society), 120
truth, 74, 96, 109, 121; love of, 116;
moral, 198
truth-telling, see veracity
Turgot, 341, 341n, 342, 342n
tyrannicide, 283, 285, 285n
tyranny, political, 320, 342, 350; of
rules, 247, 247n

ultimate ends, 146, 203, 217, 217n, 338
uncertainty, 157-58
Unger, Roberto Mangabeira, 73n
uniformity, historical, 341; of human
nature, 21, 37, 84-85, 88, 90, 92, 94,
121, 147, 158, 193, 302, 305, 369;
moral, 193-94, 197, 211, 217, 225,
234, 284, 311, 356; of moral experience, 280; of nature, 8, 18, 23, 25,
50, 53, 55, 72, 82, 84, 87, 92, 112,
185, 279-80, 296-99, 301, 307, 309-
310, 334, 339, 344-45, 347-48, 356;
in observance of moral rules, 226,

248-49, 265, 279, 335; social, 232,
346, 355. See also future, resemblance
to past; nature
Urmson, J. O., 201n
useful qualities, 200, 208-210, 212, 218.
See also agreeable qualities; utilitarianism; utility
utilitarianism, 4, 10, 21, 28-29, 102n,
164n, 207, 211-17, 217n, 221, 223,
227, 232, 234, 239, 241n, 242, 254,
258-59, 267, 281, 304, 312, 316-17,
332, 343, 353, 365-66; act-, 229n;
conservative, 349, 365-67, 367n; cumulative effect-, 230n; rule-, 229n
utility, 22, 30, 80, 102n, 143n, 160,
202, 211-17, 212n, 220-21, 223n,
227-33, 232n, 239, 243, 254-55,
267n, 276, 278n, 279-85, 306, 309-
311, 309n, 317, 319, 321-22, 330,
337-41, 357, 365-71; -maximization,
145; mutual expected, 261n; of practices, 226n, 317; public, 285, 317
utopianism, 130, 343-44

value(s), 124, 192, 197, 207, 214-17,
221, 246, 277, 288, 297, 304-305,
314, 322, 347, 361; judgments of, 19,
46, 190, 204, 210-11, 310; political,
190, 203, 358, 362; public, 232;
study of, 7, 194-95; theory of, 196.
See also fact and value
Vaughan, C. E., 162n
vault, justice compared to a, 248-49,
265n
veracity, 90, 120-21, 204, 223, 226n,
230, 231n, 244n, 283
Vernière, Paul, 248n
violation(s), of justice, 249, 265, 268-70
visionary action, 346
vivacity, vividness (conceptual), see liveliness (conceptual)
volition, 78, 112, 132, 139-46, 161-67,
177, 185, 193, 198, 202, 262, 279,
286, 305, 339
vulgar, the, 64-65, 74, 87, 106-107,
115, 145, 298-99. See also ordinary
people, opinions of; wise person

wall, benevolence compared to a, 248,
265n

war, 178, 186, 224, 234, 238, 259, 264. *See also* military affairs

Wars of the Roses, 320

Watkins, Frederick M., 195n, 323n, 349n, 356n

wealth, national, 107; personal, 150, 153-54, 156, 166-67, 171, 235. *See also* riches, the rich

Weber, Max, 80

welfare, *see* happiness

well-being, *see* happiness

Wertz, S. K., 94n

Wexler, Victor G., 314n, 318n, 321n, 327n

Whelan, Frederick G., 113n, 233n

Whigs, Whiggism, 318n, 319, 325, 326n, 327, 340-41, 340n, 353, 356-57, 360, 373

Whitehead, Alfred North, 39n, 84n

Wiles, Peter J. D., 166n

Wilkes, John, 341n, 359

will, popular, 319; rational, 332. *See also* free will; liberty and necessity; motivation; sovereignty; volition

Willey, Basil, 69n

William III, 320

Williams, Bernard, 145n, 280n

Wilson, Fred, 42n

wise person, 18, 20, 120-21, 129, 144, 299, 306; contrasted to vulgar, 110, 120, 145, 226n, 242n, 309, 336. *See also* reasonable person

wit, 151

Wittgenstein, Ludwig, 54n

Wolff, Robert Paul, 42n

Wolin, Sheldon S., 177n, 293n, 339n, 351n, 354n, 368n

Wollaston, William, 162n, 198n

women, position of, 239, 240n

Woozley, A. D., 240n

xenophobia, 154

York, House of, 320n

Library of Congress Cataloging in Publication Data

Whelan, Frederick G., 1947-
  Order and artifice in Hume's political philosophy.

  Revision of the author's thesis (Ph.D.)—Harvard
University, 1976.
  Bibliography: p.
  Includes index.
  1. Hume, David, 1711-1776—Political science.
2. Hume, David, 1711-1776. A treatise of human nature.
I. Title.
JC176.H9W47   1985   320'.01   84-42554
ISBN 0-691-06617-5 (alk. paper)